D1599234

In the Absence of Don Porfirio

Francisco León de la Barra and the Mexican Revolution

In the Absence of Don Porfirio

Francisco León de la Barra and the Mexican Revolution

PETER V. N. HENDERSON

A Scholarly Resources Inc. Imprint
Wilmington, Delaware

First published 2000
Printed and bound in the United States of America

Scholarly Resources Inc.
104 Greenhill Avenue
Wilmington, DE 19805-1897
www.scholarly.com

Library of Congress Cataloging-in-Publication Data

Henderson, Peter V. N., 1947–
In the absence of Don Porfirio : Francisco León de la Barra and the Mexican Revolution / Peter V. N. Henderson.
p. cm. — (Latin American silhouettes)
Includes bibliographical references and index.
ISBN 0-8420-2774-2 (alk. paper)
1. Barra, Francisco L. de la (Francisco León), 1863–1939. 2. Mexico—History—1867–1910. 3. Mexico—History—Revolution, 1910–1920. I. Title. II. Series.
F1235.5.B36H46 1999
972.08'16—dc21 99-20439
CIP

∞ The paper used in this publication meets the minimum requirements of the American National Standard for permanence of paper for printed library materials, Z39.48, 1984.

To

Courtney

and her

grandmother,

Sydney Henderson

Contents

Francisco León de la Barra. *Courtesy of the Centro de Estudios de la Historia de México*

Introduction

The Mexican Revolution of 1910, one of the most dramatic episodes in all of Latin American history, conjures up images of Pancho Villa's mustachioed cavalry charging fearlessly into the demoralized federal army or of Emiliano Zapata's "pajama"-clad *campesinos* (people of the fields) clutching their rusty rifles, determined to retain land wrested from the great estates. This volatile, popular rebellion has captured the fancy of journalists, filmmakers, and historians alike, including the first generation of professional commentators such as Frank Tannenbaum and those who have more recently revived his interpretation of the revolution. In many ways this popular revolt, certainly one of two major currents of the revolution of 1910, contained elements of a nostalgic quest for a past perhaps more imagined than real. And although the popular uprising failed to restore the good old days, perhaps oversimplified as a demand for more local autonomy in the north and the restoration of village lands in the south, its legacy for modern Mexico is substantial. One purpose of this book, then, is to examine the early manifestations of the popular revolution.

The more prosaic and largely middle-class "revolution" that ultimately triumphed in 1920 had a great deal more in common with the dictatorship it overthrew than its leadership cared to admit. The new elite never doubted that capitalism, properly directed by well-educated technocrats, would provide the answer for Mexico; they simply wanted more opportunity, especially for people from the provinces. Creating a larger economic pie ultimately would benefit all Mexicans, they reasoned. At the same time, the new elite, joined in many instances by members of the former provincial Porfirian elites, advocated a program of social reform designed to placate the land hunger and wage concerns of the rural and industrial laborers and to promote democracy to a greater or lesser degree depending on the circumstances and the administration involved. Yet the rhetoric of reform often seemed to outweigh the government's performance. Do these precepts also hold for the early revolution?

The revolution of 1910 rekindled parochial fires of provincialism that Porfirio Díaz, Mexico's ruler from 1876 to 1911, thought he had quelled. From 1910 to 1920 the republic lived up to its reputation as a mosaic that in troubled times like these tended to crumble. Even in 1911 the rationale for revolt varied widely from state to state. This book has profited enormously from the extensive regional studies that have dominated the historiography of the Mexican Revolution in recent decades. But, as Alan Knight reminds us, the revolution was, after all, a national phenomenon, and so, while not ignoring action in the states, I focus on Mexico City and the national government, where the subject of this study had his greatest impact.

Francisco León de la Barra was certainly much better known in his own time than he is now. As president during the transition from Porfirio Díaz's dictatorship to Francisco Madero's "revolutionary" administration, and as a cabinet member in Victoriano Huerta's regime, de la Barra maintained a high profile. But such political prominence was not really to the liking of this rather modest, mild-mannered attorney who viewed himself as primarily a scholar and a diplomat. Vilified by nearly every historian who has examined the revolution, de la Barra has received kinder treatment from those who have examined him more methodically.[1]

For this study I have sought to be objective, balancing de la Barra's foibles against his obvious abilities within the context of the Mexican Revolution. Yet an examination of his life, particularly his political biography, poses some of the same problems that Penelope Lively describes in her recent novel about a literary biographer: "Each of us sees through a glass darkly, impeded not just by the frailties of memory but by our own convictions. We see what we persuade ourselves that we have seen."[2] Historians tend to color their vision of Mexico in 1911 with their knowledge of the events that came after; the dramatic "revolution" that, whatever its meaning, forever altered Mexicans' perceptions of themselves and their land.

Few in 1911 foresaw the coming decade of violence. Most Mexicans had little more than fuzzy memories of the days before Porfirio Díaz took office, and those few who had clearer memories recalled those troubled times with misgivings. In the absence of a strong figure such as Díaz, many Mexicans in 1911 were uncertain. Would the new era bring greater equity, progressive reformism, and a brighter future to the populace at large? Or would Díaz's prophetic remark that the revolutionaries had unleashed a tiger herald a return to the misfortunes of the nineteenth century, a time of wanton violence and economic decay? As a result of the events of May 1911, de la Barra had to try to resolve this dilemma without benefit of crystal ball or tarot cards.

De la Barra's life spanned a significant time in Mexican history even though, whether because of diplomatic assignment or personal choice, he often observed Mexican events from foreign shores. Chapter 1 describes him as a man of the belle époque, urbane, sophisticated, well educated, and professionally successful, who became Mexico's premier diplomat because the Porfirian system based rewards at least in part on merit. Chapter 2 examines de la Barra's accession to power as the accidental result of a process of negotiations, which for both Díaz and rebel political leader Francisco Madero seemed the only logical method of ending the civil war.

The bulk of this story is about de la Barra's presidency, its accomplishments and failures. Like most other chief executives, de la Barra outlined his objectives during his inaugural address. Since he believed that future prosperity rested on a foundation of social order, he promised to restore peace. In so doing, he ran headlong into the unarticulated objectives of the rural peoples, who often employed violence as their only means of redressing longstanding grievances. De la Barra and most of the civilian leadership believed in the rule of law and, as described in Chapter 3, had little patience with those such as Emiliano Zapata who tried to create change by extralegal means. De la Barra's second goal, to promote civil liberties and democracy and to provide the country with honest elections, discussed in Chapter 4, met with no verbal but some de facto dissent. And although free elections meant different things to different people, they had important repercussions for federal-state relations. Finally, de la Barra hoped to remedy the social injustices that had intensified during the dictatorship. Chapter 5 traces the reformist ideas discussed and partially implemented during his presidency, including attempts to assist labor and provide land to the rural poor. Chapter 6 looks at the remainder of de la Barra's life, most of it spent as an outsider and in exile, during which time he promoted the efficacy of international law and arbitration as a means of dispute resolution. By the time of his death in 1939, Mexico, too, had come full cycle and, to some observers and revisionist historians, openly espoused many of the values and principles of the dictatorship that had nurtured de la Barra.

One of the attractions of writing about Francisco León de la Barra and his role in Mexican history is the multitude of sources available on his life and career. Not only have his presidential and personal papers survived intact but so also have the papers of some of the leading figures associated with his presidency. His acquaintances tended to be prolific writers and thus produced considerable commentary on his term of office. Foreign observers —American, British, and French—provided thorough descriptions of what they perceived as extraordinary events. They asked whether de la Barra was tough enough, experienced enough, and savvy enough to handle the job of president, to be the "iron hand" in the absence of Porfirio Díaz. Because of the countless sources commenting on the events of 1911, the biographer derives some idea of the flesh-and-blood person who may well have been over his head in national affairs but who nevertheless struggled to administer the progressive consensus, a vision of reform held by many members of the old elite and by some of the new blood. Obscuring de la Barra's precise reflection are other aspects of his time and personality. People of the Victorian age, particularly those who styled themselves "gentlemen," as did de la Barra, tended to be less self-promoting than public figures of the 1990s. In addition, de la Barra's diplomatic training meant that he usually hid his innermost thoughts and never permitted himself uncontrolled bursts of passion. He preserved a polished, dapper exterior on all occasions, keeping his idiosyncrasies private. He was, however, a personable, well-meaning, and responsible public servant, as the evidence shows.

In the course of working for many years on this study, I have incurred many debts. For financial and professional assistance, I wish to thank Winona State University, which, as a result of various funding initiatives, paid for research trips to Mexico, Europe, and California. Darrell Krueger, president, Doug Sweetland, then vice president for academic affairs (now president of Southwest State University), and Dean Bonnie Buzza managed to channel some monies into research despite the severe budgetary problems of the 1990s. They also generously granted me a sabbatical leave for 1995–96 to complete this project; and so for their help and friendship I am most grateful. To my good friends David LaFrance, Douglas Richmond, and William Beezley, who read an early version of the manuscript in its entirety, and Jonathan Brown, who read a portion of it, I owe an immense amount of gratitude. The final version of this book has been considerably strengthened as a result of their influence. I also would like to thank Friedrich Katz, Alan Knight, Michael Meyer, Friedrich Schuler, Steve Bunker, Sam Brunk, and Stephen Haber, who offered suggestions on my research. Finally, I would like to thank William Beezley and his graduate seminar at Texas Christian University and Jonathan Brown and the members of his graduate seminar at the University of Texas-Austin for helping to sharpen my ideas and analysis.

The personal debts I owe are also numerous. My colleagues in the Department of History at Winona State University have been strong supporters over the years. I owe a particular debt of gratitude to several archivists and librarians who opened their collections and offered advice to this gringo. In particular, I would like to thank Sra. Clotilde Lucio Avila of the Universidad Autónoma de México, Josefina Moquel Flores of the Centro de Estudios de la Historia de México, and General Manuel F. Vadillo Trueba of the Secretaría de Defensa Nacional, all of whom allowed me access to relevant materials and facilitated my research efforts. At the University of Texas, I want to thank Laura Gutiérrez-Witt, Carmen Sacomani, and the entire staff of the Benson Collection. In libraries from Paris to Palo Alto, Winona to Cholula, I want to thank the many librarians who generously lent their advice. My sister Sarah Wiehe and my brother, Skipper, put me up (and up with me) during my two West Coast stays. Jeff and Eileen Marston extended their warm hospitality during my research trip to Washington. My sister Anne Finucane contributed artwork that considerably enlivened the book. Finally, I owe considerable gratitude to Lis Leader, who convinced me to give up the law for my true love, academia; to my mother, Sydney Henderson, who provided the maps and a refuge in Cape Neddick, Maine, during several Augusts where I could write in peace; to Roberta Lucas for her work on an early stage of this project; and to Lori Beseler, Michelle Huling, Shirley Wheat, and Joan Valentine, who word processed all too many versions of this manuscript. To them all, I can only say thank you.

Taft-Díaz interview arranged by Francisco León de la Barra. *Courtesy of El Paso Historical Society*

1

Scholar and Diplomat

It was the best of times, it was the worst of times, . . . it was the age of foolishness, . . . it was the spring of hope, it was the winter of despair.

—Charles Dickens, *A Tale of Two Cities*

The short but dapper and distinguished president of Mexico, Francisco León de la Barra, stepped down from the presidential train to the cheers of thousands of his countrymen and a shower of confetti. As bands played the national anthem, the president, Governor José Septién, and the official party rode through the streets of Querétaro that were decorated for the occasion with green, white, and red bunting and headed for the substantial house near the main square, de la Barra's birthplace.[1] De la Barra began to reflect on his life. How had a man born in the provinces risen to the presidency in the early twentieth century when the glamour and influence of Mexico City so dwarfed the rest of the country? Did a person like him succeed because of his lineage, because of his connections with influential people, or on his own merits? And as the parade continued to wend its way through the streets, de la Barra also recalled his hometown's illustrious history.

Querétaro had enjoyed an important role in colonial Mexico, serving for three hundred years as the woolen goods capital of the country. Indians locked in the *obrajes,* or sweatshops, had produced the coarse material that clothed the poor.[2] Although Querétaro's economic importance declined in the nineteenth century, the city, by sheer coincidence, hosted two events that marked the beginning and the end of Mexico's most serious time of troubles from 1810 to 1867, not to suggest that all of Mexico's troubles miraculously ended in 1867. The first of these events, Miguel Hidalgo's unsuccessful conspiracy in favor of independence, germinated about a block and a half from de la Barra's birthplace. Father Hidalgo and a group of alienated criollos (Spaniards born in the New World) plotted to overthrow their colonial masters because of a perceived policy of discrimination preventing them from advancing to important positions in the state and church. Unfortunately for the would-be rebels, Spanish intelligence officers ferreted out their plans and ordered a troop of soldiers to arrest the leaders. One of the conspirators, the wife of a high-ranking local official thereafter known to her countrymen as La Corregidora, momentarily foiled the Spanish police by whispering a message through a keyhole to a servant, who rode to the town of Dolores to warn Hidalgo.[3] Although most of the drama of the Hidalgo movement played itself out elsewhere, Querétaro justly claimed fame as one of the birthplaces of Mexican independence.

It would be patently unfair to blame La Corregidora for Mexico's ills during the next sixty years; however, political, economic, and social conditions in Mexico worsened for decades after independence. While granting the nation the autonomy it deserved, independence did create economic dislocation, particularly in the area just north of Querétaro known as the Bajío. During these decades, Mexico experienced the evil triplets of militarism, factionalism, and imperialism. From its position as the jewel of Spain's empire in the eighteenth century (or at least its silver tiara), Mexico backslid and became one of the most troubled of all Latin American nations. Antonio López de Santa Anna, the quintessential unprincipled caudillo, or military leader, personally led the country down many of these steps to disaster with his coups, countercoups, and selfish bravado. A greedy northern neighbor, anxious to fulfill its manifest destiny, took advantage of Mexico's inner turmoil to further its own lust for territorial expansion, abetted by Santa Anna's ineptitude in defending the nation. Finally, one of Mexico's hardest fought civil wars, begun in the late 1850s, coupled with another foreign invasion led by the French under Emperor Napoleon III, completed Mexico's political misery. It was at this last critical juncture that the León de la Barra family became involved in Mexican affairs.

The Family and the Reform Era

Although the latter twentieth century places little stock in the belief that family lineage plays a role in determining one's fitness for office or profession, the idea enjoyed great currency in the nineteenth century. Most of the nations of the European world, including Victorian England, still followed the time-honored traditions of monarchy and aristocracy, reserving the most prestigious roles in their political, economic, and social worlds to those of high birth. Although Mexico had adopted the republican form of government, which theoretically decried these practices, in reality the elite remained paramount in social and economic circles. At the turn of the twentieth century, sharp distinctions still divided the *gente decente*, the upper classes, from the *pelados* or *los de abajo*, the underdogs. The *gente decente*, disparagingly referred to as the "perfumed ones" by *los de abajo* because of their habit of using cologne, sat in the shade when they attended bullfights and adopted European high fashion, manners, mores, sports, and culture. Elegant dress and refined tastes underscored the *gente decente*'s desire to emulate the European fin-de-siècle beau monde.[4]

Like other Spanish-American elites, the León de la Barra family pointed with pride to its antecedents to reinforce its *gente decente* status. Tracing its ancestry to an illegitimate son of King Alfonso IX of the medieval kingdom of León, the noble family fought for the kingdom during the long years of the Reconquista, the battle to retake central and southern Spain from the Muslims. Members of the León family emigrated to Chile in the sixteenth century. Two hundred years later, one of them married into an influential upper-class family, the de la Barras from the northern Spanish city of Burgos, thus creating the entire patronym. The family remained among Chile's notables until and beyond the time of independence.[5]

Francisco León de la Barra's grandfather, Juan Francisco, fought for the patriots during the Wars of Independence under the command of Bernardo O'Higgins, the hero of Chilean independence, participating in the famous crossing of the icy Andes mountain pass from Mendoza, Argentina, and the decisive battles of Chacabuco and Maipú. After independence, Juan Francisco returned to Argentina as a special agent of the Chilean government, at which time he married an Argentine woman and eventually sired seventeen children, including Bernabé, Francisco's father.[6] Fleeing from a tyrannical dictator in the late 1830s, Juan Francisco León de la Barra reestablished his family in Chile, where he became involved in international trade and commerce. As a visionary entrepreneur, León de la Barra hoped to expand Chile's commercial interests throughout the Pacific, and so with some government largesse, including the loan of three ships captured during its 1830s war with Peru, he started a transpacific livestock business. He sent Bernabé, his third son, then a sickly youth of nineteen, to work as the purser of the first expedition, as it crossed the "desert of water."

Bernabé's recollections of the Pacific voyage seem less than enthusiastic, given the range of locales and adventures that he experienced. After spending six months in Tahiti, the small fleet sailed on to Australia but then shipwrecked on the New Zealand coast, where Bernabé barely escaped death at the hands of the cannibalistic Maoris. After several weeks, a ship rescued the survivors, who promptly returned to Chile. Bernabé's surviving letters make no reference to the beauties of the South Seas, the exotic flora and fauna, or the friendly islanders, all of which impressed other travelers to the region.[7] Instead, Bernabé reported in a businesslike manner about the sales of the cattle and horses. He remained in Chile for several years while his father returned to Argentina. His next venture abroad carried him to California, where he joined the early wave of forty-niners not as a gold miner but as a merchant selling foodstuffs to the camps in the area around Sutter's Mill. After the gold rush ended, he took the business southward, trading cattle and horses with ranchers in northern Mexico, particularly Sonora and Baja California.

Then a curious episode occurred. For eleven years, Bernabé did not communicate with his family, which presumed that he had been killed somewhere in Mexico. Whether his father had expressed disappointment in the path of his son's career or whether Bernabé was determined to drop out of sight for some other reason cannot be decided from the few letters that the family preserved. Reading through Bernabé's rather detached and formal letters from the 1840s, one could speculate that a coldness had grown between father and son. Whatever the reason for his disappearance, he resurfaced in 1861, only because his cousin, on a business trip to New York City, happened to recognize his voice as he stood on a street corner talking with friends. Bernabé's subsequent apology to his family for his long years of silence seemed sincere, but he offered no real explanation for his failure even to write. Instead, he related his adventures in Baja California, which created opportunities for him in Mexico.[8] Apparently Bernabé never discussed this difficult period of his life with his children; the aforementioned cousin revealed these details only after Bernabé's death in 1893.[9]

Bernabé eventually prospered but in a career, the military, very different from the one his father had intended for him. What precipitated his deeper involvement in matters Mexican was William Walker's invasion of Baja California. Walker, "the grey-eyed man from Tennessee" better known for his exploits in Nicaragua later in the decade, led two filibustering expeditions against Mexico in the early 1850s, one to Baja California and the other to Sonora.[10] Nor were Walker's actions unique. Adventurers from France, too, sensed that Mexico was ripe for plucking and lured by tales of fantastic riches easily had sought to grab the silver tiara. But Bernabé León de la Barra and a group of volunteers turned Walker and his forces away at La Paz, driving him back to the United States. Acclaimed by the Baja Californians for his role in defeating the hated Yanquis, de la Barra was invited to confer with President Ignacio Comonfort about further employment just as the great civil war, the War of the Reform, broke out in 1857.

By entering into the service of a foreign country, de la Barra joined the small clan of internationalists, or Spanish Americans as one author calls them—that is, members of notable families such as Bernabé who, recognizing the common heritage, traditions, and problems of the Latin American nations, felt free to serve a nation other than their homeland. The best-known Spanish American, Ecuador's Vicente Rocafuerte, became a Mexican diplomat and political philosopher in the decade following independence before returning home as president in 1834.[11] No doubt a less well-developed sense of nationalism in the early nineteenth century also contributed to the phenomenon of Spanish Americanism. Finally, the romantic view of adventure and the individual as hero influenced men such as Bernabé and Giuseppe Garibaldi, with whom Bernabé was already well acquainted, to fight for liberal principles outside their own country.

Bernabé's internationalism, and his years of business dealings in the United States, uniquely qualified him to become the arms purveyor for the liberal cause. According to his cousin, the job proved thankless, however, because the liberals had no cash to spend, even though they controlled the customs revenues in Veracruz. The government needed these limited funds internally, and Bernabé therefore had to seek credit to purchase guns. Eventually, he acquired ten thousand rifles for the liberal army with assistance from U.S. sympathizers and returned to Mexico in time to participate in several battles in the later stages of the war. He served under the command of General Alejandro Quijano of the Yucatán and in 1862 married the general's daughter, María Luisa. As a reward for his services during the Reforma, Bernabé received a high-ranking post within the War Department rather than land, the reward given to many other liberals.

The bliss of the honeymoon, for both Bernabé and Mexico, had scarcely worn off, however, when war broke out afresh. Recalcitrant conservatives, determined to resurrect their cause, sought European assistance to resume the struggle. While conservative military bands raided the countryside, murdering and looting, their agents wooed the ambitious French emperor, Napoleon III, enticing him with the vision of an American empire rivaling his uncle's continental successes. An Austrian prince on a Mexican throne under French control would secure the empire. Other Frenchmen, particularly those bankers to whom the conservatives owed money, dreamed again of the illusory riches of Mexico. The combination of French and conservative flattery proved too much for the guileless Austrian Archduke Maximilian and his new wife, Carlotta, whom the French duped into believing that the Mexican people wanted them. Maximilian contributed to his own folly, disregarding warnings from his brother the emperor of Austria. Only later did Maximilian realize that the chimera of empire rested upon the military might of the French army.

Even facing a major European power the liberals fought hard, registering Mexico's most famous military victory, the Cinco de Mayo, in 1862 when Ignacio Zaragoza and Porfirio Díaz defeated the French army just outside the city of Puebla. Despite this heroic triumph, the French military could not be denied. Reinforcements and a more cautious commander reversed the outcome of the Cinco de Mayo about one year later. The French promptly swept across Mexico, scattering the liberal forces northward. General León de la Barra scarcely had time to gather up his young wife and their fifteen-day-old baby, Francisco, and flee first to Monterrey, then Matamoros, and ultimately across the border into the United States. The family never returned to Francisco's birthplace in Querétaro. Many other liberals joined the de la Barras in exile, although President Benito Juárez managed to maintain a tiny liberal nook that now bears his name in northern Chihuahua. After two years in the United States, Bernabé and his family returned to Mexico in 1866, although he did not become militarily active again until February 1867 when the empire was in its death throes. Bernabé fought in the final battle of Querétaro, which resulted in the capture and then the much-debated execution of Emperor Maximilian and two of his principal conservative generals on the Hill of the Bells on the outskirts of the city.

Perhaps because Bernabé played such a tardy role in the defeat of the French, he received only a minor reward for his services in the years of the "Restored Republic," as the Benito Juárez-Sebastián Lerdo de Tejada governments from 1867 to 1876 were labeled. President Juárez appointed him customs collector in Campeche, where his wife's family owned property. For several years, young Francisco enjoyed the warm tropical breezes and slow-paced life of southeastern Mexico. Then the government transferred Bernabé to Matamoros, Tamaulipas, where he again served as customs agent, until March 1876 when the Lerdo government appointed him commander of the garrison there, a promotion that ultimately proved to be his downfall.[12] Quite unintentionally, Bernabé figured prominently in Porfirio Díaz's destruction of the Restored Republic and the creation of the Porfiriato, Díaz's dictatorship from 1876 to 1910. Rebelling against President Lerdo in 1876 under a slogan calling for "effective suffrage and no reelection," Díaz enjoyed his first military successes against Bernabé's garrison at Matamoros. With about five hundred men, Díaz attacked the fortifications, which promptly surrendered to the frontal attack. Research has revealed that the defeat was not Bernabé's fault but occurred because Díaz had suborned one of the officers, Jesús Toledo, who encouraged others to defect. After a brief pro forma resistance, Bernabé fled across the Río Grande to the United States, thereby ending his military career.[13] Soon thereafter Bernabé moved his entire family to Mexico City. He took advantage of his citizenship of Chile to become that country's consul to Mexico (as well as Bolivia's) and otherwise dedicated the remainder of his life to the education of his seven sons.[14] Whatever the state of his personal fortunes in the late 1870s, Bernabé conferred *gente decente* status on his children.

Education and Scholarship

Just as Bernabé León de la Barra exemplified the characteristics of his age, achieving social position through military service, so his eldest son, Francisco, personified the values of the Porfiriato. Although lineage and personal connections to important figures in the dictatorship, including Díaz himself, helped Francisco León de la Barra to advance, he owed his success primarily to his abilities as a lawyer and a diplomat. The assumption always has been that the dictatorship, in its later years, offered little opportunity, perhaps because photographs of Díaz and his cabinet in 1910 show a group of old men well past the age when most men would have retired, making room for a new generation. But there was in fact more opportunity in the lower ranks of the bureaucracy than traditionally believed. Like bureaucrats today, most civil servants at that time were well educated and from urban areas, particularly Mexico City. That meant the vast majority of the population was excluded.[15] Opportunities such as those available to Francisco León de la Barra existed because Díaz changed Mexico for the better in many ways.

During the Porfiriato, Mexico left its rather desultory past and in many respects achieved relative greatness in the eyes of contemporaries, becoming one of the most economically advanced of all the Latin American countries. Díaz presided over a period of great political stability, which in turn encouraged foreign investment and economic growth. With the assistance of foreign capitalists, many of them from the United States, Díaz created a modern infrastructure including a rail system that was the envy of Mexico's neighbors to the south (except possibly Argentina) and a communication network that linked the most remote village (as long as it was economically viable) with the capital. The regime modernized Mexico City as well as many of the provincial capitals. Further, as a result of Mexico's new prosperity the middle class expanded, taking on many of the new jobs in the government.

People such as Francisco León de la Barra succeeded in part because their educational experiences permitted them to seize newly created opportunities and capitalize on them. Díaz purposely expanded the public education system that Gabino Barreda had introduced in the Restored Republic. Barreda and other anticlerical liberals believed that traditional parochial education must end because its instructors often "poisoned" their students' minds with religious dogma. Instead, Barreda advocated secular primary and secondary schools that were state funded and practiced the new "scientific" principles of education. *Científicos* (proponents of scientific principles like Barreda's) hoped to use education to reconstruct society; their slogan was Progress Through Order. As a laboratory for the experiment, Barreda created an elite academy, the National Preparatory School, and recruited the country's top students. The new curriculum placed a heavy emphasis on the sciences and mathematics, while downplaying and nearly disregarding the traditional humanities. A course in logic served as the students' capstone experience in their senior year, tying together all of their earlier learning. Barreda also created separate postsecondary professional educational institutions for law and medicine. After his tenure in office expired, others, most notably Justo Sierra, a former Greek history professor at the institution, modified some of the rigidity of the early scientific curriculum, although that curriculum remained controversial to the end of the Porfiriato.[16]

The new philosophy of education molded Francisco León de la Barra, both as a student and as a teacher, and, in that sense, made him philosophically a *científico*. After completing primary school, de la Barra enrolled in the National Preparatory School, which was located in the former monastery of San Ildefonso in Mexico City. The beautiful colonial facility, now the site of some of José Clemente Orozco's greatest murals, had an open courtyard where students could mingle and discuss ideas. When de la Barra graduated at the age of twenty-one, Joaquín Baranda, minister of education and foreign relations, appointed him as an instructor in a first-year course of mathematics at the school, where he taught logic and mathematics for the next fourteen years. De la Barra received the appointment, despite his youth, because he was at the top of his class scholastically and because he was Minister Baranda's nephew. In 1897, de la Barra was appointed to the chair in logic.[17] He must have been a good teacher, because years later a number of his students remembered him kindly.[18] While teaching at the National Preparatory School he finished his law degree at the Escuela Libre de Derecho (where he subsequently lectured), specializing in international law.[19] His thesis, later published, was, like most such works, narrow and technical. It condemned the reciprocity provision of the Civil Code (part 4 of Article 3288) that pertained to extradition and called for its repeal.[20] De la Barra continued to study the intricacies of the law of extradition and published a more sophisticated work on the topic a decade later.[21]

De la Barra also studied the rights of neutral nations in times of war and published a scholarly monograph on the topic that was filled with classical allusions.[22] Taking a historical and scientific approach in this book, he surveyed the contemporary state of the rights of neutrals. While arguing that the proper behavior for the neutral nation was to avoid any interaction with either belligerent, de la Barra elaborated on the practical difficulties (for example, a private citizen engaged in commerce with one of the belligerents) that made this ideal position difficult. As with his earlier work on extradition, de la Barra would return to his study of the rights of neutral nations later in his career, producing in 1917 his most memorable work in international law. This last monograph gained him recognition in Europe as well as in the United States as an authority and led to his participation in both academic conferences and the arbitration courts mandated by the Treaty of Versailles in post-World War I Europe. While the scholarship of de la Barra's books was sound, current legal scholars find his style bombastic and pretentious. But at the time, lengthy allusions were much in vogue. Measured by the standards of nineteenth-century education, de la Barra stood out from most of his colleagues; his scholarship vaulted him to prominence in the Mexican academic community and ultimately opened up a career for him in the public sector.

During the 1890s de la Barra held other public and private positions that indicated his growing stature in Porfirian Mexico. De la Barra never described his first meeting with Porfirio Díaz, although Díaz recalled being present at de la Barra's baptism in 1867. Probably they first became acquainted through Baranda. Díaz arranged de la Barra's election as a Mexico City council member and then for three terms as a member of the national Chamber of Deputies. Historically, and particularly after Benito Juárez emasculated the legislature in the 1860s and 1870s, congress played only a nominal role in national affairs. Basically, it rubber stamped the president's proposals, although occasionally it also served as an effective debating society where the administration could test controversial ideas. De la Barra's three terms in congress gave him some experience with national issues and provided proof of his friendship with Porfirio Díaz. He also had access to the dictator, clearly a boon for his private law practice. Clients experiencing legal difficulties who came to de la Barra found that he could open doors to Chapultepec Palace.[23]

Was De la Barra's rapid advancement the result of his contacts or his abilities? Both contributed. His ability increased his access to important people. Although his uncle, Joaquin Baranda, gave him his first break, de la Barra also befriended Baranda's successor, Ignacio Mariscal, who remained in Díaz's cabinet until ill health forced him to resign in 1910. A signatory of the constitution of 1857, Mariscal had gained respect as one of Benito Juárez's close associates. Besides knowing Díaz himself, de la Barra also knew Díaz's father-in-law, Minister of the Treasury Manuel Romero. De la Barra's association with influential *científicos* in the regime, and his belief that international law could be codified scientifically, suggest further that he could be labeled a *científico*. But the term *científico*, referring to Porfirio Díaz's positivist-oriented circle of advisers, lacks precise definition. Participants in the Mexican Revolution viewed the *científicos* as primarily political and branded all Porfirians with that label. Probably they are better described as the technocrats of their day.[24] In 1892 they introduced a program to revitalize the dictatorship based on their liberal ideology, but the dictator rejected the idea.[25] Francisco León de la Barra, in keeping with his education and experience, concurred with several *científico* ideas. Nevertheless, he lacked the political prominence to be considered part of Díaz's inner circle.

Another issue on which de la Barra agreed with the *científicos* concerned the creation of an independent judiciary, which still provokes controversy now just as it did in the early years of the republic. Proponents of an elected judiciary pointed out the advantages of a judicial system more responsive to the democratic electorate that could be voted out of office if unsatisfactory. Critics responded that under such a system judges would lose their ability to function independently, because a politically unpopular but legally correct decision could cost them their career on the bench. In Mexico, the issue had been further complicated by the failure of democracy in the nineteenth century. The national trend over the course of the century was to strengthen the executive, and so judges had lost their power to act independently. De la Barra, like many of the *científicos,* believed in an independent judiciary and advocated this reform when he became president. Like some of the *científicos,* he also believed that immigration would solve the nation's problems by providing a work force, imbued with the proper values of hard work and thrift, that would positively influence the Indians.[26] De la Barra, as a product of positivistic education, thus thought that many of Mexico's problems could be reformed scientifically. But because the Porfiriato was a personalistic dictatorship, Díaz did not endorse all of the *científicos'* ideas, and they certainly did not control him.

De la Barra's secondary role in the regime did not affect his status as a member of the Mexican beau monde. In fact, most of the rich and powerful members of high society, including Mexico's largest landowner, Luis Terrazas, and its best-known general, Bernardo Reyes, were never admitted to Díaz's inner circle. Díaz even excluded members of his own family, such as his favorite nephew, Félix, from the governing clique.[27] De la Barra and the king of the *científicos,* José Yves Limantour, shared a relationship with the exclusive French colony: Limantour by birth and de la Barra by marriage, to his first wife, María Elena Borneque, the daughter of a wealthy businessman. Although few in number, the French entrepreneurs exerted a disproportionate influence in Mexico because of their financial dealings.[28] After 1892 the French colony grew in importance when Díaz, following the death of his father-in-law, promoted Limantour to finance minister. To many observers, Limantour deserved credit for the wizardry behind the economic growth of the country during the final decade of the nineteenth century. Although his French birth meant that Limantour was constitutionally barred from seeking the presidency, his presence in government nevertheless lent further prestige and influence to the French bankers.

De la Barra's family life evidenced a set of traditional Hispanic values, which the French colony shared. When his sickly wife died in 1909 leaving him with two sons, Francisco and Julio, neither of whom survived to adulthood, de la Barra married his widowed sister-in-law, Refugio Borneque, after a proper mourning period. When the marriage took place in February 1911, the wedding topped the society pages. Porfirio Díaz himself served as one of the four witnesses required for the mandatory civil ceremony, and the archbishop of Mexico presided over the religious nuptials. De la Barra and his new wife were happy. They made quite a splash in Washington society, bringing some youthful gaiety (through their children) to an otherwise staid diplomatic group. De la Barra's two boys played with President William Howard Taft's youngest son and were apparently welcome at all times in the White House.[29] In his private life, de la Barra exuded warmth; in public, he was more formal and reserved. De la Barra and his second wife had one son of their own, Carlos, who also died in his youth. Despite these personal tragedies, the couple lived together compatibly until de la Barra's death in 1939.[30] De la Barra's two marriages also in part explain his affinity for France, where he would spend his last years in exile. His marriages also meant that he had some money beyond what he had earned professionally but did not make him a major property owner like many of the elite during the Porfiriato. Nor did he become an investor in the new businesses that the prosperity of the Porfiriato created; instead, he remained a fairly typical member of the *gente decente*, relying primarily on one or two steady jobs and his wits to provide an income for his family.

Diplomatic Service

Because teaching was considered a part-time career, de la Barra also wanted to find employment in the public sector. His expertise in public international law led Ignacio Mariscal to hire him as a special consultant during the 1890s to help resolve pending diplomatic issues. In this service, de la Barra, like other members of the meritocracy, became one of the "technocratic managers of the new social order." The first of his consulting jobs involved conflicting claims by the United States, France, Mexico, and Great Britain to a deserted Pacific Ocean coral island, called Clipperton Isle, after an eighteenth-century English pirate who used it as his base. Although the island had been mapped as part of the viceroyalty of New Spain, as the Spanish territory north of Panama had been delineated before independence, both England and France asserted their less historical titles because of later but better documented acts of possession. De la Barra finally convinced the British and U.S. representatives to withdraw their claims and France to agree to international arbitration with the king of Italy as arbitrator.[31] As occurred in all too many instances of agreed arbitration in the late nineteenth century, the decision maker failed to decide, and in 1912 the two nations still awaited a resolution.

De la Barra's second assignment had him toiling over a treaty of friendship, commerce, and navigation with the Low Countries, as Belgium and the Netherlands were still called in the late nineteenth century. During these negotiations, he proposed revisions of the Mexican-Netherlands-Belgian treaty to clarify language pertaining to territorial waters and most-favored-nation status, language so precise that other treaty makers copied it. On his third assignment, de la Barra's legal scholarship convinced Italy to revise its extradition treaty with Mexico and to base extradition on broad principles rather than on a list of specific crimes that might be capriciously altered by legislative enactment. De la Barra's accomplishments qualified him as a technically expert international lawyer, whose merits the Foreign Relations Department quickly grasped.

Foreign Minister Mariscal also employed de la Barra as Mexico's delegate to various international conferences, some ceremonial and others more substantive, dealing particularly with the use of arbitration to resolve international disputes, a cause that de la Barra pursued for his entire life. De la Barra represented Mexico in 1892 when Spain hosted the quadricentennial of the discovery of America. In Spain he enjoyed an audience with Queen Isabella II, met many literary and artistic luminaries of the time, and toured the country with his brother, a resident of Barcelona. On this occasion he received the first of his many medals when he was inducted into the Order of Carlos III. Over the next twenty years other rulers, including the king of Italy and the emperor of China, bestowed medals and honors upon him.[32] Conferring medals on visiting dignitaries was part of the diplomatic ethos of the Victorian era. Whether this atmosphere of ceremony and gentility prepared de la Barra for the rough-and-tumble politics of the Mexican Revolution is quite doubtful.

In addition to ceremonial meetings, de la Barra dealt with serious policy issues at international conferences such as the second International Peace Conference held at The Hague in 1907, and the Pan-American Conferences of 1902 and 1906. These conferences carried forward the idea of arbitration and the judicial resolution of international disputes born at the first International Peace Conference of 1899 also held at The Hague, where Mexico (but not de la Barra) was the only developing nation in attendance. As Mexico's budding international law expert, de la Barra was a logical selection to attend these sessions. Although he played a very minor role in the conference proceedings, the meetings reinforced his belief in the notion, widespread at the time, that arbitration would provide the best path for the resolution of international disputes. But the efficacy of the mechanisms of international arbitration would rightly be questioned by a later generation of diplomats who complained that arbitrators tended to delay decisions interminably, hoping that in the interim the disputing parties would settle the issue themselves.[33]

Perhaps most significantly, de la Barra seconded the vocal harangue of Brazil's Ruy Barbosa that less powerful states should be entitled to a greater representation on the arbitration court, an issue that threatened to disrupt the second Hague conference.[34] Léon Bourgeois, a prominent French politician and former premier who became a good friend of de la Barra's, led the majority, who wanted to create the first permanent Court of Arbitration, dominated by the great powers and with a single justice selected from the developing world. The conference also debated whether arbitration should be voluntary or compulsory. Although the members could never agree on compulsory arbitration, ultimately the delegates increased the number of judges from smaller countries on the court of arbitration. De la Barra was certainly pleased with the tenor of the discussion at The Hague meeting, and he continued to endorse many of its ideas for the next thirty years.[35]

De la Barra pursued his country's interest in arbitration in the new rounds of Pan-American conferences. In 1902, he served as one of nine Mexican delegates at the second Conference of American States, which took place in Mexico City. The Pan-American spirit, evident at the time of this meeting, differed radically from the individual Spanish Americanism of his grandfather and father's era, and more closely resembled Simón Bolívar's dream, which expressed itself in the failed Congress of Panama in 1826. The delegates not only cited the need for a mechanism to resolve problems between Latin American states in order to avoid wars but also eventually agreed to sign the first Hague convention supporting voluntary arbitration. At the third Pan-American meeting in Río de Janeiro in 1906, where de la Barra presided over the Mexican delegation, the members agreed to create a permanent organization, and every Latin American country volunteered to send a delegate to the second Hague Conference. The delegates also agreed on the need to codify international law, another project that de la Barra heartily endorsed. The meetings engendered a new spirit of cooperation among the Latin American nations.[36]

During the Porfiriato, Francisco León de la Barra became the nation's premier diplomat. His prior service as consultant and emissary earned him consideration for a diplomatic post shortly after the turn of the century. During the 1890s, as a result of Mexico's growing prestige, the dictator decided that he needed to expand and improve the foreign service. In particular, this meant establishing new diplomatic posts where none had previously existed and elevating the status of some of Mexico's consuls to ministers. Whereas in earlier times the government had been content to dispatch special envoys to resolve particular diplomatic disputes on an ad hoc basis, now the dictator wanted full-time employees in diplomatic posts throughout the world. Following the French model, these diplomats were young gentlemen of letters who identified themselves with the Porfirian inner circle. For the first time the government assigned two ministers to South America, one to the Atlantic side (Argentina, Brazil, Paraguay, and Uruguay) and one to the Pacific (Chile, Peru, Colombia, and Ecuador). De la Barra received the more important of the two positions, in Buenos Aires. His salary of 15,000 pesos was a considerable amount of money for a public servant.[37] He accepted his new assignment enthusiastically, although he delayed his departure to Buenos Aires for several months because a yellow fever epidemic was decimating the population of the port city. By the fall of 1902, however, he had arrived at his first full-time diplomatic post.

Argentina in the early twentieth century basked in its greatest period of prosperity and success. With the age of the caudillos now a distant memory, and under the leadership of competent oligarchs,

Argentina had become a haven for refugees and an important source of grain for Europe, as well as a fertile ground for foreign, particularly British, exports. Buenos Aires rebuilt itself into an ultramodern city, whose denizens liked to compare it with Paris. The wave of immigrants who had rushed to its shores from Italy and Spain, establishing barrios such as La Boca with its brightly colored metal houses that preserved the immigrants' ethnic identity, in many ways had transformed Argentina.[38]

The impact of immigration on Argentine development and the burst of capitalistic energy in the beef-packing and wheat-processing enterprises so impressed de la Barra that he published a monograph about it. For him, Argentina provided an example of how a Latin American nation could mature from historical origins as chaotic as Mexico's; in 1910 the Argentines enjoyed the fifth highest standard of living in the world, ranking above European nations such as Italy, Spain, and Sweden. Had de la Barra been more influential in government circles, he might have done more to incorporate the Argentine experience into Mexico. But there is no evidence that his analysis of Argentine immigration ever had a significant impact on Mexico, which never attracted European immigrants in the same way that the southern-cone nations did. As a result, he had to content himself with fulfilling his responsibility of creating amicable relations between Mexico and Argentina and its neighbors, which he did. Even a journey to isolated Paraguay, eight days by boat up the La Plata, did little to dampen his enthusiasm for the region.[39]

Having acquitted himself well in South America, in 1904, de la Barra received a promotion to minister to the Low Countries, where he performed similar duties. Besides promoting Mexican commerce, he engaged in diplomatic colloquy and attended stately social affairs designed to evidence Mexico's arrival as a mature nation. For example, Queen Wilhelmina of the Netherlands responded cordially to his remarks at the time he was presented to her, stating how pleased she was at Mexico's progress during the Porfiriato. King Leopold of Belgium, equally gracious, wanted to promote a new shipping line to Mexico. De la Barra's four-year stint in Brussels permitted him to travel to various parts of Europe and his first wife to spend time with her French relatives. De la Barra was also conveniently present for the 1907 International Peace Conference at The Hague, which proved such a formative event for him.

In the name of the Mexican government, de la Barra purchased a house that doubled as his home and the site of the new ministry in Brussels. Befriending other diplomats stationed in Brussels, he proved socially adept, as usual. One of his new acquaintances, U.S. Minister Henry Lane Wilson, who would later serve as ambassador to Mexico during the early revolution, praised de la Barra's manners and social graces. Privately, de la Barra expressed serious reservations about Wilson's abilities as a diplomat, calling him overly excitable. Professionally, however, relations remained warm and cordial.[40] In his memoirs, de la Barra also severely criticized the Belgian king, Leopold II. Cold and businesslike, Leopold failed to generate much popular sympathy, among either his own people or the diplomatic corps.[41] Ever the diplomat, de la Barra kept his criticisms of Leopold private because to voice them would have destroyed his ability to carry out his ministerial functions.

De la Barra's four-year stint in Europe turned him into a confirmed Francophile, a trait that he held in common with many other Mexicans. For most of its modern history, Mexico had looked to France as the source of its culture, whether it be opera, fashion, or philosophy. Thus, de la Barra's decision to move to France following the demise of his political career was in keeping with an ideal shared by many of his affluent countrymen. But at this juncture in his life, de la Barra was not fated to remain in Europe. In 1908 Porfirio Díaz recalled Enrique Creel from Washington, leaving the ambassadorship to the United States vacant. Both Ignacio Mariscal, who would soon retire because of ill health, and Porfirio Díaz believed that de la Barra deserved the appointment to Mexico's most prestigious foreign service post, even though he would be the youngest ambassador in Washington.[42] Certainly, his personality lent itself to the diplomatic service. Observers agreed that his manners and civility, coupled with his charm and acute intelligence, made him an ideal representative for Mexico. Only the diplomatic appointment to the United States carried with it the title "ambassador"; all other Mexican diplomats were "ministers." The distinction was more than a formality; historically Mexico's most vital diplomatic relations were with the United States, a truism as accurate in 1908 as in the 1830s.[43]

While the United States had caused many of Mexico's problems in the early part of the century, it had provided the mixed blessing of its investment capital in the Porfirian era. U.S. Secretary of State Elihu Root seemed most pleased with de la Barra's appointment, perhaps because they had met and become friendly at the second Hague Peace Conference.[44] Before actually taking up residence in the United States, de la Barra traveled to Mexico to consult with Díaz and Foreign Minister Mariscal about the diplomatic issues that Mexico faced. Mariscal informed him about the disputes dividing the two nations, and Díaz instructed him to "avoid any friction that could prejudice relations" between the two nations. Fully briefed, he departed for Washington. Although many Mexicans perceived a minor crisis in the relationship between Mexico and its neighbor to the north, de la Barra hoped to follow his instructions to improve relations between the two countries. To that end he dedicated his time in the United States.[45]

Ambassador to the United States

During his three years in the United States, de la Barra worked diligently on four problems that threatened Mexican-U.S. relations. The first, the so-called Chamizal dispute, resulted from the meanderings of the "imperialistic" Río Grande, which had carved a new bed further to the south in Mexican territory. Under the terms of the 1848 Treaty of Guadalupe Hidalgo, the new territory, most of it in the area around El Paso, now belonged to the United States. The Mexicans, unwilling to give up any additional territory to their northern neighbor, bitterly protested any shift in the border. De la Barra, taking a position consistent with his lifelong beliefs, ultimately convinced his own government to enter into binding arbitration over the boundary. Unfortunately, this arbitration came to naught when the United States refused to abide by the Canadian arbitrator's decision, and the dispute only found resolution under the Lyndon Johnson administration in the 1960s.[46]

A second issue that de la Barra negotiated with the United States concerned the rights to the waters of the Colorado River. As U.S. farmers moved into the southwest, they began to divert the waters of the Colorado for irrigation, thus depriving riparian property owners downstream in the state of Sonora of a much-needed water supply. This matter, too, remained contested for many years until the nations reached an equitable solution for shared water usage by treaty in 1944, although the quality of water remained an issue for decades more.[47]

The third issue involved a troublesome Nicaraguan dictator, José Zelaya, whom President Taft wanted removed in the name of restoring order in Central America. De la Barra, again in keeping with his lifelong beliefs, urged the United States to forgo intervention and informed Secretary of State Philander C. Knox that Mexico would not participate in a joint intervention. De la Barra saw Central American discord as an opportunity for the United States and Mexico to demonstrate their deep friendship for one another.

The fourth, and in some ways the thorniest of all the diplomatic problems, resulted from rumors circulating about a potential Japanese lease of Magdalena Bay in Baja California, an issue that immediately raised the hackles of the United States, whose military experts were concerned about the safety of the Panama Canal. In this instance, de la Barra was able to report to the United States that Díaz had not entered into a secret arrangement with Japan.[48] Further, de la Barra convinced Secretary Knox not to ask Mexico to renew the Magdalena Bay lease with the United States, at least until some of the anti-American hostility in Mexico had cooled down.

De la Barra's most important diplomatic initiative was to arrange a meeting between Díaz and President Taft to show the world that, despite the recent tensions, relations between the two nations remained cordial. He claimed that he got the idea when he heard that Taft intended to make one of his rare trips from Washington. De la Barra convinced Díaz that he should also take a train to Ciudad Juárez, and in October 1909 the two presidents clasped hands midway across the bridge over the Río Grande. Although the meeting was largely symbolic, it proved most useful at a time when relations between the United States and Mexico seemed more volatile than they had been at any time since 1876. De la Barra believed that the meeting would provide some good public relations and would negate some of the "earlier libels" that threatened to poison relations between the nations. Thereafter, de la Barra saw this achievement as the culmination of his diplomatic career.[49] He also enhanced his country's relations with the United States by befriending Taft and the members of his cabinet on a personal level. De la Barra particularly liked Attorney General George Wickersham, with whom he could discuss topics of international law. He worked well with Secretary of State Knox, also a Wall Street lawyer, although he believed the secretary to be too susceptible to political influences. De la Barra's bête noire, however, was Undersecretary of State Huntington Wilson, whom he characterized as a man of mediocre intelligence.[50] To de la Barra, Wilson played an inflated role in the department because Knox was frequently absent from Washington, for both matters of business and rounds of golf.[51]

Although Porfirio Díaz's foreign policy in 1910 was predicated on balancing European and U.S. influences, the dictator realized that Mexico relied heavily on American capital to develop new businesses. As a result, de la Barra was also charged with responsibility for promoting investments, a job that he ably performed. He served as honorary president of New York's Mexican Club, which included among its membership Andrew Carnegie. De la Barra also knew Carnegie personally from the latter's interest in the peace movement, and the two remained friendly for years. The ambassador apparently resuscitated confidence in Mexican investment, which had seriously declined since the onset of the 1907 depression. The downturn in the U.S. economy had had a profound effect on Mexico, throwing many individuals out of work and making borrowing difficult. De la Barra's job was to convince would-be investors that the economic slump was merely temporary, and that Porfirio Díaz possessed both the will and the wizardry to lead Mexico to recovery. To do this, de la Barra embarked on promotional tours across the United States, speaking to large urban business organizations.[52] The message played well even in Peoria, although the coming of the revolution in 1910 would again make Americans skittish about investing money south of the Río Grande.

De la Barra's diplomatic career through 1910 exemplifies the opportunity available to a skilled technocrat in the Porfirian bureaucracy.[53] De la Barra had proven himself a thoroughly professional diplomat, fully worthy of the esteemed rank that he had achieved. He had distinguished himself on numerous occasions, usually by demonstrating his expertise in international law. In this sense, he was typical of the many highly skilled professional technocrats, who, through a combination of connections and ability, rose to occupy the second echelon of public service in the late Porfiriato but never the very top ranks of government. The older generation of Porfirians, including the dictator himself, did not have the good sense to retire at a reasonable age and make way for a new generation of leaders, men whom they themselves had trained and imbued with the values of the dictatorship. Thus, during the late Porfiriato, the lawyers, journalists, educators, and other intellectuals who had ambitions for high office developed a malaise that would contribute to Díaz's downfall.

As ambassador, Francisco León de la Barra was a serious, career-oriented person who worked diligently, although, like his father, he made time for his children and, according to the society pages, was a devoted parent. He also epitomized Mexico's *gente decente,* exuding polish and good manners. He excelled at ceremonies and was always able to make pleasant conversation and to deliver the bon mot. One would expect no less from a highly successful diplomat. But one might wonder whether his love of ceremony and show outweighed the intellectual substance he brought to the job. For at least one renowned diplomatic historian, de la Barra lacked decisiveness.[54] At this point in his career he seemed more the sailor than the captain, although he did display initiative once he became ambassador. At times he seemed a slave to protocol. For example, he canceled a speaking engagement at the Chamber of Commerce in Toledo, Ohio, because the Spanish minister had been given preferential seating at the dinner table, an affront to de la Barra's dignity as ambassador.[55]

On more substantive matters, de la Barra embraced and advocated important principles and ideals such as arbitration and nonintervention, which the dictatorship endorsed. As a Porfirian, he believed in the well-ordered state and the tenets of material development. Through 1910 he had demonstrated no interest in domestic politics, but clearly he accepted many of the values of the Porfiriato, as his presidency would demonstrate. His tact and his belief in negotiations in all situations probably did not render him or Mexico good service during his presidency. Unprepared for the Mexican Revolution and for the emotional, rather than rational, outlook of some of its participants, de la Barra erroneously expected people such as Emiliano Zapata to act like European diplomats. Certainly, de la Barra looked the part of a president. Throughout his life he lived up to the dapper image that he had cultivated while a student. Most photographs show him in formal evening wear, adorned with the medals that foreign princes had awarded him, "the diplomat of story in appearance and manner."[56] Like his father, Francisco León de la Barra was a man of his age. His Porfirian career symbolized Mexico's transition from a society dominated by swashbuckling soldiers to a land where sophisticated lawyers and technocrats helped to modernize the economy and society. But would de la Barra's image and his technical skills as a diplomat prove to be an asset when Porfirio Díaz faced his ultimate crisis, the rebellion in November 1910?

José María Pino Suárez, Francisco Carvajal, and Francisco Vázquez Gómez at the Peace Grove Conference speaking to reporters. *Courtesy of El Paso Public Library, Southwest Collection*

2

Revolution by Negotiation

The Treaty of Ciudad Juárez

Some are born great, some achieve greatness, and some have greatness thrust upon them.

—William Shakespeare, *Twelfth Night*

On May 25, 1911, Victorian Mexico, the world that had nurtured Francisco León de la Barra and other members of the Porfirian elite and middle class, whimpered to an end. Its demise occurred not because hordes of armed, screaming revolutionaries drove Porfirio Díaz from the National Palace but because the Porfirians and the civilian maderistas signed an agreement negotiated over the course of several months. The compromise placed Francisco León de la Barra in the presidency. In the end, months of fighting did little more than reverse the bargaining positions of the two sides. Both the Porfirians and the civilian followers of Francisco Madero agreed fundamentally that the dictatorship had accomplished much that should be preserved; continuity in many respects would prevail over change. Nevertheless, the mystique of the revolution of 1910 as a violent upheaval that ousted Díaz from his comfortable quarters into penurious exile and created a totally new nation remains central to Mexican national consciousness today.

This chapter challenges the idea that Francisco Madero and his civilian supporters conceptualized a radically different Mexico from the one in which they had matured. The challenge is based primarily on evidence about how Porfirio Díaz transferred power to Francisco Madero, scion of one of Mexico's wealthiest families. Indeed, can a major social revolution, as some claim the revolution of 1910 to be, result from a negotiated settlement with the old regime?

Possibly, if a negotiated settlement could be a temporary strategy to remove a potentially dangerous outside force, as was the strategy of the North Vietnamese in negotiations with the United States in the 1970s. But Mexico in 1911 faced no real threat of foreign intervention. Yet, from the outset of the insurrection, the civilian maderistas and the Porfirians never wavered from the principle of negotiation. This chapter also introduces the theme that many members of the Porfirian elite, including most of the civilian maderistas, had reached a consensus by spring 1911 about the social reforms that Mexico needed in order to achieve a more equitable society. Both Madero and (more reluctantly) Díaz concurred with the progressive consensus. What separated the two leaders, and made the military struggle in 1910 and 1911 last for six months, was not, therefore, a debate over social policy but a purely political issue: who should govern Mexico, Díaz or Madero? On this topic the two men and their followers disagreed fundamentally, thereby making violence inevitable.

Traditional revolutionary historiography has identified the negotiations that led to the Treaty of Ciudad Juárez ending the Díaz dictatorship as Madero's first huge mistake.[1] According to this point of view, Madero erred in not completing the revolution and in leaving various Porfirian institutions, particularly the legislature, judiciary, and most significantly, the army, intact. Madero's subsequent actions during the interim regime and his own presidency make sense only if one rejects this traditional argument and accepts the notion that Madero and his civilian followers never intended to sweep away the establishment in Mexico, even though, as nearly all historical accounts correctly point out, Porfirio Díaz and his principal minister, José Yves Limantour, were the prime movers in the negotiations.[2] This chapter explores the reasons both sides believed negotiations would benefit Mexico.

Traditional historiography has also argued that the process of negotiation proved that the dictatorship had weakened since its tough old days and thus in turn encouraged the insurrectionists. This analysis fails to recognize that because the Madero revolution differed from all previous national anti-Díaz revolts, a negotiated settlement was the objective from the outset, and that the violence was merely a means to an end. Only Díaz could make peace through effective concessions, assuming Madero was unwilling to surrender. Initially, Díaz's supposed military might tipped the scales heavily in his favor, but as rebel military victories mounted, Díaz had to pile additional concessions on his side of the fulcrum in order to restore balance. At the same time, military successes encouraged the civilian maderistas to ask for more. When the scales finally tipped, putting Francisco León de la Barra into the presidential chair, the progressive consensus that had emerged during the negotiations set the tone for his entire presidency.

The Electoral Campaign of 1910

The negotiations offered Díaz an opportunity to extricate himself from a sticky mess of his own making. Basking in the glories of what many observers perceived to be the most stable political system in all of Latin America, with the possible exception of the elitist regime in Argentina, and perhaps more than a little flattered by the fulsome praise of his fellow-president Theodore Roosevelt, who had referred to Díaz as "the world's greatest living statesman," Díaz in 1908 granted what ultimately proved to be a fateful interview to James Creelman, a correspondent for *Pearson's Magazine*. In the interview Díaz stated that Mexico had matured sufficiently to assume the responsibilities of democracy. Therefore, he encouraged the development of an opposition party to contest the election of 1910, even though no institutional framework existed for a two-party democracy. Why Díaz advocated an opposition party and why he promised not to run, contrary to his clear intentions, remains a puzzle.

Díaz may have issued the statement to quell growing concern in some circles in the United States that Mexico was a dictatorship and not a true democracy.[3] This premise assumes that *Pearson's Magazine* did not circulate at all in Mexico (admittedly it had a small circulation), that Díaz believed that the article would not be translated and printed in Mexico, or that Díaz knew that *Pearson's Magazine*'s domestic readership would ignore an article about Mexico. These assumptions seem shaky at best. Another possibility, never previously put forward, is that the eighty-year-old Díaz, in a moment of fatigue, actually considered retiring and then later changed his mind. A third possibility is that Díaz, in keeping with tactics he had used since the founding of the dictatorship, hoped to smoke out his political opposition and then crush it.[4] The most persuasive explanation for Díaz's declaration, however, is that he was vain enough to expect Mexicans to shower him with demands to run for another term. Such behavior would certainly be the logical result of the unhealthy egocentrism nurtured by thirty-four years of his being surrounded by fawning sycophants. Whatever his motivation, Díaz soon publicly repudiated the portion of the Creelman interview in which he proffered his retirement and announced he would seek another term in 1910.

Díaz's change of heart surprised few and, more to the point, seemed to perturb almost nobody. Many reasoned that Díaz would not survive another six-year term (which in fact he did not). Thus, in deference to their leader, and out of fear of reprisals, the politically astute generally conceded the presidency to Díaz and focused their attention on the vice presidential contest. Supporters of General Bernardo Reyes, the governor of Nuevo León, tossed out his name in opposition to the very unpopular *científico* incumbent, Ramón Corral, who had been picked as vice president in 1904. Although Corral had been a competent governor of Sonora, he never attracted a personal following. Civilian Porfirians questioned his competence and his morality. Malicious rumors circulated widely about him, making him the target of considerable sarcastic commentary by journalists. Probably, Díaz selected Corral primarily because he could never outshine the dictator's glory.

Reyes's followers organized the Democratic party and campaigned actively for him as vice president. Díaz reacted quickly to the "vivas" for General Reyes and shipped him off on a military mission to Paris, urging him to renounce his vice presidential aspirations and disband his followers. As the Reyes bandwagon slowed to a walk, never again to enter the parade of national politics in any significant fashion, the Anti-Reelection party took its place. Led by Francisco Madero, the party initially asked for the right to select a vice president democratically to run alongside Díaz. When crowds swelled and the dictator's repressive agents did nothing, Madero became more ambitious and began discussing the possibility of running for president. Quickly the Anti-Reelectionists concurred and agreed that their founder, chief fund-raiser, and titular head should be the party's nominee for president.

Initially, Díaz reacted to Madero's political activities with a combination of indifference and scorn. His indifference stemmed from the fact that Madero came from the establishment; his scorn was based on Madero's many idiosyncrasies and his unlikely prospects. Squeaky voiced and an unpresidential five feet, two inches tall, Madero had supposedly been inspired to run for the presidency of Mexico after a late-night session at a Ouija board that had mysteriously predicted his ascension to the gilded chair in Chapultepec Palace. In very macho Mexico, Madero, among other things a vegetarian, seemed out of place. When a friend of the family was allegedly asked in an interview whether a vegetarian could ever become a national leader, the response was, "Not in Mexico."[5] Whatever criticisms might appropriately be leveled at Madero, one must admire his incredible courage in 1909 and 1910. As the campaign swung through the republic, repression intensified. Municipal officials denied him permits to hold rallies, police broke up crowds that came to see and hear him, and yet he persevered. The Anti-Reelection party convention held in April 1910 that officially nominated Madero for president faced various forms of extralegal coercion. Finally, just before the elections in June, the government imprisoned Madero on a trumped-up charge.[6]

To analyze the breakdown of seemingly stable regimes such as the Porfiriato, social scientists have constructed various theoretical models. One useful analysis differentiates underlying major causes, or preconditions, from "precipitants," or the moral outrage that causes the spark to be lit.[7] De la Barra would have been more comfortable using a lawyerly construct such as "proximate cause," the precise definition of which attorneys and judges have spent years debating. Courts have developed several tests for proximate cause, from the very broad idea that the event was a "substantial factor" in the result to the more narrow view that the result would not have happened "but for" the event.[8] For historical purposes, the language of the "but for" test probably leads to the tightest conclusions.

Most historians would agree that the outbreak of the revolution of 1910 probably cannot be reduced to a single proximate cause. For the civilian maderistas, the proximate cause was Madero's arrest, which cast Díaz as a tyrant and engendered sympathy for Madero.[9] Others, like de la Barra, never reached this stage in their thinking. For still others, who hoped as late as June 1910 that Díaz would substitute either his nephew Félix Díaz or the governor of Veracruz, Teodoro Dehesa, for Corral, the proximate cause was the dictator's stubborn refusal, which concluded the political campaign of 1910 on a sour note.

Civil War, Diplomacy, and Negotiations

The election of 1910 took place as scheduled, with Díaz and Ramón Corral winning a predictable victory. But because of the dictator's unwillingness to compromise before the election, many Mexicans withdrew their wholehearted allegiance to him. Some would remain nominally loyal to the government, while others would join the maderistas in rebellion. Díaz's imperious preelection behavior also had temporarily closed down the negotiation process. In order for negotiations to reopen and succeed, the Madero forces had to have some significant cards to play, which could be obtained only as a result of military victories. Thus, when Madero jumped bail and went into exile in San Antonio, Texas, violence was inevitable.

Madero issued his Plan de San Luis Potosí, which called for a military uprising against the government on November 20, 1910. Although the exile leadership was optimistic, the urban movement fizzled because of the vigilance of the Porfirian police. Much to Madero's surprise, only small, scattered bands of guerrillas in the hills of Chihuahua, followers of Pascual Orozco, a muleteer from San Isidro, and the people associated with Francisco "Pancho" Villa, won their initial engagements, administering sound thrashings to small army detachments. Madero himself, who had crossed the border in anticipation of a massive uprising, fled back to Texas when confronted by federal soldiers.[10]

The documentary evidence suggests that almost as soon as the maderista challenge began, so did negotiations. In late November, Díaz sent negotiators to Ciudad Guerrero to meet with some of Orozco's rebels. Unfortunately, Díaz also sent the army to protect the negotiators, or so he claimed, and the maderistas suspected his intentions. This action by the "old crocodile" seemed to reinforce his reputation for skulduggery. Concerns about his sincerity proved to be a major hurdle in the negotiation process. Although the actual terms of the first peace proposal were never revealed, Díaz apparently offered no more than a blanket amnesty for the rebels if they surrendered their arms peacefully. The maderistas spurned the offer. Having staked so much on their rebellion, they could not abandon it at the first sign of adversity.[11]

If Díaz's offer is viewed as the first in a series of negotiations that culminated in the Treaty of Ciudad Juárez of May 1911, one must ask why he negotiated in 1911 rather than relying on repression, as he did with other rebellions such as the PLM (Partido Liberal Mexicano) uprisings in 1906 and 1908. The most likely explanation is that Díaz knew that the Madero revolt differed dramatically from the Flores Magón revolts of 1906 and 1908 and from the occasional regional ruckus that had disturbed the Pax Porfiriana. In contrast to the challenge from Madero, Ricardo Flores Magón and the other architects of the revolutionary PLM, running the gamut of the ideological spectrum on the left from anarchism to communism, had intended a fundamental reorganization of Mexican society. Their basic objective, the destruction of the traditional order, was simply non-negotiable for Porfirio Díaz, who believed in the precepts of democratic capitalism, a model that he adopted for Mexico.

The occasional regional revolt that may have reflected the underlying stresses of modernization most often could be crushed by overwhelming force if the dictator so chose. But sometimes even those, like Venustiano Carranza's elite-led, local revolt in Coahuila in 1893, reached negotiated settlements. The Madero rebellion, however, was different. Its entire civilian leadership concurred with the notion of democratic capitalism. Madero himself, the eldest son of one of the largest property owners in Mexico, more resembled a wayward child who needed to be both chastised and coddled than a fire-breathing demagogue bent on destroying Porfirian society. Díaz knew and respected many of Madero's followers. They were professionals and educated middle-class people as well as members of the provincial elite, products of the Porfiriato themselves.

Thus, for the next six months, Díaz pursued a policy that appeared contradictory. On one hand, he threw the might of his army and rural police at the rebels. His power was far greater on paper, however, than it was in reality; Díaz was more like the Wizard of Oz than he cared to admit, able to make noise like thunder and lightning but lacking real military strength. His corrupt, elderly generals, required to consult personally with Díaz before acting, lacked initiative. The dictator had no coherent plan and tried to suppress each brushfire separately. Furthermore, he committed the strategic error of holding most of his forces in reserve near the capital rather than risking them in the north.[12] He also directed his ambassador Francisco León de la Barra to encourage the United States to unleash its legal system to repress the political exiles. On the other hand, Díaz pursued negotiations with the rebels, hoping by conciliatory words and political concessions to bring the angry, rebellious youth of his family back to the fold in order to preserve intact the material progress that he intended to bequeath to the nation. Some historians have concluded that Díaz's seeming inconsistencies resulted from old age, infirmity, or a lack of resolution.[13] These claims have been much exaggerated, although they contain a germ of truth. Díaz used his well-practiced tactics, but, unbeknownst to the rebels, his military position was inherently weak.

Both sides in the civil war played the same cat-and-mouse game. Thus, in a letter dated December 3, barely two weeks after the rebellion began, Madero's first representative to the United States expressed his wish that after a few military victories, which hopefully would allow the maderistas to establish a de facto government in Mexico, the United States would recognize their legal status as belligerents. Recognition "would be a great step to initiate peace negotiations." To further this end, Madero's attorney, Sherbourne Hopkins, suggested that provisional president Madero send an official envoy to Washington.[14] Ultimately, Madero would follow this advice and designate his vice presidential running mate in the election of 1910, Francisco Vázquez Gómez, as his ambassador to the United States. Vázquez Gómez would have a considerable impact on the negotiations that ended the Porfiriato.

At first, Vázquez Gómez expressed reluctance to accept the position, because, as he put it, only "Pancho on one side and General Díaz on the other" could approve the terms of peace and therefore using intermediaries meant delay. Vázquez Gómez and Díaz both understood another strategic implication: official negotiations would elevate the insurgents' status in international law. Therefore, Díaz would insist that negotiations remain "unofficial" until May 1911.[15] Nevertheless, as early as December 1910, both Madero and Vázquez Gómez agreed on the desirability of a negotiated settlement. Neither demanded the complete military destruction of the old regime; each was willing to preserve aspects of the old dictatorship. The political issue alone separated maderistas from porfiristas.

Both sides knew that the key to successful negotiations lay in the military campaigns being waged in the north. Generally, during the first few months of the rebellion, the insurgents won local fire fights, made hit-and-run attacks on small communities, and successfully disrupted rail and telegraph service, particularly in the state of Chihuahua. Soon maderista rebellions erupted in other states; for example, Emiliano Zapata declared his insurgency in Morelos in January 1911. But the federal army won decisively the only formal pitched battle of the early campaign at Casas Grandes in Chihuahua on February 25, 1911. In that engagement, Madero himself took command of the troops for the first and last time. He proved himself no match for a trained federal general and nearly was killed. Madero's wounds healed slowly; he was still wearing a bandage on his hand, his red badge of courage, as late as the end of April.

After Casas Grandes, however, both sides had reason to hope for ultimate military victory—the federales because they had just won their sweetest triumph, and the maderistas because revolts were erupting in several states. This hope, which ultimately proved false for the Díaz government, was in part responsible for the collapse of a second round of negotiations, which occurred in late February. Díaz had sent a close friend, Iñigo Noriega, along with Madero family members Ernesto Madero and Rafael Hernández to meet with Madero's father and brother in Corpus Christi, Texas. The battle of Casas Grandes, coupled with Vázquez Gómez's refusal to join the negotiations because of the presence of so many Madero family members, led these talks to fail.[16] Preliminary discussion focused primarily on Ramón Corral's resignation as vice president and the replacement of some cabinet members.

Meanwhile, in Washington, Ambassador Francisco León de la Barra had begun his frustrating task of urging the United States to enforce its neutrality statutes, which created a misdemeanor for anyone who "sets on foot, or *provides or prepares the means for* a military expedition against any foreign state" (my emphasis). Madero's agents in the United States freely recruited and purchased arms there and marched back and forth across the border, seemingly without interference from the United States. Some historians have concluded from these facts that President William Howard Taft and his Republican administration hoped that Madero would triumph and oust Díaz. As further evidence for this conclusion, these historians point to a series of episodes they believe had made the United States hostile to Mexico, including the nationalization of the Mexican Railway, which U.S. capitalists had largely owned, and the recent granting of preferred privileges to British petroleum investors such as Lord Cowdray, as well as the diplomatic irritants that de la Barra had tried to smooth over with a handshake, as described in Chapter 1.[17] Followers of this school of interpretation also point to the contrast between the ease with which the Madero rebels operated in the United States and the harassment of the PLM rebels of 1906 and 1908. In those years the U.S. government prohibited the sale of the PLM newspaper, *La Regeneración,* and arrested the Flores Magón brothers before they could fully implement their revolutionary plans, whereas in 1910 Madero's friends printed and distributed their literature throughout the southwest and freely exported weapons for their insurrection.

Ambassador de la Barra certainly believed that the United States was not doing enough to forestall the maderistas along the Río Grande. Madero operated with impunity; only after three months of pleading could de la Barra persuade the Justice Department to issue a warrant for his arrest. De la Barra also pointed out that detectives hired by the Díaz government had turned over to U.S. authorities, on numerous occasions, information about political rallies at which civilian maderistas had recruited, purchased weapons, and distributed anti-Díaz information. But the authorities had taken no action. Detectives had informed local agents about groups of Mexicans arriving in border towns, presumably poised to cross the Río Grande and begin fighting for the rebellion, again to no avail.[18] Secretary of State Philander C. Knox responded to de la Barra's requests for more stringent enforcement by stating that traffic in arms and ammunition constitutes mere "commerce," that political meetings cannot be disrupted because the First Amendment guarantees free speech, even to aliens, and that the transport of armed men out of the United States to a foreign country is not illegal unless the armed men are using the United States as a military base.[19]

With this very narrow interpretation of the neutrality statute, de la Barra and the Mexican government clearly could expect little assistance from the United States in arresting the rebels before they entered Mexico. Thus, Taft's interpretation of the neutrality statute lends some credibility (though, I would argue, inappropriately) to the interpretation that the United States wanted the Madero revolution to succeed. In his own defense, Taft stated, with some logic, that the burden ultimately rested with the Mexican government to patrol its own border, and that the solution to Mexico's unrest lay in Porfirio Díaz's hands. In frustration, de la Barra finally discharged the Furlong Detective Agency, which the Mexican government had used for some years for surveillance and identification of neutrality violators in the United States, because their efforts in 1910 and 1911 had borne no fruit.[20]

Did de la Barra do a credible job as ambassador when Mexico needed his services, and more important, did the U.S. attitude toward the insurgents matter? Over the winter months, de la Barra deluged the State Department with complaints, presented in formal diplomatic language, and blanketed Knox's desk with "evidence" of neutrality violations as the Mexican government saw them. Knox always replied politely, although privately he complained about de la Barra's "howling for strict enforcement of neutrality."[21] Even de la Barra's private meeting with Taft brought no change of policy. Only when Joaquín Casasús, a personal emissary from Díaz, met with Taft did Mexico finally elicit a promise for more agents to curtail illegal arms shipments.[22] In sum, de la Barra had been polite, legalistic, and rational but unable to convince. In fairness to him, however, one should point out that even had the U.S. authorities sealed the border, the popular maderista insurrection ultimately would have defeated Díaz.[23] The sheer number of rebels, most of them supplying their own military equipment, would have taken down the dictatorship.

Finally, although the accumulation of these apparent violations of neutrality may lend credence to the argument that the United States favored the Madero rebels,[24] logic dictates otherwise. Two Wall Street lawyers such as President Taft and Secretary of State Knox, who had dedicated their lives to the preservation of the principles of law and order, could not rationally have promoted rebellion in a friendly country.[25] Their behavior seems far more logical, however, if one looks at their belief that all statutes ought to be strictly construed to avoid excessive governmental interference in the lives of the citizenry. During the PLM experiences in 1906 and 1908, a different person, with a very different judicial philosophy, had occupied the White House. Theodore Roosevelt, even though also a Republican, never felt constrained by rules when issues of right and wrong, as he perceived them, were involved. Therefore, in Roosevelt's opinion, the neutrality statutes had to be broadly interpreted to squelch dangerous revolutionaries such as the PLM. Roosevelt was inclined to believe that the ends justified the means, and so he proved willing to use the power of the federal government against dangerous "subversives" such as the Flores Magón brothers. But unfortunately for Porfirio Díaz, Taft was president in 1910 and he believed in a narrow interpretation of statutes.[26] The U.S. government's view of the neutrality statutes, coupled with lax enforcement in the borderlands by lower-echelon officials who, along with 90 percent of the people in the region, did have pro-Madero sentiments, left the frontier wide open. Díaz probably realized that neither his counterinsurgency program nor his diplomatic efforts would succeed. This realization gave him another reason to continue negotiations in March 1911.

The New York Negotiations and Their Aftermath

Higher-level negotiations, though still unofficial, took place on March 12 and March 15, 1911, in New York City, with Francisco Vázquez Gómez, Madero's father, Francisco Sr., and brother Gustavo on one side against Finance Minister José Yves Limantour on the other. Limantour had spent almost six months in Europe, reaching an agreement for a temporary loan for Mexico with French bankers. Because the insurgency had already weakened investor confidence, thereby making further business difficult to transact, and because Díaz needed to consult his most important minister, Limantour agreed to cut short his trip and return to Mexico by way of New York, where he could meet informally with the revolutionaries.[27] The conferences took place privately in Ambassador de la Barra's sitting room at the Hotel Astor. Díaz clearly hoped that a deal could be struck. Likewise, many of the civilian maderista leadership were ready to compromise.[28] The remainder of the Madero family was not as keen on Francisco's rebellion as he was, and the disaster of Casas Grandes was fresh in everybody's minds. Further, Limantour had been a close friend of Francisco Sr.'s for many years and Díaz obviously hoped that the father could persuade his eldest son to capitulate before Porfirian Mexico collapsed. Finally, the maderistas were concerned about rumors that Limantour had talked with General Bernardo Reyes in Paris. They assumed that the two men had discussed Reyes's return to Mexico, which could have had a profound impact on the fate of the Madero rebellion.

Although Limantour and Reyes, the former contender for the vice presidency under Díaz who had been exiled earlier on a "military mission," disagreed on many issues, they both agreed that Porfirio Díaz's continued presence in Chapultepec Palace was vitally important for Mexico. Reyes certainly recognized the need for reform and hoped that Don Porfirio would take strong measures to get rid of the "pernicious influences," by which he meant the *científicos,* that surrounded him.[29] Because no evidence exists about the content of the Reyes-Limantour discussions, historians have speculated that they talked about conditions under which Reyes would be permitted to return to Mexico to lead government forces against the rebels. They may also have reached some agreement on the social and political reforms that the government would propose. After that meeting Limantour leaked his private thoughts about his country's situation to the press and suggested that the great estates in the north (among which he probably meant to include those belonging to the Madero family) ought to be divided and sold in small plots to the peasantry.[30]

Some of the content of the "secret" informal talks in New York became public information because the participants granted interviews to the press. One issue that the negotiators discussed freely in the press was the recent dispatch of twenty thousand U.S. soldiers to the border on "routine maneuvers." Both Porfirians and maderistas feared U.S. intervention. The maderistas believed that

Taft, in keeping with U.S. dollar diplomacy, would invade Mexico to squelch the revolt, while the Porfirians feared an invasion for the reasons cited earlier. Taft's public utterances did not reveal his actual intentions. The degree of disorder in Mexico concerned him, leading him to reach the opinion privately that the Díaz government could not by itself contain the maderistas. Ambassador Henry Lane Wilson's visit in early March had triggered the decision. Wilson claimed Díaz was "sitting on a volcano" and needed U.S. assistance. Taft also felt the need to scare the insurrectionists and thereby protect U.S. investments in northern Mexico. Thus, it seems very likely that he had decided to do precisely what the Mexican government had requested back in November, to dispatch additional troops to the border in an attempt to enforce the neutrality statutes, or, in Taft's own words, "to hold the hands of the existing government."[31]

De la Barra initially reacted to the mobilization negatively, but by the time he joined the meeting at the Hotel Astor, he seemed more reassured about U.S. intentions. He had conferred privately with Taft and State Department officials, who told him that the mobilization meant nothing more than a commitment to patrol the border more effectively, thereby preventing neutrality violations, in addition to routine war maneuvers.[32] Publicly, at least, de la Barra seemed convinced, and he issued a statement of friendship for the United States and acquiescence with Taft's policy. In his meeting with the president and his cabinet, de la Barra asked about the reason that so many naval vessels had been sent to Mexican ports if the United States did not intend to intervene. Taft responded that the ships' arrival was a coincidence; they were only fueling and would be ordered out of Mexican ports immediately. Since both the maderistas and the Porfirians feared U.S. intervention, and Limantour played upon that fear, the U.S. military presence motivated both sides to continue negotiations. According to de la Barra, Taft also recommended that Díaz make concessions to the rebels.[33] And since both sides really wanted a signed accord, Taft's action in fact hastened the peace process.

In addition to expressing concerns about the U.S. "threat," the New York conferees also discussed possible cabinet changes and other internal political reforms. General Díaz had initiated local political change in late February when he dumped the immature scion of the Terrazas family as the governor of Chihuahua and replaced him with a known reformer. Díaz would continue to implement personnel changes unilaterally throughout the spring, removing unpopular *científico* governors and appointing the loyal Porfirian opposition to their places. The question of a second level of political reform, replacing the cabinet members, surfaced for the first time in the Hotel Astor meetings. Francisco Vázquez Gómez favored a clean sweep that would include the removal of Finance Minister Limantour. The Madero family was not willing to go that far, particularly where their friend Limantour was concerned, and Madero Sr. argued that Limantour was indispensable for the implementation of the reform program. The most significant cabinet change discussed in March was the substitution of Francisco León de la Barra for Enrique Creel as secretary of foreign relations, ranking member of the cabinet, and constitutionally next in succession for the presidency after Vice President Corral.[34]

The conferees did not select de la Barra's name randomly or without considerable forethought. Francisco Vázquez Gómez recollected that after meeting de la Barra on several occasions, he became convinced of the ambassador's political neutrality. Because de la Barra was not committed to any political faction, Vázquez Gómez believed he could be trusted to act fairly. As a result, Vázquez Gómez decided to recommend de la Barra as an acceptable choice for secretary of foreign relations. Later, he regretted the decision.[35] De la Barra also seems to have been the choice of Porfirio Díaz. When de la Barra returned to Mexico in January to remarry, he had a productive meeting with Díaz, after which the dictator commented publicly and very favorably on his ambassador's abilities. According to Limantour, Díaz became convinced at that time that de la Barra ought to be offered a cabinet position when a vacancy occurred.[36]

During the course of the negotiations from March to May, both sides indicated that they were comfortable with Francisco León de la Barra as at least the number two man in Mexico, Vice President Corral's resignation being a foregone conclusion. The maderistas continued to accept him even though he occasionally issued some harsh press releases, such as that of March 16 in which he claimed that the rebellion was insignificant, that its ideas were meaningless, and that it would soon be crushed by the federal army.[37] Presumably, the rebels understood that de la Barra was only doing his job, and downplaying the maderistas' strength was part of the ambassador's public relations responsibilities.

Another interesting question worthy of some consideration is whether Díaz anticipated that de la Barra would become an interim president of Mexico. Díaz certainly perceived de la Barra as a man of merit whose services might prove useful, and although it seems unlikely that in January Díaz foresaw his own resignation two months later, the situation had clearly changed. Díaz's papers do not reveal his innermost thoughts at this moment, but he probably considered the possibility that he might be forced from office. Thus, Díaz understood the significance of the selection of the new minister of foreign relations who might eventually become interim president. Certainly, many other observers speculated that de la Barra would soon occupy the presidency. De la Barra recalled a year later that Taft stated at the time of their final interview, "I think that soon you will be president of Mexico," to which de la Barra responded politely that he doubted it since he was not politically known. The British ambassador in Washington, however, did not think de la Barra would be up to the job. He believed that while de la Barra was a solid diplomat, he lacked initiative and "was not the sort of man one would run to in a crisis."[38]

Although debate about the turnover of cabinet members occupied much of the discussions in New York, Limantour recollected that his most important concern was convincing the Maderos of the imminent danger of foreign intervention and therefore the importance of compromise. To end the revolt and forestall intervention, Limantour agreed to take the insurgents' written demands back to Mexico although he believed them to be exorbitant.[39] Vázquez Gómez's meeting notes, supposedly written by Luis Lara Pardo, reflect the civilian leadership's state of mind in March. In addition to three cabinet positions (not including finance), the maderistas demanded ten governorships and Ramón Corral's resignation. The rebels would be granted amnesty and all political prisoners would be freed. Congress would resign and new elections would take place. Finally, they wanted a constitutional amendment prohibiting the reelection of the president or governors.[40] Madero Sr. left the meeting pleased with the discussions. He and his son Gustavo traveled down to the border, hoping that they could meet Francisco Madero and continue the dialogue. Eventually, many of the terms proposed in March were in fact accepted, as well as a few other conditions that were added as the tide of battle swung in favor of the maderistas.

When Limantour returned to Mexico, he reported immediately to Díaz. While the cabinet debated the likelihood of winning the war, and concluded that compromises and negotiations were necessary, the dictator unilaterally began to implement many of the insurgents' demands within the next two weeks. Limantour also apparently suggested that Díaz propose some additional reforms, such as those Limantour had suggested to the press in Paris, to reduce the attractiveness of the maderista program to those who were vacillating. Thus, in a major speech to Congress on April 1, Díaz announced sweeping changes for Mexico. By offering more than the rebels had demanded, Díaz hoped to win back the fence-sitters. Díaz's package eliminated the *científicos*, Limantour excepted, from the cabinet. Corral resigned as minister of the interior and left for Europe, although formally retaining the vice presidency. (He left the text of his vice presidential resignation with President Díaz, who hoped that the document would serve as his trump card.) The president pledged, with the assistance of state governments, to end the abuses associated with local officeholders, the infamous jefes politicos. He promised an independent judiciary, as well as a statute, if not a constitutional amendment, that would prohibit the reelection of any official holding an executive post. Finally, Díaz advocated the division of the great estates on "terms that were fair" to both owners and workers.[41] Díaz's agrarian reform proposal would have granted plots of five, ten, or fifteen acres per family, depending on the number of family members. The breadwinner was eligible for a government loan to purchase the property, which would have to be repaid in ten years. Although more modest than most of the land reform programs that would emerge later in the revolution, Díaz's scheme was the first specifically designed to redistribute private property belonging to individuals, rather than just to parcel out public lands.

In a single message, therefore, Díaz appropriated for himself nearly all of the Anti-Reelection campaign program and more, including in his remarks specific social reforms as well as political changes. Except for his continued presence in Chapultepec Palace, a major point of contention, Díaz showed that a progressive consensus had developed among educated Mexicans about the direction in which the nation should evolve. Although many historical accounts leave the impression that Andrés Molina Enríquez's famous *Los grandes problemas nacionales* was the only contemporary book that expressed concern about Mexico's land problem, in fact numerous works about land reform appeared in the late Porfiriato. Even establishment figures such as Limantour knew that a land problem existed. Thus, Díaz's social reform proposal of April 1, 1911, was nothing radical or unexpected; it was something that had been on the minds of thoughtful Mexicans for some time.

Nevertheless, it is important to consider the effect of Díaz's reform package on Francisco Madero and his presidency. Díaz's action essentially co-opted the social changes acceptable to the civilian maderistas, leaving Madero with little new to offer during his term. Because Madero was unwilling to go beyond the progressive consensus in his thinking about social reforms, his presidency was doomed to failure as far as the militant popular maderistas were concerned. A very real issue after April 1911 for the civilian maderistas was whether Porfirio Díaz could be trusted to implement the promised reforms and whether he ought to continue in office as president.[42] Almost all of the maderistas were skeptical about both issues, and with good reason. Díaz had made promises in the past, but more than once had failed to fulfill them. His incumbency was becoming more and more controversial, and rebel military successes made it increasingly likely that Díaz would have to resign. Ultimately, the dictator's unilateral concessions failed to end the insurgency.

From Informal to Formal Negotiations

Díaz's shuffling of personnel had proved one thing, that he was willing to compromise at last. His not-so-subtle message sent a host of would-be unofficial negotiators brimming with optimism to the border. But their informal discussions there met with no success. The first talks, with Rafael Hernández and another Madero brother, Salvador, representing the government, took place with the exiles in San Antonio at the end of March. Then Madero's father, hurrying south after the New York meeting, stopped in El Paso to see whether their suggestions would meet with civilian maderista approval. Neither proposal succeeded. By now, the Texas-based exiles, in communication with Madero, insisted on Díaz's resignation as a sine qua non for a negotiated settlement, a position that Francisco Vázquez Gómez endorsed.[43] As a result, Madero eventually disavowed any agreements for anything less. Equally unpalatable and ineffective was U.S. Ambassador Wilson's offer to use his good offices to end the civil war. Foreign Minister de la Barra thanked Wilson but noted "that it would be badly received to allow a foreign power to mediate our domestic disputes."[44] Other indirect negotiations proved so cumbersome that Díaz ultimately had to concede that they were unworkable.[45] Communications sent to Madero by way of the governor of Chihuahua, Miguel Ahumada, and maderista sympathizer Silvestre Terrazas also failed.[46]

Fortunately for Díaz, at this opportune moment two other eager and able volunteers came forward to see whether they could get the talks moving again: Oscar Braniff, a banker and the brother of Mexico's most important industrialist, and Toribio Esquivel Obregón, one of the early Anti-Reelectionist leaders who had disagreed with Madero over the idea of revolution and had therefore remained loyal to Porfirio Díaz. Braniff explained his motives for undertaking a peace mission in late April 1911. He believed that the rebellion had occurred because of a desire for "effective suffrage and justice, a more logical distribution of land, [and] more active public instruction," reforms that the government had just granted. Once Díaz made these concessions, Braniff believed, violence was no longer justified. Now "the public considers that the Revolution has won out morally and has no reason for continuing to be active."[47] For his part, Esquivel Obregón made no statement, but his prior actions as well as his subsequent writings made it abundantly clear that he preferred to work within the system rather than to overturn it by violence.[48]

After a lengthy conference with Díaz, Braniff and Esquivel Obregón traveled to Washington, where they interviewed Vázquez Gómez, who encouraged them to deal with Madero himself.[49] Upon arriving at the San Isidro Ranch where Madero was headquartered, Braniff and Esquivel Obregón reiterated their position that the insurrection had essentially succeeded and that further bloodshed and property destruction were unnecessary. Madero publicly disagreed, reminding his followers that Díaz had made promises in the past that he had not always kept.[50] Madero again enunciated his demands, which, in addition to the terms previously discussed with Limantour, included another cabinet position, four additional governorships, and the resignation of the state legislatures. He wanted the federal army to evacuate the northern tier of states: Chihuahua, Sonora, and Coahuila. He demanded compensation for the victims of the civil war, the freeing of all political prisoners, and payment of the rebel forces for time served in the maderista army. Finally, he wanted de la Barra to remain as minister of foreign relations. Esquivel Obregón and Braniff duly transmitted these demands to the dictator.[51]

Notoriously absent from Francisco Madero's list was Porfirio Díaz's resignation, probably a result of the presence of the Madero family at San Isidro. This omission well may have encouraged Díaz to stiffen his resistance to resignation and also to agree to send an official peace commissioner, Francisco Carvajal, to formalize the negotiations. The appointment of Carvajal, a forty-five-year-old supreme court justice with a sterling reputation, represented a major concession for Díaz. In effect, Díaz was now conferring face-to-face with the rebels, essentially accepting their status as equals, although Carvajal was given lengthy instructions about how to avoid recognizing the maderistas as "belligerents."[52] Carvajal managed to weave his way successfully through this legal minefield and still have useful talks. Meanwhile, because the negotiations looked promising, the unofficial envoys signed a temporary armistice with Madero to prevent further bloodshed and property loss for the duration of the peace talks. To complicate matters further, the recent arrival, Francisco Vázquez Gómez, perhaps because of his own ambition, as detractors claimed, or because Madero's resolve needed strengthening, now added a new set of opinions to the discussions.

Carvajal did not arrive at the border until May 3, sometime after Vázquez Gómez, and so for about a week the maderista leadership cooled its heels. The would-be negotiators had no choice but to sign an armistice extension until May 6. Madero himself agreed that the armistice was a good idea, as did Vázquez Gómez.[53] Some of the soldiers, however, grew impatient with the waiting and demanded action. But the talking continued. In these "Peace Grove Conferences," so named because they took place in a cottonwood grove, Carvajal initially asserted that he would not consider the notion of Porfirio Díaz's resignation. While at times the maderistas, sometimes Madero himself, privately waffled on this point, ultimately the rebels would hold firm to the idea that Porfirio Díaz must resign. Not long after Carvajal arrived, newspapers published an interview with Díaz in which he promised to resign as soon as peace was reestablished. Carvajal and his volunteer assistants, Esquivel Obregón and Braniff, argued that Díaz deserved an opportunity to resign with honor and suggested that the rebels should agree that his resignation be delayed until peace was restored.[54] But this compromise required trust, and Madero had no trust in the dictator's promises.

After a long meeting and considerable debate, the maderistas decided not to accept the offer. Francisco Vázquez Gómez was the most strident voice calling for Díaz's immediate resignation; Madero was willing to wait. Finally, the rebels refused to be persuaded that Díaz should delay his resignation.[55] The maderistas became even more perturbed when Carvajal admitted that he had no authority to make a deal, and when they learned that Díaz had set no certain date for his resignation, the question of whether he could be trusted was raised once again. When Carvajal conferred with Limantour and Díaz, they also rejected the proposal that the soldiers in the rebel army in the northern three states would become rurales and that elsewhere they would enlist as public security forces.[56]

On May 6, with the negotiations at a stalemate, Carvajal broke off his talks with Madero, who, in response, ordered his army south. A day of pleading for more negotiations by Rafael Hernández, Braniff, and Esquivel Obregón proved useless.[57] Madero's forces were already restless, spoiling for a fight, in the spirit of Carlos Fuentes's character Tomás Arroyo in *The Old Gringo*, who asserted that the essence of revolution is movement. If a revolution stagnates in a single place, momentum is lost, and the revolution dies.[58] The Madero revolution was stuck while the negotiators talked, and for men of action such as Francisco "Pancho" Villa and Pascual Orozco, the talk was pointless.

At this moment, then, the two segments of the Madero insurrection became separated one from the other, not to reunite until much later in the decade. The first group, Madero, Vázquez Gómez, and other civilian politicians, were the talkers and the compromisers. They saw value in the Porfirian civilization and wanted a place for themselves in the political process, and they wanted to see the social goals of the progressive consensus implemented. The other segment of maderismo was that of the men of the countryside, *los de abajo*. For them, the Porfiriato represented inequity and oppression. While unable to articulate precisely what they wanted, they knew that change was important and that up to this point, all the talk had accomplished little. Their needs differed, region to region, and hence they had a much more difficult time finding common ground.

Madero, bitterly disappointed with the failure of the negotiations, knew that now he had to win another military victory in order to strengthen his bargaining position with Porfirio Díaz. Fearing that an attack on Ciudad Juárez might provoke a U.S. response if any of its citizens were killed or wounded, Madero decided that Chihuahua City might be a safer objective. The local U.S. military commander helped persuade Madero to make this decision by warning that an attack on Ciudad Juárez could only lead to international implications, including possible military intervention.[59] The decision to retreat southward was a rational one. But to the men in the field the decision could not be defended rationally; they thirsted for immediate action and they saw a choice target in front of them. The insurrection had stalled at Ciudad Juárez and the popular maderistas felt it important to seize the city.

In one sense, what happened next proved to be a microcosm of the Madero presidency. Madero could not control his nominal followers from rural Chihuahua, and when he saw that he had lost command of the situation, he weakly acquiesced to their actions. Many contemporaries saw Madero's vacillation at the time of the battle of Ciudad Juárez as a sign of impending problems. They were probably correct, although the more charitable would view Madero's actions as driven by expediency. In the end, Madero's army simply disobeyed him and, led by Pascual Orozco and Pancho Villa, opened a withering fire on the border city on May 8. When Madero found he could not dissuade his troops from the attack, he gave the order to continue firing. Certainly Madero's actions set a precedent for a second mutiny later in the week, when the military leadership wanted to execute federal commander Juan Navarro. Madero on that occasion successfully stood up to the generals, but the first incident had been enough to diminish his prestige among some of the soldiery. Some writers would see in the animosity generated by these two episodes, coupled with Madero's apparent indifference to his wounded soldiers in El Paso hospitals, the seeds of the rebellion that Pascual Orozco would lead against Madero in 1912.[60]

The battle of Ciudad Juárez from May 8 to May 11 proved to be the turning point in the negotiations, dealing Madero sufficiently good cards so that he could win the final hand with the dictator. Vázquez Gómez, too, was pleased with the practical results, because the rebels now controlled a border city, and this, as he had suggested all along, permitted guns, food, and medical supplies to flow freely into rebel hands. Ciudad Juárez marked the first time the rebel forces had defeated the Porfirian army in a pitched battle. One could sense the momentum shifting toward the maderistas, and although the outcome of the civil war could not be predicted with complete certainty, the likelihood was that the dictatorship would ultimately lose.[61] Yet almost as soon as the battle ended, the talks started again.

Why did the maderistas continue to negotiate even though a total military victory now appeared possible? There are several reasons. First, Madero's family, or at least some members of it, which had provided the better part of the funds, had begun to run out of money.[62] Although some writers have speculated that Madero's lawyer, Sherbourne Hopkins, persuaded Standard Oil of New Jersey to pump resources into insurgent pockets in exchange for preferred treatment once the revolution had succeeded, the evidence is murky at best. Further, reports from the field indicate that the rebels lacked weapons and ammunition, especially where unskilled commanders such as Orozco were wont to waste bullets in the heat of a battle.[63]

Second, Madero's political advisors feared the arrival of General Bernardo Reyes, the much-acclaimed iron man of the Mexican military establishment. According to rumors, Reyes was en route from Paris, anxious to take to the field and crush the rebels, a matter of no small concern to the maderistas, who certainly believed that a reinvigorated Porfirian army represented a significant military threat.[64] Third, the rebels could not be certain that their successes in a remote border city could be repeated in a pitched battle for the capital, where federal resistance would likely be stronger. Finally, and most important, Madero and the other civilian maderistas admired the Porfiriato and its achievements and had no interest in seeing Mexico devastated. They wanted to use the infrastructure of the state that Porfirio Díaz had built, not destroy it. Consistent with their actions from the beginning of the fighting, the rebels preferred a negotiated peace.

In the aftermath of Ciudad Juárez, however, the relative strength of the two sides engaged in the debate had changed. Díaz's stubbornness notwithstanding, the issue no longer was whether Porfirio Díaz would resign, but when. At first, the dictator refused to face reality; he decided to try one last colossal bluff. He proposed withdrawing federal forces from the three northern states where three thousand rebels would take over the maintenance of law and order by serving as a rurales corps but balked at the notion of paying the rebels from the moment they entered military service against the government. Ten governorships would change hands. All remaining insurgents would muster out, and Corral would resign. A noreelection bill would be submitted to congress, along with amnesty legislation. Díaz threatened that this was his final offer.[65] The problem with Díaz's proposal from the rebel perspective was twofold. First, as Francisco Vázquez Gómez had noted shortly before, Díaz offered little to the southern rebels, who had few incentives to respect the peace. Second, the proposal said nothing about his resignation. That meant, without question, the insurgents would not accept. Madero urged the dictator to resign by the end of the month to prevent further bloodshed.[66]

At this juncture, talks broke off momentarily so that Díaz, who had been suffering from a toothache, could undergo emergency oral surgery. Because of Díaz's key role in the regime, his absence delayed any further decisions until after May 17. Much has been made of this episode; some accounts even suggest that Díaz had been so ill for so many months that he had been unable to cope with the rebellion.[67] According to documentary evidence, however, this was the first time Díaz was too debilitated to work, and this episode lasted only a single day. All other contemporary reports suggest that Díaz was still relatively physically vigorous, despite his advanced age, and that other factors were responsible for the fall of the dictatorship.

The Treaty of Ciudad Juárez

Meanwhile, Carvajal and Madero had begun to talk again, sparring verbally while Díaz pondered the realities of his situation. Madero signed an additional five-day armistice, assuming that the news of the disastrous defeat at Ciudad Juárez, coupled with the ability of the rebels to import munitions freely into Mexico, would suffice to persuade Díaz to give way.[68] Unlike the earlier armistice, Madero agreed that this one would apply nationwide, so that theoretically the fighting in Morelos and other southern states would cease as well. Despite Madero's signature on the armistice, the violence increased. Some rebels claimed that they never received word of the cease-fire from their commanders. Other Mexicans seized the opportunity to declare themselves in rebellion, for possibly two reasons. With the coercive power of the dictatorship in check, those who had been cautious about joining the revolt now found the courage to do so, knowing that the federal army would not retaliate against them. And, perhaps more important, the two strands of the Madero movement, those of the civilian politicians and the rural poor, continued to diverge. For those who joined the rebellion to remedy a local grievance against a landlord or jefe politico, the talking at the national level made little or no difference. These men, many of whom declared themselves in revolt in late May and even June 1911, believed that the activities of politicians such as Madero were essentially irrelevant. At best, the civilian leadership of the insurrection provided no more than a legitimizing label for these people seeking resolution of local grievances.

It may not be productive, therefore, to debate whether a unified social revolution took place in Mexico during spring 1911.

Instead, it may be more appropriate to consider the differences between two distinctive threads of the anti-Díaz movement. Madero's political revolt, at least in May 1911, seemed to have only a superficial connection with the agrarian social movements that had commenced regionally. The *gente* of Zapata were as far removed from Madero's control as they were from Porfirio Díaz's. The chaotic, dualistic nature of the Madero movement concerned Díaz officials; they wanted the fighting to end and assumed that Madero had the power and influence to halt the violence.[69] He did not, and the mid-May armistice failed.

The growing and open dissent provided the rationale for Díaz to sign a peace treaty rather than fight to the bitter end to defend his dictatorship, as, for example, Fulgencio Batista would do in Cuba in 1959. Age, infirmity of purpose, and a serious toothache do not adequately explain Díaz's motives in giving up the struggle before a major battlefield loss had occurred in central Mexico. Díaz assessed his chances for victory realistically in late May. He knew that the tide of public opinion, even in conservative Mexico City, had turned against him. Catcalls filled the Chamber of Deputies, and people in the streets openly discussed the end of the regime. But far more weighty for Díaz's decision was his own sense of historical importance and pride in the dictatorship's achievements. As Limantour stated, "We did not want to destroy the accomplishments of the past twenty-five years."[70]

The issues that the intermediaries resolved during the final round of negotiations included the names of the six new cabinet officers and the fourteen governors that Madero wanted state legislatures to appoint. The rebels expressed considerable concern about the new minister of war; they made it abundantly clear that they did not want Bernardo Reyes to have that position. Further, they insisted on Limantour's resignation. Carvajal asked the maderistas to appoint someone living in Mexico City to work out these details with Díaz, which the rebels did.[71] Manuel Amieva, a mutual friend of Vázquez Gómez and Díaz's who had open access to the president's house, carried messages back and forth. The final issue to be resolved was the date of Díaz's resignation, which the dictator purposefully had left vague. Limantour now authorized Carvajal to promise that Díaz would resign before the end of the month, thereby granting the last major concession that the rebels sought.[72]

With agreements reached on the identity of the cabinet members and the resignation of the governors, as well as a relatively firm date for Díaz's departure from the presidency, Madero and Carvajal signed the formal document that has become known as the Treaty of Ciudad Juárez (see Appendix A).[73] The Treaty of Ciudad Juárez is extremely vague, containing none of the specifics that had been debated orally (for example, how many governors had to resign) and that had bogged down earlier discussions. Instead, the Treaty of Ciudad Juárez called for all of the rebel armies to be mustered out and sent home, with the exception of a few soldiers who might be given positions in state police organizations or the rurales as local circumstances dictated. Madero clearly believed that Porfirio Díaz's and Ramón Corral's resignation ended the underlying reason for the civil war, and that the Porfirian military would maintain peace. In fact, Madero assumed that his rural followers would return to their villages, since the objectives of the 1910 revolt, as far as he was concerned, had been accomplished with Díaz's resignation. Some of the other participants in the civil war, however, later voiced opposition to the settlement for a variety of reasons.[74]

Finally, although not mentioned specifically in the treaty, Madero insisted that the governors, but not the state legislatures, be replaced with people sympathetic to him. Madero wanted to reward his followers and hoped that his friends would instill democratic ideals at the state level. Cynics, however, would assert that these governors controlled state political machines, which in turn counted the ballots in local and federal elections. Thus, an earlier period of Mexican history, the Restored Republic of the 1860s and 1870s, has been reinterpreted as a period when machine politics prevailed and strong presidents used precisely these tactics in order to perpetuate themselves in power.[75]

Although both parties had signed the Treaty of Ciudad Juárez on May 21, Díaz took no action for several days. Calls for his resignation now rang louder in the galleries of the Chamber of Deputies; people milled around the Zócalo in downtown Mexico City shouting vivas for Madero. On the night of May 24, a huge crowd gathered outside the presidential palace, demanding Díaz's resignation. The dictator responded with one last show of force; an army battalion fired into the throng, killing a few of the demonstrators and sending the remainder fleeing for their homes. But it was Díaz's last hurrah. The next morning he entered the Chamber of Deputies and delivered his resignation and that of Ramón Corral. Only two deputies voted against Díaz's resignation, one of whom, Benito Juárez Maza, was a member of Madero's coalition. Under the terms of succession set forth in the constitution and as agreed upon in the Treaty of Ciudad Juárez, Francisco León de la Barra acceded to the presidency.[76]

De la Barra's short inaugural address was meant to reassure his countrymen that the interim presidency would restore peace and supervise the transition to democracy. In the speech de la Barra emphasized that he would enforce the laws, particularly the electoral laws, and that under no circumstances would he be a candidate in the presidential or vice presidential elections. He pledged freedom of action to political parties. In addition, he articulated the necessity for peace and the importance of restoring the calm that had lasted for a generation so that all Mexicans could prosper in the new age. Finally, he pledged to work for democracy and "a common aspiration for peace and progress."[77] These stated objectives became the goals that de la Barra set for himself for the interim presidency (see Appendix B).

Both Madero and Francisco León de la Barra were pleased that the long battle of proposals and counterproposals had now ended. De la Barra thanked Madero profusely for "his patriotic and dignified attitude" and pledged his cooperation in creating a new era of peace and progress.[78] Madero in turn congratulated de la Barra on his accession to the presidency. He also requested that all political prisoners be freed and that the new provisional governors be seated in accordance with the agreement. De la Barra fulfilled the request.[79] Although relations between the federal army and the insurgents were particularly tense in some urban areas where they stood face to face, generally, Mexicans welcomed peace. De la Barra and Madero both pledged to cooperate for the transition period and, at the moment, appeared to be of a single mind.

Meanwhile, Porfirio Díaz had slipped out of Mexico City, bound for Veracruz. Undoubtedly Díaz had been hurt by his countrymen's disloyalty and the disrespect manifested in the demonstrations of late May. But he left the nation a proud man. When his train was attacked by maderistas in the state of Veracruz, Díaz ordered a counterattack, and his troops drove off the rebel band after a minor skirmish.[80] When Díaz arrived in Veracruz, he resigned his commission in the Mexican army, returning to civilian status in exile. He did request his military pension, which de la Barra granted in very respectful terms, but he refused British investor Lord Cowdray's offer that he live at an English estate and spent his years in exile in rather modest circumstances.[81]

As Díaz stepped aboard the *Ypiranga,* which would eventually take him to exile in Paris, he reputedly stated, "Madero has unleashed a tiger. Now let us see if he can control him." This statement underscored one additional reason that Díaz had been so reluctant to yield the presidency. Madero had no executive experience. He had never administered anything other than a family estate. Díaz was not alone in his concerns. Other foreign observers also thought that "Madero was of little weight," and too much of a "dreamer," or idealist, but that his courage in opposing the dictatorship had made his name a rallying point for most Mexicans.[82] Whether courage and a love of democracy would be enough to make him a competent president remained to be evaluated.

And what about de la Barra, this person who had been thrust into the presidency? He, too, had no political experience, though he had long engaged in diplomatic affairs and was accustomed to observing politicians in action. According to an inside account, de la Barra did not want the presidency, the cabinet had to badger him into accepting it (although of course some outsiders saw him as a schemer).[83] De la Barra's hesitancy was not false modesty. As he said in his inaugural address, he had no intention of running for office, and in fact he resigned before his allotted term expired. Assuming, then, that mere ambition did not drive de la Barra, was he competent to govern Mexico? Would it be possible for a good man, but perhaps not a great one, to be strong enough to replace an iron hand like that Porfirio Díaz wielded where the state lacked an adequate institutional framework?

The British certainly felt more confident than they had in April. Their minister proclaimed that de la Barra had handled the recent crisis very well and that he had displayed "qualities of energy and resolution of which one would not have believed him to be possessed."[84] De la Barra was certainly intelligent and industrious. But both the British minister and his American colleague also noted that de la Barra tended to be naively optimistic at times. For example, in early May Ambassador Wilson said, "As [de la Barra's] zeal for the accomplishment of peace is so strong, he has frequently permitted the wish to be father to the thought," a problem that would plague him during his presidency. Yet, as a former colleague in the cabinet remarked, de la Barra appreciated delicate situations and was not obstinate by nature; he preferred to compromise, and that quality was exactly what the civilian maderistas appreciated in him.[85] He certainly looked like a president. But would a compromiser and diplomat have the political skills to govern Mexico and fulfill his inaugural promises in the absence of Porfirio Díaz?

3

The Quest for Order

Down, down I come, like glist'ring Phaeton,
Wanting the manage of unruly jades.

—William Shakespeare, *Richard II*

Francisco León de la Barra's highest priority in June 1911 was to tame the tiger to which Porfirio Diáz had referred and restore peace. But to govern Mexico without an institutional framework in place required more than just an iron hand like the one Díaz had used. It also required approval of government policies by a majority of the politically active population.[1] Part of the difficulty de la Barra faced was determining whom he had to please, whether the politically viable included the campesinos and workers as well as the traditionally dominant elite and the growing middle class. In a sense, de la Barra's dilemma reflects the recent historiographical debate about the very nature of the Mexican Revolution: Was it a popular rural, agrarian, social revolution as the first generation of scholars believed, or was it a rebellion full of sound and fury, signifying little more than the replacement of an old political elite by a newer one, as the revisionists would have us think?[2]

This chapter examines the military disturbances that confounded de la Barra's inaugural promise to restore peace and presents some reasons why the quest for order met with only limited success. Further, this chapter tests the hypothesis that pacification largely failed because the myriad of revolts that plagued Mexico in summer 1911 were symptomatic of popular, rural discontent and demands for immediate change that would intensify during the next few years. Clearly, few people in 1911 took the popular uprising as a demand for social change, perhaps because no articulate popular leadership had yet emerged. Instead, de la Barra and

Popular maderistas in 1911 in Chihuahua. *Courtesy of El Paso Public Library, Southwest Collection*

Madero assumed that they and their colleagues of the middle and upper classes would agree on a paternalistic reform program to benefit the underprivileged. In the meantime, the two wondered what to do about the rural maderista army with its penchant for violence.

Traditional historiography asserts that Francisco Madero made his second colossal blunder by permitting interim president Francisco León de la Barra to demobilize the rebel forces in accordance with the Treaty of Ciudad Juárez. These authors argue that the de la Barra government then connived with the federal army to derail Madero's "revolutionary" program and that this derailment in turn led to a decade of bloodletting, fraught with the loss of millions of lives and the destruction of considerable property.[3] The revolution finally succeeded in 1920, according to this interpretation, only because the new revolutionaries would not stand for the sorts of compromise that had tarnished Madero's leadership. As their most persuasive example, these authors focus on de la Barra's insistence on demobilization in Morelos, which precipitated Emiliano Zapata's revolt in August 1911 and plunged southern Mexico into another round of civil war.

This chapter explores the complex contours of the government's pacification policy. It presents the thesis that the rural revolutionaries resisted disbanding primarily because they were interested in full employment at good rates of pay, which their traditional jobs as agricultural laborers could not guarantee. The de la Barra government, including Madero and his civilian colleagues, as pre-Keynesian participants in the progressive consensus, did not concede that the federal government had a major role in insuring employment for the masses. Further, the financial burden of the rebel army on the national treasury, coupled with numerous incidents proving that this army threatened private property, forced those who had reached a consensus about reforms to call for demobilization to forestall further violence. Thus, the conceptualization of the pacification program, given the intellectual predilections of the largely middle-class civilian maderistas and remaining Porfirians such as Francisco León de la Barra, made perfect sense to them although its implementation proved unsuccessful. The pacification problem ultimately boiled down to issues of trust and credibility. The popular maderistas did not believe that de la Barra and the civilian maderistas would implement agrarian reform and labor reform once order was restored, while neither the government nor Francisco Madero trusted the popular maderista insurgents' promises that they would disband (rightly, the evidence suggests). Suspicion led to further conflict, and especially because of what happened in Morelos, the prospects for peace dimmed.

The Crescendo of Revolutionary Violence: The Rural Maderista Expectations

The scent of the dying Díaz regime in May 1911 drew great numbers of popular maderista fighters, and they came like a swarm of vultures, eager to dismember the carcass. The sheer numerical increase of rebel bands in the last month of the dictatorship eventually would have ended the regime militarily even had the leadership on both sides not been determined to reach a negotiated settlement; by May 21 at least forty thousand rebels faced a much smaller Porfirian army. These rebels by themselves would have presented the government with problems of disorderliness and cost increases, at least in some regions. But still more damaging to de la Barra's quest for order was the large number of even more unruly bands that entered the fray after the signing of the Treaty of Ciudad Juárez on May 21, and the further number who rebelled after Porfirio Díaz resigned four days later, thereby swelling insurgent ranks to sixty thousand or seventy thousand soldiers, according to very unreliable estimates.[4]

While some of these late insurgencies possibly can be attributed to the poor state of communications that existed because many telegraph lines had been cut, most occurred more purposefully. These rebels knew that they enjoyed near immunity in making their declaration of rebellion; they knew that because of the treaty, no federal army would fire on them, unless provoked. Yet many of these johnny-come-lately rebels were at least as vociferous about recovering a share of the rewards as their more timely, and perhaps braver, comrades. The rural maderistas had several motives for continuing their warlike ways in May and June. Because Porfirio Díaz had surrendered before losing a major battle, some insurgents felt cheated of their victory and wanted an opportunity to take out their frustrations with the Porfiriato on the federales. Specifically, these rural maderista jefes wanted to take the cities that symbolized the Porfiriato and garrisoned their enemy. As a result, despite the armistice, conflicts emerged at the gates of several major cities and many small towns. The following narrative of just a few such incidents provides a good sense of the state of the hostilities in June 1911.

For example, the garrison in Durango had held out against approximately three thousand popular maderistas for well over a month until after the peace treaty was signed. Signing the treaty of Ciudad Juárez did not deter the rebels, who demanded the surrender of Durango. As one rural maderista said, "Oh yes, we know about the peace, but the war is not over yet."[5] On the 31st, after Emilio Madero arrived to exert some control over the insurgents, the federal army allowed their former enemies into the city. Over the next two weeks, looting and armed robberies took place, shocking foreign residents. Compared with some other communities, however, in Durango the transition was relatively peaceful.[6] In Cholula, Puebla, a band of popular maderistas tried to enter the city on May 29, provoking a conflict with the federal garrison. The minister of war told his commander to parley with the rebels and suspend hostilities.[7] But despite the commander's hope for a peaceful entrance into Cholula, the maderistas freed all the prisoners from the jail, burned the archives, and stole the municipal treasury.[8] Throughout the north and center particularly, maderista forces demanded entry into the cities and towns, with looting and other forms of lawlessness characterizing their takeover. Urban riots contributed as well to the malaise of many urban dwellers, particularly the *gente decente*.[9] Ironically, the most peaceful transitions took place in Chihuahua, where, despite fears of the former Porfirian governor, the insurgents occupied the capital city without incident.[10]

Another factor that contributed to the disorder of the early interim period was the almost volcanic nature of the celebrations accompanying the fall of the dictatorship. Despite the ideals of temperance among many of the civilian maderistas, often the rural maderistas engaged in lengthy drinking bouts to celebrate their triumphs. In their state of intoxication, the rural maderistas shot up homes, tore up shops and stores, and even killed and wounded some of the *gente decente*. The civilian maderistas found that their attempts to quell these disorders by introducing statutes of prohibition was out of step with the mores of their rural counterparts. For example, Abraham González, governor of Chihuahua, ordered the saloons and gambling casinos of Ciudad Juárez closed, all to no avail.[11] Not only did the town's tradition as a bawdy border community contribute to the statute's failure, but also the idea of prohibition flew in the face of Mexico's own cultural traditions, particularly in rural communities. Although one could occasionally find a teetotaler in rural Mexico, such as Francisco "Pancho" Villa, the norm was someone like Emiliano Zapata, who enjoyed a regular *copa* or more.

This brings us to the central thesis of this chapter. I suggest that the rural maderista revolt can best be described as the *revolution for full employment*. Studies have shown that rural Mexico experienced a serious increase in unemployment rates and a decline in take-home pay in real terms in the early twentieth century. Wages declined, while the price of staples rose dramatically.[12] The documentary evidence about the demobilization question in the de la Barra presidency shows that as much as anything else, the rural maderista wanted a decent-paying job. Payment meant more than a regular wage for soldiers; after all, that was available to enlistees in the Porfirian army. For these soldiers, receiving decent pay also meant taking the opportunity to right past wrongs by occasionally looting and pillaging, by ceasing to pay taxes, and by holding a job that provided some prestige. As one British consular officer observed, "Many of the men feel that [military service] cannot be relinquished willingly . . . as the alternative offers drudgery and 50 centavos per day, with little outlet for the grosser inclinations." A popular jingle put it more bluntly: "Less work, more money, cheap hooch. Hurrah for Madero."[13] For others, decent jobs meant the acquisition of a piece of land where they could raise corn, beans, squash, and chili on their traditional milpas. Contemporary Mexicans understood the quest for full employment, and peppered de la Barra with suggestions about how his government could find ways to put these idle hands to useful work.

The de la Barra government lacked the vision, or perhaps more fairly the philosophical bent, to adopt full-scale employment public works projects. It is interesting to speculate, however, whether the bloodshed of the following decade might have been averted had the federal government invested resources in these public works schemes. Probably not, because in addition to their general quest for employment, many of the rural maderistas had a specific type of employment in mind, either military service or a better living in their own pueblo. It is important to note that for many rebels, few economic alternatives beyond the military existed. A temporary downturn in the southwestern U.S. economy meant that most of those who went to the United States returned home unemployed.[14] Likewise, opportunities at home remained scarce for poorly educated and unskilled rural maderistas.

For a variety of reasons, the rural maderistas preferred military service to other types of employment, although of course the aforementioned alternatives never came to fruition. Many of the rural maderistas hoped to enlist in the rurales.[15] Although the documents reveal no individual motives other than financial behind requests for continued military service, a number of other motives come to mind. The armed rebellion had allowed many men to travel beyond the confines of their villages. It allowed them to break away from the dull routine of village life and also gave those who wanted it the opportunity to carouse and to seduce women. Finally, military service offered these restless men a chance to even scores against those who had abused them in the past, to acquire a horse and put some cash in their pockets. The combination of these factors meant that military employment was far preferable to unemployment or underemployment as a *peón* on a hacienda.

The new governors understood the need to provide all of these soldiers with meaningful employment. The interim governor of Guanajuato recommended that the rural maderistas be incorporated into the regular army or rurales with their military ranks intact unless they voluntarily returned home. Abraham González, the well-known reformist governor of Chihuahua, expressed his concern about the rapidity with which the federal government proposed to muster out the veterans of the struggle against Díaz, who had no employment prospects and, alarmingly, were not turning in their real military hardware as required. González recommended that the remaining troops be discharged at a rate of 10 percent each fortnight so that society could absorb them with less dislocation. Other civilian maderistas wanted to convert as many of the insurgents as possible into state forces while the remainder were mustered out.[16] But the de la Barra government refused to accept gradual demobilization as a general rule, although it did make an exception for Chihuahua.

Clearly, the men who enlisted in the maderista forces wanted to maintain their ranks so that they would continue to be fed and paid. Some simply refused to muster out because the government offered so little compensation to do so. Others wanted to stay in arms so that they could continue the process of social leveling. "Socialist" ideas were spreading in the rural areas, and the innumerable breaches of public order were often the workings of inarticulate social revolutionaries.[17] Thus, while the rising crescendo of violence is easily demonstrable, especially in June and July 1911, the interpretation of the reasons for this new wave of turmoil depended on one's perspective. For many of the rural maderistas, the violence meant opportunities for employment, redressing old grievances, and moving forward their social agenda.

The de la Barra Government's Response

President de la Barra pledged to restore order throughout the countryside. Perceiving himself at first as a caretaker president, he assumed that Madero would play a major role in the pacification process. Specifically, he erroneously believed that Madero could control the popular maderistas; that once he told them to holster their arms and return home, they would do so. Neither de la Barra nor Madero understood the distance between the political and popular rebellions. As a result, the de la Barra government tended to discount the social content of the popular movement in May and to see the violence as illegal attacks on property. For de la Barra, since the rebellion was "over" once Díaz resigned, the latecomers' military "contributions" to the end of the Porfiriato were meaningless. Further, because these latecomers violated property interests without any sort of legal process, he and the civilian maderistas branded them as troublemakers and bandits. The government refused to countenance the argument that the insurgents' continued military presence guaranteed the gains of the anti-Díaz revolt, which in de la Barra's mind had already been accomplished. De la Barra believed that the government was obligated to control these last-minute insurgents, particularly when they confronted the federal army in the cities and threatened riot and destruction.

Some of the demobilization controversy occurred because the government tended to attribute the actions of disorderly last-minute maderistas to all insurgents, even those with greater service. While it would be simplistic to label the former "bandits" while ascribing popular social revolutionary characteristics to the latter, there is some truth to this generalization. Civilian maderistas noted a great deal more discipline in the ranks of Pascual Orozco's battle-hardened veterans than among the ranks of the last-minute insurgents of the center and south of Mexico.[18] De la Barra asked Madero's "peace commissioners," who included Alfredo Robles Domínguez, a civilian maderista who had spent most of 1911 in a Porfirian prison, to dissuade the insurgents from further violence.

The peace commissioners even forbade the rural maderistas to accompany Madero on his triumphal march to Mexico City or to enter the capital to greet Madero when he arrived on June 7. Their action explains why Emiliano Zapata and other southern leaders came without their *gente*.[19]

Madero arrived in Mexico City the hero of the hour. Heavenly portents seemed to shine on him. Halley's comet had crossed the country just as the negotiations reached their final stage, and now an earthquake struck Mexico City. Even the mountains tremble at Madero's arrival, his friends asserted.[20] Thousands of people greeted Madero at the train station, showering him with adulation and strewing flowers in his path as he made his way through the streets. The newly appointed governor of the Federal District, Alberto García Granados, posted notices requesting order, and the demonstrators complied. Madero finally made his way to the National Palace to talk with Francisco León de la Barra. The two greeted each other warmly, and on this rather auspicious note began a partnership that, though quite troubled at times, lasted through half of the interim period. At least initially the two men agreed on issues, particularly pacification.

They agreed, for example, to convert a select few popular maderista chiefs and some of their gente into rurales squadrons, while discharging the vast bulk of the maderista forces. Certainly the *gente decente* welcomed this policy as the next step toward the restoration of law and order. But the rich were not alone in their complaints about the violence. Poor people as well resented the increase of lawlessness that so recently had become part of their lives. Villagers in Campeche asked their governor to pacify the countryside because the popular maderistas were ruining their farms.[21] Another group of villagers complained that foraging maderista troops had stolen two of their cattle, which they could ill afford to lose.[22] As Eric Hobsbawm suggested many years ago, the line between bandits and social revolutionaries is a thin one, at times a tiny, penetrable membrane.[23] Often, then, the label "bandit" or "social revolutionary" depended on one's perspective. Clearly the level of violence in rural Mexico in June 1911 far exceeded that of the preceding year.

In sum, several factors contributed to the continuing rural disorders, beginning with the orgy of celebration. Beyond that, Francisco León de la Barra lacked both the reputation for firmness that made Díaz's iron hand so effective and any real coercive forces, such as a sizable and efficient military and police that would have transformed his wish for peace into a reality.[24] Lacking the military means and the support of many of the popular maderistas, the national government could not end the violence. Nor did the de la Barra government consider immediate and radical social reform programs as a means for achieving peace. While de la Barra and the civilian maderistas had some sympathy for social reforms, the pace of these progressive measures would not be rapid enough to satisfy the popular maderistas. Further, the members of the progressive consensus agreed that peace had to precede reform.

Mexicans with a criminal past probably also played a role in the increase of violence during early summer 1911. One of the customary maderista tactics during the conflict had been to empty the jails after capturing a town. Likewise, the Treaty of Ciudad Juárez had partially condoned this practice by calling for the release of all political prisoners. Over the years, Díaz had jailed many of his opponents, although certainly not all prisoners in Mexican jails were there for political reasons. The popular maderistas all too frequently failed to observe the niceties of this distinction and simply opened every cell and invited all inmates to join their forces. On one occasion, the soldiers did string up a "cold-blooded killer" but allowed the remainder of the jail's occupants to sign up as soldiers.[25] Without drawing any conclusions about the rates of recidivism for these released prisoners, for which no specific evidence exists, the records do reveal that the popular maderista groups these prisoners joined did continue to act in a disorderly fashion, destroying property and threatening, and sometimes taking, lives.

Along with the escalating violence, the other factor that influenced the interim government to advocate disbanding the revolutionary army was the sheer expense of maintaining the military machine. Francisco Madero clearly agreed with this concern. The disproportionate cost of the military establishment compared with the expenses of other departments of government had been one of Mexico's endemic problems since independence. Generally ineffectual in resisting foreign invasion and constantly involved in palace intrigues, the Mexican military's record through 1876 had been pretty abysmal; plenty of historical data showed the high political and economic costs of a bloated military payroll. For example, one of the causes for the failure of Agustín de Iturbide's empire was the expense of paying for a military filled with high-ranking officers, an army that exceeded in size many European countries' professional forces. Antonio López de Santa Anna further besmirched the honor of the military by selling national territory to pay military salaries.

In more recent times, governments had devised other stratagems to deal with a military fattened by troubled times. The gorged military of the Restored Republic needed trimming, and so one of Benito Juárez's first acts following the French Intervention was to discharge most of the liberal army, setting a precedent for de la Barra's policy (although to be fair Juárez also mustered out all of the conservative army). Juárez's policy was not popular. When the size of the army increased dramatically again as a result of Porfirio Díaz's successful revolt in 1876, Díaz reduced it gradually and voluntarily. Although the ostensible size of the army in 1910 was about thirty-five thousand soldiers, in reality the army could muster about half that number. Since the Treaty of Ciudad Juárez required that the federal army remain intact and that some of Madero's irregulars would be commissioned as rurales and supplement these numbers, clearly President de la Barra's military payroll had increased significantly. Thus, de la Barra and many others believed that the size of the military had to be reduced to avoid squandering the carefully accumulated treasury surplus.

The popular maderista demands on the federal treasury for supplies and salaries in June were significant and made de la Barra doubly aware of the problem. The governor of Durango, for example, where relatively late fighting had occurred, asked for a loan from the federal treasury of about 200,000 pesos, about 32,000 of which was directly attributable to the cost of demobilizing the maderista army, not to mention the cost of their maintenance while the mustering-out process was being negotiated.[26] One of Alfredo Robles Domínguez's jobs as the principal "pacifier" of the central states was to make good on the receipts that maderista officers signed when they commandeered horses and weapons. Local maderista military leaders bombarded Robles Domínguez with handwritten drafts drawn on banks from which the rebels had appropriated funds.[27] Thus, the second great incentive for the demobilization program from de la Barra's perspective was to reduce federal military expenditures to a more normal and reasonable level.

To reduce the size of the military budget permanently by mustering out the rural maderistas, the de la Barra government had to increase expenditures temporarily because of the agreed-upon policy of a one-time payment of twenty-five to forty pesos to revolutionary "veterans," regardless of the nature of their actual service in the maderista ranks. Congress appropriated funds specifically for these payments and, more controversially, to reimburse Gustavo Madero for revolutionary expenses.[28] As mentioned previously, the policy made good sense for those soldiers who had actually fought for the cause and risked their lives. But as a practical matter it was difficult to distinguish between long-term soldiers and the johnnies-come-lately who might have rebelled even after all the shooting had stopped. Furthermore, the amount of salary paid for a day's service far exceeded the amount most peasants received as day laborers, creating a disincentive for popular maderistas to muster out quickly. Thus, the financial rewards cost the treasury significantly and created additional problems. Despite the difficulties in some districts, the demobilization proved relatively successful.[29] Although some former insurgents complained that the government offered them insufficient compensation for their weapons and some who had already agreed to accept the standard sum later felt that they had been cheated because other soldiers received more, others simply stacked their arms, picked up their pesos, and walked away.[30]

Nevertheless, the de la Barra government found itself in a no-win situation. Some citizens argued that paying the soldiers was a waste of money (a total of 8 million pesos was budgeted), especially those soldiers who joined the revolt after the fighting stopped.[31] Madero himself felt this way. He was shocked by the number of latecomers seeking rewards, and he concurred with the idea that the sizable number of troops who took up arms after the treaty ought to be discharged.[32] But others claimed that the de la Barra government and Madero were being penny-wise and pound-foolish, that without payments the discontented would merely rise up in arms again and cause more economic damage than the pay-off itself would cost.[33] For the civilian maderistas and the Porfirians, the violence proved that the countryside had fallen victim to a wave of criminal activity. For them, the only rational solution entailed the mustering out of the popular maderista troublemakers and the imposition of order by the Porfirian military.

With the civilian maderistas' concurrence that the numbers of rural maderista forces had to be reduced, de la Barra and Madero agreed on a process for carrying out the demobilization almost immediately. Alfredo Robles Domínguez and other peace commissioners coordinated the discharge process.[34] Madero himself reiterated the agreed-upon terms under which a limited number of rural maderistas could operate as police and the remainder would be mustered out. De la Barra, growing impatient, issued a controversial but ineffectual decree stating that demobilization had to be finished by July 1; otherwise, popular maderistas remaining in arms would be considered bandits.[35] But the process failed. Violence continued, and large numbers of popular maderistas remained on the federal payroll. President de la Barra slowly lost confidence in Madero because of his inability to control the rural maderistas' behavior, particularly following an unnecessary incident in Puebla in July, the bloodiest conflict over an urban occupation.

The Puebla Incident

The city of Puebla, sometimes known as the Rome of Mexico because of the extreme religiosity of its people, lies about two hours (by modern transportation) southeast of Mexico City. Built as a Spanish enclave in the sixteenth century, the city is famed for its dark-blue tiles and local cuisine specialties such as *mole poblano*. By the time de la Barra became president, Puebla had experienced its share of major conflicts. Mexico's most dramatic patriotic incident took place there in 1862 when the Mexican army defeated French invaders on the outskirts of the city on Cinco de Mayo. During the Porfiriato, Puebla underwent a major transition as it became Mexico's most industrialized state, specializing in textile production. Consequently, Puebla had a larger urban working class than any other state, and that created special circumstances for the maderistas in 1910. The state's great maderista hero, Aquiles Serdán, came from lower-middle-class origins. A humble shoemaker whose family was socially mobile in the wrong direction (his grandfather had been a landowner and governor), Serdán's presence and that of his working-class associates lent a more radical tint to the civilian maderista faction in Puebla compared to other states. Because Serdán had been among Madero's earliest supporters, Madero hesitated to undermine his leadership, even though the two disagreed on many of the goals of reform in 1910.

Two days before Madero had scheduled the November revolt to begin, the Puebla city police closed in on Serdán, acting on a tip that he was preparing to rebel. Serdán refused to surrender, and in the ensuing fray, the police killed him. The leaderless civilian maderistas drifted inactively for several months until spring, when the popular maderistas commenced their rebellion. Rebel numbers escalated in May, forcing the civilian maderistas into action. The latter were not necessarily unhappy with the newly appointed governor who had replaced the despised, long-time incumbent Mucio Martínez, but they did see the need to prevent the popular maderistas from gaining power. Thus, the lawyers, bureaucrats, and businessmen in Puebla, as in many other states, positioned themselves to move into leadership roles once Díaz resigned. By May, Díaz's fall seemed inevitable, as a mere fifteen hundred troops guarded the state's main cities against an estimated army (probably exaggerated) of about twenty thousand rural rebels fighting in the countryside. After the signing of the Treaty of Ciudad Juárez, the Puebla state legislature, at the urging of Francisco León de la Barra and with Madero's blessing, appointed the lawyer and civilian maderista Rafael Cañete to the governorship.[36] Thus, Puebla, like many other states, ultimately experienced a political revolution that unseated the Porfirian governor because of the impetus of the rural revolt.

Cañete's first task was to calm the revolutionary waters. The new governor solicited help from Agustín del Pozo, a latecomer maderista rebel with impeccable credentials (from the civilian maderista viewpoint) to pacify the state and implement the demobilization policy. Del Pozo was not a typical rural maderista; like Manuel Rincón Gallardo in Guanajuato, he was a large property owner who joined the revolution late in the spring. His selection as commander of the revolutionary forces disappointed many of the popular maderistas, who hoped that one of their own would take charge.[37] At first, del Pozo had little luck with pacification, as the Cholula incident previously described indicates. He could do little in neighboring Tlaxcala, where the Porfirian governor Próspero Cahuantzi refused to resign until rebels toppled him, more than a week after Díaz signed the treaty. Puebla's popular maderistas, however, were ordered to stand clear of Tlaxcala.[38]

Despite the changes in the Puebla governorship and notwithstanding all efforts at both the state and national level to stop the fighting and demobilize the state, the rural violence continued through June and July. Alfredo Robles Domínguez told del Pozo to take strong measures against groups of bandits, but the job was difficult.[39] Emilio Vázquez Gómez expressed his concerns about the prevalent disorder in the Puebla countryside, first by complaining to the popular maderistas that they were "embarrassing the revolution" by their actions, and later by ordering del Pozo to put a halt to these activities.[40] President de la Barra begged Madero to use his influence to restore order.[41] The situation did not better itself in July, and rural Puebla remained torn by violence. One landowner thought that changing ministers of the interior would help. He also solicited permission to form a rurales corps locally in which he offered to serve as a "simple soldier."[42]

The *poblanos'* motives for remaining in arms mirrored popular maderistas' feelings in other states; they were concerned about reforms but even more about economic opportunities that would be lost if demobilization occurred. Maderista soldiers in Puebla continued to be paid, and when the monies did not arrive from Mexico City, they requisitioned food, cash, and equipment from hacendados. Military service opened the door to a better way of life. Further, the military employment did not have to be full time. Many of the *poblano* rebels apparently tilled their crops during summer 1911 and used their military service as a means of supplementing their income.[43] Thus, the planned, quick mustering out in Puebla failed because of the reluctance of popular maderistas to accept the demobilization plan.

Puebla's most notorious violent incident took place in July and provided de la Barra with the excuse to fire Minister of the Interior Emilio Vázquez Gómez. De la Barra blamed Vázquez Gómez for the pitched battle that took place between the maderistas and federal troops billeted in Puebla city under the command of Colonel Aureliano Blanquet, later to be identified as one of the major villains of the Mexican Revolution. The incident began when Emiliano Zapata's secretary, sent to Puebla to uncover the facts about an alleged assassination plot directed against Madero, incarcerated several members of the old Martínez regime while he ascertained if enough evidence existed to try them. Emilio Vázquez Gómez reluctantly ordered the prisoners released because of the president's concern about the presumption of innocence and the infringement of personal freedoms that the arrest created.[44]

Three days later, on July 12, a car containing "a well-dressed group of individuals" fired some shots at a maderista guard billeted outside the city's bullring, where a large crowd of popular maderistas had gathered in anticipation of Francisco Madero's arrival for a speech the following day. The maderistas gave chase to the automobile, which sped off in the direction of army headquarters. At that point, a battle ensued in which the Twenty-ninth Battalion under Blanquet drubbed the maderistas. According to several of the maderistas, Colonel Blanquet compounded the tragedy by shooting several women and children. The death toll eventually reached forty-six.[45]

Although Madero no doubt grieved over the shedding of so much blood, his subsequent actions demonstrated where his sympathies lay. Unlike Díaz, who doubtless would have stayed above the fray, at a banquet the next evening Madero gave the traditional *abrazo*, or hug, to Colonel Blanquet and promised to promote him to general. To make matters worse from the popular maderistas' perspective, Madero then told the maderista soldiers that they ought to go home without their weapons, because the federal army was the only legitimate army in Mexico. He stated that he would remain in Puebla to assist with the mustering out of any remaining soldiers.[46]

The speech and Madero's gesture were consistent with the policy that he and de la Barra had agreed on in late May. In their minds, Puebla was no place for the riotous, disorderly popular maderista soldiers. In this instance, although the maderista soldiers had been provoked, they had precipitated the conflict by chasing the car toward army headquarters with their guns blazing. Madero and de la Barra believed that had the insurgents been properly discharged as ordered, the incident never would have occurred. Still, Madero hoped, perhaps too optimistically, to reconcile the hard feelings by requiring the federales and the remaining popular maderista soldiers properly in rurales units to march together on the Juárez birthday parade on the 18th.[47] Francisco Vázquez Gómez also tried to smooth ruffled feathers and to encourage the maderistas to demobilize. He happened to stop outside of Cholula the next day as a large group of popular maderistas were threatening to march on the state capital. He persuaded them to disband and promised he would look into matters surrounding the Puebla incident.[48]

The Puebla incident also created an international problem because a group of fleeing maderistas engaged in a shoot-out with the foreign managers of a textile mill called La Covadonga. In the exchange of gunfire, five foreigners were killed, four Germans and a Spaniard. The German minister to Mexico demanded action and repeatedly requested that the de la Barra government apprehend the murderers. De la Barra did his best to comply, urging Governor Cañete to proceed rigorously with the investigation.[49] Unfortunately, no witnesses came forward to identify the culprits, and although everybody suspected that Benigno Zenteno and his group of popular maderistas caused the deaths, arrests were slow in coming. The Covadonga matter dragged on through Madero's presidency, replete with jailbreaks and a bungled prosecution, and contributed to Mexico's unfortunate new image as a lawless land where violence went unpunished. Madero's ineptitude in handling this case may have persuaded the German minister to side with the anti-Madero forces in the February 1913 coup.[50]

A second controversial trial involved former governor Mucio Martínez and his sons, who, the government suspected, were behind a multitude of anti-maderista plots, including a foiled assassination attempt against Madero himself as well as the provocative July 12 incident. Witnesses eventually linked two of the Martínez sons to the Puebla massacre, identifying them as passengers in the automobile that precipitated the conflict. As a result, the government arrested Martínez, who was hiding in Mexico City, and extradited him to Puebla, where he and his sons stood trial.[51] In response to concerns raised, President de la Barra made certain to protect the former governor's safety, especially during his transfer back to Puebla.[52] Nevertheless, Martínez's attorney complained that the deck was stacked against his client, charging that the testimony of prostitutes and washerwomen enjoyed full credibility and that the judge permitted innuendo to creep into the trial record. The attorney also made a technical argument, questioning the court's jurisdiction because of the type of judicial appointment that the magistrate held.[53] De la Barra was not swayed by the attorney's convoluted reasoning on the issue of process, although he did insist that the trial be fair. Whether Martínez received favorable treatment because of executive pressure is hard to prove, particularly because his actual trial occurred after de la Barra's interim presidency had ended. The evidence against the former governor was circumstantial at best and may well be the reason for his eventual acquittal.

These incidents in the state of Puebla echoed many of de la Barra's concerns about demobilization elsewhere. He believed that popular maderistas had behaved badly and that the passage of time had not helped to cool them down.[54] Madero also showed his frustration after the mid-July massacre when, rather than expressing his sympathy for the dead soldiers, he begged the popular maderistas to simply lay down their arms and return home. Nowhere else did the bad feelings between the military victors and the vanquished reach such a level of intensity. The blood shed near the bullring on July 12 was symptomatic of the tensions throughout the republic. Worse, from the popular maderista perspective, was the idea that their national leader had sided with de la Barra against them. Hard feelings remained. Pacification had not really worked in Puebla. The battle in the streets of Puebla provoked the first cabinet crisis and resulted in the elimination of Minister of the Interior Emilio Vázquez Gómez and Minister of War Eugenio Rascón.

The First Cabinet Crisis: The Emilio Vázquez Gómez Controversy

De la Barra's cabinet, chosen in consultation with Madero between May 18 and 21, also has provoked many unfavorable comments. Because Porfirians supposedly dominated the cabinet, its selection has been called Madero's third major error. According to this school of interpretation, only three of the cabinet members (Emilio Vázquez Gómez at interior, Francisco Vázquez Gómez at public education, and Manuel Bonilla at communications) were bona fide maderistas. The remainder of the cabinet (Ernesto Madero at treasury, Rafael Hernández Madero at justice, Manuel Calero at development, Eugenio Rascón at war, and Francisco León de la Barra at foreign relations) were Porfirians. Allegedly the Porfirian majority then worked its wiles to subvert the revolution.[55]

This argument rests on several shaky contentions, among them that a bitterly divided cabinet fought incessantly over many issues, with the three maderistas losing a show of hands on each occasion. In fact, except for the contentious issue of demilitarization over which two of the maderistas (the Vázquez Gómez brothers) strongly disagreed with their colleagues, the cabinet seemed to work together relatively harmoniously.[56] Further, this argument presumes that Madero's uncle Ernesto and his cousin Rafael voted against his wishes, an exceedingly unlikely occurrence particularly since both continued to serve him through 1913. Eugenio Rascón, the only holdover from Díaz's last cabinet other than de la Barra himself, had stayed on because Madero could think of nobody to replace him. De la Barra did count Rascón as his closest associate in the cabinet, but only because they had become acquainted after March 1911. In sum, the cabinet was not predisposed to subvert Francisco Madero's plans for reform.

The cabinet members responsible for pacification, Rascón and Emilio Vázquez Gómez, did fail to accomplish their mission, with the result that both de la Barra and Madero became increasingly disenchanted with their job performances. Vázquez Gómez was certainly the more annoying of the two for several reasons. Born to an impoverished campesino family in Tamaulipas, he struggled to get an education and eventually became a successful attorney in Mexico City, perhaps one reason friends called him the twentieth-century Juárez. His credentials as a long-time opponent of Porfirio Díaz's endless reelections to the presidency were impressive. In 1892 while Madero was touring Europe and the United States and playing at being a student, Vázquez Gómez wrote a tract opposing Díaz's third consecutive term of office. The election of 1892 was the first (and until 1910 the only) time that the issue of reelection raised a real furor, with the *científicos* along with many other members of the establishment leading the clamor against Díaz's third consecutive term. After this brief foray into politics, Vázquez Gómez returned to his private law practice, only to reemerge in 1909 when his anti-reelection tract was republished.[57]

In 1909 Emilio Vázquez Gómez was among the first to join Madero's Anti-Reelection party while the organization was still operating in the shadow of the reyistas, whom his brother Francisco supported. Presumably, Emilio wooed Francisco into the Anti-Reelection party once the Reyes campaign waned. Despite their obvious filial loyalty, the two brothers differed on some political issues and should not be dubbed the "Tweedledee and Tweedledum" of the Mexican Revolution, as one journalist has done.[58] Both brothers displayed considerable independence from Madero, a fact that became clear when the November 1910 uprising began. Francisco quite belatedly decided to join the revolution and serve as its unofficial envoy to the United States in Washington, while Emilio maintained an even lower profile in exile in Texas.[59]

In some ways, then, Madero surprised many observers when he picked the two brothers, Emilio as minister of the interior, next in line after the minister of foreign relations for the presidency and the cabinet officer in charge of the rural police, and Francisco as secretary of public education. Perhaps Madero assumed that Emilio would maintain his timid demeanor and defer to Madero. Equally likely, Francisco, who played such an important role in the final stages of negotiations, advocated his brother's candidacy.

Emilio Vázquez Gómez initially annoyed de la Barra because he presumed to act independently on a host of issues, some of them well beyond the ordinary purview of the Interior Department. For example, he issued directives encouraging communities to replace long-standing officials with newcomers after consulting popular opinion (but not necessarily holding an election), and he made a lengthy suggestion about public works projects. He also attempted to persuade state legislators to appoint his friends to some governorships. Vázquez Gómez's failure to consult with either de la Barra or Madero, and his meddling in local politics, caused considerable irritation.[60]

De la Barra also eventually blamed Emilio Vázquez Gómez for the high costs of the military establishment. The terms of the Treaty of Ciudad Juárez had implied that an unspecified number of the insurgents would transfer into the rurales with their rank intact. Every local rebel who attacked a hacienda or an undefended pueblo with eight or ten of his friends styled himself a general, or at least a colonel. Thus, the disproportionate number of high-ranking officers among the rural maderistas, with their large salaries, further increased the price tag of the armed forces and heightened resentment among career army officers, many of whom had not been promoted in decades. Adding to the expense, Vázquez approved unquestioningly every popular maderista commander's requisition of food, guns, and cash from local haciendas, stores, and banks with nary a word of moderation. The cabinet tried to halt what they saw as the squandering of the treasury by requiring War Secretary Rascón to countersign each of Vázquez's drafts. But Vázquez subverted this process by shipping a mass of requisitions over to Rascón, which he compliantly signed in blank.[61] De la Barra could not have been pleased with either of these ministers, but for the moment he decided to do nothing.

Most problematically, during June, Emilio Vázquez Gómez used his cabinet position to slow the demobilization process in direct contradiction of official government policy. Contemporary observers assumed, and historians generally agree, that he did so out of personal ambition, in the hope of creating a following among the popular maderistas.[62] If so, the evidence is murky, because at times he issued, probably disingenuously, strict-sounding directives instructing the popular maderistas to be orderly, asserting these soldiers were "embarrassing" the "revolution" by creating disorder.[63] But despite these verbalized concerns, Emilio Vázquez maintained most of the forces intact; he converted many popular maderistas into rurales, one thousand of them in the state of Tamaulipas alone, where very little fighting had occurred.[64] Apparently Vázquez Gómez's plan, which typically he never shared with the cabinet, was to muster out a few of the most disorderly insurgents in June and then to incorporate the remainder as rurales as of July 1, thereby keeping a large number of former rebels in arms under his authority as minister of the interior.[65] Furthermore, when the bill for June's salaries and requisitions for the popular maderistas came due, Vázquez Gómez indicated he was willing to pay all claims.[66] This in itself was enough to raise de la Barra's hackles.

Finally, de la Barra had all he could take. Vázquez Gómez had the audacity at a cabinet meeting on July 12 to demand de la Barra's resignation (a prime example of his self-serving ambition, according to critics) because, he said, the interim president was not fully in sympathy with the "revolution."[67] His speech, which reportedly caught the entire cabinet off guard, could only have infuriated de la Barra. To make matters worse for the minister of the interior, the cabinet expressed its confidence in de la Barra. Coming on the same day as the Puebla disaster, which seemed to prove the danger of leaving popular maderistas in arms, the speech left de la Barra determined to fire Vázquez Gómez.

Because this decision had political ramifications, the president cleared his proposal with Francisco Madero. Madero agreed with de la Barra, though perhaps for different reasons, but asked that the request for Vázquez Gómez's resignation be delayed until an inspector-general for the rurales had been appointed who could take over the command of the troops and preside over demobilization until a new minister of the interior could be appointed. Quickly the administration produced the name of General Clemente Villaseñor to be the inspector-general. The candidate, who, like virtually all of the Porfirian military, had remained loyal to Porfirio Díaz, had since expressed his political sympathies for the civilian maderistas.[68]

De la Barra then summoned Emilio Vázquez Gómez to Chapultepec Castle for what turned out to be a confrontation. De la Barra asked his minister for an accounting of the demobilization funds and an explanation for the belated process. Getting no satisfactory response, de la Barra demanded Vázquez Gómez's resignation. The next day Madero confirmed that Emilio Vázquez ought to be out by the end of the month.[69] A curt note from de la Barra asked that the outgoing minister document which units had been mustered out, to whom they had surrendered, and where their arms were stored.[70]

Emilio Vázquez Gómez's dismissal marked an important turning point in the de la Barra presidency. In his first month in office, de la Barra had taken a ceremonial, almost passive attitude toward the presidency, viewing himself more as a stakeholder acting in formal capacities than as the policymaker. As such, he undoubtedly felt that the de facto holders of power, Madero and his civilian followers, ought to play the dominant role in policy determination. Playing the secondary role was not particularly difficult for the relatively ambitionless de la Barra, because, after all, the maderistas had won the civil war and, further, the Porfirians and civilian maderistas agreed on almost all major policy issues. By mid-July, however, de la Barra became convinced that he needed to act decisively, especially when he realized that Madero could not restrain Emilio Vázquez Gómez's maverick behavior. After a discussion, Madero gave in and granted de la Barra "an entirely free hand."[71]

The dismissal of Emilio Vázquez Gómez did not go unnoticed, especially by the popular maderistas, whom the former minister had coddled with expectations of full employment. Three insurgent generals, Juan Andreu Almazán, Cándido Navarro, and Gabriel Hernández, objected to the firing and demanded that the interim government reinstate him. When they came to the palace, de la Barra ignored the fears of his presidential guard and let the generals walk into his office to talk about the matter. Emilio's brother Francisco wrote several lengthy letters to Madero protesting de la Barra's action and claiming that the dismissal would divide the "revolutionary party" and permit the Porfirians to regain power. According to Francisco Vázquez Gómez, the "revolution" required his brother's presence in the cabinet.[72] Madero responded by asserting that Francisco Vázquez Gómez's letters greatly exaggerated his brother's importance to maderismo. Madero stated that he agreed with President de la Barra, and he urged Francisco to desist from further efforts on his brother's behalf. De la Barra had been "completely loyal to the principles of the revolution," and so he deserved the civilian maderistas' cooperation. Madero also argued that Emilio's replacement should belong to the maderista party, so the civilian maderistas would not lose a voice in the cabinet.[73]

Finally, Madero quashed any further discussion of the matter by telling his brother Gustavo, the toughest of the clan, to inform the insurgent generals that he fully agreed with the decision and that he would sanction the use of the Porfirian army against them if they continued to protest. To Francisco Vázquez Gómez, Madero stressed the importance of keeping the military out of policymaking roles, a problem that had frequently plagued Mexico since independence.[74] With this rebuke, the military officers stopped complaining and reaffirmed their support for Francisco Madero. Emilio Vázquez Gómez took his medicine in a sulky fashion. In his formal resignation he conceded the need for order as a first priority[75] and supported the electoral process in September, apparently hoping that his forced resignation would galvanize popular support for him rather than Madero in the presidential campaign. When that hope failed to materialize, Emilio Vázquez Gómez went into exile in the United States, where he began to plot his own rebellion, a movement as unsuccessful as his ministry.

In the meantime, de la Barra and Madero discussed how to fill the cabinet vacancies. Replacing Rascón proved relatively easy; the undersecretary, José González Salas, enjoyed both the confidence of the president and the advantage of being a Madero in-law. Naming Emilio Vázquez Gómez's replacement was not so easy. Madero and de la Barra each vetoed the other's first suggestions.[76] De la Barra then proposed Alberto García Granados, successful governor of the federal district since June and a civilian maderista whose credentials were at least as impressive as those of Emilio Vázquez Gómez. García Granados had achieved notoriety as an opposition journalist jailed for his outspoken criticism of Díaz's 1892 reelection, and although a latecomer to maderismo, he enjoyed a sterling reputation as an anti-Díaz reformer. García Granados was also de la Barra's only personal friend in the cabinet, and for this reason as well as for his credentials, Madero accepted him, saying that he was one "whose ideas are entirely in agreement with our party's."[77]

Later, García Granados gained a reputation as a petulant, quarrelsome man, lacking any diplomatic skills. He was widely quoted as saying "the shot that kills Madero will save Mexico." Ultimately, his vituperative nature led him to a tragic end. In 1914, when a successful revolutionary movement claiming to be the heirs of maderismo took Mexico City, some soldiers snatched García Granados from his sick-bed, tied him to a chair, and executed him. But all that was still in the future. In late July 1911 both Madero and de la Barra thought García Granados would be a vast improvement over Vázquez Gómez as interior minister.

Was the appointment of García Granados a mistake from Madero's point of view? Did the two replacements demonstrate a philosophical shift to a more "conservative" cabinet, thereby subverting the goals of the "revolution," as some have suggested?[78] Clearly not in Madero's eyes—he believed he had gained a strong voice in the cabinet with González Salas's elevation to secretary of war, and, too, so did any number of civilian maderistas, including Juan Sánchez Azcona, and at least one rural maderista, who thought that Emilio Vázquez Gómez's departure was good riddance.[79] What the government had gained was not a more "conservative" cabinet but unity and agreement on the resolution of the pacification problem. Further evidence demonstrating the absence of a "conservative" plot is the complete silence of the communications minister Manuel Bonilla, the other supposed "revolutionary" in the cabinet. Bonilla uttered not a single word of protest against Vázquez Gómez's dismissal. Further, de la Barra seemed to get on well with Bonilla, despite the fact that Bonilla uprooted many Porfirian bureaucrats in the post office and telegraph offices and replaced them with civilian maderistas. De la Barra seems not to have responded to complaints from Porfirians along these lines, or to claims that Bonilla had unfairly raised wharf taxes and to charges that he had seduced a young woman working in his home as a seamstress.[80] He certainly never suggested replacing Bonilla. In short, the first cabinet crisis occurred because of the failure of the two ministers in charge of demobilization to pacify the country, not because of anyone's political agenda.

At the same time, de la Barra and Madero discussed appointing new undersecretaries in justice and interior. Interestingly all the names discussed for these positions, Federico González Garza, José Vasconcelos, Miguel Díaz Lombardo, Luis Cabrera, and Roque Estrada were youthful civilian maderistas. Only González Garza took the new job, which represented just a change of departments for him. The others turned down the offers, preferring to pursue their private careers.[81] Eventually another civilian, Jesús Flores Magón, the brother of Mexico's most famous radical, whose career is discussed later in this chapter, accepted the job of undersecretary of justice. The tenor of this discussion between Madero and de la Barra, properly focused on having a cabinet in place that would help de la Barra carry out his inaugural pledge to pacify the country, again, should lay to rest the myth that de la Barra had political motives for changing his cabinet in late July.

De la Barra's new interior minister took a no-nonsense approach to the demobilization issue. García Granados's attitudes coincided with those of many of the other civilian maderistas and Porfirians. And although some of the civilian maderistas had doubts about him, de la Barra convinced Madero that García Granados was loyal. García Granados simply could not understand why the insurgent army had been permitted to remain in arms for so long, stirring up trouble and bombarding the treasury with demands for salary and benefits. Once he assumed office in early August, the mustering-out process sped up noticeably. First, he simply closed section 4 of his ministry, which had been responsible for paying out funds to popular maderistas still in arms. Without funding, many insurgents just went home. Elsewhere the hammer of the ministry fell quickly, in Celaya and Guadalajara, where the Porfirian military disarmed the rural maderistas.[82] García Granados's most notorious use of firm tactics occurred in the state of Morelos, as we see later in this chapter. Not all of the ministers agreed with García Granados's assessment of the situation and the need for speedier demobilization; his undersecretary, Federico González Garza, eventually resigned his post over the issue.[83]

But in all fairness, García Granados had a more complex solution in mind; he was willing to negotiate, as he did, for example, in San Luis Potosí, when he believed that talk might lead to a lasting resolution of a bona fide dispute.[84] In Chihuahua, where the authorities had relatively little trouble with the insurgents despite the fact that the longest and hardest military struggle had occurred there, García Granados and Abraham González apparently agreed on a plan to muster out a portion of the revolutionary army every month.[85] But García Granados was not willing to procrastinate further when there was evidence of bad-faith dealings, which he perceived happening in the state of Morelos.

De la Barra's get-tough policy produced results in most instances. The sheer volume of marauding rural maderistas clearly declined in late summer 1911. The reason may have been that some respect for central authority had been reestablished, that the celebratory mood had passed, or that the harvest season approached. What is clear, however, is that many observers attributed the new success to the tougher measures, thus reviving and adding credence to the myth of the iron hand, the idea that only the exercise of force could restore order and the Porfirian peace. For proponents of this idea in particular, Francisco León de la Barra deserved accolades because of his decision to remove Emilio Vázquez Gómez from the cabinet.

At the same time, observers of the Mexican political scene who subscribed to the philosophy of the iron hand became more convinced than ever of Madero's incompetence and foolish idealism. They had good grounds for this conclusion: Madero had no governmental or administrative experience even in the private sector. De la Barra, after trying to work with Madero for a month, determined to play a stronger role in the government simply because be believed that Madero should have been able to discipline his popular followers.

De la Barra's mood switched to one of cautious optimism by fall 1911. With the exception of the Morelos problem, he and García Granados had successfully overseen the demobilization of large groups of troublemakers and had reduced the frequency and severity of incidents of property destruction. De la Barra's letters to influential Mexicans living abroad brimmed with undue optimism that pacification had been accomplished.[86] While his national policy now had a greater opportunity for success because it was being carried out consistently, much depended on whether the administration could maintain the progressive consensus that it had achieved in mid-May with the civilian maderistas and win over the hearts of the population at large. That consensus called for the government to place pacification before democracy, and elections before social reforms. To see whether that occurred, the story must now shift from the National Palace and an examination of general policy guidelines to the provinces, where feelings about demobilization ran the highest. Events in the states of Chiapas, Sinaloa, Baja California, and Morelos provide the most striking examples of the complexities of the pacification issue that faced the de la Barra government.

Chiapas: The Issue of Where to Locate the State Capital

The violence of the 1910 revolution also provided the excuse for long-standing regional feuds within states to resurface, disguised in the political rhetoric of the revolution. Events in Chiapas, on Mexico's southern border with Guatemala, exemplify this phenomenon. Rivalries building for nearly two decades erupted into rebellion in September 1911, creating another pacification problem for the de la Barra government. The clash pitted the elite of San Cristóbal las Casas, the traditional capital of Chiapas from colonial times through most of the nineteenth century, against the businessmen of the new capital, the more economically modernized community of Tuxtla Gutiérrez. As the Porfirian leadership transformed the economy of the state, making it a garden of tropical export products such as coffee, cacao, mahogany, and rubber, the commercial establishment successfully petitioned for the transfer of the capital to Tuxtla Gutiérrez. While lacking the charm of San Cristóbal, Tuxtla did enjoy commercial ties to Mexico City rather than to Guatemala, San Cristóbal's traditional trading partner. Regional rivalry continued unabated beneath the political surface for two decades, with Tuxtla successfully resisting San Cristóbal's attempts to reverse the decision of the 1890s.[87] But the demise of Porfirian stability allowed the two cities to revisit the issue in 1911, with violent results.

Unlike many other states, Chiapas had local legislative elections scheduled for summer 1911. Presumably, a new, freely elected legislature, under the guidance of a sympathetic governor, could reverse the decision made twenty years earlier, or so the citizens of San Cristóbal believed. They therefore concentrated their efforts on the selection of a favorable interim governor, who would then appoint pro-San Cristóbal jefes politicos in the districts. The jefes supervised the voting for the legislature, which in turn verified the results of the gubernatorial election. The fact that control of the interim governorship would probably determine which city was to be the capital, explains the contentiousness of the two factions that led to the election of four interim governors during the summer. Madero's second choice, Policarpo Rueda, took charge in July with the promise of restoring order. Rueda proved a moderating influence, lessening the tension and dealing even-handedly with both factions. But in August, the compromising Rueda resigned just before the legislative elections, possibly to make himself eligible for a full term as governor.

The outcome of the legislative elections only intensified the conflict. Although the returns were close, the majority of seats in the Chiapas legislature remained in the hands of supporters of Tuxtla Gutiérrez. Disgruntled San Cristobalenses prepared to fight, calling on their old retainers, the Chamula Indians, who lived in the villages around San Cristóbal, to take up arms in rebellion.[88] The rebels "pronounced" on September 14 a significant state holiday commemorating Chiapas's peaceful annexation to the Mexican nation. Actual fighting broke out shortly thereafter, as the rebel campaigners occupied a number of small and medium-sized communities. What particularly concerned many citizens, however, was the possibility of a race war, or "caste war" in local parlance, especially with reports that the Chamulas had cut the ears off thirteen of their prisoners before tossing the victims onto a bonfire. These notions dredged up fears and vague memories of a similar conflict that had occurred during 1868–69.[89] Like much of southern Mexico, with less middle-sector mestizo influence than in the north, the disparity of wealth between the Hispanized elite and the Indian masses made the political leadership wary. The state nervously sat and waited for de la Barra to act.

De la Barra, as in other instances, insisted on proceeding constitutionally. One solution that had occurred to him was to ask the interim governor to resign and to recall Policarpo Rueda. The sitting interim governor resisted the suggestion, arguing that Rueda was responsible for much of the unrest and denying any "irregularities" in the administration or in the supervision of the election.[90] The machinations of the state legislature did not help; it tried to appoint as governor a federal legislator (Querido Moheno) who complicated matters further by refusing the office. He complained loudly in the Chamber of Deputies about his proposed nomination, blaming Alberto García Granados for violating the state's autonomy. And so, when the issue of the capital's location came to a head, Chiapas was stuck with an unpopular and possibly unconstitutionally seated interim governor, with a resultant conflict raging between him and the legislature.

Finally, de la Barra consulted with a chiapaneco politician whose judgment he trusted, who advised him to use the army to restore order and guarantee free elections for the permanent governorship.[91] The tough stance fit compatibly with de la Barra's predilections after August. He had General Eduardo Paz stationed on the state border, poised and ready for action. On October 8, Paz engaged the poorly armed rebels in what would prove to be the decisive battle in a short-lived campaign. After a bloody victory at Chiapa de Corzo, the federals and the state militia retook the remainder of the state in four days with many casualties on the other side. The easy triumph did much to boost the federal army's morale, something de la Barra had tried to accomplish before through public ceremony and praise.[92]

One of de la Barra's greatest pacification triumphs thus occurred in Chiapas. He hoped that garrisons of federal soldiers, coupled with a binding plebiscite, would resolve the issue of the location of the state capital once and for all.[93] No doubt he also hoped that the resolution of the troubles and the presence of outside forces would guarantee a free and honest election for governor, another goal of his presidency.[94] According to the leading authority on the state, the gubernatorial candidate who won had good reason to want federal supervision because the legislature refused to confirm his election and instead seated his opponent.[95] By that time, however, de la Barra had left the presidency, and Francisco Madero had to walk the thin line between respect for local autonomy and insistence on democratic principles.

Sinaloa: A Shadow of Morelos

Sinaloa, on the Pacific coast, had only begun to develop when the revolution of 1910 began. Speculators compared its coastal plain to the valleys of southern California and predicted that its fertile soil would flourish under the cultivation of bananas, sugar cane, cotton, and corn. Sinaloa's ties to the outside world were through its port, sun-drenched Mazatlán, and a railroad connecting it to the state of Sonora to the north. But the rugged peaks of the Sierra Madre, pitted with remnants of miners' camps, effectively isolated Sinaloa from central Mexico.[96] This state also experienced a popular uprising somewhat similar to the one that occurred in Morelos and manifested the problems de la Barra had in achieving pacification in 1911. Like so many other states, Sinaloa experienced conflict when the Porfirian old guard tried to prevent the insurgents from entering the capital. The popular maderistas, led by tough Juan Banderas, nicknamed "Stoopy" because of his bad posture, finally took Culiacán, the state capital, after a bloody battle.[97]

The prominence of the popular maderistas led to an incident in early August when Banderas simply took over the state governorship, stirring up a ruckus in the Mexico City press, which blamed local son Manuel Bonilla's meddling for the coup. Bonilla disclaimed any responsibility for the takeover and told de la Barra that the press sensationalized the story to sell papers. Further, he urged de la Barra to support the Banderas coup, even though "Banderas's personality is not what we want." To do otherwise, Bonilla thought, would be to intervene in local matters, which would only increase resentment. De la Barra agreed completely, at least for the moment.[98] Banderas enjoyed considerable support even among bankers and the business community because he seemed able to restore order.[99] But Banderas angered Madero over his out-and-out attempt to influence the gubernatorial election in favor of José Rentería, the official civilian maderista candidate.[100] Nevertheless, on September 27 Rentería took the oath of office as Sinaloa's new governor, and Banderas returned to his field command.

In that role Banderas became embroiled in a battle with another rebel commander, but this time he was not entirely at fault. Minister of the Interior Alberto García Granados ordered a non-local detachment into Sinaloa without consulting the governor (presumably in response to some complaints about property damage), and Rentería protested strongly that he, and not Mexico City, ought to control the rurales.[101] García Granados defended his decision and sought to absolve himself with his friend de la Barra by claiming that the new rurales commander had been ordered to respect the local authorities and do nothing hostile to Rentería.[102] Meanwhile, Banderas had left Culiacán to do battle with the invader, whose drunken and disorderly conduct concerned law-abiding citizens.[103]

Madero declared that García Granados had overstepped the bounds of prudence in intervening in local matters. He urged de la Barra to order the forces to refrain from attacking one another and asked García Granados to halt troop movement in the state. De la Barra decided to remove both of the contentious commanders and replace them with a third party, José María Cabanillas. The new leader quieted things down and completed the process of bringing Banderas to his knees by arresting him for the murder of the federal commander in Culiacán the previous June. Banderas remained in prison in Mexico City until February 1913, when he escaped.[104] Thus, the Sinaloa experience saw the popular maderistas crushed and overwhelmed, at least for the moment, by a combination of outsiders and the military. Nevertheless, the countryside had quieted down only for the harvest season. Before long, new local revolts would prove once again that in Sinaloa de la Barra's pacification program had failed.

Baja California: The PLM Radical

De la Barra's pacification program did succeed in Baja California, where the PLM (Partido Liberal Mexicano), an anarcho-syndicalist group, attempted a rebellion. Here pacification meant handling not popular maderistas but ideologically driven radicals and filibusters who had nothing in common with the Madero insurgency. Thinly populated and with few riches to attract either Mexican or foreign capitalists, Baja California remained the most isolated area of Mexico during the Porfiriato. The PLM focused its revolution in Baja California and in neighboring Sonora in part because Baja's proximity to Ricardo Flores Magón's headquarters in Los Angeles made communications relatively simple, and the peninsula's military governor had only about one hundred soldiers under his command, many of whom were poorly trained conscripts. Further, Madero had never campaigned in Baja, and thus no civilian maderista organization could compete with the PLM to any degree. Elsewhere, when the two fought head to head, in Chihuahua, for example, the more broadly based maderistas had simply overwhelmed the radicals, encouraging their soldiers to defect or defeating them in battle.

But Flores Magón did not intend to surrender simply because Díaz fell. He wrote, "El Chato signed the peace, but the revolution will continue. Now it is the Liberal party against Madero and de la Barra."[105] The first PLM expedition in Baja had taken the small city of Mexicali at the end of January 1911, when the Madero insurgency was sputtering in Chihuahua. At that moment, the PLM seemed to be a serious rival for Madero, although each passing month made it clear that the PLM would be confined to Baja California and a few isolated locations elsewhere in the north while the remainder of the country fell under the maderistas' sway. To complicate Flores Magón's situation further, a group of U.S. and European radicals, Wobblies (Industrial Workers of the World members), socialists, and adventurers flocked to Baja California in support of the PLM, helping them to capture Tijuana in early May. As a result of these volunteers, non-Mexican participation in the PLM army crept up to as much as 80 percent, opening up Flores Magón to the charge that he and the PLM were the agents of U.S. filibusters who hoped to annex Baja California to the United States.

Thus, the de la Barra government faced an ideologically based challenge to its desire for peace. Scholarly research has shown what contemporaries could not have known: the PLM threat was greatly exaggerated, particularly the feared independence day revolt in Sonora that never materialized.[106] Believing the worst, Madero and de la Barra determined to use force to disperse the magonistas after Jesús Flores Magón's efforts to induce his brother's surrender failed. Tactically, this decision created problems because the virtually nonexistent Mexican navy could not ferry troops to Baja, and no overland railroad passage from central Mexico existed except through the United States. The possibility of Mexican troops crossing U.S. soil raised diplomatic issues that took some time to sort out.[107] De la Barra initiated his request for permission for troop transport with the State Department on May 27, and at the same time impressed on Madero the significance of the forthcoming campaign. Madero had already been visited by U.S. businessmen with vested interests in the Imperial Valley who expressed their concern. The two Mexican leaders planned a joint invasion of federales and rural maderistas under the command of maderista general and Boer War veteran B. J. Viljoen.[108] Military preparations got under way promptly, and soon government forces were poised in Ciudad Juárez, waiting for permission to cross the U.S. frontier.[109]

Meanwhile, the PLM forces had begun to self-destruct. Army commander Caryl Ap Rhys Pryce, feeling, correctly, that the Flores Magón leadership in Los Angeles had not been fully supportive of the military efforts, determined to entrain for the City of Angels to confront the boss. Wishing to avoid arrest, having been detained once before on grounds that he had violated the U.S. neutrality statutes, Pryce left at night without informing his army of his whereabouts. He never returned. In his absence, the soldiers panicked, and Hollywood actor Dick Ferris, involved for months on the fringes of the action, strode onto center stage. His friends in the army nominated him for president of the Republic of Mexico even as Pryce parleyed with Flores Magón. Ferris's publicity stunt cost him dearly; despite refusing the office, he was arrested in Los Angeles for violating the neutrality laws. As a result of the arrest of the two principal foreign leaders, the Mexican elements in the PLM regained control over its revolution after June 3.[110] But shortly thereafter, authorities also arrested the PLM civilian leadership, including Ricardo Flores Magón, further complicating the situation of the few PLM soldiers who remained in control of Mexicali and Tijuana.

Finally, the United States granted official permission for Mexican soldiers to cross its territory to fight the few remaining red flaggers and the filibusters. De la Barra and Madero also may have had political motives for sending soldiers to Baja California because the governor, Celso Vega, did not seem willing to cooperate with the new government, and reputedly was corrupt and arbitrary. Allegedly, he hoped to preserve an autonomous Porfirian enclave, which did not fit Madero's plans.[111]

As it turned out, the federal reinforcements were unnecessary. As a result of some bargaining, the PLM troops in Mexicali agreed to muster out for the price of ten dollars apiece, a sum not dissimilar to those offered rural maderistas in other parts of the republic. Similar attempts at demilitarization failed in Tijuana, however, when the foreign commander demanded ten times the price. As a result, Colonel Vega finally had his chance for revenge, and with numerical superiority and better supplies, he administered a sound whipping to the PLM army.[112] Thus, the PLM revolution ended with a crushing defeat, although the specter of magonismo, in many ways more fearful than the reality, lurked in the minds of Mexican politicians through the remaining months of the de la Barra presidency.

The Mexican government insisted that its agents keep a watchful eye on magonista suspects. Groups with PLM leanings were believed still to exist in Los Angeles and El Paso, fanning the fears of officialdom, although no significant invasions of Mexican soil ever occurred. It appears that government operatives such as Julián Alvarez convinced at least some of the magonistas that further activities would be fruitless. Even more important, the de la Barra government worked hard to erode Flores Magón's natural foundation of support, the working class. Not only was a new and progressive labor code sent before the legislature but friends of the government persuaded influential U.S. labor leader Mary Harris ("Mother") Jones to lend her efforts on behalf of peace. She agreed to come to Mexico to speak with workers and interested officials and then to intercede with Flores Magón to convince him to forgo any future military efforts against the de la Barra government.[113] Thus, the combination of force and the promise of progressive reform brought peace to Baja California. These tactics would not work, however, in the country's most troubled state, Morelos.

Morelos: The Zapata Rebellion

By far the most conspicuous failure of Francisco León de la Barra's pacification policy occurred in the state of Morelos, where three unsuccessful attempts to muster out Emiliano Zapata's revolutionary army led to a wave of violence that lasted from August 1911 to 1920. Traditionally, historians have portrayed the breakdown between the progressive consensus and the popular maderistas of Morelos, henceforth referred to as the zapatistas, as the result of false promises, betrayals, and invidious motives on the part of the central government.[114] Given Zapata's subsequent image as the personification of the Mexican Revolution, and particularly as the champion of the aspirations of the downtrodden campesino for agrarian reform, the traditional characterization of the interim government is logical. But there are two sides to every story, and the civilian maderistas and de la Barra's view of what was happening in summer 1911 deserves to be told as well.

To understand fully the events of that fateful summer, one has to review the long sweep of history in the state, particularly in the eastern region of Morelos that most of the zapatistas called home. There, the conflict between hacienda and village for land, water, and labor had been ongoing for centuries. The land proved particularly fertile for raising sugarcane, and from the time of Hernando Cortés in the 1530s much of the state's land had been given over to sugar production. Cortés set the standard for many generations. With him as an example, Morelos hacendados lived an opulent life-style, often as absentee landlords visiting their plantations sporadically, and then enjoying the pristine pleasures of the countryside rather than assuming the roles of true managers and supervisors. Periodically, hacendados began to usurp the villagers' land, initially for the sake of the land itself and to limit the campesinos' access to water, a process that the planters stepped up during the Porfiriato. The planters in the end took the land not because they needed more space for sugarcane, since much of their estates lay fallow a good part of the time, but to deprive the campesinos of the ability to be self-sufficient. When the villagers found that they could not raise enough corn and beans on their milpas to feed their families, economic exigencies forced them to labor on the sugar plantations to make ends meet.[115] Both state and federal governments acquiesced in the land grab because the sugarcane planters epitomized modern Mexico, bringing fancy technology to their plantations and raising the level of production significantly. As far as the planters were concerned, cheap labor was essential for the efficient production of their crops, and the Porfirian land policy guaranteed a steady labor pool. The land acquisitions increased so severely by the end of the Porfiriato that the villagers began to protest, led by the campesinos from Anenecuilco and their newly elected council president, Emiliano Zapata.

Zapata and his followers had good reason to object after 1909, because for them, the political picture in Morelos had also worsened, boding ill for the few acres they still controlled. Their rough-and-tumble veteran governor, in many respects a man of the people, died suddenly. Although he was genuinely mourned by both planters and campesinos, the planters saw his passing as an opportunity to solidify their position in the state and really turn the screws on the campesinos. Therefore, they urged Porfirio Díaz to appoint to the governorship one of their own, Pablo Escandón, chief of protocol for the dictator and a member of high society who spent much of his time abroad. The "election," however, was scheduled after Porfirio Díaz's public promise to restore democracy and permit free elections, and so the slowly coalescing political opposition, known generally as the Democratic party, decided to run an opposition candidate, Patricio Leyva, the son of a local hero of the nineteenth-century War of the Reform.

Díaz had always tolerated some local dissent as a means of ensuring that his governors enjoyed at least a modicum of popularity. But actually to oust an incumbent, or elect an opposition candidate, an elite protest group had to have somebody on the inside, close to Díaz, who could cut a deal. In Morelos, in 1909, the reformers hoped that inside pressure on the venerable dictator could keep Escandón out of the governor's palace. Díaz, however, decided to let the planters' choice stand. The long and bitter political campaign did nothing to soothe the feelings of the campesinos and, from the central government's perspective, could not have come at a less opportune moment. To make matters worse, Escandón proved every bit as incompetent and intransigent as the reformers feared. Taking a completely pro-planter position, he approved new legislation requiring the pueblos to reregister their lands, thus revaluing small properties to increase their taxes. Coupled with a court case that Anenecuilco lost in 1908, the new taxes bolstered the villagers' determination to defend their lands at all costs.

Meanwhile, the Madero political campaign failed to take root in Morelos. With the Leyva faction out of business, no Anti-Reelection leaders emerged, and so Morelos remained tangential to Madero's national plan. Especially after the arrest of Madero's Mexico City agent, Alfredo Robles Domínguez, and the death of Aquiles Serdán in Puebla, the focus of Anti-Reelection activity swung northward, leaving the southern political insurgency to develop its own personality and leadership. Morelos's rural character, too, made the state an unlikely center for a Madero-style political movement. Nevertheless, Zapata and the villagers did respond to the Madero revolution, albeit rather late, in March 1911. During the intervening months they had sent their spokesperson, Pablo Torres Burgos, to San Antonio, Texas, to confer with Madero, obtain commissions for the principal military officers, and discuss the meaning of article 3 of the Plan de San Luis Potosí. That provision called for a restitution of lands unjustly seized from Indians once the *disputed titles had been reviewed*. For campesinos still smarting over the aggressive acquisitiveness of the planters, such words provided some hope. But the Morelos movement took another unexpected turn when federal troops surprised Torres Burgos and shot him to death, leaving the state revolution leaderless. Zapata, in part by default and in part because of the inherent respect he had won from his followers, became the military head of the revolutionary movement of the south, a rather grandiose title considering his influence was limited to the eastern portion of Morelos and bits of the neighboring state of Puebla. Two days before Madero signed the Treaty of Ciudad Juárez, Zapata recorded his only major victory: his troops occupied the city of Cuautla. The federal commander, outnumbered ten to one, decided to retreat after a devastating six-day siege.[116] But with no important civilian maderista emerging in Morelos, and outsiders from Guerrero occupying the state capital, Cuernavaca, Zapata had as much claim as anybody to the leadership of the state.

At this juncture, Zapata became fixated with the idea of appointing the interim governor. Three times he wrote to Alfredo Robles Domínguez asking for the authority to make the appointment.[117] Zapata's correspondence does not reveal whom he had in mind for the post, or the reason for his sudden concern with politics. Whether it was to have a favorable governor who would approve the informal land seizures that Zapata had already authorized, or whether he had aspirations for political office himself, the records do not reveal. What was clear, however, was that Madero had no intention of granting Zapata the authority to appoint. The pattern from other states was certain; Madero chose as interim governors middle- or upper-class civilian politicians who had actively participated in the Anti-Reelection political campaign of 1910 and not the military veterans of the revolution. Based on this criterion, neither Zapata nor any of his followers qualified for high office. Furthermore, Morelos had been so unimportant in Madero's scheme of things that the state had not even appeared on the list of governorships he was negotiating with Porfirio Díaz in April and May, although after May 21 every state and territory except Baja California received a new governor anyway. As far as Madero was concerned, the new governor could well be a planter since he could think of no suitable Anti-Reelectionist candidate. Ultimately, Manuel Asúnsolo, a representative of the respectable Figueroa brothers who had captained the maderista movement in neighboring Guerrero, influenced the choice of the governor. He selected Juan Carreón, a banker from Chihuahua who had lived in Cuernavaca since 1905 but who had not been affiliated with the old regime.[118] Apparently Zapata concurred with the choice, because his representative, his brother Eufemio, had met with representatives of Asúnsolo and Robles Domínguez to make the final decision.[119]

Meanwhile, complaints about lawlessness, property seizures, and violence in the Cuautla region surfaced in Mexico City. A Madero supporter, fleeing his hometown, wrote to Madero about the bad impression that the "bloodthirsty" Zapata had created in Cuautla.[120] Even the municipal president whom Zapata had chosen for Cuautla protested the lack of order in the city. According to him, after occupying the city Zapata had looted the homes of the wealthy citizens, claiming they were all *científicos*. His soldiers set fire to the municipal archives (where notarial records and disputed land titles would have been located) as well as the Hotel Morelos, now serving as a hospital, where nineteen wounded federal soldiers were recuperating. All died in the ensuing blaze. Zapata's soldiers, who were supposed to act as the police force for the community, were often drunk, and in that state they stole from stores and cavorted with "women of ill repute." When the municipal president tried to impose order on his own by returning stolen horses and informing the campesinos that they had to apply to the civil authorities for their land titles and not rely on Zapata's military dispositions, Zapata ran him out of town.[121]

Reports of zapatista lawlessness occurred outside Cuautla as well; property owners demanded that rurales stop the thievery, and Governor Carreón, who claimed to sympathize with the civilian maderistas, expressed grave concerns about the negative effect Zapata was having on local businesses.[122] Zapata, however, probably did not have the ability to control all his followers, any more than Madero could control all the rural maderistas. Emilio Vázquez Gómez shared these worries; he ordered Zapata to cease his attacks on peaceful communities and end the bloodshed.[123] Clearly, the popular maderistas in Morelos were interested in something more than political change. For the politicians, including the civilian maderistas and de la Barra, however, Zapata's callous disregard for human life and property interests raised grave doubts about his trustworthiness.

Zapata's interpretation of the purposes of the 1910 struggle clearly differed from that of Francisco Madero, a difference readily revealed during the course of the discussion the two men had in their first face-to-face meeting in early June. Zapata said that he was interested in land reform; Madero said that demobilization had to take place first. Then, "Zapata stood up, and, carrying his carbine, walked over to where Madero sat. He pointed at the gold watch chain Madero sported on his vest. 'Look, Señor Madero,' he said, 'if I take advantage of the fact that I am armed and take away your watch and keep it, and after awhile we meet, both of us armed the same, would you have the right to demand that I give it back?' Certainly, Madero told him, he would even ask for an indemnity. 'Well, 'Zapata concluded, 'That's exactly what happened in Morelos, where a few planters have taken by force the villagers' land. My soldiers—the armed farmers and all the people of the villages—

demand that I tell you, with full respect, that they want the restitution of their lands gotten under way right now.' "[124]

Zapata's analogy, which John Womack, his biographer, relates movingly, was not quite apt, however. The planters had not taken possession of the villagers' land by force of arms; instead they held legal title, or at least legal color of title, however unethically obtained. To undo the planters' aggression would require, at least in the eyes of the civilian maderistas, some sort of legal due process with evidentiary hearings and judicial review. Article 3 of the Plan de San Luis Potosí set forth these due process requirements by stating that previous dispositions of lands granted by the Ministry of Public Works or the courts would be subject to review. When Womack claims that Zapata met this provision of the plan by subjecting the land disputes to his own personal review, he glosses over Zapata's clear misinterpretation of article 3. Madero consistently insisted on observing the legal formalities of due process regarding land reform, and hence his interest in creating a land commission to establish procedures for adjudicating land disputes.[125] This basic disagreement over the nature of the 1910 revolution would contribute to the division between Zapata on one hand and de la Barra and the civilian maderistas on the other and would be a primary factor leading to the bloodshed of August 1911.

Madero and de la Barra had a straightforward response to the disorders caused by social revolution in Morelos: disarm the zapatistas. This, of course, paralleled the solution that they applied in other states where armed popular maderistas had proven themselves to be troublemakers. Thus, in mid-June, the government began the demobilization of the zapatistas. Emilio Vázquez Gómez sent funds to Robles Domínguez's brother Gabriel to supervise the mustering-out process, and by the end of the week of June 21, the first demobilization had taken place.[126] The demobilization cost the government approximately 47,500 pesos and yielded 3,500 weapons, at least temporarily. The next day, however, Zapata seized five hundred rifles from the government, apparently of newer manufacture than those turned in, claiming a forthcoming appointment by Madero as chief of the state police. The job never materialized, nor did Zapata return the rifles, stating "the only government I recognize is my pistols." To de la Barra and the civilian maderistas, Zapata had shown bad faith by remaining armed. Zapata claimed that his forces consisted only of the fifty-man personal escort that Madero had authorized; nevertheless, the planters considered this force to be excessive and one that fomented "pernicious" influences around the state, chilled the business climate, and dissuaded workers from laboring.[127] But for the time being, de la Barra and Madero did nothing about the failed demobilization.

Zapata's motives for resisting discharge paralleled those of other popular maderistas. During the early part of June, Zapata's forces had been paid well. Zapata had written receipts for everything he had requisitioned, which included horses, food, and weapons, and the government had paid.[128] Zapata was also interested in finding permanent employment for his followers as auxiliaries to the state forces. In a sense, Zapata was recreating the General Reserve or Second Reserve, a popular military reform Bernardo Reyes had sponsored in 1900. The reserve, modeled on the German *landwehr*, was intended to protect the state in the event of invasion and was very popular with local communities until the *científicos* persuaded Porfirio Díaz to abolish it.[129] Most important, Zapata of course wanted to keep his men in arms to guarantee the retention of plantation lands already seized and to protect the autonomy of their region from the centralizing forces of Mexico City. In 1911, Zapata, just as he had been throughout the decade of violence, was prepared to fight for the land. That desire ran counter to the de la Barra government's policy to have an unarmed citizenry that would obey any laws that the civilian authorities established. As villagers later confessed, one of Zapata's most fundamental premises was to keep the villagers armed to defend their property.[130] This policy made no sense to Madero and de la Barra, and even to some of the other popular maderistas. Some of these soldiers lamented the fact that Zapata remained armed, while "good guys" like Manuel Asúnsolo had retired to the quiet life of farming.[131] Despite the failed demobilization in June, however, Madero continued to believe that Zapata was a true follower and not a "traitor," as the planters had suggested.[132]

Perhaps a less naive person than Madero would have sensed Zapata's growing disenchantment with the interim government. Madero continued to hope that his personal diplomacy would iron out the points of disagreement. While on vacation in Tehuacán, Puebla, a popular warm water spa, he invited Zapata on several occasions to come and visit and discuss Morelos. Zapata refused, first on grounds of ill health, which Madero jollied him about, and then because he claimed that he feared assassination.[133] Zapata clearly no longer trusted Madero since the latter wanted him to relinquish his personal escort and sided with de la Barra on the demobilization policy. Zapata showed his disenchantment with the course of events in mid-July by rearming more of his veterans and using the Puebla incident as his excuse. In response to the incident in the bullring, Zapata recruited troops and volunteered to march to Puebla in support of the maderistas. Immediately, he received orders to remain where he was.[134] Neither de la Barra nor Madero wanted Zapata's help in resolving the Puebla problem; the federal army and Francisco Vázquez Gómez did just fine. But despite orders to remain where he was, Zapata did not discharge his followers once the crisis had passed; instead he continued to enlist men in the Army of the South. From the perspective of the government, Zapata had for the second time demonstrated bad faith. In de la Barra's opinion, there had been no need for Zapata to rearm; he had simply disobeyed his superiors. The planters well could argue that the government had squandered the 47,000 pesos on the Morelos disarmament with no concrete results to show for it.

Zapata also seized upon the dismissal of Emilio Vázquez Gómez from the de la Barra cabinet as another justification for remilitarizing the state. Although the evidence is unclear, Vázquez Gómez apparently began to supply the zapatistas with munitions in early July. Whether these allegations contributed to de la Barra's decision to fire Emilio Vázquez is not certain.[135] What is clear is that from the government's vantage point, Zapata continued to disregard de la Barra's obvious intent to separate the zapatistas from their weapons. Thus, the groundwork was laid for a major showdown, which began almost immediately after the new minister of the interior, Alberto García Granados, took office in August. His new policy called for the immediate and forceful disarmament of the zapatistas to restore order in the state. Since both de la Barra and Madero had subscribed to the idea of using force to demilitarize other states when no alternative seemed to exist, naturally they could with consistency apply the same policy in Morelos. Now all they needed was a soldier who was sufficiently tough to implement the policy, a man of strong will. They found him in Victoriano Huerta.

At the same time, Madero, de la Barra, and Zapata were all willing to compromise on political issues, because nobody was satisfied with Governor Carreón's performance in office. The zapatistas probably hoped for a governor who would endorse agrarian reform measures, and the planters clearly wanted someone who was tougher on crime, as they defined it. Carreón, in part because he was an outsider, lacked the popularity to lead reforms and the muscle to enforce the campaign against banditry. As a result, the planters asked de la Barra to consider replacing Carreón with a prestigious local man who would prove more effective.[136] The planters and the zapatistas agreed on the need for a local man, but still no local civilian maderista leader had emerged. Only Zapata had the requisite stature and name recognition, but of course most of the planters would never accept him. Interestingly, a few planters did approach Zapata and ask that he run for governor. Zapata refused.[137] Did he refuse because he believed that if he accepted a candidacy proffered by planters he would lose credibility with the campesinos he represented? Did he suspect that the planters were attempting to mold him for their own purposes, as the wealthy landowners of Chihuahua were attempting to do with the maderista general Pascual Orozco? Or did Zapata simply feel that he lacked both the education and the necessary experience to be an effective governor? Unfortunately, Zapata never explained why he declined the office, nor have his biographers, who note, however, that throughout his career he never aspired to political office. In some ways, the refusal seems illogical, because if Zapata wanted to implement his agrarian reforms, probably the best way to do that would be by becoming governor.

In the absence of a local candidate, Madero and de la Barra decided that a fellow southerner and maderista would have to suffice, and so they proposed Ambrosio Figueroa from Guerrero as Carreón's replacement. When Madero wrote to Figueroa and offered to secure his appointment as interim governor and commander of the state's forces, he explained the need for pacification. "Zapata must be put in his place," he said.[138] Figueroa refused the job, although his brother Francisco offered to mediate the dispute between Zapata and Madero.[139] Zapata never would have accepted Ambrosio Figueroa as governor in any case because of the deeply felt animosity between the two.[140] Nevertheless, the lack of a popular governor posed an additional problem.

By now Madero, as well as the government, had lost patience with Zapata. De la Barra and García Granados ordered Huerta and his forces into Morelos on August 9; four days later Madero sent Zapata a very curt telegram, complaining that Zapata had ignored Madero's earlier orders to meet to discuss their differences. "Come immediately," Madero ordered, adding that Zapata must begin to muster out his forces very quickly.[141] Zapata refused for the third time to visit Madero, who had to be satisfied with telephone calls. Meanwhile, de la Barra and García Granados concluded from Huerta's invasion that Zapata would respond only to threats of force. Huerta reported a victory after a skirmish with Genevevo de la O's forces and attributed the bad situation in Morelos at least in part to the inept governor, Carreón.[142]

The telephone conferences of August 14 and 15 went very well, according to Madero. Zapata asked that the present secretary of state, a native son, be named as interim governor (even though Madero expressed his preference for General José de la Luz Blanco, a popular maderista veteran from Chihuahua). He also asked for the removal of federal troops on the grounds that their presence violated state sovereignty. Madero optimistically and perhaps naively asserted that Zapata would ultimately agree to de la Luz Blanco as governor as long as a small percentage of the zapatistas were offered jobs in the state police under an officer chosen by de la Barra and Madero. De la Barra remained more skeptical, noting that he wanted "definite guarantees of peace" from Zapata. The president also suggested another candidate for governor, unfortunately someone whom Zapata had specifically rejected the day before.[143] De la Barra did not care much who became governor or held other offices; his real concern was with disarming the zapatistas. Thus, he willingly accepted Madero's suggestion of Pedro Santos Mendiola, who had performed a similar role in Tamaulipas, as the chief of the state forces. But de la Barra insisted on appointing Santos Mendiola and removing the federal troops only after Zapata had disarmed.[144] Thus, while Madero seemed willing to accept Zapata's promises about disarmament at face value, de la Barra insisted on actions to prove Zapata's good faith. Over the next two weeks, however, those actions, from de la Barra's perspective, were not forthcoming.

The telephone conference between Madero and Zapata continued the next day, August 15. The more Madero discussed the Morelos situation with Zapata, the more conciliatory and indecisive Madero became. Suddenly he decided that the worst way to supervise the demobilization was with federal troops—better to bring in maderista volunteers from any state except Guerrero, where the Figueroa rivalry still rankled Zapata. Despite the delay that bringing rurales from Veracruz or Hidalgo would occasion, Madero thought that if these conditions enhanced the possibility of a lasting peace, they were but minor concessions. He did not seem to consider the possibility that Zapata interposed these conditions to delay and possibly forestall demobilization. Madero also thought, quite erroneously, that the only major stumbling block to Zapata's submission was the choice of governor. Zapata insisted on a local candidate, but this condition Madero never seemed willing to concede. Finally, to break the impasse, Madero decided that he would travel to Cuautla personally to negotiate with Zapata yet again. Such a gesture of goodwill, he believed, would melt the ice.[145]

De la Barra concurred that a peaceful solution was preferable to a violent one and again expressed indifference about the gubernatorial choice. Yet de la Barra suspected Zapata's motives far more and would have preferred that Madero remain on the sidelines. De la Barra noted that Zapata was, according to military reports, taking advantage of the army's halt to recruit and build up his own forces, yet another apparent act of bad faith. De la Barra reminded Madero that the government had agreed to the hard-nosed approach in Morelos because it believed that lives and property must be protected.[146] In another telegram, de la Barra pushed for results. He reiterated his determination to provide law and order in the state and expressed concern about prolonged negotiations, suggesting that they were a mere ruse to prevent disarmament from ever taking place. He went on to tell Madero that he had given Huerta orders to proceed with the military option if demobilization did not begin immediately. De la Barra insisted on results, not more talk, especially with someone of Zapata's ilk, whose past behavior made successful overtures of peace unlikely.[147]

Madero seemed to heed de la Barra's words. Although he was now negotiating with Zapata, he had clearly not been completely won over by Zapata's claims of innocence. For example, he asked Zapata to refrain from attacking any haciendas or pueblos while he returned to Mexico City, showing that he did not entirely trust Zapata.[148] Huerta, for his part, shared de la Barra's skepticism that anything would come of Madero's negotiations.[149] Nevertheless, the president ordered Huerta to hold steady in Cuernavaca.[150] De la Barra believed, as did Huerta, that the presence of the federal army would bring Zapata to the bargaining table and conclude the discharge process. Madero and Huerta did agree on a military strategy. They decided not to complain that Zapata was calling his forces together from all over Morelos and nearby Puebla, a fact that had deeply bothered de la Barra, because, in Madero's words, if the negotiations failed and hostilities broke out, "it is better to have [the zapatistas] all together so as to give them a decisive blow."[151] Madero went on to say that he would return to Mexico City to confer with de la Barra before heading for Cuautla on the 18th to make final arrangements with Zapata. Thus, Madero and de la Barra appeared to be of a like mind again about Zapata. Delays made them impatient, and both Madero and de la Barra were prepared to use force if negotiations failed to bring the desired result.

The talking continued the next day, much to Huerta's discomfiture. In the late afternoon, de la Barra repeated his order for Huerta to stay put in Cuernavaca, specifically stating that he should suspend any military operation that could be considered offensive.[152] Huerta obeyed the letter of de la Barra's instructions if not its spirit by moving his troops in a "maneuver" in the direction of Yautepec, closer to the scene of the action. Speaking "plain soldier" like Henry V, Huerta asserted that in all honesty Madero's discussions with Zapata would have no results unless Huerta moved his forces into position, displaying his overpowering military superiority to cow the zapatistas into submission.[153] Huerta's remarks were consistent with the plan of action that Minister of the Interior García Granados and President de la Barra had initiated earlier in the month. The general continued to believe that Zapata would respond only to threats of force. Up to this point the talks between Madero and Zapata had yielded no concrete results; no satisfactory gubernatorial compromise candidate had been selected, and not a single soldier had been mustered out of Zapata's army. On hearing about the federales' advance, however, Zapata telegraphed Madero to find out whether he was being attacked. Madero replied that he was as surprised as anyone by Huerta's troop movements, and issued orders for Huerta to cease his advance.[154] But Zapata had flinched, or so it seemed to Huerta.

Zapata fired off an apoplectic and emotional telegram to the president, blaming the "*científico* hacendados" for starting the trouble and the presence of federal soldiers for upsetting the people of Morelos. He asserted that the villagers wanted to be listened to and have their rights respected and that if bloodshed resulted, history would judge the guilt of the offender.[155] De la Barra did not reply.[156] Obviously, he had not changed his mind. The only solution, as far as he was concerned, was immediate and total demobilization. If Madero's talks proved unsuccessful, then the military option remained. De la Barra clearly placed no credence in Zapata's statement that the state's troubles were caused by someone other than himself. Nevertheless, as a civilian and as a lawyer who believed in the process of negotiation and arbitration, de la Barra favored a peaceful resolution if possible. At the same time he did not take Zapata's grievance about federal troop movements very seriously, since, in modern parlance, it was clearly a situation of no harm, no foul.

Meanwhile, Huerta remained encamped on the Yautepec road.[157] De la Barra carefully explained his puzzling, and arguably even inconsistent, policy to his commander. The cabinet had conferred at length about Morelos and, convinced by Madero's assurances that Zapata would surrender and disarm immediately, had outvoted García Granados and given Madero a chance to accomplish demilitarization without combat. The president assured Huerta, however, that if Zapata did not surrender immediately, he would send orders directing the army to continue the military operation.[158] Huerta, no doubt, was disappointed even at the smallest delay, because he believed that the show of force had been the factor that had brought Zapata to the bargaining table. As further evidence for Huerta's view, twenty armed zapatistas surrendered to his soldiers that afternoon.[159] Meanwhile, Madero had boarded a train for Cuautla. He sent Zapata two telegrams telling him about his plans and stating, "You must have faith in me as I do in you."[160] Given Madero's agreement to the proposed military solution and his earlier letter to Figueroa, the statement is at best disingenuous. But probably Madero did hope that he would be able to reach a peaceful accord with Zapata that would obviate the need to unleash the hammer of the Porfirian army.

The meeting with Zapata on the 18th went well, at least superficially. Zapata agreed to all of Madero's demands, even though he again asserted the need for local people to hold office. According to Madero, Zapata was willing to accept Eduardo Hay, another northern revolutionary general, as governor, and Raúl Madero, Francisco's younger brother, as a commander of the state militia. One wonders how carefully Madero listened to Zapata's concerns and how honestly Zapata spoke about his intentions. Zapata's acceptance of Madero's suggestions may have been simply a ploy made in the hope that Madero would then order the federal troops out of the state, permitting Zapata to return to business as usual. Later events suggest that this interpretation has some merit. Madero also reported in his agreement that the mustering out would begin on the morrow, August 19, with 250 former rural maderista soldiers from the state of Hidalgo supervising. He also requested that de la Barra order Huerta and his forces to return to Cuernavaca.[161]

At this point it is worth considering why Zapata was so insistent that the federales withdraw and that other rural maderistas supervise the mustering-out process. Did he have a genuine fear that once disarmed, the federales would massacre the zapatistas to teach them a lesson? If so, he seems to have had no grounds in reality for his paranoia. The federal army had never attacked unarmed former revolutionaries. Even the Puebla incident that was described earlier in this chapter was a battle between two armed factions. Passions had not yet reached the level that they would in 1913 and 1914 when wholesale massacres did occur. Thus, the past performance of the federales made Zapata's fears seem unwarranted. Further, the distance from Yautepec to Cuautla was more than a day's march, certainly a sufficient amount of time to resist or retreat if the federales had shown evidence of bad faith. Still, Zapata asserted the possibility of treachery.

For their part, the federal government asked themselves whether Zapata's demand that the federales withdraw suggested that he hoped to engage in yet another act of deceit regarding demobilization. As Warman tells us, one of Zapata's basic premises from the outset was that the zapatista should never relinquish their weapons. Zapata probably hoped that the former maderistas would be less dogmatic about enforcing the mustering-out process, since many of them disagreed with the policy in the first place. Finally, as all concerned mentioned, should some "misunderstanding" occur over whether Zapata had surrendered all of his weapons, the former maderistas would be less likely to fire on the zapatistas than would the federales. Each of these interpretations is somewhat speculative, and while one does not want to engage in counterfactual history, the evidence is certainly not incontrovertible that the government had some mischief planned for Zapata once he completed the mustering-out process.

To heighten the tension further, perhaps inadvertently, Governor Carreón again reported disturbances in eastern Morelos. De la Barra informed the governor that Huerta had orders to crush all such disturbances.[162] Whether the reports of outbreaks of fighting to the east were accurate is difficult to tell. Both Huerta and Madero agreed throughout this crisis that the rumors about banditry were greatly exaggerated but had some basis in fact. As far as de la Barra was concerned, Carreón's report provided further evidence of Zapata's untrustworthiness. Nevertheless, because of the cabinet's decision and Madero's promise, de la Barra continued to hold Huerta in his position, encamped on the road to Yautepec. Huerta obeyed.[163] De la Barra did not accede to Zapata's request to withdraw the troops because such a request seemed unnecessary, and because the government premised its policy on the notion that Zapata's compliance with demobilization had to be coerced.

De la Barra's response to Madero's optimistic news of settlement is highly instructive. De la Barra did not concern himself with the details of the governorship or command of the state forces. His response was single-minded, almost as though he had not heard Madero mention the terms. His sole concern was the process for restoring order, not the steps or concessions Zapata demanded before he would disarm. De la Barra told Madero that once order had been restored and the demobilization accomplished, he would remove the federal army from the state.[164] Like Zapata, then, de la Barra had a single purpose foremost in his mind, disarming the zapatistas. All other issues, including the identity of the governor of the state, were irrelevant.

August 19 dawned hot, and in the steamy environs of Cuautla, the cordial three-month alliance between Madero and de la Barra began to unravel over the Zapata affair. Madero, his hopes buoyed by his face-to-face discussions with Zapata on the previous day, felt optimistic about the compromise. The disarmament process had begun, albeit slowly. But President de la Barra fundamentally disagreed with Madero's policy of appeasement, probably because he harbored deep suspicions of Zapata's intentions and did not believe the latter would demobilize. An informant had told him that Zapata had no intention of disarming, and if he did, that he would simply rearm, just as he had in June and July. For de la Barra, the evidence of Zapata's untrustworthiness was simply too strong to ignore. He believed that Zapata and his men had acted intolerably, and he expressed his intention to establish order "whatever it costs" as Huerta began his advance to Yautepec.[165] Madero, who did not agree that his negotiations had failed, was worried that de la Barra's decision would destroy his labors. He repeated his belief that Huerta and Blanquet ought to be sent to Cuernavaca, not Yautepec, away from the zapatistas and not toward them. Madero asserted that some of the alleged troublemakers actually were in Cuautla with him, thus expressing his doubts about the veracity of de la Barra's sources.[166] The dispute came down to a matter of trust. Madero believed in Zapata, and de la Barra did not.

Madero also claimed to see political motives in Huerta's advance. He suspected that Huerta's troop movements were part of a plot by his presidential opponent, General Bernardo Reyes, to embarrass him.[167] The evidence for political machinations is sketchy at best. It is true that Huerta admired Reyes, but so did many military officers. At this point in his career, Huerta had not shown any political ambitions and would scarcely have followed Reyes blindly, as his subsequent refusal to participate in either of Reyes's military plots to unseat Madero proved.[168] More likely, Madero was simply experiencing the pre-election jitters that every candidate in a contested election experiences. Evidence of Huerta's involvement in a reyista conspiracy is so weak, therefore, that the idea must be dismissed, if only because his future actions show he was out only for himself.

The government accepted two of Madero's suggestions. De la Barra asked Ambrosio Figueroa to station his Guerrero state troops along the border to prevent zapatista disturbances in the region where Governor Carreón had reported trouble. Figueroa agreed to do so, and his men seemed to do the job.[169] The second suggestion, to halt Huerta and Blanquet's march on Yautepec, de la Barra ultimately accepted,[170] although apparently reluctantly. Madero's uncle Ernesto, the secretary of the treasury, telegraphed his nephew to express the cabinet's concern about holding back the military solution. In their opinion, based on the thin information gleaned from de la Barra's informant, Zapata was not disarming, and they agreed with de la Barra that if this were true, then order had to be imposed by force.[171] But Madero advocated his disarmament policy despite the evidence of a lack of compliance and so persevered in his appeasement of Zapata.

Meanwhile, a minor skirmish had broken out between the federal forces and zapatistas. The combat proved indecisive and ended quickly. Huerta informed de la Barra that he intended to remain in his present location anyway because he needed forty-eight hours to prepare the Yautepec road for the passage of his heavy artillery pieces. Therefore, the zapatistas would enjoy a two-day respite before the federales would begin to advance again and Madero had his additional time. After the two-day delay, Huerta intended to have the army press forward immediately once the road was ready "because the only reason the bandits will surrender is by force of arms."[172] Thus, the military exigency happily coincided with the political decision that de la Barra and the cabinet made in deference to Madero on August 20. They agreed to give Madero the last chance he requested to work out terms that would allow Zapata to surrender peacefully. They directed Huerta to suspend all forward advances for two days. The zapatistas were to proceed to Cuautla to disarm. General Casso López was ordered to remain at his present location. Finally, former maderistas from Veracruz and Hidalgo would oversee the actual discharge.[173] Therefore, Zapata had one final opportunity to show good faith by discharging his men in the additional two-day respite the government had granted.

Even as de la Barra conceded the two days to Zapata and Madero, however, he made explicit expectations of what must happen by August 22. He expected a quick surrender of all the zapatista arms (just as he had on August 9 when the advance into Morelos began) because in his mind it made no sense for the zapatistas to remain armed. Once order was restored, he specified that the government would look at the agrarian issue "that Zapata is exploiting."[174] He conceded again that he would agree to whatever gubernatorial candidate Madero and Zapata selected. De la Barra personally telegraphed Huerta his new orders, as Madero's uncle confirmed.[175] De la Barra probably had little hope that Madero's plan would succeed, but he had pledged to prevent bloodshed, at least for the next two days, and the military alternative was not available until the 22nd anyway.

Madero had decided to remain in Cuautla to observe the discharge. He commented that the zapatistas were quite disturbed by Huerta's presence outside Yautepec.[176] Madero pleaded again for orders returning Huerta to Cuernavaca, while Cándido Aguilar and the other rural maderistas from Veracruz supervised the discharge.[177] De la Barra refused another change of plans and authorized Huerta's advance to Yautepec, having learned from Madero that the zapatistas had already evacuated the town for Cuautla and thus no possibility for a skirmish between the two forces existed.[178] Later in the day Madero again said that Huerta ought to retreat to Cuernavaca, but he remained optimistic that the demobilization would continue in the morning. Further, he approved of the government's decision to recall General Blanquet.

While Madero believed that his compromise arrangement was proceeding on schedule, de la Barra drew other conclusions. A newspaper correspondent reported that only forty zapatistas, a paltry number, had actually been discharged during the first day of demobilization. Was Zapata going through the charade of demobilization for the second time, only to have his forces reappear as a military problem once the federal army departed from the state? Such events had happened before in Mexican history and would again in the future.[179]

Certainly Huerta believed that Zapata's move was a mere ploy. His source told him that the discharge was an effort to get more money out of the treasury, and nothing more. Supposedly the zapatistas were turning in knives, clubs, and unusable rifles as their "weapons," and Madero was accepting these "weapons" instead of demanding their field equipment. Huerta's blunt response to what he viewed as another example of Zapata's bad faith was to advocate the use of military force to eliminate Zapata, either by hanging him or by forcing him into exile.[180] De la Barra's views were close to those of Huerta. He reminded Madero of the importance of verifying the discharge of the zapatistas and pointed out to Madero that the federal army had been completely loyal to him.[181] The implication, of course, was that the zapatistas were less trustworthy. Thus, because Madero and Huerta disagreed about the success of the discharge, the government had to choose between the hard line and conciliation.

Because Huerta believed in Zapata's duplicity, his forces advanced on Cuautla on August 23. Publicly, Madero blamed Huerta for misconstruing his orders and exonerated de la Barra from any share of the blame in the disaster.[182] Possibly the responsibility for Huerta's advance lay with Minister of the Interior García Granados, who had consistently advocated a hard line in the cabinet. But García Granados controlled only the rurales, and so while it is convenient to blame him, it seems unlikely that Huerta would have received his orders from García Granados. Possibly de la Barra ordered Huerta to advance, on the assumption that the mustering-out process was a farce, as Huerta reported. But, curiously, given the encyclopedic file on the Morelos case, no document exists to suggest this possibility. Therefore, Madero's conclusion probably was accurate; Huerta exceeded the letter of his instructions, doing what he thought was best for Mexico. If Huerta had received copies of de la Barra's correspondence with Madero, which he did in some instances, he may have found implicit approval of the advance in de la Barra's insistence on independent confirmation of the zapatista demobilization. Madero had won a concession on this point from Zapata, who had agreed reluctantly to verification. De la Barra clearly believed verification to be vital.[183] Simply put, he would not abide the breakdown of law and order, and he insisted that the demobilization of the zapatistas precede any other change in the state.[184] De la Barra's position was reasonable given Zapata's clear reluctance to muster out his forces. To de la Barra, the man of honor, deeds proved words, and Zapata's past history had shown him to be untrustworthy. Despite Madero's hope that peace lay just around the corner, de la Barra was more skeptical. Nevertheless, on the 24th he gave Zapata one last chance by issuing Huerta orders to stay in Yautepec and sending General Casso López to occupy Cuautla instead.[185] By this time Madero had returned to Mexico City to plead Zapata's case. But for Zapata the identity of the federal commander was not important; he wanted to be left alone, and so the two sides had reached a stalemate.

As further justification for Casso López's advance, Huerta received a report that the few zapatistas recently discharged had attempted to recover their arms by force.[186] The report, coupled with the expressed fears of a member of the Cuautla town council, goaded the government to further action.[187] Huerta asked de la Barra for permission to take the zapatistas by surprise at night and relieve them of their weapons. Huerta guaranteed that if the government followed his plan, then Zapata and his "bandits" would no longer be able to impose their conditions on the government. He argued that the government's policy had called for the quick demilitarization of the state.[188] As a result of Zapata's prevarications and delays, nearly three weeks had passed since the demobilization orders were issued, and the government seemed no nearer a solution than it had been in June. De la Barra concurred, stating that Huerta had been both prudent and firm, and that the "banditry had to be fought formally." He asked Huerta to continue to coordinate his efforts with those of General Figueroa. De la Barra urged Huerta to "show one more time that the army was the effective guardian of order and the loyal defender of laws and property."[189] Raúl Madero telegraphed his brother the next day from Cuautla, asserting that the orders to advance made a conflict inevitable,[190] but Madero was unable or unwilling to do anything. De la Barra and Huerta concluded that only a military solution remained.

Serious military operations began on August 30, three weeks after the adoption of the get-tough policy. Huerta's forces marched into Cuautla, although he himself did not enter the city, while his soldiers waved white flags in an effort to minimize the concerns of the citizenry. Other federal detachments left Cuernavaca for Jojutla.[191] Zapata protested, claiming that all his men had been mustered out, that he had kept only the small escort that Madero had permitted him, and that he was still loyal to the government. At least two of these assertions were inaccurate, but Zapata "was not temperamentally up to being fair."[192] Huerta knew that Zapata was hiding at the hacienda of Chinameca and had sent Federico Morales to capture him. Morales failed, charging precipitously through the front gate of the estate rather than surrounding the house first and thereby permitting Zapata to escape by the rear door. Zapata had been declared an outlaw by the de la Barra cabinet, and in the eyes of the government, he had now formally crossed the line to banditry.[193] Thus, both Zapata and de la Barra held to their principles to the bitter end; Zapata insisting that the villagers remain armed and de la Barra insisting that the villagers surrender their weapons and restore peace.

Uniformly, de la Barra's decision to attack Zapata has been declared a mistake, the greatest failure of the "Madero government" and a blot on the name of the revolution's first hero.[194] A more important point, however, is whether the policy was a failure in its conception or just in its execution. One way to examine the issue is to see how the victorious "revolutionaries" handled the Zapata problem. In 1919, "revolutionary" president Venustiano Carranza's right-hand man, General Pablo González, occupied the state of Morelos where Zapata and his soldiers were still creating disorder. González, with Carranza's consent, concocted an elaborate plot to trap Zapata. One of his officers, Jesús Guajardo, pretended to rebel in favor of Zapata. Guajardo proved his loyalty by attacking carrancista units and killing some soldiers loyal to the government. Guajardo then requested a face-to-face meeting with Zapata, ironically at the same hacienda, Chinameca, where he had nearly been killed in 1911. When Zapata arrived at the appointed meeting place, Guajardo greeted him with machine gun fire. Thus, the revolutionary leaders succeeded where de la Barra had failed in 1911.

González then went even further. He deported zapatista dissenters to the Yucatán, forcing them into plantation labor. As a result of the decade of violence and the deportations, Morelos was depopulated dramatically by 1920.[195] Thus, one could argue that de la Barra did nothing more and nothing less than Carranza by trying to kill Zapata. Of course, had Huerta succeeded in doing so he would have deprived the revolution of its most potent symbol. Like de la Barra in 1911, Carranza also insisted on imposing order and asserting federal primacy before institutionalizing land reform. Further, Carranza and his successors did not return land to the campesinos as Zapata had hoped. The federal government granted very few petitions for restorations, although it proved more willing to grant petitions for new ejidos, thus demonstrating its supremacy.[196]

The aftermath of the August 1911 fiasco proved at least the short-term wisdom of de la Barra and Huerta's policy. The number of disturbances diminished for a while, although Zapata made some important gains in recruiting new soldiers in October. In

September, Huerta marched uncontested throughout the state, despite the resentment of the villagers. Huerta told the government that he heard great sentiment from the middle and upper classes in favor of order and expressed shock at the amount of destruction he witnessed.[197] By the end of the month, when Juan Andreu Almazán surrendered, Huerta considered the state to be completely pacified. The two men impressed each other. Huerta considered the ambitious Almazán smart and competent and suggested that he be given a position as the state's rurales commander.[198] Many, including President de la Barra and some of the citizens of Morelos as well, congratulated Huerta on a job well done.[199] Some former maderistas thought in September it might be easy to persuade Zapata to surrender, and even Zapata's official declaration of his "counterrevolution" implicitly confirmed the weakness of his position by recognizing the legitimacy of the de la Barra government.[200] But peace would not come that easily to Morelos. Once harvest season had passed, the villagers returned to the zapatista fold, swelling the ranks of his army and enabling him to attack Cuautla.[201] And so the de la Barra government passed its final days of existence, frustrated by the failure of its pacification policy in Morelos.

The other effect of the Zapata incident was to drive a wedge between Madero and de la Barra. Foreign observers wrote about the rift. De la Barra told several of them that he resented Madero's untimely interference at the very moment when the get-tough policy in Morelos seemed to bear fruit and attributed the failure to muster out Zapata's troops to Madero's meddling. De la Barra felt betrayed and threatened to resign unless Madero stopped interfering in matters of state. Madero responded with an angry letter, blaming the cabinet for the breakdown of law and order, in both Morelos and the nation as a whole. This disharmony surfaced in the press and in the Chamber of Deputies by the end of October.[202] There, Alberto García Granados testified that Madero's influence paralyzed the operations in Morelos, while González Salas blamed Huerta and stated that the zapatista problem would end within three days of Madero's inauguration.[203] The debate precipitated the second cabinet crisis (the resignation of García Granados, González Salas, and Francisco Vázquez Gómez) and de la Barra's decision to resign somewhat earlier than planned. The frequency of correspondence between de la Barra and Madero diminished, even on projects in which they were in agreement, and their salutations no longer included the words, "My very esteemed and distinguished friend." Thus, the Morelos campaign ended on a sour note for all concerned and demonstrated the impossibility of the task of pacification in 1911.

Conclusion

The first pledge de la Barra made to the citizens of Mexico in June 1911, to restore peace, failed to bear fruit. His government had taken several unsuccessful measures designed to eliminate banditry and to pacify the countryside. Even as the interim presidency wound down, new outbreaks of fighting occurred. In Juchitán, Oaxaca, the local jefe politico led a revolt against the civilian maderista governor to protest his interference in local affairs.[204] Despite de la Barra's cautionary words, fighting broke out and the local federales detachment soon had a tough battle on their hands.[205] Nor was this an isolated incident. In fact, rebellions against the national government provide one measure of the continuity between the de la Barra and Madero administrations.

The failure of de la Barra's pacification policy leads to two questions: Did the policy fail simply because de la Barra lacked the nerve to use the iron hand to tame the tiger and reincarnate the Porfiriato in the absence of Porfirio Díaz? And, more important, would the iron hand, in and of itself, have sufficed to calm Mexico and control its "unruly jades" in 1911? While some political observers described de la Barra as vacillating and acting like "a marshmallow," others (mainly the former maderistas) found him too harsh and uncharitable, at least toward the popular maderistas.[206] Probably the conciliatory and unambitious de la Barra did as well as anyone could under the circumstances, because, simply stated, the iron hand by itself was no longer sufficient to govern Mexico. The Madero insurgency had loosed new forces; many of the soldiers preferred "the free life of the campaigns" because there was "none of the humdrum drudgery of work."[207] The desire for higher salaries and greater freedom spelled doom to the Porfirian policy, as one contemporary journalist pointed out.[208] In sum, peace would not return to Mexico until its president had leadership ability and represented the aspirations of a majority of the population.

Finally, did the endemic violence of the months of the de la Barra presidency rise to the level of a social revolution? Assuming that a social revolution can be defined as a social movement where either the ownership of the means of production changes hands (by campesinos acquiring title to land from haciendas or by industrial laborers gaining ownership of the factories where they work) or where the popular classes gain some significant nonmaterial rewards, the mere violence and manifestations of popular discontent in summer 1911 did not in and of themselves rise to the level of a social revolution. For a final determination, however, we need to hold this question in abeyance until after the next two chapters, which measure the level of change in Mexico in 1911.

Francisco León de la Barra casting his ballot in the presidential election. *Courtesy of Honnold Library, Claremont College*

4

Sowing the Seeds of Democracy

Democracy is the worst form of Government except all those other forms that have been tried from time to time.

—Winston Churchill

Mexicans today revere Francisco Madero as the courageous initiator of the revolution of 1910 and the father of Mexican democracy. From the outset of his presidential campaign in 1909 until the last days of his life, Madero constantly preached the dogma of democracy. What is seldom discussed today, however, is that Francisco León de la Barra and many other Mexicans, including Porfirians, believed just as much in the ideals of democracy. Critics, both contemporary and modern, have scoffed at these attestations to a belief in democracy, pointing to what they charge was duplicitous conduct during the elections in 1911 to prove that the commitment to democracy was more rhetorical than real. Did Mexico transform its traditional authoritarianism into a democracy consistent with "progressive" ideals as its leaders professed? Were civil liberties and the political rights of opposition candidates fully respected? This chapter argues that because the level of political partisanship in the elections of 1911 was so high and because Mexico lacked the requisite institutional heritage and political culture, the democratic practices proved more ephemeral than real.

Mexico also lacked the cultural traditions to support a flourishing democracy in 1911. Although the nation had modernized dramatically at the end of the nineteenth century, Mexicans did not have the general literacy (theirs was far below 50 percent) and per capita income level common to successful democracies. Democracy also requires citizen participation through universal suffrage and elections contested between viable political parties. Institutional indicators of democracy include civil liberties, universal suffrage, competitive political parties, free and fair elections with alternative candidates for office on the ballot, and governance by the winning party. Tactics such as censorship, rigged elections, coercion, and harassment of the opposition tend to negate democracy.[1] This chapter examines the use of these tactics during the de la Barra interim presidency and suggests that familiar patterns of authoritarianism, dressed in well-intentioned democratic idealism, prevailed in 1911.

This chapter also looks for the institutional indicators of democracy, asking specifically, did the society endorse the idea of widespread political participation and protection of the rights (civil liberties) of those who dissented? Although some recent studies describe an underlying democratic tradition in Mexico,[2] this chapter suggests that such traditions were not deeply ingrained. For much of the nineteenth century, elections were charades. Rarely did a government in power lose an election, and even the great liberal patriot Benito Juárez stooped to tampering with ballot boxes in order to secure reelection.[3] Nor did matters change much during the Díaz years, despite the continuation of the formalities of regularly scheduled presidential, congressional, and gubernatorial elections. Thus, Francisco Madero and the reformers did not invent the procedures of Mexican democracy. Some rudimentary democratic practices did exist, but the political culture that would have promoted democracy was not in place.

Historians often cite the 1911 elections as the first truly democratic ones in Mexico's history, drawing conclusions that may exaggerate the nature and extent of democratic practices, as argued above. Uniformly, however, writers give no credit to Francisco León de la Barra for overseeing these elections, which occurred during his administration.[4] Instead, they credit Madero with initiating the democratic ideal and making sure that the government observed democratic tenets in the very elections in which he was a candidate. But because of the apparent contradiction between this idealism and the reality of the election results at the time, opponents charged Madero with electoral fraud. After all, they argued, he had a vested interest in seeing the traditional system function as usual. Not only did he want to be elected president, but he wanted close friends and political associates to be chosen in the gubernatorial contests. And sweep these elections the civilian maderistas did, with only an occasional loss, which added more fuel to critics' fire.

This chapter partially rebuts these critics and suggests that de la Barra deserves considerable credit for carrying out the second of his inaugural promises: holding "democratic" elections in 1911. At the same time, however, the text attempts to soft-pedal Madero's severest critics and show that he and his followers, right down to the local level, had genuine democratic aspirations for Mexico. Simply to credit de la Barra rather than Madero would not create a deeper understanding of Mexican democracy in 1911. Instead, the evidence shows that the belief in democracy was among the dominant notions within the progressive consensus. Mexicans generally agreed with Porfirio Díaz's statement in the famous 1908 *Pearson's Magazine* interview with James Creelman that the nation was sufficiently mature to practice democracy along the lines of the Anglo-Saxon model, contested elections and all, although at times the realities of politics overwhelmed the ideal. Neither de la Barra nor Madero deserves exclusive credit for this achievement. Democracy was an idea whose time had come in 1911.

A third historiographical issue that this chapter debates is the idea that the interest in democracy in Mexico belonged exclusively to the middle- and upper-class civilian maderistas. Proponents of this idea usually claim that lower-class Mexicans were concerned primarily with the struggle for their daily bread and therefore focused their demands on social issues, while the well-to-do classes enjoyed the luxury of the more esoteric quest for democracy.[5] This chapter suggests, however, that the quest for democracy permeated all social classes, and that even the poorest villager held democratic aspirations and believed that the popular will, expressed in constituted elections or some quasi-democratic process, could oust local tyrants. During 1911, many local entities (but not all—some local Porfirians were popular) changed their political masters with Madero's and de la Barra's approval and a minimal amount of fraud and imposition, proof of the widespread acceptance of democracy as a principal element of the progressive consensus. In their own words, popular leaders believed that the insurrection of 1910 allowed them to recover their lost liberties.[6]

The picture of democracy in 1911, however, should not be painted in rosy hues. A myriad of complaints fill the presidential archives with reports of political repression at the local and national levels. People campaigning for political outsiders often found themselves imprisoned, and on other occasions suspected that their ballots were not counted.[7] Madero freely placed his friends in the interim governorships, leading to charges that his appointees rigged subsequent elections to secure full terms.[8] At times, interim governors and state legislatures considered engaging in skulduggery such as delaying elections until a moment when a more politically propitious result could be arranged, a tactic that President de la Barra prevented in the national elections.[9] Madero's political supporters, the civilian maderistas, expected preferential treatment in their quest for employment, which sometimes included elected offices.[10] The spoils system operated openly and shamelessly. Thus, any description of democratic practices in 1911 must recognize considerable continuity with the past. The traditions characteristic of Mexican politics—a single party dominating the political scene, ballot tampering, favoritism, and repression of opponents—all certainly occurred in the elections of 1911. Yet, the democratic process in 1911 provided Mexicans with their first taste of liberties in a generation; and, when all is said and done, the elections proved to be a vast improvement over what had gone before and, some would argue, what has occurred since then as well. Losers from both sides—Porfirians and maderistas—complained, but not every close election was lost because of fraud and coercion.

The Guarantee of Personal Freedoms

The nation's hallowed constitution of 1857 in principle provided all citizens with generous portions of liberties. Theoretically, the liberal democratic state that the document created prevented authorities from imposing arbitrary and capricious demands on an unwilling citizenry. Drawing on the precepts of the U.S. Constitution, rather than earlier failed Mexican precedents, orators at the constitutional assembly in 1857 talked at length about cherished notions such as free speech and freedom of the press, all of which had been notoriously absent during the dictatorship of Antonio López de Santa Anna.[11] But the ideals of the framers proved illusory for all except a few brief moments during the remainder of the nineteenth century.

Juárez and Díaz pressed the argument that the exercise of these freedoms subverted the orderly course of government, that criticisms of administrations led to disrespect for the authorities and ultimately to rebellions. Rather than permit such a sequence of events to occur, a government, they argued, could take justifiable steps to prevent chaos by ignoring or silencing political opponents, jailing them, or even putting them to death. Thus, the reality of the

Juárez and Díaz dictatorships was that these governments stifled criticism. Naturally, Díaz's critics believed he should have permitted more political freedom, as the events of 1909 and 1910 demonstrated. No wonder Mexicans fought to regain these "lost liberties" during the insurgency in 1911 and then insisted on the right to exercise them once the dictatorship fell. From the closed environment of the Porfiriato, then, a major attitudinal change took place that became part of the progressive consensus and that did have some concrete results, specifically, the restoration of civil liberties.

Freedom of speech, the right to assemble for political purposes, and freedom of the press were among the most cherished of liberties that Mexicans regained under the de la Barra administration in 1911. Unlimited freedom of the press was the most obvious change from the days of the Porfiriato. De la Barra cultivated this liberty by ending governmental subsidies to all newspapers, granting members of the press open access, and admitting reporters into the presidential palace regularly for interviews, in marked contrast to practices of the Díaz era. To observers he appeared willing to answer all questions, even those that seemed fairly critical.[12] Independent publications flourished in 1911 and 1912, sprouting up particularly in Mexico City like wildflowers after a spring rain. More important, de la Barra and Madero both permitted journalists critical of their actions to operate freely. Barbs and satires about the "White President," as de la Barra was popularly called—not because of his complexion but because of his alleged political nonpartisanship—appeared regularly in the Mexico City press, especially after the Emiliano Zapata fiasco in August.

Madero lent himself more obviously to caricature than did de la Barra because of his squeaky voice and unimpressive physical appearance, his inability to make tough choices, and the innumerable relatives he put in office. Some supporters suggested, and later biographers have agreed, that Madero granted too much license to the press, that the Mexican press was too immature to editorialize responsibly, and that the constant attacks undermined the respect that citizens normally felt for the presidential office and ultimately destabilized the government.[13] This argument fails to account for the fact that the absence of these traits during the Porfiriato was one of the primary reasons the dictatorship drew fire. A more logical conclusion is that de la Barra and Madero were right to advocate a free press. Naturally, critical editorials and sensationalist commentary sold more papers, but the merits of a free press outweighed any political damage it caused.[14] Had Madero not made so many errors in judgment, and been possessed of fewer foibles, the press probably would have been kinder to him.

De la Barra also committed his administration to protecting citizens' rights to assemble and speak freely without censorship. The president at one point reprimanded an interim governor for jailing a state legislator and told the minister of the interior to issue orders to free him. His administration stood for "effective individual freedoms," he proudly stated. He also apparently reinstated a government employee fired because he criticized the minister of development (Manuel Calero) in a letter to the press, and he made himself accessible to any Mexican citizen wishing to speak with him by holding open house three afternoons each week.[15] After some of Madero's overly zealous partisans used physical force to disrupt an opponent's presidential campaign speech on September 3, de la Barra offered the candidate full-time police protection for the remainder of the campaign.[16] De la Barra was supported by many of the civilian maderistas in his desire to protect free speech and political activity. For example, at least two interim governors reprimanded jefes politicos under their jurisdiction for interfering with free speech, instructing them that political rights must be respected, even of those people "who profess ideas contrary to our cause." Madero told the exiled Luis Lara Pardo, who later wrote very nasty books about him, that he could come home and enjoy full freedoms, and he chastised a friend who was using his power as interim governor to attack his gubernatorial rival.[17] These examples, among many others, of the federal government's willingness to protect the political speech of dissenters were a notable change from the practices of the Porfiriato. The other freedoms that de la Barra guaranteed his countrymen were more nebulously articulated in Madero's original campaign slogan, "Sufragio efectivo y no Reelección," ironically, the same phrase Porfirio Díaz had used to describe his revolution's goals when he swept to military victory in 1876 over the "dictatorship" of Sebastián Lerdo de Tejada. Clearly, the slogan, which has been translated into English in various ways, embodied political rights that went to the very core of democracy. Yet the literal translation, "effective suffrage and no reelection," is ambiguous.[18]

Effective suffrage basically meant that every ballot would be counted, and that all those eligible to vote would be allowed to do so. Congress debated the idea of universal suffrage at great length in 1911, arguing against literacy requirements and European models of property. Tampering with ballot boxes was a problem endemic in the country. Military dictators frequently sent soldiers to "guard" the ballot boxes and supervise the counting, thus ensuring that their governments won those elections. With no provision for a secret ballot in Mexico, the presence of soldiers tended to intimidate citizens whose signatures (or names if they were illiterate) appeared on the flip side of the ballot. Such accountability could lead to arrest or at a minimum to a discarded ballot. To clean up elections one citizen proposed that each voter fill out a two-part perforated ballot with one half serving as a receipt, stamped by the election official. After the tallying took place, the results would be posted along with each man's vote, and then voters could check to make certain that their votes had been properly recorded. While solving one problem, the proposal still did not insure the secret ballot, a goal of a majority of the reformers. De la Barra was sufficiently interested in the issue of balloting that when a U.S. salesman offered to demonstrate a tamper-proof ballot box that he had invented, de la Barra granted him an interview.[19]

To insure effective suffrage, congress considered a number of electoral reforms, including the direct election of deputies, senators, and supreme court justices. Concurrently, U.S. progressives advocated the direct election of senators, ultimately ratified as the Seventeenth Amendment to the U.S. Constitution in 1919. Direct election in Mexico caused little controversy and became law in May 1912.[20] Fraud had also occurred in the past because the federal government interfered in local elections, especially during the Díaz dictatorship. De la Barra was clearly committed to the idea of one man, one vote and to noninterference in state and local elections, as he stated on many occasions. "I am resolved," he once told a friend, "that in all the republic the citizens will vote in an entirely free manner."[21] But a part of the problem was that many Mexicans had no experience voting. One citizen offered to hold educational meetings, especially for the illiterate, to instruct them on the niceties of democracy.[22] De la Barra's concern for "effective suffrage" was a strong indication of his belief in democratic principles.

The other half of Madero's campaign slogan, "No reelection," has been imaginatively rendered by one historian as "no boss rule."[23] The translation certainly addresses a basic political practice that the reformers wanted to change. Even worse than the urban political machines of the United States, Porfirian governors and jefes politicos dominated the municipal councils, who directly controlled local taxes and perquisites. Jefes politicos often remained in office for extended terms during the Porfiriato. Local squabbles tended to be the most bitter, perhaps because the official and the citizen probably knew one another personally, and favoritism was more obvious. Boss rule permitted a political elite not only to perpetuate itself in office but also in many instances to enrich itself. Those who were among the "outs" in the Namierite sense felt their exclusion deeply, and in 1910 many joined the insurgency seeking recourse to boss rule.

"No reelection" would also include the modern notion of term limitations, an idea that gained much viability in the later twentieth century in the United States because of problems paralleling the Mexican experience. Feelings about term limits were so pervasive after the Juárez dictatorship that Porfirio Díaz refused reelection in 1880 because it would have resulted in a certain rebellion. Only after he became "irreplaceable" did he formally amend the constitution to permit indefinite reelection, and then in the midst of the most critical political discussions of his administration before the 1910 campaign. The abuse of interminable incumbencies occurred not only in the presidency, however, but also in the cabinet and in state and local offices. While most local Mexican politicians did not have campaign reelection war chests, local pork barrel projects, and congressional privileges to sway voters, they could resort to a more naked form of coercion, intimidation, and fraud to secure their reelection.

By 1910 Mexicans clearly wanted new leadership at all levels, and Madero's slogan, tired as it was, appealed to many. While Madero negotiated with Díaz to change only some of the governorships, once the dictator left Mexico City, all governorships changed hands (see Appendix C). The sentiment for term limits grew to almost absurd proportions; the de la Barra government, with Madero's agreement, stated that interim governors could not seek "reelection" for a full term even though congress had not yet passed the electoral reform statute. The reasons for de la Barra's policy were obvious to all; he wanted to prevent the interim governor from using the power of his office to arrange election results. For the same reason (as well as some personal factors), de la Barra refused to be a candidate for the presidency, setting an example for his fellow citizens. The Chamber of Deputies formally enacted the no-reelection statute, proposed in April 1911, on the day after Madero took office.[24] Thus, the Porfirian consensus included an agreement on term limits that, because of past abuses, was adhered to very strictly.

The issue of political and individual freedoms, admittedly having differing meanings for the middle and lower classes, underlay the insurgency of 1910 and provided the cornerstone of the progressive political consensus. If democracy were truly to become a part of the political scene, individual freedoms had to count for more than mere rhetoric. Vested interests who felt either that they deserved to retain the control they had enjoyed for a generation, or new interests who thought that their participation in Madero's rebellion entitled them to political office regardless of any other considerations, did not always agree with, or abide by, this sentiment. As a result, the de la Barra government's record in preserving and protecting individual liberties is mixed. All too often the president was called on, as in the Reyes campaign, to correct an abuse after it had taken place and when no real remedy was available. Even more frequently, the complaint was highly exaggerated and partisan. Further, de la Barra's belief in federalism limited his willingness to intervene in local matters. Despite questions about de la Barra's effectiveness in controlling political abuses, the evidence suggests that protecting personal liberties was extremely important to him. He promised a free election in his inaugural speech, and he did his best to make it happen. Whether practice conformed to rhetoric, however, must be determined case by case.

State and Local Elections: Progressive Reforms

Politics at the state and local level took on more pragmatic overtones than the theoretical discussion of liberty and freedoms. Putting the ideals into practice meant identifying those who would get jobs and power. Because of the undisputed popular sentiment in favor of "no reelection," the negotiators of the Treaty of Ciudad Juárez orally agreed to appoint interim governors and hold new gubernatorial elections in every state. Although, in some states the local legislatures had to be coerced into selecting an interim governor acceptable to the maderistas, the process took place. By mid-June, Madero and de la Barra had further agreed that the principle of no reelection also required these interim governors to resign if they intended to be candidates for the full-term elections, and many of them did so. The two simply transferred to the local level their national agreement. De la Barra had repeatedly declared that he would not be a candidate for the presidency or the vice presidency, and Madero had resigned the provisional presidency to which the

Plan de San Luis Potosí entitled him so that he might run in the presidential contest of 1911. The agreed-upon policy was then forwarded to each of the governors along with instructions to clarify election requirements and to begin scheduling the balloting.[25] Naturally, these orders precipitated a round of resignations by interim governors, especially those who, like Abraham González and Venustiano Carranza, anticipated being elected to full terms of office.

González did not resign, however, until late August when the popular balloting had already taken place. His action raised some eyebrows among those inclined to hold Madero and his followers to the letter of their promises. Initially, three candidates had appeared to challenge González's almost certain election. The first of these, Miguel Bolaños Cacho, a lawyer and a Porfirian politician from Oaxaca with business ties in Chihuahua, quickly withdrew his challenge, complaining that Abraham González's control over the interim governorship made the results a foregone conclusion. Bolaños Cacho further stated that he was withdrawing from the contest because he did not want to cause civil strife in the state, but as a practical man he no doubt realized his chances of success were few. The other outside candidate, Federico Moye, a prominent businessman and hardware merchant, discovered he was not eligible because of his foreign birth.[26]

The third opposition candidate presented a real threat because he enjoyed at least as much popularity as González. This person was Pascual Orozco. If Chihuahua was the "cradle of the Mexican Revolution," then Orozco's was the hand that rocked the cradle, particularly in early infancy. Orozco enjoyed tremendous personal appeal among the military veterans of 1910, the same humble battlefield veterans who would respond to his call to rebel against Madero in 1912. He had little intellect and probably would have made a poor governor; already he was falling victim to the blandishments of the Terrazas family, which went out of its way to befriend him.[27] Orozco's lapses found their way into the newspapers, yet his courage and his willingness to stand firm for popular maderista principles against what some perceived as Madero's vacillations and compromises with the Porfirians made him a popular candidate.[28] But the civilian maderistas found a constitutional technicality to thwart his candidacy; Orozco was not yet thirty years old and therefore was ineligible to run.

González's statements about his commitment to democracy show at least a rhetorical interest in the idea. As he told some acquaintances, he was resigning the interim governorship "principally because the electoral campaign must be democratic, with full guarantees of liberties for my opponents." To another he wrote, "I must resign within a short time in order that the people may have a free election and none can say that I took undue advantage."[29] The verbal commitment to democracy that González shared with Madero and de la Barra was an essential component of the progressive consensus of 1911, although the temptation to practice authoritarianism caused inconsistencies.

The picture was no prettier in Coahuila. In late May, Madero had to threaten to use force to persuade the state legislature to install Venustiano Carranza in the first place. Carranza delayed appointing a replacement even after he knew he would be a candidate for the permanent job. Only a week elapsed between Carranza's resignation as interim governor and the election, and so while he technically complied with the no-reelection provision, the presence of a close friend as interim did not hurt his chances at the polls. Furthermore, on election day his supporters trucked hacienda peons in from the countryside to vote, even though they were not registered in Saltillo.[30] Past practices died hard even in the north, where the civilian maderistas had won the confidence, for the most part, of the campesinos.

Madero's agreement with de la Barra on political issues drew fire, however, from supporters who were critical of his "political compromises" with former members of the Porfirian establishment. These rabidly partisan civilian maderistas argued that Madero ought to have insisted on a wholesale political housecleaning, requiring the election of new federal and state legislatures and the replacement of the bureaucracy and the judiciary. The absence of this clean sweep, they argued, impeded the progress of the revolution.[31] Madero and de la Barra did not insist on the resignations of the federal deputies for several reasons. For one, the redistricting of the federal Chamber of Deputies following the census of 1910 remained uncompleted.[32] Therefore, it made some sense to postpone new congressional elections until 1912 when the redistricting process had concluded. Nor did de la Barra convene special elections for the vacancies that existed in congress in fall 1911 despite a petition from the Chamber of Deputies that he do so.[33] Significantly, Madero did not protest this decision, probably because legislative bodies never (right up to the present) had carried much weight in the Mexican political system. They routinely approved executive mandates and listened uncritically to administration proposals. One observer, from Sonora, stated it well when he asserted that the legislature was "trained" to do what the executive wanted.[34] Nothing in Madero's experience suggested otherwise. As a result, the sitting federal congress supported electoral reforms, served fairly as the electoral college, and proposed social reforms consistent with the civilian maderistas' ideas. Thus, Madero saw no real need to cleanse the national legislature in 1911, because it endorsed the progressive Porfirian consensus.

Likewise, the state legislatures across the nation had uniformly buckled under pressure from Mexico City to appoint maderistas to the interim governorships. Some states, including Chiapas and Veracruz, did schedule new legislative elections, but this, in de la Barra's federalistic view, was properly a matter for local initiative and not national dictate. State legislators enjoyed no more power than their federal counterparts. Therefore whether new elections were held made little practical difference. But as with the national chamber, the absence of new deputies at the state level felt wrong to many maderistas, some of whom complained loudly. At least one outgoing governor believed that the Porfirian state legislators would make trouble for his civilian maderista replacement.[35]

The idea of changing judicial personnel was even more anathema to de la Barra, who believed in an independent judiciary. Since at least the eighteenth century, Mexicans had debated the proper tenure for judicial officials. The question was whether judges ought to serve "at the pleasure of the king" or for their lifetime based on "good behavior." Mexicans throughout the nineteenth century complained that judges were mere tools of the executive, that the judiciary had not achieved the independent status that most jurists agreed was essential. De la Barra and many of the Porfirian legal community believed that Mexico needed to follow the example of the United States and establish an independent judiciary not beholden to the administration. If this policy were to be adopted, replacing the judiciary because of the insurgency in 1911 seemed to send the wrong signal.

So strong was the progressive consensus on this point that congress passed a reform measure guaranteeing lifetime positions to supreme court justices, who could be removed only for just cause. De la Barra concurred with the proposed reform and refrained from exerting pressure in prevailing cases. After all, he had been one of the independent judiciary's principal theoretical supporters in 1892 when the *científicos* first proposed the idea. Working with Minister of Justice Calero, de la Barra also made certain that only high-caliber lawyers, in contrast to the all-too-frequent corrupt political hacks of the past, were appointed to judgeships.[36] Despite some partisan demands for the removal of Porfirian judges, the civilian maderistas, in the light of contemporary progressivism, preferred instead to make them independent and professional.

What critics of Madero's "compromise" failed to recognize was that, although many of the legislators and judges kept their offices, other elected and appointed political and administrative officials were removed in large numbers. Minister of the Interior Emilio Vázquez Gómez began issuing directives urging the replacement of local officials, especially the jefes politicos, beginning on June 10. As he said in his second circular, "a change in the political authorities, both federal and local, is necessary for the public peace." Vázquez Gómez urged that such changes be democratic where required by the constitution; otherwise, they ought to be consistent with public opinion.[37] Vázquez Gómez followed with a third memorandum on July 7, alleging that his orders had been carried out in Guanajuato and a few other states, but not universally. As a result, he again ordered that "all the local authorities [be replaced] by others who are to the liking of the people."[38] Most, if not all, interim governors appear to have responded. In the state of México, the interim governor gradually replaced all political employees in accordance with the directive.[39] In San Luis Potosí, the wheels turned a little more slowly. Rafael Cepeda, a Madero loyalist, had to ask local authorities which villages had made changes before he could report he was in compliance with the policy.[40]

The jefe politico stood at the base of the administrative hierarchy created by the constitution of 1857. Under Porfirio Díaz, the jefes worked as the local arm of the dictator and state governors, circulating decrees, collecting local taxes, drafting dissidents into the army or rurales, and generally imposing the Porfirian will. The jefes often infringed on the autonomy traditionally enjoyed by the elected town council, or ayuntamiento, which sometimes saw the jefe politico installed as its president or at least as its informal boss. Because the jefes enjoyed the authority to transfer municipal lands and waters, and to sell public lands, these Porfirian officeholders often became the focal point of local resentments. After May 1911 communities reasserted their desire to control taxes locally and to have their own militia and their own parish church. No wonder local insurgents called for the wholesale replacement of jefes politicos or the abolition of the office altogether as happened immediately in several states in 1911 and nationally in 1914. The transfer of local offices in 1911 occurred sometimes as a result of proper elections and sometimes by popular acclamation, at least in the state of Guanajuato, the only state where the institution has been studied systematically.[41] The multitude of documents on the removals of jefes politicos in 1911 underlines the intensely local nature of the Mexican Revolution.[42]

Some historians see Emilio Vázquez Gómez's directives as part of his attempted power grab when taken in conjunction with his reluctance to disarm the popular maderistas and his demand at a cabinet meeting that de la Barra resign and leave him in charge of the country.[43] The evidence disputes this interpretation. De la Barra reviewed a draft of Vázquez Gómez's directive before it was issued and approved of its contents. In a very candid letter he revealed that he agreed with the idea that old political officials be replaced, as long as the process was legal and any decisions to replace local officials were not made simplistically. The president pointed out that not all of the previous government employees were evil or unpopular, and that qualified and well-liked employees who agreed with the principles proclaimed by the maderistas ought to be retained. Further, he reiterated these ideas, including the notion of abolishing the office of jefe politico, in a press conference on July 17.[44] A close examination of Vázquez Gómez's three directives indicates that he too avoided a simplistic analysis of the issue. Nonetheless, because of the assumption that the jefe had to be local and because of the limited number of candidates from among notable families—the only candidates acceptable to civilian maderista governors—the change in jefe politicos often resulted in the return to office of someone who had served at some earlier point in the Porfiriato.

The discussion about who to retain and who to dismiss quickly became highly partisan, especially when the focus of change shifted from political officeholders to bureaucratic functionaries who worked in the various federal and state agencies. Civilian maderistas seemed to accept the idea that competent Porfirian civil servants ought to be retained. Emilio Vázquez Gómez, the supposed radical who wished to eliminate all the bureaucratic Porfirians, even secured a promotion for a former Porfirian friend of his.[45] No doubt for several reasons Madero and de la Barra believed that the entire state and federal civil service should not be terminated wholesale.

One source of their belief may have been the example of the United States. As most of the civilian maderistas and Porfirians looked north, they saw the benefits that had emerged from the civil service reform initiatives of the Progressive era. No longer did the U.S. government operate on the spoils system, with political appointees seizing the opportunity provided by their patrons' four-year terms to graft their way to financial security. Instead, the civil service had become significantly professionalized and better paid, and, theoretically, it did a better job because of increased job security and benefits. The educated leadership of Mexico clearly wanted to emulate this success, and in fall 1911 the congress passed a civil service reform law. Madero and de la Barra also realized that the bureaucracy needed a certain amount of continuity to function efficiently. For example, a member of the board of directors of Mexico City's public water supply urged that while clearly the chair of the board (Limantour) had to be replaced, the remainder of the officials ought to keep their jobs because otherwise their work, and the city's service, would be disrupted. De la Barra agreed.[46] Thus, the directive of June 16 particularly seemed to carry out the policy objective of infusing the bureaucracy with necessary new blood while retaining essential employees still doing a good job.

Interim governors took very seriously the business of replacing selected Porfirian bureaucrats. Abraham González implemented the national policy in Chihuahua, making certain he appointed political personnel whose beliefs were compatible with those of the populace at large, but retaining competent Porfirians, especially in the customs house in Ciudad Juárez where certain skills were important.[47] Deciding which jobs were political and which were bureaucratic proved controversial. One pawnshop controller, a veteran of twenty-nine years, lost his job as did several postal and telegraph employees.[48] Madero also proved willing to urge the undersecretary of at least one department to have his lawyers conduct an investigation into abuses allegedly committed by department members in Porfirian days.[49] Thus, the evidence shows that some civil service jobs and nearly all political offices changed hands in 1911. Equally important, the notion of changing personnel did not pit civilian maderistas against reactionary Porfirians; it was a policy consensus.

The state gubernatorial elections in 1911 drew the loudest cries about political imposition and electoral fraud. There the stakes were much higher than in local elections, and civilian maderistas won almost unanimously. Critics denounced the de la Barra government and Madero personally, accusing them of spouting democratic rhetoric while retaining traditional tactics of violence and intimidation as tools for political repression of opponents. These tactics were used in the Reyes presidential campaign, discussed later in this chapter, and in elections in the state of Michoacán. Like much of the rest of western Mexico, Michoacán only belatedly became involved in the maderista insurgency. Not long after May 25, the state legislature deposed the Porfirian governor and replaced him with Miguel Silva, who generally appealed to most of the political factions within the state. Silva's very success bred problems. The civilian maderistas quickly endorsed him as their candidate, allowing the opposition to coalesce around two rivals. Displaying their partisanship, Silva's followers felt that they could legitimately intimidate the opposition, particularly the very viable Catholic party candidate, and take other ethically questionable steps to insure Silva's victory. Both of these practices lent credence to claims of electoral fraud.[50]

Silva's friends used violence to threaten and intimidate his principal opponent, Francisco Elguero. Elguero, an intelligent, conservative attorney, had become one of the national leaders of the Catholic party, a conservative opposition party that had emerged at the end of the Porfiriato. The Michoacán Catholic party nominated Elguero as its standard-bearer, and when his candidacy seemed to strike a responsive chord, Silva's campaign handlers decided that they had to do something to diminish the threat.

On the night of August 12, a large crowd of Silva backers gathered outside Elguero's house, tossing rocks and shouting "mueras" to the candidate. Although Elguero himself was apparently not at home, his relatives in the house were clearly frightened by this ugly turn of events. Two family members are said to have come out onto the balconies and fired shots at the mob. Police finally arrived and drove the crowd off. The next morning, Silva appeared and delivered an impassioned speech to the reassembled crowd about the need for law and order, telling the crowd that it was morally offensive to shout "mueras" to the opposition in an attempt to intimidate. At the same time, however, the government issued a warrant for Elguero's arrest, allegedly for wounding someone in the crowd.[51] The issue for Michoacán was whether the hostile demonstration actually affected democracy adversely. Ultimately, Elguero did withdraw his candidacy, and so the intimidation succeeded.[52]

On these occasions the structural indicators of democracy frayed, revealing Mexico's longstanding authoritarian tradition. In another case an interim governor asked for permission to suspend constitutional guarantees in his state during the election period and impose martial law in order to prevent violence.[53] While such a policy superficially met the goals of de la Barra's law-and-order scheme, it conflicted fundamentally with his desire to see the democratic, free franchise operate, a subject about which his convictions were nearly as sensitive, and so the answer to the interim governor's request for troops was no.

Other questionable state practices included waiving technical requirements on behalf of favored candidates while imposing them on the opposition and bending rules on the eve of the election to secure the desired results. For example, neither the opposition candidate in San Luis Potosí nor the maderista met the constitutional requirements. The opponent was too young and Rafael Cepeda had not been a resident for five years, but for Cepeda the interim state governor waived the barrier.[54] The gubernatorial elections in Querétaro presented a different problem. Apparently, all three candidates enjoyed a significant following and therefore none received the required majority for election. Although de la Barra had apparently anticipated this problem and proposed a convoluted solution involving the electoral college, Madero did not agree. He suggested that the state legislature select his candidate, who had won a plurality, because that represented "the will of the people."[55]

Few practices smacked more of fraud than delaying the scheduled elections. Unlike the U.S. system of declaring the first Tuesday in November as election day for all races in all years, the Mexican practice was to permit the state legislatures to set the time of elections. But because the legislature was often subservient to the governor, this constitutional provision led to widespread fraud during the nineteenth century. The ability to delay elections clearly hampered democracy. If the governor did not like his party's chances in the prevailing political climate, then he would simply persuade the legislature to delay the elections until a more propitious moment. This did not always work, of course, because sometimes electoral delays prompted rebellions.

In several instances in 1911, interim governors did try to delay elections to improve their party's chances. In Sonora, rumors that the *científicos* were planning to delay elections drew the wrath of the maderistas, who were confident of victory.[56] Probably the worst case of proposed election manipulation occurred in Oaxaca, where Madero questioned the competence of both declared candidates. His antipathy for Félix Díaz, nephew of the deposed dictator, is understandable, but he also publicly doubted the abilities of his own candidate, Benito Juárez Maza, whom he considered a bit of a fool. Madero proposed to de la Barra that the elections be delayed a month so that a third candidate could be selected, someone both capable and loyal. De la Barra stated that Madero's arguments for delay were not persuasive, even though he probably agreed Juárez Maza was a dolt, and Oaxaca elected the maderista candidate at the scheduled time.[57]

In Jalisco, as the scheduled date for gubernatorial elections approached, the governor decided to postpone them, mostly because the Catholic party's candidate, the well-known author José López Portillo y Rojas, seemed likely to triumph. Madero feared the election of a conservative.[58] One of Madero's counselors encouraged him to back Alfredo Robles Gil, certainly the favorite of the business community.[59] He delayed the elections as long as possible but to no avail. José López Portillo y Rojas won by a decisive margin, and the Catholic party took control in Jalisco in 1912.[60]

This discussion brings us back to the questions with which this chapter begins. To what degree does the evidence support the claims that Madero, de la Barra, and the civilian maderistas brought democracy to Mexico in 1911? Were the discussions of democracy mere rhetoric to hide traditional authoritarian practices? The preliminary answer seems to be that, while professing belief in democracy, Madero and de la Barra sometimes sent mixed signals to state governors who then interpreted the new rules as they saw fit. Although Madero espoused democracy and free elections, he also wanted his political allies ensconced in the gubernatorial mansions throughout the republic.

De la Barra also favored certain candidates, though not always the same ones favored by Madero.[61] De la Barra, however, refrained from fixing elections for his friends, saying, "There will not be an official candidate because I am resolved that everywhere in the republic the citizens will vote in an entirely free manner."[62] Because de la Barra remained aloof from the elections, neither seeking office nor overtly supporting a particular party, he had much less at stake than did Madero, and thus his commitment to democracy seems genuine. His most controversial declaration, repeated in several state races, was that he desired "strongly that the results of the election be favorable for the welfare and progress of the state." Although basically noncommittal, this statement does suggest certain values.[63] Generally, de la Barra came out strongly for democracy and "effective suffrage," a phrase he repeated endlessly as the nation prepared for the many electoral contests in 1911.[64]

The general principles reveal a certain commitment to democracy by Madero and his partisans and by the Porfirian members of the consensus. All agreed that Mexico needed new political blood, that for too long the same people had monopolized positions of power and influence, creating a petrified forest of administrators (see Appendix C). Thus, the new philosophy made it possible for an outsider to win. For example, in Tlaxcala a rather desultory gubernatorial campaign between two civilians emerged. Both allegedly had links to the old regime, and both desperately wanted to forge a relationship with Madero. Neither was popular, leaving many citizens of the state wondering what the revolution had brought them. To make matters worse, the original interim governor had been thrown out of office for constitutional irregularities. Fortunately for the state, however, a highly respected judge named Ramón Maldonado agreed to serve as the new interim governor and preside over the state elections in September.[65] With no viable local civilian maderista of the *gente decente* available, intellectuals and civilians with connections to Puebla took charge. They organized a convention in the state capital in early September to find a candidate.

Many of the convention's participants were industrial workers and hacienda day laborers, further proof that interest in democracy extended far beyond the middle class. These novice politicians carried the day and, under the direction of the intellectuals, many of whom were rural school teachers, nominated a forty-year-old industrial worker from the "lowest class," Antonio Hidalgo, who had played a minor leadership role in the labor unrest of 1906 as their symbolic leader. In addition to choosing Hidalgo, the Tlaxcala convention drafted a platform filled with radical social goals without considering the expenses of these programs. The convention stayed orderly, but the interim governor feared the worst and called for military reinforcements for the days ahead.[66] Hidalgo's platform did endorse radical change, but its second plank called for the establishment of democracy.[67]

Hidalgo's "socialistic and communistic" notions sent a shudder through the political establishment. Local "perfumed ones" feared that Hidalgo's program would propel the state in the direction of Morelos, which they certainly did not want to happen. Worse yet, from their perspective, Hidalgo seemed unbeatable in the election because nearly every worker and day laborer, the overwhelming majority of the population, would vote for him. Although some observers hoped that the two civilian maderista candidates could smooth over their petty ideological differences and jealousies to present a united front and a single alternative to Hidalgo, the feud ran too deeply.[68] The elections took place quietly, and the interim governor's call for additional troops proved unnecessary. Neither the feared invasion from Morelos nor the mass assassination of the state chamber of deputies occurred, apparently because the interim governor assured the electorate that the balloting would be free and fair, and Antonio Hidalgo, the most popular candidate, won the election.[69]

Tlaxcala's election is in some ways the most interesting of all the state elections because it is the only one in which a true outsider won. The establishment civilian maderistas clearly did not want Hidalgo, and after the election they worked successfully with the remaining Porfirians in the state legislature to extend Maldonado's interim term as long as possible, until December 1.[70] Tlaxcala even then did not become the nation's blueprint for radical social change. But Tlaxcala's election is also very significant because it offers convincing proof of Madero's and de la Barra's commitment to democracy. Neither participated in the machinations of the local civilian maderistas, intervened in the state to nullify the election results, or influenced the state legislature to postpone the election until a more moderate popular candidate emerged. Granted, Tlaxcala was not an important state in the union; had Hidalgo been the gubernatorial candidate in Puebla or Jalisco perhaps Madero and de la Barra might have acted differently. The national leadership may also have remained aloof because the process was peaceful, popular, and democratic. Tlaxcala did not experience the rounds of violence that accompanied the cry for change in Morelos and that so clearly angered the president. He probably reasoned that any intervention on his part in Tlaxcala would only disrupt the peace that his administration had pledged to preserve. Madero, too, deserves praise for keeping his hands off the Tlaxcalan election in fall 1911. Thus, Tlaxcala remained an outstanding example of the progressive consensus in favor of democratic change in action although later local politicians would try to derail Hidalgo's reforms.

Policymakers encouraged the interim governors to hold local elections where possible, usually for municipal councils, and to appoint nonelective officials who met with popular approval or "the will of the people." No doubt many members of the consensus felt the influence of U.S. progressivism.[71] Where elections were contested, and the successful candidate close to those in power at the time of the election won, claims of electoral fraud did arise. In keeping with a longstanding political tradition that undoubtedly will continue into the twenty-first century, an overwhelming percentage of those befriended by interim governors won their races. Nevertheless, the results suggest that de la Barra and his interim government kept his inaugural promise to preside over fair and honest elections.

The Vice Presidential Election

The vice presidential elections drew criticism because the loser raised claims of electoral fraud that many observers found believable. Because of Madero's oft-repeated commitment to democracy, opponents pointed to questionable practices that made him seem hypocritical. His critics took umbrage at the results of the vice presidential election because of what appeared to be a disturbing parallel to Porfirian practices, the imposition of an unpopular, unknown nominee over what appeared to be a more popular choice. As the U.S. ambassador noted, Madero had sharply criticized Porfirio Díaz's electoral methods, which the maderistas showed "a facile willingness to emulate at the first opportunity."[72]

De la Barra stayed aloof from much of this controversy because the dispute over the selection of the vice presidential nominee arose within Madero's political party, to which de la Barra did not belong. The subsequent victory of that nominee against his interparty rival and an unwillingly drafted de la Barra created a second controversy over the vice presidential election in 1911. The evidence suggests, however, that despite some highly suspect circumstances, the popular Madero did persuade the electorate to give his candidate the job.

The vice presidential debate arose because of the on-again, off-again relationship between Francisco Madero and his original vice presidential running mate from 1910, Francisco Vázquez Gómez. Madero had chosen Vázquez Gómez originally for two reasons. He would be a bridge to the rapidly disintegrating Democratic party, the followers of Bernardo Reyes, who represented a significant force within the electorate in 1910, and he had been Porfirio Díaz's personal physician and presumably was on sufficiently close terms with the dictator to mollify some of his wrath. In short, Vázquez Gómez's nomination did not result from his long and active service to the Anti-Reelection party. It was a gesture of expediency, designed both to broaden support and appease the dictator. Not long thereafter, as early as fall 1910, Madero and Vázquez Gómez began a falling out. Vázquez Gómez had some doubts about the wisdom of taking to the battlefield. He remained in Mexico City while many other party members fled to Texas and began to plot the uprising. Although Vázquez Gómez joined the insurrection two or three months later and served in the important post of de facto ambassador to the United States, as outlined in Chapter 2, his procrastination in fall 1910 caused some maderistas to question his loyalty.

Madero's brother Gustavo, his closest political kinsman and the political tough guy of the family, led the charge against Vázquez Gómez. In part, the animosity arose because Francisco Vázquez Gómez made disparaging remarks about the omnipresent Madero clan during the Ciudad Juárez negotiations. Madero's family certainly occupied a disproportionate share of the offices in the de la Barra and Madero governments. Two of Madero's relatives, his uncles Ernesto Madero and Rafael Hernández, served in de la Barra's cabinet at treasury and development, respectively. A relative of his wife's, Jóse González Salas, held a third cabinet post as secretary of war. His brothers Raúl and Emilio became rurales commanders, the latter severely criticized because of the expenses run up under his command in Torreón.[73] Others, like Gustavo, entered the congress. Gustavo, a minister without portfolio, also served as Madero's political manager and organizer of the Porra, a group of heavies who enforced the Madero political orthodoxy. The sheer number of Madero's relatives in office draws to mind William Faulkner's Snopeses. Of course, nepotism extended beyond the Madero family. Both Vázquez Gómez brothers found high-level appointments. Likewise, Luis León de la Barra, the interim president's brother, received a promotion to a consulate a week after his brother became president, and another brother, Ignacio, remained as director of public works for the Federal District.[74] But the Madero family took the brunt of the criticism, probably because Gustavo Madero's responsibilities included leaning on Francisco Vázquez Gómez and the other mavericks who questioned Francisco Madero.

Nor did the allegations stop with nepotism. Complaints of corruption headlined the press, especially after Gustavo received reimbursement in June 1911 for revolutionary expenses that came in the form of 600,000 pesos he had embezzled from French investors in a family business enterprise.[75] Gustavo did observe all of the formalities, and the "Porfirian" Chamber of Deputies and the senate authorized the expenditure. Nevertheless, Gustavo's reimbursement created an appearance of wrongdoing. Vázquez Gómez further alienated himself from the Maderos by discussing publicly the appropriateness of the congressional action. Whatever the original cause, Francisco Vázquez Gómez and Madero had fundamental disagreements by summer 1911.[76] For Madero, the question became whether an independent-minded maverick (Vázquez Gómez) made a better vice president than a sycophant. Rumors became rife in July 1911 that Madero, not surprisingly, would dump his original vice presidential nominee.

Vázquez Gómez, who clearly wanted to hang onto his official candidacy, pleaded for party unity, as did some others who had been close to the two men during the preceding year.[77] By late July, Madero still had not announced the identity of his running mate. Some felt Alfredo Robles Domínguez would be chosen because of the torments he underwent for the cause in prison and his relative success as the peace advocate for central Mexico. Others supported Fernando Iglesias Calderón. Certainly the man eventually nominated for the office, Governor José María Pino Suárez of the Yucatán, qualified as a dark horse. Although rumors surfaced in late July about his possible selection, Pino responded that he still belonged to the old Anti-Reelection party, and therefore he would be supporting Francisco Vázquez Gómez for the vice presidency.[78] Vázquez Gómez pleaded with Pino Suárez to do the "patriotic" thing and advocate party unity.[79] Unless Pino Suárez was being totally disingenuous, he did not know that his name had surfaced because of Madero himself.

Madero responded that Vázquez Gómez should not be so worried about dividing the party. The party's central committee had decided on its own to hold a new convention and to rename the organization the Constitutional Progressive party. The name Anti-Reelection party now seemed irrelevant since neither Porfirio Díaz nor Francisco León de la Barra was seeking reelection. Further, according to Madero, Vázquez Gómez should have every expectation of being renominated by the new party, although again this statement by Madero seems misleading. Finally, Madero suggested that the new convention would bring various factions together and would include some more recent converts who had not attended the April 1910 meeting.[80]

That Madero was not being totally honest with Vázquez Gómez seems pretty clear. He asked Vázquez Gómez to remain in the de la

Barra government (which he did) and clearly hoped the soothing remarks would mollify him (which they did not). The rationale for calling a new convention seemed unconvincing, and the numerous rumors of alternative candidates must have made Vázquez Gómez suspicious. Madero's veiled intentions became a little clearer at a meeting between the two men on August 11. There Madero bluntly repudiated the old Anti-Reelection political clubs, which he turned over to Vázquez Gómez. Madero stated that the Constitutional Progressive party (PCP) would create its own clubs to rally support at the polls. Madero must have been convinced that he did the right thing by dumping Vázquez Gómez when, at a press conference, he told reporters that the two had settled their differences, only to have Vázquez Gómez publicly contradict him.[81]

The PCP convention scheduled for August 27 proved to be a banner day for Madero and his family and friends. The convention formally adopted the new party label and then nominated Madero for the presidency. The reunion, just a few weeks before the election, certainly fired up the enthusiasm of the rank and file. One observer called it the "first untrammeled political convention ever held in this country," where platform planks were hotly debated and discussion was open. The vice presidential nomination was the most contentious issue. Pino Suárez led Vázquez Gómez by only five votes on the first ballot, requiring Madero to do some arm-twisting to get his way.[82] The party now had a viable organization in every state and territory, with gubernatorial candidates active in every contest. But the good mood of the convention had dissipated over the bickering about dumping Vázquez Gómez.[83] In the end, the convention nominated José María Pino Suárez, as Madero instructed, leaving some voters feeling that their representatives at the convention had betrayed them by joining the stampede for Madero's choice against the wishes of many party members.[84]

Was Pino Suárez's selection an imposition similar to Porfirio Díaz's imposition of Ramón Corral in 1910, as some of Madero's critics charged? As in the United States, the selection of the vice presidential running mate was the personal choice of the successful presidential nominee. Madero did not have to choose someone who was popular or well-known to run on the ticket with him, just someone with whom he was comfortable.

Even if Pino Suárez's nomination was an "imposition," it was well within Madero's prerogative and not contrary to democratic practices. Madero apparently valued loyalty over name recognition. Pino Suárez had been with Madero in Texas from the beginning and had always complied with Madero's directives. Madero may have chosen Pino Suárez also because of Mexico's historical problem with vice presidents acting contentiously and independently. During the early republic, vice presidents so often rebelled against the chief executive that the office was abolished in the constitution of 1857. Francisco Vázquez Gómez displayed some of the same disturbing characteristics as earlier troublesome vice presidents, and therefore Madero was both justified and reasonable in replacing him with somebody who was loyal. As Madero told the British minister, it was important to have a vice president of "total fidelity" who could be his alter ego.[85] Besides, the nomination alone did not seal the matter; Vázquez Gómez's name still appeared on the ballot as the vice presidential candidate of the Anti-Reelection party, and conceivably he could win the office even without Madero's endorsement.

Although only a month remained before the polls opened, Madero bestirred himself from his summer holidays at the baths in Tehuacán to campaign for Pino Suárez. In Guadalajara, he introduced Pino Suárez to a crowd of some twenty thousand people, who roundly booed him. In the crowded Degollado Theater, after a series of pro-Pino speeches, Madero made the mistake of inviting Roque Estrada, a close friend of Francisco Vázquez Gómez's, to the podium. Apparently to Madero's surprise, Estrada talked about Vázquez Gómez's virtues and his sympathy for him to loud applause from the audience.[86]

Pino's reception in various cities in Veracruz was even chillier. In Jalapa, catcalls interrupted Madero's introduction of him, and each time the vice presidential candidate stepped forward, the boos drove him from the podium. The crowd also tore down all the Pino Suárez posters.[87] Similar responses met the campaigners in Orizaba and in the port city of Veracruz. The rally at the Dehesa Theater backfired when the crowd shouted choruses of "Madero-Vázquez Gómez."[88] All along the campaign trail, the party was met with the chant, "Pino no, Pino no." Because Mexico had no equivalent of the Gallup polls in 1911, scientifically measuring this anti-Pino sentiment is impossible. Officially, according to the results, both Jalisco and Veracruz voted for Pino Suárez and not Vázquez Gómez (see Appendix D). But did the maderista machinery at the state level tamper with the ballots?

Vázquez Gómez was not the only name on the ballot with Pino Suárez. In addition to two irrelevant also-rans who garnered a smattering of votes, Francisco León de la Barra appeared on the ballot as the vice presidential nominee of the Catholic party. Although de la Barra had stated in his inaugural address and many times thereafter as well that he would not run for the presidency or the vice presidency, he could not persuade the Catholic party to remove his name from the ballot. De la Barra's candidacy was unwilling, forced on him over his strenuous objections, and he later said that had he been elected, he would not have served.[89]

The elections took place amidst the usual cries of fraud and coercion. Pino Suárez won a bare majority; even with all the fuss (see Appendix D).[90] One district in Sonora, reputedly pro-Vázquez Gómez, was represented by only Pino Suárez candidates in the electoral college.[91] One of de la Barra's supporters reported his friends were barred physically from voting, while in another location the Pino Suárez team complained that they had lost because of the heavy-handed tactics of local pro-Vázquez officials.[92] Thus, clean elections did not occur everywhere, and undoubtedly in some districts local officials coerced the voters. Certainly the Veracruz and Jalisco results seem skewed. Nevertheless, a plurality of the voters probably accepted Madero's personal choice for the vice presidency.[93] Congress promptly confirmed the election results, and Pino Suárez became the last person to serve as Mexico's vice president.

Because Franciso Vázquez Gómez continued to be outspoken in his criticism of the electoral process, he ultimately lost his cabinet post amid allegations of disloyalty to the government.[94] His brother Emilio, after being rejected as president in the same election, slipped into exile in the United States and began plotting a rebellion. The government suspected that as early as August the two had been in cahoots. Supposedly, a damning telegram from Emilio to Francisco provided evidence of Francisco's complicity. Francisco Vázquez Gómez denied all charges and even requested that the minister of communications search the telegraph office's duplicate file for the original telegram, but the search proved inconclusive.[95] Vázquez Gómez's resignation from the ministry effectively ended his role in the Mexican Revolution. Living quietly in Mexico City for the remainder of the Madero presidency, Vázquez Gómez fled once the Huerta dictatorship took power in 1913. After years in exile, he reemerged as an intellectual in Zapata's camp, where he advised on agrarian reform issues before drifting into obscurity and exile once again.

The vice presidential election raised many of the same questions the gubernatorial elections raised—whether the Madero clan stooped to Porfirian tactics of fraud and coercion to obtain the desired results at the polls. Certainly choosing one's own running mate did not constitute an imposition, and probably a majority of Mexicans were willing to approve Madero's choice. Whether Madero made a political error by rejecting his compatriot from the 1910 ticket is another matter. But loyalty is a valued quality in a vice president, and Francisco Vázquez Gómez had demonstrated over and over again that he lacked that quality. What Francisco Vázquez Gómez failed to recognize was that he had been every bit as obscure and undeserving in 1910 as Pino Suárez was in 1911. Ultimately, the decision about the vice presidential nominee rested with Madero, and he clearly felt more comfortable with Pino Suárez than with Vázquez Gómez. A large number of Mexicans agreed to respect his wishes and chose Pino Suárez.

The Presidential Race

The presidential election raised some of the same issues as did certain state races about the practice of democracy in 1911, especially concerning interference with civil liberties. The intrigues surrounding the presidential candidacy of General Bernardo Reyes produced the most virulent criticisms of the new democracy. In particular, Madero's friends and especially his brother Gustavo came under attack for intimidating Reyes and forcing him to drop out of the contest. Otherwise, Reyes's political behavior in 1911 was every bit as incomprehensible as it had been in 1908. Back then, after the Creelman interview, Reyes seemed to be the most popular and most logical candidate to run for the vice presidency, a sure winner. But Díaz would have none of it; he feared Reyes as a rival. So when Díaz told Reyes he could not have the vice presidency, the general accepted his assignment as a special military envoy to Europe.[96]

Reyes's planned return to Mexico in 1911 caused fear and loathing among the civilian maderistas, fear because initially they believed it possible that the miracle man might turn around the military situation in May (which he could not have), and loathing because once the Madero insurgency ended, Reyes remained a viable political alternative (or so they thought). As a result, during the negotiations at Ciudad Juárez, the rebels insisted that Reyes be detained in Havana, Cuba, until the contending factions sorted out the domestic situation and leadership had changed hands. When Reyes finally landed in Mexico in June, he was an anachronism, though few recognized it at the time. His return to Mexico City attracted a great deal of attention, and in June crowds flocked into the streets to get a better look at him. Reyes's fame rested on his reputation for grit and activity, but as events during summer 1911 would prove, he had character flaws as well.

When Reyes returned, because of his apparent popularity, Madero made a warm gesture of reconciliation. He met with Reyes under de la Barra's auspices at Chapultepec Castle and offered him the cabinet post of minister of war in his postelection administration. Madero believed that Reyes would prove useful, and that he could "facilitate our work of pacifying the country and strengthening foreign confidence."[97] Madero knew Reyes's reputation for organization, and thought his talents would be useful in reforming the war department according to progressive principles. Further, Madero did not fear Reyes, because he had acted professionally and loyally to his commander in chief.[98]

The proposed compromise drew a lot of negative commentary. Madero's followers complained that Reyes had duped Madero and doubted he could work in a democratic world. Further, they anticipated the worst, assuming that Reyes was hatching dark plots with his military friends to take leadership away from the weak and naive Madero.[99] In short, the whole notion of compromise with Reyes was anathema to many of the civilian maderistas. Interestingly, at least one former reyista shared this view. He had long admired Reyes's discipline and professionalism but believed that the general's hour had passed. Now, he asserted, the government ought to be made up of men who had participated in the insurgency.[100] Despite these criticisms, Madero's policy made sense. Many people, both in and out of the military, revered the general. For them, his presence in the new government would have soothed bad feelings and broadened the civilian maderista-Porfirian coalition. Madero also defended his idea by stressing the advantages of the arrangement.[101]

For Reyes, the compromise should have made sense, too. His day had passed, and the proffered service gave him an opportunity to resuscitate his reputation in the eyes of friends and foes alike by proving he could work within the democratic context. But Reyes had the poorest sense of timing of any of his contemporaries in the Mexican Revolution. His popularity had clearly waned from 1909; and he should have recognized that Madero had won over many of his old Democratic party followers.[102] But Reyes resisted logic, and his efforts to return to the Mexico of 1909 made him a laughingstock. He was vain, and instead of reacting logically to his changed circumstances, he took the bait some friends offered and decided to abandon Madero's generous compromise in favor of a more ambitious but less practical plan to challenge Madero at the polls.

Madero, too, had some second thoughts about his offer once his colleagues' objections started pouring into his office. Nevertheless, he probably would have held firm for the compromise had not Reyes taken the initiative to break it off. Only days after the agreement was reached, Reyes informed de la Barra that he would "disentangle himself from the compromise of serving as secretary of war." He asked the president to rescind any orders returning him to his military mission in Europe.[103] Soon Reyes was explaining his new plan, the run for the presidency, with his old friend, Madero's uncle Ernesto, the secretary of the treasury. Naturally, word quickly got back to Francisco Madero, as Reyes undoubtedly intended.

In a letter in mid-July, Madero freed Reyes (and himself) from the earlier agreement. After reiterating his reasons for seeking Reyes's cooperation, Madero stated that he had not intended to bribe Reyes with a cabinet position in order to prevent him from making a run at the presidency. Instead, Madero asserted, he thought that Reyes's organizational skills and their agreed-upon concern about dividing the country at its time of crisis had been good reasons for the original compromise offer. If Reyes chose to run, Madero hoped that the campaign would be clean and democratic.[104] Although the two men seemed cordial at this moment, the tensions of the campaign would soon lead to rancor between them. Madero noted, in response to the new intransigence of the reyistas, "we need people in the cabinet with absolute fidelity to the principles of the revolution."[105] Foreseeing the rising tempers, President de la Barra asked Madero and Reyes to meet personally to resolve their differences and rationally approach the coming presidential campaign.

De la Barra took his cue from Reyes, who had requested the session to make certain that the playing field was level.[106] Accordingly, Reyes and Madero met on August 2 in the presence of Ernesto Madero. Francisco Madero confirmed what he had written in mid-July, that Reyes was free to campaign for the presidency. Reyes assured Madero that for his part the campaign would be democratic and that he would remain absolutely loyal to the government. He pledged his services to the government regardless of the results. Reyes asked that Madero in turn confirm his earlier guarantee of electoral freedom and offered the vice presidency to Ernesto

Madero, who declined with thanks. Francisco Madero responded warmly to the session, stating that he hoped that the two would remain friends and that he would still consider bringing Reyes into his government although he would no longer promise to do so. Both candidates exuded effusive warmth at the end of the interview.[107]

De la Barra had nothing but praise for the results of the meeting, stating to the two candidates, "I applaud the compromise you made for a clean, democratic campaign. I assure you that the government will provide protection and will be impartial. My policy is clear. It is to make sure that the popular will is respected and to guarantee order."[108] Thus de la Barra again made a strong commitment to the democratic principles that were at the heart of the uprising of 1910. Whether the presidential rivals would be able to maintain the aura of good feelings for each other, however, remained to be seen.

Within weeks, the campaign became vituperative. Reyes soon showed his thinly disguised contempt for the mousy Madero, whom he believed to be weak and incompetent. Reyes's followers organized the usual political clubs and held rallies in local communities. The reyista party planned a national convention for early September to rally additional support and to select a vice presidential nominee.[109] Quickly, however, the party leadership began to complain that local officials, mostly maderistas, were interfering with organizational efforts. The jefe politico in El Oro, state of México, for example, arrested the author of pro-Reyes leaflets on the grounds that he was inciting riots, ignoring arguments about freedom of the press.[110] A local politician who wanted to lead a Reyes demonstration was arrested and ultimately let off with a fine, simply for having expressed his political opinions.[111] In Saltillo, the reyista club fared no better, especially after Governor Carranza made an impassioned speech denouncing the general.[112] The secretary of the interior (again the allegedly "counter-revolutionary" Alberto García Granados) overrode Nuevo León's governor and issued a parade permit in one community for an anti-Reyes demonstration.[113] Not that the reyistas were above using the same tactics themselves when they held the upper hand. In one town, drunken reyistas shot up a pro-Madero rally, scattering the participants.[114]

The worst was yet to come. On September 3, some of Reyes's followers planned a political rally in the center (now the historic district) of Mexico City. As the parade began, a group of maderistas, supposedly members of Gustavo Madero's infamous Porra, accosted them. Reyes tried to calm the hot tempers, but the maderistas picked up stones and, in a most unseemly episode, began heaving them at the general. The police apparently stood by and did nothing to stop the fracas. Reyes already had some misgivings about the efficacy of his campaign in the light of alleged maderista repression. With many electoral districts in the hands of the civilian maderistas and with Madero's popularity, he doubted he had much chance at the polls. And he was acutely aware of the street fighting that had occurred in several towns.[115]

The stoning of Bernardo Reyes in early September changed the tone of the entire campaign for the worse, and once more opened up Madero to charges of electoral manipulation. Nothing his enemies could have done would have more seriously tarnished Madero's luster than the actions of his own brother. Reyes now had to consider whether he was willing to risk his life on the campaign trail, and what measures he should take to protect himself. Further, he now held the higher moral ground, and he could argue that Madero's actions freed him from his promise of absolute loyalty to the victor in the elections.

Reyes's first thought was to arm himself and his friends. He wanted to protect not only his followers but also his family, all of whom felt extremely vulnerable after the stoning. Therefore, Reyes asked de la Barra for permission to gather a small arsenal in his home.[116] Strictly speaking, of course, such a request violated de la Barra's policy of preserving order by keeping weapons out of private hands; but he did not want Reyes to be murdered while he was president. And so de la Barra agreed to let Reyes have the guns. Reyes pledged he would use the weapons only under extreme duress, and then only when the police failed to do their job.[117] Arming the candidate was not much of a solution. It raised the likelihood of escalating violence and ran counter to the democratic objective de la Barra had in mind. As a result, the president decided on a more rational means of dealing with Reyes's concerns for personal safety; he suggested an arbitration meeting of party leaders to discuss the parameters for behavior during the remainder of the campaign.

As a result, on September 8 representatives of the Madero family (Francisco's uncle Ernesto, and his cousin Rafael Hernández, and Miguel Díaz Lombardo) met with the reyista party leaders (José Peón del Valle, Alonso Mariscal y Pina, and Alfredo Rodríguez). President de la Barra himself presided over the two-day session, so important did he deem the work. He asked that both parties moderate their partisanship and think about ways to insure their opponents' political liberties. After due deliberation, the parties decided to hold no more anti-reyista or anti-maderista political rallies whose purpose was to create disorder. Both sides agreed to abide by the voters' decision without resorting to violence. Both agreed to end the calumny in the press. All concurred, at least in theory, that Mexico really wanted a democratic campaign. With everyone in apparent accord, de la Barra thanked the delegates for their wisdom and patriotism and asked them to sign the agreement, which they did.[118] But the rational solution did not prevail. Within a few days, the reyistas complained that the document was meaningless because it had not been published the next day, by which time more ugly anti-reyista lampoons had appeared and the newspaper *Nueva Era* had published another editorial highly critical of Reyes. The maderista commissioners thought these charges unjustified and responded that Reyes's own bellicose attitude caused all the trouble.[119]

De la Barra tried mightily to hold the agreement together. He forwarded the reyista complaints to the maderista commissioners, who denied any wrongdoing.[120] By now, the remainder of Reyes's popular support seemed to have drifted away, and only a few military men remained outspoken in his behalf. The U.S. ambassador compared Reyes to the British politician Lord Salisbury, calling him "a lath painted to look like iron." Reyes himself was bitter and angry. In a public address in his hometown, Monterey, Reyes intemperately blasted de la Barra's "vice presidential ambitions" and, in a statement that boded ill for Mexico's peace, told the assembled crowd he could "defeat" the government.[121] Reyes then took the rash step of dropping out of the race and instructing his followers to boycott the polls.

Next, Reyes went to visit friends in San Antonio, Texas. He assumed that the United States border offered him a safe haven from which he could plan a military coup.[122] De la Barra tried to dissuade Reyes by informing him that the government was investigating the culprits who staged the anti-Reyes demonstrations and offering the candidate complete police protection. De la Barra also repeated publicly that the election would be fair.[123] He wanted Reyes to remain in the race to prevent charges that democracy had not been respected. To so admit would suggest that he had partially failed to carry out yet another of his inaugural pledges.

Not long after Reyes arrived in San Antonio, both Mexican and U.S. agents in the borderlands reported suspicious doings. Well-dressed men met clandestinely with Reyes and purchased large amounts of weapons and ammunition. Informants implicated the sheriff of Webb County in the Reyes plot. No doubt President de la Barra suspected that Reyes planned a revolt, as many observers had predicted earlier in the summer. One of Reyes's longstanding political enemies, General Gerónimo Treviño, had sent his agents to San Antonio to watch the military preparations and inform the government. Treviño also offered to organize a volunteer force to meet the reyistas as they crossed the border.[124] In a last attempt to head off the invasion, de la Barra sent his brother Luis to talk to his old acquaintance Reyes. Luis reported that despite Reyes's flowery promise "to work in conformity with national interests," the general's attitude was "suspicious."[125] Apparently, Luis did elicit a promise from Reyes that he would defer his insurrection until the conclusion of the de la Barra presidency.[126]

Reyes's aborted coup in late November 1911 has been well studied.[127] The United States helped the Madero government defeat Reyes by arresting him for neutrality violations, thus discouraging the plotters and disrupting their plans. Released on bail, Reyes fled back to Mexico, hoping that his presence on Mexican soil would arouse the military to his side. But after a month of wandering around nearly friendless in the cold deserts of northern Mexico, Reyes surrendered in December 1911.

The Madero government and some of the president's more nervous partisans were much relieved, believing a major threat to the government's existence had ended. In reality, however, Madero's (and Henry Lane Wilson's) earlier assessment of the Reyes phenomena was extremely accurate. In a remarkable letter, Madero stated that if Reyes resorted to a rebellion after the popularization of democracy in 1911, he would have a credibility problem with the Mexican people. Madero went on to say that although critics occasionally attacked him and his supporters, sometimes even unfairly, those attacks were part of a free, democratic tradition.[128] Although Madero is sometimes criticized for being naive, his assessment of Mexico's political situation, and especially Reyes, was extremely accurate. Reyes basically self-destructed and in the long run proved an inconsequential factor in political matters.

The other broadly based political party, the Catholic party, also participated in the presidential election. Founded in the dying days of the Díaz dictatorship in 1911, the Catholic party grew out of the new Roman Catholic social action popularized after the 1892 papal bull "Rerum Novarum." A national Catholic organization had met several times during the decade and debated contemporary social injustices. Specifically, the party hoped to better the lot of workers and peasants without fomenting class conflict, thereby safeguarding family values by providing an alternative to Marxism. Further, the party endorsed democracy as articulated in the civilian maderista program. No doctrinaire reactionary group, the Catholic party represented a solid alternative to the ideas of the more anticlerical civilian maderistas.[129]

The Catholic party leadership originally wanted someone less anticlerical than Madero to run for the presidency on their ticket, and so they turned toward de la Barra, who was devoutly Catholic. During summer 1911, de la Barra was inundated with letters from citizens, many associated with the Catholic party, urging him to run for the presidency. These letters ranged from those filled with simple flattery to one calling him the "candidate of God."[130] To all these letters de la Barra had a simple response—no. He patiently explained time and time again that his resolve was firm. If he ran for president, he would be accused, and rightly so, of trying to impose his electoral victory. In his memoirs, de la Barra referred to these blandishments as "the voices of Macbeth's witches."[131] Many of his countrymen agreed with him and urged de la Barra to keep his inaugural promise lest he contaminate democracy.[132]

Finally accepting de la Barra's adamant refusal, the Catholic party nominated Madero for the presidency. Although Madero's candidacy was a real compromise for many of the delegates, partly because he was a Mason, the Catholic party leadership believed it very important to disassociate themselves from Bernardo Reyes.[133] De la Barra's name appeared on the Catholic party ticket as the vice presidential candidate, without his blessing to be sure, which pleased those conventioneers upset with the endorsement of Madero. Unfortunately, after the convention Madero tried to persuade the Catholic party leadership to substitute Pino Suárez's name for de la Barra's. The party refused.[134] The incident underscores one of the problems facing Mexican democracy in 1911. Madero in theory wanted an opposition party, but he did not want any of its candidates to threaten his party's monopoly of offices.

De la Barra was also asked to head the ticket of the Popular Evolutionary party, a new organization dreamed up by Porfirian intellectual and former cabinet member Jorge Vera Estañol. Although some observers thought the party had formed to support Reyes, ultimately it too turned away from the general and looked to de la Barra as a potential candidate, drawn by his tact and the all-important factor of name recognition.[135] The interim president agreed with the principles of the new party, its belief in a national government rather than a personalistic one, and its support of order, liberty, and justice. He liked its emphasis on primary education for the masses and its interest in agrarian reform. But de la Barra reiterated that under no circumstances would he become a presidential candidate. No doubt journalist Luis Cabrera's stinging editorial opposing de la Barra's "reelection" contributed to his decision to make public his refusal of the Popular Evolutionary party candidacy.[136] Fellow citizens tried to dissuade de la Barra from his resolve with arguments that the will of the people should not be thwarted since de la Barra had proven his good intentions about no reelection. Further, one of Mexico City's leading newspapers endorsed him.[137] One analyst has suggested that the most interesting question the presidential race raised was whether de la Barra would run.[138]

In many senses, the presidential election of 1911 was de la Barra's finest hour. Despite the importuning (which must have been very flattering) of influential citizens and two parties (a new Liberal party also nominated de la Barra for president), de la Barra kept his promise to remain aloof from politics and to do "all in his power to secure an impartial and unfettered election."[139] Realism undoubtedly played a role too, since de la Barra knew he had no chance of beating Madero had he chosen to run.

The last maneuver of the scattered anti-Madero forces, led by Vera Estañol's friends, was an attempt to persuade the Chamber of Deputies to postpone the elections from October 1. The conservative paper *El Imparcial* had been suggesting this strategy since July.[140] As time passed and Madero's popularity dwindled, delay seemed a sound strategy to those determined to keep Madero from the presidency. But de la Barra would not countenance a delay, even though he could have spent some additional time in the presidential office. All the preparations had been concluded. Early that summer the interim government had ordered each state to establish electoral districts in accordance with the recently completed census of 1910.[141] The government never wavered from its intent to hold elections on October 1, as the allegedly reactionary interior minister

Alberto García Granados oversaw the prompt division of villages into precincts, the posting of voting lists, and the naming of an individual in each community to register voters.[142]

The popular elections took place on October 1, and the electoral college met two weeks later. Madero took almost 95 percent of the vote, with a few scattered votes for de la Barra and Emilio Vázquez Gómez. As noted previously, Pino Suárez won the plurality of the vice presidential votes with de la Barra running second and Francisco Vázquez Gómez a distant third (see Appendix D). Thus, Mexico experienced a relatively free and democratic election, although at the time a few of the participants, particularly the vazquistas and the reyistas, cried foul. Nonetheless, the revolutionary victor and his vice president had won the endorsement of the Mexican electorate.

Conclusion

Proving one way or the other whether the elections of 1911 were free and fair is difficult, perhaps impossible. Certainly large segments of the population wanted democracy. Students became actively involved in the campaign of 1911. Towns where balloting had never occurred before held elections.[143] An old man wrote about his years of observation of the Mexican political scene and concluded that "Madero's work must not be futile."[144] A wave of idealism spread throughout society as part of the spirit of liberation from the Porfirian tyranny. Yet appearances of electoral manipulation continued to exist for those who had suspicious minds, a natural result of a century of such practices. Madero told a military man to "watch carefully" a general who was politicking on behalf of Emilio Vázquez Gómez.[145] Should a democratic leader have made such a request? Did Mexico measure up to a social scientist's definition of a democracy in 1911?

Based on an examination of the indicators associated with democracy (civil liberties, universal suffrage, competitive political parties, free and fair elections with alternative candidates on the ballot), the elections of 1911 fell short on most counts. Abuses of civil rights, from the rock throwing in front of Francisco Elguero's house and Bernardo Reyes's hotel to the jailing of political opponents, were all too common. Madero certainly did nothing to encourage the participation of competitive political parties, seeing both the reyistas and the Catholic party as threats to his political success. He was scarcely the first, however, to sacrifice his idealism to ambition. Despite having universal suffrage (for men), voter turnout was quite poor, with fewer than twenty thousand people voting in the general election.[146] Nevertheless, de la Barra and Madero made considerable improvements over past practices, even though the authoritarian tradition had ultimately triumphed.

Madero's desire to bring democracy to Mexico is undeniable. Over and over he wrote to his supporters cautioning them about being too partisan. As he told his former vice presidential running mate, who constantly complained that the revolution was being betrayed, "We must not be alarmed by the democratic questions; that is precisely what the revolution is about. What is happening is something new for us and should not alarm us."[147] Most civilian maderistas shared Madero's desire, even though occasionally they were also torn with election jitters. Francisco León de la Barra and many of the Porfirian intellectuals also clearly supported the principles of democracy. The interim president wrote consistently in favor of free elections and liberty. He congratulated Madero on the PCP's clean convention and its adherence to democratic principles.[148] As he reflected on his presidency, de la Barra was extremely proud that he had contributed to the growth of democracy in Mexico.

Perhaps the discrepancy between professed democratic ideals and actual practice existed in part because democratic values had not yet reached deep into Mexico's soil. Two examples of the absence of the appropriate political culture may suffice to prove this point. The first is the well-known story of two campesinos watching Madero and his wife make their way through the streets of Mexico City. " 'What is this *democracia* we are shouting for?' [one] asked of the other. 'Why, it must be the lady who accompanied Madero,' replied his companion."[149] In Sinaloa, a reporter asked a campesino what "effective suffrage" meant to him. The young man replied that he assumed that it meant that the *tienda de raya* (company store) on the hacienda where he worked would pay wages in cash and not scrip.[150] In short, the progressive consensus believed in the ideal of democracy, but its practice was so foreign to most Mexicans that authoritarian traditions could not be changed overnight. Indeed, looking long term at Mexico, one could argue that authoritarianism, with the important exception of the principle of no reelection, lasted until the 1990s. Yet for many Mexicans in 1911, democracy offered primarily a means to greater social justice, and it is to that story we turn now.

Francisco León de la Barra visiting a workers' club. *Courtesy of Honnold Library, Claremont College*

5

Social Change in Mexico in 1911

The evil that men do lives after them,
The good is oft interred with their bones.

—William Shakespeare, *Julius Caesar*

After a hesitant beginning under Francisco Madero, most of Mexico's social revolution, according to traditional historiography, took place much later, during the 1920s and 1930s, following the framing of the milestone constitution of 1917. Proponents of this interpretation argue that the Madero years and, by implication, the de la Barra interim presidency initiated little more than cautious, faltering steps down the path of social change.[1] Others argue that even in the long run the Mexican Revolution accomplished little in the way of meaningful social change. They see the Madero and de la Barra period as typical: rhetoric on behalf of social justice was plentiful but accomplishments were few.[2] This study cannot resolve this complex debate, but it can clear up some of the misunderstandings that surround the first year of the revolution. The debate over the nature of the revolution is highly charged, and certainly will continue for years. For now, however, because the Mexican Revolution has commonly been billed as Latin America's first social revolution, the issue of social change merits further discussion.

This chapter presents evidence that social change did begin to occur during summer 1911 in the midst of the de la Barra presidency. Two distinct streams of social change emerged. Members of the working class, whether employed in factories or in fields, manifested a new discontent with their traditional socioeconomic status by taking part in land seizures and strikes. They exhibited some xenophobia and a remarkably peculiar indifference to the moral crusade of the civilian reformers. In contrast, the civilian policymakers discussed ideas, reflective of U.S. and European progressive reformism, about how to achieve social change and social justice that ultimately would contribute to a lasting peace. Aware of the gross inequities of the Porfirian world, they understood the necessity for change and they had ideas about how to achieve it.

These civilian reformers were not willing to concede, however, that all of the basic premises of the Porfirian system needed to be altered. They continued to believe (rightly, I would argue) that developmental capitalism—the infusion of private investment, even from foreign sources, to expand the economy and provide jobs—offered the only realistic solution to Mexico's problems. As a result, they continued to seek and protect investors who wanted to participate in the growth of the Mexican economy. They urged restraint on those who would radically transform the status of urban wage earners and the rural dispossessed. Reforms, in their opinion, had to be carried out legally, justly, and gradually. Further, they believed that the nation's poor needed a moral uplifting, and thus they added education and temperance to their list of necessary social modifications.

The authors of traditional accounts assume that Francisco Madero introduced these moderate reforms. The evidence indicates that these changes began during the presidency of Francisco León de la Barra and that more of them were implemented during his last two months in office when Madero had become less involved in the government.[3] Certainly de la Barra hoped to be remembered as a reformer. As he told reporters, he saw his legacy to Mexico in the labor department, the school lunch program, and the National Agrarian Commission. According to the reinterpretation this chapter presents, de la Barra does not personally deserve all the credit for reformism in 1911. Instead, like the idea of democracy, such changes were mutually agreed on by significant numbers of both Porfirians and civilian maderistas as necessary for the country's well-being.

Social Conditions in June 1911

The economic growth of the last two decades of the nineteenth century catapulted Mexico from the ranks of the economic also-rans in Latin America into a position of recognized leadership. According to most statistics, based on a western European model, Mexico now found itself in the heady company of the ABC nations (Argentina, Brazil, and Chile) and Uruguay in the forefront of economic development in Latin America. The changes that put it there included urbanization, industrialization, a dramatically improved GNP, the development of modern systems of transportation and communication, and the artistic and architectural mimicry of European tastes. For good measure, democracy and a policy of universal public education also contributed to a nation's ranking.[4] The elite of Latin America and the foreigners who accepted these indicators of course ignored (at best) the achievements of the ordinary people of Latin America, sometimes referred to as the "folk." And although an interesting case may be made that the western industrial capitalist model operated to the detriment of the folk,[5] the assumption here is that Latin America, and Porfirian Mexico specifically, made the correct choice in adopting the developmental model.

Economic development was the most significant indicator of progress, but Mexico in 1880 lagged too far behind western Europe to develop autonomously, or so policymakers believed. As a result, Mexican financiers, such as José Yves Limantour, looked to foreign capital. But before development predicated on the infusion of massive doses of foreign investment could occur, Mexico had to prove itself sufficiently mature in the eyes of prospective investors by creating a stable political environment. Without peace there could be no progress. The Porfirian peace of the 1880s gradually convinced investors that long-term prospects looked good and that the risks of putting money in Mexico were relatively few.

Like the citizens of the United States when its industrial revolution began, Mexicans themselves lacked sufficient capital to pay for costly machinery and modern industrial buildings. As a result, the *científicos* expended their efforts coaxing foreigners to risk their dollars, pounds sterling, francs, and marks in various industrial and agricultural enterprises. The premise that Mexico needed a healthy business climate went unchallenged during the Porfiriato. No voices suggested that Mexico could achieve growth after modest accumulations of domestic capital over long periods; policymakers were far too impatient for such a long-term initiative to be persuasive. Instead, the prevailing view held that Mexico needed massive influxes of capital immediately to catch up with the European industrialized world.[6] To a degree not previously known, large sums of money and foreigners appeared in late nineteenth-century Mexico, and both would challenge traditionally held values and interests.

With the advance of new industry and agriculture, old social patterns faded out. Although some smaller factories could accept the paternalistic work patterns that had persisted for centuries, larger plants could not, even if the capitalistic mentality permitted such thinking. Wage earners, fresh from the country, had to learn new labor behaviors and withstand long hours of toil and harsh conditions that included few if any accommodations to cultural traditions. Mexican workers were expected to fit into the western European industrial model. But despite the new work conditions, they flocked to industrial centers, some because they had been forced from their traditional occupations as small agricultural producers on village lands, others because they were drawn by the lure of high wages and the promise of a better life than rural Mexico could offer.

Conditions were often bad in the industrial workplace. Management cared little about safety, because providing safe conditions cost more money. They refused also because of the cost to implement any sort of workers' compensation system for those injured on the job. And further, the bosses denied labor's right to organize and strike and decried the presence of radical agitators among the workers, be they socialist, anarchist, or communist. Probably the workers could have tolerated the situation had not real wages declined after 1900, causing a flurry of strikes and labor demonstrations. Although the regime's response to these actions varied, in general Porfirio Díaz perceived himself as the neutral mediator in labor disputes such as the famous Río Blanco textile mill strike of 1907. But Díaz, at least so the workers perceived, seemed to favor management and certainly tolerated no additional worker disturbances once he had arbitrated the labor dispute.[7]

By the time the insurgency of 1910 broke out, labor in Mexico was of two minds, just as it was in the United States. A vocal minority rejected capitalism and agitated for radical change in the socioeconomic system based on theories of anarcho-syndicalism, communism, and other intellectualized doctrines of European extraction. The vast majority of Mexican labor, however, favored the gradualist approach of Samuel Gompers and the American Federation of Labor (AFL), which had chosen to strike for changes such as better wages and working conditions, shorter hours, and an end to exploitative female and child labor. Labor played a very small role in Madero's victory but, like other groups in Mexican society, hoped to take advantage of the fruits of May 1911.

A second policy initiative of the Díaz period that would draw a reaction in 1911 was the purposeful concentration of land and water resources in the hands of a diminishing number of individuals. Díaz's advisors held that large landowners, particularly agribusinesses, were more efficient and productive custodians of the land than Indian villages, peasants, and campesinos. As a result, the government pursued the idea, begun at an earlier time, of divesting the pueblos of their lands and selling national public lands to developers who promised to create wealth. Earlier liberal legislation required communally held lands to be divided among the users, who were then given titles to their individual plots. In the 1880s and 1890s many campesinos gave up their land, either because they were defrauded or because they legitimately sold their interests to others. Further, the great national lands were sold cheaply, often to foreigners, on the promise that agricultural colonies or plantations would make "unoccupied" land bloom.[8] By 1910 fewer people owned a greater proportion of the land than ever before. No other single policy of the Díaz administration caused more dissent than the land policy. Thus, to dissatisfied campesinos, the period following the signing of the Treaty of Ciudad Juárez was an opportune time to recover what they had lost. At the same time, Porfirian intellectuals were well aware of the long-term implications of the land policy and had begun to rethink national priorities.

Finally, the Porfirian modernization scheme brought with it a great outcry to reform Mexico's moral ills, largely what the middle class perceived as the decadence of the working poor. The condition of the illiterate and frequently dissolute rural poor troubled many Porfirian intellectuals. Some, like Francisco León de la Barra in his formative years, suggested that the solution lay in encouraging energetic European immigrants, a policy that had clearly worked in Argentina. Yet most Mexican intellectuals in the latter Díaz years opposed ignoring the "Indians," a designation that often referred more to a class than a race, for two reasons. First, encouraging foreign immigration had not succeeded to the extent hoped for by 1910, and furthermore, the newcomers had been lopsidedly North American, raising fears of possible territorial annexation by the United States. Second, the indigenous population was far more numerous and more sophisticated in Mexico than in Argentina and could not realistically be ignored.

For the late Porfirian reformers, moral uplifting would include educating the rural peoples in particular. Díaz's record in providing rural education was weak. The dictator had built fine schools in the capital and some of the territorial cities, but both the relatively small size of the public treasury and the intellectual and constitutional limitations of federalism prevented Díaz from spreading public education benefits equitably throughout the nation.[9] Although Mexico's rate of literacy improved slightly during the dictatorship, it still hovered around 20 percent, an embarrassing statistic for the government. The squalor of rural living conditions and the dissolution of the rural poor also proved embarrassing to the modernizers. Indians still tended to get drunk at religious festivals and in some regions even during Mass. Such behavior led to the persistence of stereotypes of indolent "natives" unable to progress through work to achieve modern civilization. The Díaz administration had neither the interest nor the revenue to resolve these problems; they could only pretend they did not exist by banning Indians from entering the capital city in their traditional garb when foreigners showed up for the centennial celebration of 1910. Since most Indians were too poor to own store-bought European-style clothes, Díaz's policymakers hoped by this restrictive ordinance to prevent foreigners from seeing the other side of Mexico. As a result of Díaz's failed policies, after 1911 some Porfirians would join the civilian maderistas in an attempt to extend the moral crusade, uplift these "unfortunates," and imbue them with middle-class values.

The Labor Movement in 1911

To analyze the changes that occurred in the labor sector in 1911, the historian must examine two different types of activities. On one level, the inchoate protests of workers demonstrated the frustrations that they felt with Porfirian paternalism. Like other popular elements in Mexican society, labor expressed its restiveness after the dictator fell, and in summer 1911 engaged in an orgy of strikes and organizational activities. The de la Barra government responded to these acts fairly consistently, approving orderly protest but denouncing violence. Further, the progressive consensus willingly mediated with labor leaders philosophically aligned to the Samuel Gompers AFL moderates but not with socialists or anarchists. The second and unrelated labor activity centered on the articulated labor program of the interim government and the policy changes it proposed through legislation. Most authors when discussing the creation of the new labor department and its bureaucracy attribute its creation and development incorrectly to Francisco Madero rather than to de la Barra. That detail aside, the more important question is whether the interim government's labor proposals constituted real change or simply a formalization of past Porfirian policies and attitudes. Was de la Barra's labor department an agency for mediating strikes and a blueprint for the progressive labor codes that ultimately were incorporated into the constitution of 1917, as one author has asserted?[10] Or was the creation of the labor department merely a political gesture to hide the fact that the government was essentially pro-business, as another historian contends?[11]

To get a sense of the activity of workers themselves, one needs only to count the number of strikes and compare labor's new freedom to express itself with conditions in 1910. Strikes proliferated in summer 1911, especially during June and July in the heyday of the celebratory mood, even though few industrial workers had participated in the fighting against Díaz. Workers certainly had justification enough to strike. Wages were depressed everywhere and hours were long. Workers at one mill petitioned de la Barra to intervene with management to trim their workday to twelve hours; they were clocking in at 5:30 A.M. and out at 8:00 P.M. daily.[12] Others protested the common management device at the mill of keeping wages down by paying reduced piecework rates. These laborers complained that their families were starving on the 18 centavos per blanket they earned during their shifts at the factory.[13]

Two industrial sites that saw violence in 1907, Orizaba and Río Blanco, had workers on strike for much of the summer in 1911. By late August, with the strike fund exhausted and families in desperate straits, the strikes were settled, largely because de la Barra and the popular maderista Rafael Tapia were able to negotiate an agreement.[14] But management retaliated by firing thirty-three former strikers and, worse yet, by blackballing them so that they could not be hired by other factories in the district. In response, some workers went out on a short-lived sympathy strike, and, in a replay of past Porfirian practices, de la Barra again was asked to intercede on their behalf.[15] Workers elsewhere simply struck over wages. For example, the dock workers in Tampico demanded an increase of their daily wages to three pesos.[16]

Mexico City also experienced a rash of strikes in July 1911. The most serious involved a walkout by the trolley car operators, stranding commuters and shoppers in downtown Mexico City on July 3 and rendering urban transportation difficult (the already expensive taxis raised their fares to meet the new demand). De la Barra stated that the governor of the Federal District, then Alberto García Granados, had to arrange the settlement between the strikers and management. The three-cent-an-hour raise granted workers was a significant percentage of the trolley operators' base pay of between ten and fifteen cents an hour, and the vast majority accepted their new contract and returned to work. A small minority tried to derail the settlement by physically preventing the trams from starting up. Here de la Barra and García Granados drew the line, and the police arrested the violent agitators. Other Mexico City strikes, such as those involving bakers and cigarette makers, resolved themselves peacefully.[17]

As the details of these strikes indicate, the great mass of laborers essentially were interested in bread-and-butter issues rather than theoretical and political issues involving ownership of the means of production. Pragmatic issues could be negotiated between labor and management, while only violent revolution could alter ownership of the means of production. For de la Barra and the progressive consensus, the latter alternative was simply unthinkable. De la Barra felt very comfortable drawing on the ideas of Roman Catholic social action, which in its broadest sense urged the reconciliation of capital and labor along the lines suggested in the papal bull "Rerum Novarum." Four Catholic congresses in the late Porfiriato had focused on workers' problems and sought ways, through the formation of mutual aid societies and legislation, to better labor's position in society.[18] Mexico's leadership also encouraged secular, peaceful alternatives to anarcho-syndicalism. Madero met with Mary Harris ("Mother") Jones, the U.S. labor icon friendly to Gompers, who offered to unionize Mexican miners and to speak, unsuccessfully as it turned out, to Ricardo Flores Magón to try to persuade him to give up attempts to revolutionize Mexico. Philosophically, de la Barra and the progressive consensus supported the betterment of labor's condition through the organization of craft unions, bargaining, and negotiations.[19]

Workers also seemed eager to follow the more moderate course. They were relieved that the Díaz tyranny had ended, because they believed it had contributed to their past harsh treatment. In the Porfiriato, management had interfered with labor meetings and with attempts to organize. Real wages declined after 1900; the average wage of 1.25 pesos a day barely kept a family fed. Worse, management often engaged in the practice of fining workers for minor infractions, thereby reducing pay even further. Workers looked forward to the dawning of a new day in May 1911 and appreciated de la Barra's frank discussions in the media about the workers' plight and potential remedies. They applauded his public statement that workers deserved a just contract that would prevent conditions of neo-slavery.[20] Conceptually, de la Barra and other proponents of the progressive consensus were willing to listen to the workers. They recognized the justice of the workers' demands for shorter hours, their right to organize and strike, and their need for better wages. This progressive, reformist attitude clearly had its limits, however, since de la Barra also balanced these ideals against management's complaints about labor violence.

For labor to retain de la Barra's sympathies, its protests had to be orderly. Many entrepreneurs feared that striking workers would turn into Luddites, threatening the expensive capital equipment and the buildings that housed it. Hence, mill owners frequently asked the government for soldiers to protect their factories. At Cananea, another hotbed of labor contentiousness during the Porfirian period, violence seemed imminent in summer 1911 because the thirty-five hundred workers were heavily armed and the government had little physical presence in the community. As a result, the civilian maderista governor called for a military force to protect the foreign-owned property interests and prevent bloodshed.[21] At least one owner, sensing the changing attitude of the government, had begun to reform conditions in his mine himself without interference from Mexico City or the state capital. He voluntarily closed the *tiendas de raya* (company stores) at the Mazapil Copper Company, which had been the focal point of much of the dissent. Yet, he claimed, "outside agitators" continued to make trouble, even though wages had increased and the town now boasted a hospital that cared for injured workers.[22]

One of the lengthiest strikes during summer 1911 involved the Mexican Railway, which Díaz had nationalized in 1906. Díaz took this unusual step because of the high-profile presence of foreigners in the operation who would not toil for the same wages as Mexicans and who refused to learn Spanish. The union in 1911 would not tolerate the presence of foreign employees who earned more for performing the same task as Mexican workers. The Mexican Railway had made great progress in Mexicanizing the work force, even though upper management remained British. Nevertheless, complaints about the preferential treatment of foreigners were still heard in 1911. In response, management claimed that they had retained only one foreign conductor, and he received a higher wage because of his long-term contract, not his national origin. Some foreign-born technicians were said to be receiving higher wages than their Mexican counterparts because they possessed special skills. By 1911, the company reported that 87 percent of its work force on the trains was Mexican because Mexicans had been given preferential status in hiring.

The railworkers' union also griped about the low wages its members received. But, management argued, the company simply could not afford to increase wages. The recent Madero insurgency had lessened cargo traffic, decreasing revenues for the railroad. Management asserted that the railroad was doing its best to maintain full employment, and increased wages would result in the layoff of workers.[23] The strike began in July when railroad employees stopped a train three kilometers from a station. Responding to the inconvenience to passengers, President de la Barra came out in favor of the right to work and the public interest that the strike threatened. Workers then settled for a 7 percent pay increase.[24] Thus, concern for the protection of private property and the public interest influenced de la Barra's analysis of the dispute. His responses to labor were quite consistent. Disorder was the factor that led to a coercive response. For example, when a strike in the El Oro district degenerated into disorder, specifically a robbery and some rioting, the governor of Mexico state sent soldiers to handle the crisis. President de la Barra offered more soldiers if the disorder continued.[25] He worked with the popular maderista commander Rafael Tapia to prevent violence from breaking out at Río Blanco. "You must continue your work calming the feelings of the workers so as to avoid disturbances of the public order," he wrote.[26]

Labor and management expected government intervention in the strike process, especially when disorder threatened. Under de la Barra's new emphasis on states' rights, usually state governments tried to resolve the dispute locally, although as a last resort federal action was possible. The president paternalistically served as the ultimate arbitrator, who, if called upon, would impose a unilateral and hopefully fair judgment that both sides would accept. De la Barra's temperament and past experience fitted him perfectly for this role. When strikers threatened order he did not hesitate to use force, but in times of peace, he favored labor over management when fairness so required. For example, when the stevedores of Veracruz appealed to him for assistance in resolving their strike after bargaining had broken down, the president agreed to help, welcoming a delegation of laborers from Orizaba who came to Mexico City to discuss their problems with management.[27] He listened to workers at the Hércules Factory in Querétaro complain about their supervisors and told the owner, "if the stories are true you will remedy them."[28] Another group of workers told him about the long hours and low wages they endured, and the system of fines that reduced them to penury. De la Barra himself wrote to the factory owner and asked him to look into the workers' allegations before the government did.[29]

De la Barra's paternalistic attitude was typical of the progressive consensus and manifested itself time and time again in the Madero presidency as well. Madero, for example, told his brother to intervene in labor disputes in Torreón in order to preserve law and order.[30] Governor Venustiano Carranza followed the same policy in Coahuila.[31] As a result of these paternalistic yet benevolent attitudes toward workers, Madero could assure the Workers' party that their welfare and progress would continue to be one of his principal interests once he achieved power, just as it had been for the de la Barra government.[32] In sum, both de la Barra and Madero honestly believed that they were pro-worker. In practice, well-behaved workers who reported abuses found a sympathetic, if paternalistic, ear. But once workers crossed that thin line into violence or lawlessness, the government lost patience.

At least as important as de la Barra's reaction to pending labor crises was the new legislative scheme that the government fashioned to deal with labor in the abstract. Early in his administration, de la Barra encouraged the creation of a job bank for unemployed workers. Although each state had to establish its own agency and try to place workers locally, those states that had a surplus of either workers or jobs had to contact the minister of the interior. De la Barra's idea was to respond to the law of supply and demand for workers, reducing unemployment and poverty.[33] In late September, he presented congress with the idea of creating a separate department of labor within the ministry of development, just as he had witnessed in Argentina and Belgium, where he had been stationed. Because he had carefully studied the problem during his diplomatic career, de la Barra felt comfortable suggesting the formation of the new department to congress. Specifically, the department of labor would mediate disputes between workers and businessmen. In addition, the department would formally constitute a national job bank and provide names of potential workers to employers. Like any good bureaucracy, the department was required to collect lots of data.[34] De la Barra signed the enabling legislation just before leaving office, and the department started functioning under its new director in December.

The progressive consensus intended to do more than just create another agency, and like Progressives in the United States, debated other labor-related issues, such as workers' compensation, child labor laws, and safety requirements. Although limited to workers in certain dangerous occupations, the workers' compensation scheme, borrowed from the German model, held businesses strictly liable for workers' injuries and required them to have insurance.[35] Beyond this, the progressive reformers hoped to improve the workers' lot by financially supporting workers' clubs. De la Barra agreed that the government should underwrite an athletic club for workers that would provide laborers with a place to pursue sports like gymnastics, boxing, jujitsu, and sumo wrestling. On another occasion, he spoke at the opening of a workers' dance hall, named for Jesús García, the "hero of Nacozari," an engineer who diverted a trainload of dynamite to save a town at the cost of his own life.[36]

De la Barra's proposals represented a significant shift in policy and should be recognized as such. Under Madero, the labor department began to function reasonably well and achieved some minor advances for workers throughout the remainder of his presidency and into the Huerta period. The department's existence suggests that the progressive consensus favored labor reform and that all those who had supported the exiled dictator in 1910 were not necessarily "reactionaries." After all, it was a Porfirian who suggested the creation of the department and a Porfirian congress that legislated it into existence and charged it with its responsibilities. The creation of the department of labor provided Mexico with an agency equivalent to those of other industrializing western nations and was a source of great personal pride to de la Barra. The legislation providing workers' compensation rivaled statutes elsewhere, even in the United States. Children were now, in theory, protected from abusive employers and required to attend school, if only at the job site. De la Barra and the progressive consensus also supported certain workers' movements, if they were peaceful and sought financial gain and not violent revolution. In sum, the government's pro-labor attitude and its willingness to intercede on behalf of certain strikers closely resembled the relationship between labor and the state in post-1920 Mexico.

The Growth of Business

The fate of the business community during the Mexican Revolution has kindled little interest, until recently. Less than two decades ago, John Womack pointed to the dearth of economic studies of the revolution and posited a number of generalizations that need testing. Among them was his finding that Mexico's economy remained relatively stable until 1914, when the stresses of militarization and the destruction of many enterprises set off a significant inflationary spiral.[37] This section confirms Womack's hypothesis that the economy did nearly return to normal during the de la Barra and Madero presidencies. Further, policymakers in both the de la Barra and Madero governments, though the latter is outside the scope of this study, continued the fundamentally pro-business precepts of the Porfiriato but added a progressive dimension, an antitrust act. While condemning many of the excesses of the dictatorship, particularly its repression and political fraud, most if not all of the members of the progressive consensus agreed that its economic growth had significantly benefited Mexico.

Policymakers saw themselves reaffirming the pro-business climate of the Díaz period. Explicitly, they rejected the idea that the economic growth of the later nineteenth century had negative consequences, draining resources out of the hands of ordinary Mexicans and concentrating it in the hands of a privileged few. They believed that growth and development were synonymous. They also rejected the claim, expanded on further in the next section, that foreign investment and technology had sucked wealth from Mexico into foreign lands.[38] Instead, members of the Porfirian consensus viewed business expansion positively and wanted to do their utmost to encourage economic growth, in a foreshadowing of the thinking of post-1940 Mexican governments.

As the first requirement for continued investment, businessmen demanded a return to the stability of the Porfiriato. Business leaders were not afraid of the hot political debates of 1911 between civilian members of the consensus, but the proliferation of guns, armed workers, looters, and bandits did worry them. To insure profits, entrepreneurs required a stable work force and uninterrupted production, or at least production at levels based on market factors and not intrusions of revolutionary violence. An excess of uncertainty and the climate of violence in some communities occasionally frightened businessmen into shutting down their enterprises. Therefore, the de la Barra government did what it could to assure businessmen that their factories and properties would be protected. For example, a yarn company closed after insurrectionists sacked it. The presence of popular maderistas, still armed in July, made the owners wary of resuming operations, and they asked for a detachment of the regular army to protect their property and restore order, which de la Barra sent.[39] Businessmen wanted federal troops rather than rurales because in most states the latter contained popular maderistas, who frequently instigated trouble rather than quelled it, or so the business community believed.

Railroads also clearly preferred federal troops when disorder threatened. Because of the importance of transportation links for all forms of commerce, both de la Barra and Madero did not hesitate to send the federal troops to guard railroads when trouble brewed. Madero recognized the importance of the railroads to business; hence his order in late May 1911 that the insurgents begin repairing the torn-up track and replacing telegraph wires onto the poles. The continued presence of armed popular maderistas and the outbreaks of violence in the early de la Barra period made further railroad expansion seem risky to some businessmen. At the least, the prolonged violence operated as an excuse for one company to back out of its commitment to build an additional line. Concessionaires of the Railroad Company of Nacozari, which would have linked the Montezuma Copper Company mines to market, asked for a return of their bond investment. They charged that turmoil in the region made it impossible for them to begin construction. Their attorney, the versatile Jorge Vera Estañol, argued that peace and stability were a prerequisite to development as far as foreigners were concerned and therefore asserted that the government ought to return his clients' money.[40] In this instance, even de la Barra's offer to send federal troops to the construction site would not quell the investors' anxiety, according to Vera Estañol. But the Nacozari Railroad situation was an exception. By August, the celebratory mood of most popular maderistas had ended, and the government had mustered out much of the "Liberating Army." As a result, investor confidence picked up, and business returned to more normal levels of activity.

Just as reformers in the United States targeted railroads for regulation, so too did civilian maderista Manuel Bonilla, minister of communications. Bonilla set up an informal group of consultants in his ministry and charged them with studying reforms, such as the feasibility of creating a single entity out of the National Railway holdings and regulating the rates charged on all lines. Two businessmen, three engineers, civilian maderista Miguel Díaz Lombardo, and journalist Luis Cabrera comprised the commission. Bonilla further proposed that when the advisory body completed its deliberations, permanent railroad inspectors, employees of the federal government, be hired. He and de la Barra had several conversations about this project, and the president was in complete agreement. Thus, de la Barra and the provisional government continued the Porfirian trend of expanding the bureaucracy, but in this instance to regulate the railroads.[41]

Even with some plans for increased regulation, investors felt confident, according to some reports, because after a downturn at the end of the fiscal year (July 1, 1911), the Mexican National Railway, the "barometer of business conditions," had showed a significant profit for July and August.[42] By midsummer, foreign investors resumed their interest in Mexico.[43] The British embassy reported that the "economic situation in general is notably improving."[44] Some investors even mentioned that prospects were better for business in 1911 than they had been in the latter Díaz years, largely because the notorious graft of some Porfirian officials (although the dictator himself was remarkably clean on this score) had dampened their enthusiasm.[45] Contracts that were said to have been negotiated as a result of corruption and bribery were disavowed. For example, Manuel Bonilla, admittedly a political enemy of Cecilio Ocón's, nullified the latter's contract for stevedore services and equipment in the port of Mazatlán, allegedly because Ocón won the bid as a result of a bribe. Ocón protested to de la Barra that he had obtained his rights fairly and that his competitor was an exploitative Spaniard, all to no avail.[46] The stability that generally prevailed at the end of summer 1911, at least in comparison with June and July, was enough to restore confidence and begin a new era of expansion.

Part of the reason for the renewed confidence was the clear message that business as usual, minus the graft, had resumed. Both Porfirians and civilian maderistas in de la Barra's cabinet did their best to convince businessmen that prosperity lay ahead. Francisco Madero offered one businessman assurances that tax exemptions would be maintained despite the fall of the dictatorship.[47] Madero's uncle Ernesto guaranteed Porfirio Díaz's son that he would be paid for the electrical work that his company had undertaken at the Mexico City Normal School.[48] And Enrique Creel, son-in-law of Luis Terrazas, Mexico's largest landowner, and a banker and wealthy hacendado in his own right, received word that the government would repay forced loans for which the insurrectionists had signed.[49] In short, men of property would be made whole again. Likewise, maderistas also hoped to cash in on business opportunities. Ambrosio Figueroa, the governor of Guerrero, proposed a railway project for his state that would open it up for the exploitation of its minerals, livestock, wood, and agricultural products. Figueroa foresaw a great future for Guerrero once the railroad was built that would bring benefit to all of Mexico in the long run.[50] Thus, even popular maderistas like the Figueroa brothers believed that further growth of the economy made economic sense for Mexico.[51]

President de la Barra clearly wanted to resume the growth curve of Porfirian Mexico. He insisted, however, that the corruption and graft of the dictatorship must end. Thus, when he learned that a judge and the jefe político of Mazapil were in cahoots with one businessman and using their authority to discriminate against another corporation, he acted. He wrote to the governor of Zacatecas and instructed him to intervene in the matter to prevent injustice and insure impartial treatment for all businesses.[52] He also assured the British minister that the Tlahualilo Company lawsuit would be handled fairly.[53] Like his predecessor, de la Barra did not cave in to British and U.S. pressure to resolve this legal action in favor of the company's foreign shareholders, but instead he let the court system decide the case. Ultimately, de la Barra laid out three basic principles regarding business. First, foreign capital was assured that it would be protected according to the law. Second, the federal government committed itself to protecting lives and property. Finally, de la Barra guaranteed that all concessions granted during the Porfiriato would be in full force and effect.[54] In short, de la Barra intended that business practices would continue as usual during his administration. He, as well as other members of the progressive consensus, continued to believe that the economy had to grow as it had done, for the most part, during the past three decades.

Yet the consensus also recognized that the Porfiriato had created inequitable business situations and that, as in the United States, trusts and monopolies posed a problem for small business. Not surprisingly, some members of congress expressed an interest in legislation drawn specifically on the model of the Sherman Antitrust Act. By prohibiting restraints of trade, the proposed legislation would have opened up the marketplace, or so theorists believed. The bill had a successful first reading, although its ultimate fate was decided during the Madero presidency.[55] Labor also supported breaking up monopolies on the theory that competition would provide lower prices to consumers. But the consensus belief in the small size of the state would render antitrust legislation ineffectual. Although some historians have seen a link between progressive reformism and the creation of a bureaucratic state under the New Deal in the 1930s in the United States, not all progressives believed in big government. In fact, voluntary organizations and private efforts attracted the attention of many reformers, just as they would in Mexico in 1911.

Part of the reason government remained small, in addition to the philosophical bent in favor of federalism discussed in Chapter 4, was the relative poverty of the national state. De la Barra and other governments of this period relied on import and export duties and the stamp tax as sources of revenue.[56] De la Barra never conceived of the possibility of a graduated federal income tax, a progressive reform Woodrow Wilson initiated in the United States. Tax reform remained the purview of state and local government in this period. Progressive northern governors such as Abraham González of Chihuahua and Venustiano Carranza of Coahuila reevaluated real property and shifted the tax burden from the very poor.[57] Tax reform depended on local initiative rather than federal legislation.

Tax code changes and local progressive reforms such as mandating Sunday business closings to insure workers a healthful day of rest also angered some local businessmen. One merchant disagreed with his town council's authority to regulate such matters and called on the state legislature for action.[58] Other businessmen complained about new taxes, particularly on alcohol production. One producer petitioned de la Barra for tax relief, arguing that the new duty hit him much harder than it did the three large distilleries in the neighboring town.[59] The new liquor taxes, however, may have been imposed for purposes other than the economic one. As a later section of this chapter explains, reducing the supply of available, cheap alcohol was among the moral reforms that the de la Barra government and progressive state governors hoped to pursue. Finally, one businessman argued that fundamental fairness required that small merchants and peddlers pay duties, which they currently managed to avoid. He urged de la Barra to crack down on street merchants and earn the government close to 1 million pesos a year in taxes.[60] Such a policy was no more socially acceptable in 1911 than it was in the 1990s, and street vendors remained a permanent part of the Mexican landscape. In sum, the basic federal tax structure did not change much from the Díaz period to the de la Barra period. The exception, the new alcohol tax, was as much a part of the drive to improve morality as it was to raise revenue. Thus, the maintenance of the Porfirian tax structure is further proof that the interim government desired to resume normal business practices.

By the end of Francisco León de la Barra's term of office, investors' confidence in Mexico's future had been renewed somewhat after the shock of the insurgency.[61] Much of their confidence was due to the government's willingness to use force to protect private property and especially businesses. Relatively few investors seemed to have backed out of their Mexican commitments because of a potentially troubled situation or because of any proposed new regulations of business. Even the passage of progressive legislation did not guarantee the government would or could enforce it. The members of the progressive consensus carried on as if little had changed. De la Barra and Madero both believed economic growth had to continue and hence the government's eagerness to repair railroad and telegraph lines and entertain new proposals for development. De la Barra did everything within his power to assure business that the return to prosperity was just around the corner. That he succeeded is indeed remarkable. De la Barra's assurances even extended to foreign-owned business and thus crashed headlong into Mexican nationalism.

The New Antiforeign Sentiment

The most significant achievement of the Mexican Revolution was inculcating in the Mexican people a sense of nationalism. By the 1920s, the idea of *mexicanidad* had clearly emerged, manifesting itself in the cultural flowering of the 1920s and 1930s. Muralists depicted heroic national events and personalities rather than aping European fashions, as the Porfirian artistic community had generally done. Philosophers considered the importance of the *raza cósmica* rather than adapting foreign ideas such as positivism to Mexican circumstances as the *científicos* had done. The great awakening of national spirit stemmed as much from the physical activity of the revolution as from the ideology that it stimulated. Peasants, set in motion by either fighting for revolutionary forces or fleeing from them, gained a greater awareness of Mexico beyond their village beginning with the insurrection of 1910.[62] The Porfirians and the civilian maderistas in 1911, however, had a far more restricted vision of nationalism than what would ultimately emerge by 1920. According to the traditional view, during the de la Barra and Madero periods, nationalism was limited to a call for unity, for common action for the good of the nation, and a limited sense of patriotic xenophobia.[63] Particularly, the popular classes responded more to emotional stimuli than to an idealistic image of a new Mexico.

A recent historiographical debate has emerged about the extent of "yankeephobia" in the early revolution and its role in promoting revolutionary change. One author has found rampant resentment against American capitalists and the tentacles of U.S. capitalism, which, he claims, were strangling the nation. According to this interpretation, the most important causational force during the decade of the revolution, even in its early stages, was the patriotic attempt to liberate Mexico from U.S. capitalist exploitation.[64] Another author, however, downplays the role of antiforeign sentiment as a cause of the insurrection and suggests that particularly in the early revolution, resentment against the United States was quite restrained and less significant than resentment against other groups of foreigners.[65]

The evidence from the de la Barra period supports the second interpretation. Incidents boiled up over the presence of Chinese, Spanish, and English foreigners in Mexican society in 1911; in fact, almost every national group was targeted except Americans. The de la Barra government scrupulously avoided complications with foreigners and made great efforts for two reasons to protect aliens living in Mexico. First, as suggested previously, the progressive consensus believed in continued economic growth, which required further foreign investment to stimulate development.[66] De la Barra specifically stated that he intended to cultivate European investment as a counterpoise to the United States, just as Díaz had done. Hence foreign capitalists, especially Europeans, always found a ready and appreciative audience in both de la Barra and Madero. Second, de la Barra's training as an international lawyer led him to conclude that the state had a legal obligation to protect the resident foreigner. For both these reasons, foreigners in 1911 received the government's protection.

One commonly held stereotype about foreigners in the Porfiriato is that they were all wealthy capitalists, the owners of plantations or factories, who profited by abusing impoverished Mexican workers and taking advantage of their privileged position to extract profits illicitly. But in fact, many of the foreigners who came to Mexico were themselves workers toiling at menial jobs in the mines or on the railroads. Others were genuine middle-class immigrants, who, like permanent residents in other countries, came to Mexico seeking a better future for themselves and their families. These foreigners stood out as different and, like their counterparts in other nations around the globe, including the United States, suffered discrimination.

Probably the most disadvantaged foreign residents in Mexico in 1911 were the Chinese. They frequently came to northern Mexico to work on railroads and the burgeoning agricultural plantations of the Laguna region; many settled in Torreón, opening restaurants, laundries, and other small businesses. The Chinese tended to live in a single community, stick to themselves, and resist speaking Spanish. To the xenophobes, such competitive enclaves invited violence. When the popular maderistas took Torreón in May 1911, they turned on the Chinese and massacred a significant number of them: "Neither age nor sex were spared."[67] De la Barra found such behavior inexcusable, and shortly thereafter his government sponsored meetings and a newspaper campaign to debate the legitimate interests of foreigners in Mexico. These public meetings were intended to defuse the anti-Chinese sentiment in Torreón.[68]

The Torreón massacre was not an isolated anti-Chinese incident. In Sinaloa, the Chinese buckled under to a popular maderista threat and paid a forced loan of 500 pesos.[69] Chinese colonists elsewhere feared a repetition of the Torreón incident and asked for protection.[70] At the end of de la Barra's presidency a mob of popular maderistas stoned the Chinese in Mazatlán and imprisoned a local official who tried to stop them.[71] But clearly the most serious incidents other than the Torreón massacre occurred in Sonora. In both Hermosillo and Nogales, mobs broke windows in Chinese-owned stores and proceeded to loot them.[72] While the interim governor provided police protection in that instance, the same governor's solution to anti-Chinese riots in a mining community was to fire all of the Chinese workers and replace them with Mexicans.[73] The reason for the intensity of the Mexican reaction against the Chinese in Sonora is somewhat difficult to fathom.[74] Probably, Mexican workers resented the fact that the Chinese competed successfully for employment and that their retail businesses flourished. They also no doubt resented Asian "clannishness," which made the Chinese visible targets for hostility. In terms of lives lost, there can be no doubt that the Chinese bore the brunt of the anti-foreign sentiment of 1911. Their relative or at least perceived helplessness also may have contributed to their status as the primary victims of the new xenophobia.

After the Chinese, the most frequent victims were Spaniards, who because of their language ability, often occupied positions of lower management and therefore meted out discipline on estates or in mills during the Porfiriato. They also prospered as retailers in urban centers and occasionally owned their own plantations. Thus, in a very visible way, Spaniards, too, became symbols of foreign dominance to Mexican workers and often targets of violence. For example, a Spanish hacendado was lynched when a mob assumed, erroneously as it turned out, that he had killed a popular maderista officer.[75] When another Spanish hacendado refused to give food to a crowd that marched onto his estate, they killed him. Spaniards were also ill treated in the Torreón region.[76] Farther south, in Oaxaca, Spaniards in several areas felt the wrath of popular maderistas.[77] Thus, generations of brooding resentment against the gachupines surfaced in 1911. Spaniards, despite their linguistic brotherhood, often remained culturally aloof from Mexicans and were targeted in the xenophobic rages of 1911.

Far fewer British citizens fell victim to mobs. A rare exception was the outspoken and vitriolic Harold Woodhouse, whose difficulties occupied the British legation for some time. Woodhouse, who married a Mexican woman and had nine children by her, owned an estate called La Concepción. A group of popular maderistas, led by Daniel Aguilar, rode to the estate with the apparent intent of dividing it among themselves, literally over Woodhouse's dead body. But Woodhouse resisted and shot back at one or two of his would-be assailants. He was subsequently arrested for attempted homicide and robbery.[78] When the local authorities seemed unresponsive to the British minister's complaints, he appealed directly to de la Barra, who sent a column of federal soldiers to Oaxaca and arranged for Woodhouse's release.[79]

Woodhouse and a British drifter seem to have been the only Englishmen to experience antiforeign wrath. De la Barra protected an English company in Tabasco that complained of arbitrary treatment by local authorities and reinstated a Mexican consul in Great Britain who had been particularly helpful in attracting British capital to Mexico.[80] Like de la Barra, Francisco Madero tried to maintain the goodwill of British citizens. In September 1911 he met with England's largest investor in Mexico, Lord Cowdray, and assured him that the British "would not be subject to interference should he come to power, that [British] investments in the country would be welcomed."[81] Clearly, neither de la Barra nor Madero conceived of implementing the economic nationalism that became an integral part of the constitution of 1917.

Further evidence that the xenophobia was widespread and not aimed solely at citizens of the United States are reports by an Italian and a German Chilean that their estates were sacked and that popular maderistas required them to provide a forced loan.[82] Other nationalities may also have experienced such difficulties. The correspondence of the period usually speaks of "foreigners" without identifying nationality. Thus, one politician hoped that Mexican judges would punish the "foreigners" who cheat their workers, while the Mexican consul in Ciudad Juárez reported the presence of antiforeign (not anti-American) sentiment in his district.[83] These and other contemporary reports indicate that all foreigners to one degree or another were the targets of xenophobia. Other evidence also strongly suggests that the Mexican government protected foreign economic interests.

The de la Barra government felt compelled to preserve its friendships with foreign countries, particularly the United States, as a means of attracting additional investment. While not kow-towing to the United States, the Mexican government certainly was willing to listen to diplomatic dialogues about the disputed Chamizal border area, claims-commission issues, and other matters.[84] Prominent people in government, both Porfirian and civilian maderista, generally spoke about the need to conciliate foreign opinion. For example, Francisco Vázquez Gómez and two outstanding civilian maderistas, Abraham González and Manuel Calero, talked about the importance of protecting foreign investments.[85] Only one significant figure, José Vasconcelos, believed that the claims-commission restitution process, which compensated for losses incurred during the revolutionary violence of 1911 and which was de la Barra's idea, was too favorable to the foreigners.[86] Pro-foreigner sentiment did exist and is exemplified by a demonstration that took place in Torreón perhaps to compensate for the earlier anti-Chinese massacre there.[87] Certainly de la Barra believed that foreign interests ought to be protected. He made a special effort to work with the Chinese government, investigating the Torreón affair and reaching resolution on compensation based on "sentiments of most strict justice."[88] Given the prevalent anti-Asian sentiments of the era, de la Barra's statement and actions are even more remarkable. In short, the de la Barra government saw nothing wrong with Díaz's foreign policy (which resembles Mexico's present foreign policy) and continued it.

U.S. President William Howard Taft confided to the Mexican ambassador that he looked favorably at the fact that so little animosity had been directed against Americans in 1911. The ambassador responded that all classes of Mexicans had pledged guarantees to foreigners whose presence benefited Mexico.[89] The recognition of the importance of foreigners for Mexico's future development raises important points of comparison with later administrations in Mexican history. Clearly, the revolution took a more nationalistic tone later in the decade and thereafter. The constitution of 1917 would ultimately convey on the government the power to expropriate foreign-owned property. By the 1930s, Lázaro Cárdenas would implement economic nationalism much to the consternation of foreign property owners. Yet while de la Barra and Madero's encouragement of foreign investment may have seemed out of touch during the Cárdenas years, their policy has clearly returned to vogue since the 1940s. Successive Mexican governments have seen a greater need for foreign investment in order to spur additional growth and development, just as Porfirio Díaz had done. The logical culmination of this development came with the adoption of the North American Free Trade Agreement, which will presumably result in greater U.S. investment in Mexico. Thus, the de la Barra government's policy toward foreigners was international rather than nationalistic and consistent with the goal of economic development.

Moral Reforms and Education

Much of the historiography that discusses the evolution of Mexican education puts little stock in the legislation that the Porfirian congress enacted in June 1911 to reform educational practices. Described as a last-minute Porfirian effort passed hurriedly in the final moments of the dictatorship, the bill has received little credit from historians. The most scholarly work on education in Mexico generally ignores the reforms of the Madero and the de la Barra period.[90] Once again, however, a detailed examination of the events of 1911 shows progressive educational reformism at work during the interim presidency. The members of the consensus knew that the inequities of the Porfirian educational system had to be redressed, which the June 1911 legislation clearly did. Further, the proposed reform was utterly consistent with notions of democratic change and progressive ideals and, to the reformers, would further the moral crusade that they found so necessary for the "redemption" of the Mexican people. Education would inculcate in the indigenous community such values as hard work, austerity, sobriety, and love of the democratic process.

Porfirio Díaz, contrary to traditional opinion, supported public education because he believed it would promote modernization, integrate Mexican society, increase rates of production, and improve the economic well-being of the citizenry. During the Porfiriato, however, he limited federal expenditures for education to the Federal District and the territories that the national government administered. As a result, federally supported schools received significantly more money per pupil than did those that the states provided. Also, because there was so little money available for public education, many Mexicans did not attend school at all, and those from privileged families attended private institutions, often in the capital, such as the National Preparatory School where de la Barra taught in the 1880s and 1890s. Primary education tended to focus on cities rather than rural communities, although this pattern varied from state to state.[91] Thus, the key questions are, Did the de la Barra government try to educate a broader cross-section of the population? (this section argues yes), and Did the underlying educational values and curriculum shift? (only slightly). The de la Barra educational policy had considerable merit. Much more than a hurriedly conceived concession of a dying regime, the new educational policy formed an integral part of the consensus about social change in the aftermath of the dictatorship. Madero and many of the other civilian maderistas led the fight for a greater commitment to public education.[92]

The reform enacted on June 15, conceived by Jorge Vera Estañol, mandated education for Indians and appropriated 300,000 pesos to carry out the new program. Indians within federal jurisdictions were to be instructed in the Spanish language as well as mathematics.[93] A second statute appropriately called for the creation of more rural schools, which required districts with more than twenty school-age children to establish schools under federal guidelines. The mandate thus applied only to the Federal District and the territories, but it did lead to the establishment of twelve elementary schools in Baja California, eleven in Tepic, and thirteen in Quintana Roo.[94] Late in the interim period, congress contemplated remedying the funding discrepancies by nationalizing primary education, as the French had done, for example. But conceptual difficulties with federal-state relations and budget shortfalls meant, at least for the moment, that nationalizing primary education was impossible. Progressive governors, again, took up the slack when possible.[95] Congress did, however, find funding for the school lunch program, one of de la Barra's pet projects designed to encourage school attendance.[96] In sum, the de la Barra government identified an area of failure of the Porfiriato and reformed it by increasing the number of rural schools particularly to acculturate Indians. The minister of public education, Francisco Vázquez Gómez, who generally had his hands full with political issues and a greater interest in curricular reform at the university level, provided limited leadership in suggesting these educational reforms. Whether Vázquez Gómez, who came from Indian parentage in Tamaulipas, was motivated by his own struggle to obtain an adequate education is not revealed in his memoirs.[97]

Curricular reform underwent more limited change. At the end of the Porfiriato, Minister of Education Justo Sierra had become disenchanted with the domination of science in the curriculum and had sought to restore some balance, at the revived National University and at the National Preparatory School. Responding to these concerns, congress created in October the School of Advanced Studies to emphasize the humanities and increased the number of humanities courses in the National Preparatory School curriculum. Vázquez Gómez, who had criticized in print the overly scientific content of the Preparatory School curriculum during the Porfiriato, supported these changes, although a majority of the students, content with their scientific education, did not.[98]

Francisco Vázquez Gómez also had to consider some less significant issues, such as personnel questions in the schools and in the ministry. He dismissed several Porfirian bureaucrats, some for political reasons and others because of a philosophical disagreement over policy.[99] A least one intellectual believed that both factors entered into the equation. He expressed particular concern that Vázquez Gómez sought the elimination of a special professorate dedicated to primary education, the abolition of which he believed would diminish the quality of the educational enterprise.[100] In general, however, Vázquez Gómez seemed moderately progressive in his understanding of educational issues, even though one constituent complained that he was feminizing Mexican youth by hiring women teachers.[101] In short, the de la Barra interim government adopted progressive reforms in primary education, specifically the creation of more rural schools, to further the objectives of cultural unity and democratic change. Education also helped to reinforce the moralizing objectives of the progressive consensus, including the virtue of hard work.

Like nineteenth-century Mexicans before them, the members of the consensus believed that the makeup of the country's rural population had to be transformed before Mexico could complete its process of modernization. Specifically, "character flaws" such as drunkenness and gambling and religious and cultural holdovers such as the multitude of fiestas and holidays had to be obliterated before Mexico could join the ranks of civilized nations. By 1911, officials conceded that foreign immigrants would not arrive in sufficient numbers to change the complexion of the countryside and that therefore the solution lay in transforming the values of the rural peoples. To nobody's surprise, then, the civilian maderistas exhibited in their makeup a strong element of the moral reformism of progressivism from across the border. The objective, as in the United States, was to uplift the moral values of the lower class by legislating the end of drinking hard liquor, gambling, and prostitution. By curbing such vices, the worker could then be led into a promised land of prosperity because his wages would no longer be squandered in the cantina, at the card table, or in the brothel. Increased savings would ultimately lead to investment, entrepreneurial success, and social advancement. As in the United States, where Prohibition was largely a movement of middle-class Americans directed at lower-class immigrants, in Mexico the civilian maderistas paternalistically aimed their reforms at Indians. Ever since colonial times, Mexican statesmen had been concerned about the Indian proclivity for strong drink and had condemned the ritualistic drunkenness that characterized popular celebrations.[102]

During the de la Barra government, the moral reform movement seemed to have enjoyed much more success in the north than in other parts of the nation. In Chihuahua, Abraham González banned gambling and the sale of liquor in Ciudad Juárez establishments. When local prefects refused to endorse the orders, González sent Pascual Orozco and his irregulars to smash the gaming machines and forcibly close down the gambling parlors.[103] In addition to objecting to poker and other games of chance, González also wanted to end professional boxing because of the gambling associated with it. Venustiano Carranza enacted similar reforms in Coahuila.[104]

Reformers also wanted the president to stop the construction of a race track in Tijuana, Baja California (a federal territory), whose construction had been debated for years. The original promoter had had a change of heart and had even authored a book entitled *Easy Money; or, Fishing for Suckers* to condemn the evils of gambling, but other contractors were eager to take his place.[105] The racetrack was not built, at least not in 1911. Reformers also wanted to curb bullfighting, a ritual of which both Madero and de la Barra disapproved. De la Barra attended the first bullfight of his life during his presidency, and then only because it was a charity event sponsored by the White Cross to benefit the widows and orphans on both sides of the recent fighting.[106] Moral reformers elsewhere in Mexico had fewer concerns about bullfighting. These were, after all, local decisions in a federal system, and traditions remained powerful.

Although the moral crusaders probably enjoyed their greatest success in the border states, other parts of Mexico shared their concerns with uplifting the morals of the common people, especially curbing their drinking. The Anti-Alcohol League had a significant following among the progressive consensus, including Alberto García Granados and Francisco León de la Barra, who in October was named honorary president of the league.[107] The new president of the league personally recruited de la Barra, telling him that the purpose of the league was to save Mexican youth from the evils of strong drink, as well as to improve the health of adults and workers.[108] De la Barra could not resist such altruistic goals.

The worst offenders, the progressives contended, were the small rural communities. One reformer pointed out that in his town, with a population of 150, he could count seven cantinas selling liquor. The result, he claimed, was an immoral population that caused social disturbances.[109] The minister of education was curious to know more about the work that the Anti-Alcohol League was doing in local schools.[110] Many believed that the opportunity to reform morals had its best chance for success among school-age children who could learn from their teachers. There was enough talk about moral reform going on in Mexico City that a liquor manufacturer asked the president whether he really intended to shut down the pulquerias.[111] Although north of the border the temperance movement made some headway in the Catholic community, it remained essentially Protestant and hence foreign to Mexico.[112] Some of the anti-Prohibition critiques offered in the United States would also seem to have great validity for Mexico. First, the government had relied since colonial times on liquor taxes for a significant portion of its revenue. Second, given de la Barra's reemphasis on federalism, only state governments could enact prohibition. Thus, the prohibition movement, despite its growing popularity among certain political figures, could succeed only where a determined governor like Abraham González committed to the reform.

De la Barra also expressed his sympathy for other private charitable efforts to assist the disadvantaged members of Mexican society. In late October, he visited the Asylum for the Deaf and Dumb, as it was then called, and was deeply moved when the children attempted to speak to him.[113] Public health issues also concerned him. He visited a suburban hospital, run by the famous surgeon Aureliano Urrutia, which performed operations and had modern facilities for mental patients and victims of tuberculosis, a disease that would ultimately kill de la Barra's three sons.[114] His most publicized visit was to the new penitentiary, as modern as the then state-of-the-art facility of Sing Sing in New York. De la Barra spoke to the men, agreeing to free any remaining political prisoners and urging the remainder to reform their ways and become useful citizens. He toured the facility, noting that the prisoners ate well, attended two hours of academic classes and additional vocational classes daily, and enjoyed regular exercise and baths. Conditions, reporters noted, were "rosy."[115] Clearly, de la Barra, like many Porfirians, cared about Mexico's disadvantaged and, in keeping with Catholic social action views, believed that private philanthropy and limited state action could improve their lives.

Another new public issue beginning to surface during the de la Barra period was feminism. Feminist concerns during the revolution centered on women obtaining the vote. Women's suffrage had just become an issue in Great Britain, where the Pankhurst family led the struggle; likewise, in the United States, Carry Nation had begun the battle. In addition to events in Great Britain and the United States, Francisco Madero's interest in political reform may have encouraged Mexican feminists to focus on suffrage rather than on removing other legal barriers that women experienced. In late May and in June 1911 Mexican women petitioned President de la Barra, requesting the right to vote in the upcoming elections.[116] The government did not respond to their petition, nor did Madero endorse women's suffrage. Likewise, the delegates to the constitution of 1917 denied the progressive reform of women's suffrage, then sweeping the United States, largely out of fear that women would vote for conservatives or allow the church to regain its political influence. Such fears governed the political leadership until 1953, when women finally acquired the vote in national elections.

Other issues concerned women. The Amigas del Pueblo petitioned de la Barra for divorce legislation but to no avail. (Later, however, it would be included in the constitution of 1917, partly because the constitutionalists found legislation against the church to be a politically safe reform.) The press had a field day with the divorce issue.[117] As far as de la Barra and many others were concerned, divorce was unthinkable, both because it violated one of the canons of the Catholic church and because it threatened the family. Porfirian reformers based much of their interest in morality on the defense of the traditional family.[118] Catholic social action, in particular, believed in upholding the preeminence of the family, which a legal divorce decree would certainly violate. The divorce issue had more impact on middle- and upper-class women than those of lower status, who have been well studied elsewhere.[119]

In short, the progressive consensus in 1911 shared the western world's interest in social reform. Moral redemption spurred on many of the civilian maderistas, who, like their liberal forebears of the 1860s, believed that the values of lower-class Mexicans had to be uplifted if the nation was ever to mature. A few reformers believed that women's status ought to be liberalized, although this was clearly not the majority opinion during the de la Barra interim presidency. Finally, and most important, the progressive consensus discussed and enacted changes in education policy in direct response to a well-focused, specific criticism of the Porfiriato. The government tried to do something about the inequities of primary education, although scarce resources and the constraints of federalism limited the vision and the impact of educational reform. While the topics of moral and educational reform interested some of the civilian maderistas and Porfirians, these issues were minor in comparison with the universally agreed upon importance of the land reform questions that emerged in the absence of Porfirio Díaz.

Agrarian Reform

Above all else, the invocation of the phrase "the Mexican Revolution" conjures up images of rural peoples seizing land, shooting landlords, and explicitly rejecting the Porfirian developmental scheme that favored large property owners. In 1910, Mexico remained a predominantly rural society just beginning to respond to the shocks of industrialization, urbanization, and rampant secularism. The anxieties associated with the transition to the modern world made rural people yearn for a less stressful past that may have existed only in their imaginations. Nevertheless, this "reactionary" attitude of rural peoples such as the zapatistas has only occasionally drawn comment.[120] And while the campesinos themselves often remained unable to articulate their demands, intellectuals, the "city boys" associated with each of the insurgent factions, theorized about the agrarian content of the revolution.[121] Their ruminations ultimately led to the writing of article 27 of the constitution of 1917 and the various programs for the implementation of agrarian reform that took place in the 1920s and 1930s, particularly during the first few years of Lázaro Cárdenas's administration. These policies led to significant redistribution of property rights to the underprivileged, especially in the form of ejidos (communal properties).

The dramatic reversal of this land reform policy in the late 1930s resulted from, in part at least, the unintended consequence of the reforms, particularly declining agricultural productivity. Agrarian policy needed to insure continuing productivity, in order to feed the urban population and earn export dollars, as well as further the social goals of reform. High productivity tended to conflict with the aspirations of rural peoples, whose primary concern was maintaining self-sufficiency and providing an adequate diet for their own families. Even peasant willingness to supply local markets did not help stave off hunger in the cities. These same rationales composed at least part of the reason the progressive consensus moved slowly to implement agrarian reform.

The traditional historiography has made certain assumptions about Francisco León de la Barra and the civilian maderistas' agrarian policy in 1911. One underlying assumption, based on a misquotation of an interview de la Barra gave to the *New York Times* in 1916, has been that de la Barra and the Porfirians opposed any change in the structure of rural Mexico.[122] This section of the chapter suggests that Madero, the eldest son of one of Mexico's greatest landowning families, and the other members of the progressive consensus, including de la Barra, had no intention of taking property from private owners without due process of law and guaranteed forms of compensation. While Madero was an idealist, he firmly believed in private property rights. His actions as president mirrored de la Barra's and shored up their theoretical beliefs; both insisted that property squabbles go through some sort of legal process for resolution. Nevertheless, these limitations did not mean that de la Barra and Madero opposed change in the rural sector.

This section also argues that the reformers realized that the long-standing balance between hacienda and village was out of kilter and consequently offered suggestions for redressing the problem, particularly in terms of water use policy.[123] During the de la Barra presidency, the government formed the National Agrarian Commission to begin the study of the land use problem, present legal solutions, and entertain other proposals to resolve the problems of the rural poor, particularly in certain troubled states such as Morelos. These proposed solutions might have been adequate to deal with Mexico's needs, but they were not timely enough to satisfy the impatience of the zapatistas and other popular maderistas.

Mexico's rural areas had witnessed battles over land, water, and labor since pre-Hispanic days. Both cultural and capitalistic considerations argued in favor of property concentrations in the colonial period and the nineteenth century. In the latter part of the nineteenth century, the impulse to make a profit from the land, present even in early colonial times, eventually overrode all other factors. The new modes of transportation and the new instruments of communication brought rural Mexico into contact with the larger world and opened foreign markets to Mexican agricultural products. Even where estate owners sought only to exploit domestic markets, the desire for commercial sales rather than self-sufficiency made land more valuable than ever before.

Mexican landowners capitalized on two pieces of legislation to acquire title to real estate: the Ley Lerdo of 1856, a statute designed to break down corporate land ownership and to further the liberal goal of encouraging individual property holding, and the Baldíos Laws of the 1880s. In promulgating the latter, a variation of the U.S. Homestead Act, the government hoped to attract colonists to public lands by offering to sell large tracts cheaply to individuals who would settle them. Although the Baldíos Laws led to speculation, recent literature suggests that their effect was not as detrimental as once believed.[124] Both the Baldíos Laws and the Ley Lerdo contributed to the concentration of property in the hands of a relatively small number of individuals by 1910, which created the most basic problem for the new government to face.

A second vital land use question involved the control of water resources. In a generally semiarid climate like Mexico's with distinct rainy and dry seasons, irrigation is often necessary in order to bring in a decent crop. Dry farming can succeed, but it is clearly a higher-risk proposition. The Porfiriato for the first time allocated some funding so that the government could begin to take steps to manage water resources. Again, the question of direct federal jurisdiction limited the extent of Díaz's largesse, preventing the government from building federal public works projects in the states. Díaz believed that private enterprise ought to be responsible for constructing dams and hydroelectric plants. His water development policy also encouraged large-scale irrigation works at the expense of smaller ones. Consistent with other aspects of its agrarian policy, the Díaz government continued to believe that the national interest would best be served through the promotion of large-scale, modern agricultural businesses rather than less productive small ranches or village ejidos.[125] The "city boys" would rethink this policy during the revolutionary decade.

Agricultural policymakers also had to reconsider issues pertaining to labor. Labor demands increased with the expansion of capitalistic agriculture during the Porfiriato. As more and more haciendas became plantations producing for international and national markets, they required additional labor. Some of the new export crops were also labor intensive, while other crops had more sporadic labor needs and hence were able to rely on *jornaleros*, or day laborers. As a result of the changes in the type of agriculture and the development of new regions of productivity such as Campeche and the Yucatán, plantation owners needed to transfer workers from more populated to less populated regions. The result, a controversial *enganchado* system, saw gullible or inebriated Indians coerced with honeyed promises of high wages into signing labor contracts for distant plantations, only to find on arrival that they were indebted for the costs of transportation and tools necessary for the job and then imprisoned at night so they would not be tempted to flee.[126]

Porfirian land policy in part demonstrated the close relationship between property use and labor. At least one author has reasoned that landowners expanded the great estates during the Porfiriato not only to acquire property for themselves but also to deprive neighboring villages of their land so that the inhabitants could not be self-sufficient and would be required to work on the plantations to make ends meet.[127] Estate workers were now viewed as cogs in a capitalistic machine, as wage earners toiling on an assembly line in the fields. As a result, the traditional paternalistic relationship between *patrón* and *peón* that in the past had mitigated the economic harshness of the hacienda situation had less significance. As a result, campesinos began to feel more restive and less accountable and perhaps were less willing to compromise than they had been traditionally.[128]

Concern about the crisis in agriculture was not limited to radical revolutionaries, as is frequently assumed. Mexicans from both ends of the political spectrum knew all too well that Díaz's development policies had shifted the balance of power too far in favor of the large landowners. The late Porfiriato saw a deluge of literature on the agrarian reform problem, including Andrés Molina Enríquez's monumental study, *The Great National Problems*.[129] Key figures in and out of the Porfirian government wrote these pamphlets, articles, and books. Hence, the consensus in 1911 included recognition of the necessity of redressing the balance of power in the rural areas. Conceptually, Madero and de la Barra concurred. More controversial was the question of how agrarian reform would be implemented. Madero had recognized the need for reform and provided general guidelines in Article 3 of the Plan de San Luis Potosí. Many of the rural poor fought for Madero because they expected dramatic changes in agrarian policy to take place in the new administration, and many believed that Madero had promised an immediate division of the lands.[130] As the prototype of the agrarian revolution, Emiliano Zapata, stated, "The theme of the revolution is the return of the lands to the pueblos."[131] But, as noted in Chapter 3, Zapata differed with Madero and de la Barra over the process required to return lands to the villages.

Enough of these land seizures took place in 1911 that there can be no doubt that Alan Knight is correct when he describes a popular revolution taking place.[132] These land seizures occurred all over the nation. For example, a veracruzano landlord complained about 150 Indians who had invaded his finca "with the depraved idea of making changes in my property." In the Yucatán, some "misguided Indians" had turned against their hacendados and were taking their lands. Outside of Culiacán, Sinaloa, a former "political" prisoner led his friends onto a hacienda where they uprooted sugar cane, plantains, and fruit trees to plant their corn, beans, and squash. Local authorities, including Juan Banderas, were unwilling to do anything to dislodge the trespassers.[133] And so it went through most parts of the republic—landowners reporting peasant invasions, violence, and destruction of plantation property.[134] Not all parts of Mexico experienced land seizures in 1911,[135] but enough did so that Knight's hypothesis rings true.

De la Barra responded with hostility to the informal land seizures that occurred in summer 1911. He could not accept the extralegal readjustment of property lines. Whether foreigner or national, property owners deserved protection in de la Barra's eyes.[136] When no federales or rurales were available to protect property, the president frequently asked state governors to send their forces to protect property interests.[137] Governors such as Abraham González also sent speakers to stump the state and rebut some of the ideas of the "socialist" land reformers, although sometimes the official spokespersons, too, exaggerated the nature of the reforms promised in the Plan de San Luis Potosí. Many rural peoples honestly believed that their "golden age" was here and that Madero had promised that they no longer had to work hard and pay taxes, that they would minimally earn a wage of a peso a day and be given land free.[138] Although a few petitioners claimed that the hacendados caused these conflicts over boundaries in summer 1911,[139] de la Barra and other members of the progressive consensus clearly understood the rural population as the primary actors. To de la Barra such lawlessness could not be tolerated. Land reform would take place only through legal channels.

As a result, the government found itself defending landlords of all political persuasions in 1911. A few of them were participants in the progressive consensus and advocates of land reform. For example, Esteban Maqueo Castellanos, who wrote a slim volume on land reform in 1910, ran into trouble on his Oaxaca estate during the de la Barra presidency. His property in the Juchitán district, which his grandfather had purchased from the last heir of Hernando Cortés, was invaded by a force of twenty-five popular maderistas, who stole money and stirred up the estate workers by telling them that they had been abused by the Spanish overseer. Worse, as far as Maqueo Castellanos was concerned, the popular maderistas threatened to partition the estate.[140] De la Barra ordered the interim governor of Oaxaca to provide protection for the property, although the latter had some misgivings about his ability to do so.[141] He believed that the problem arose because the overseer acted like a "Spanish viceroy" and did not pay the estate workers fairly.[142] De la Barra believed that, regardless of where the fault lay, legal process, not impromptu violence, should resolve the problem. He was not alone in wanting to protect private property from popular maderistas. Emilio Vázquez Gómez, the supposed radical, also advocated the use of force to defend estate owners and their lands.[143]

As part of the government's policy to defend property owners, de la Barra and Abraham González dispatched troops to help Enrique Creel, one of the heirs to the vast Terrazas landholding fortune in Chihuahua. During the insurrection and often afterward, the Terrazas ranches had been favorite targets for looting, probably because the vast herds of cattle represented a constant source of food for the rebels. Creel estimated that revolutionaries ate fifteen head of cattle a day for about five months.[144] In addition, as the largest landowner in all of Mexico, the Terrazases attracted the agrarian reformers as a symbol of all landowners. In spring, ranch after ranch fell to the revolutionaries, who continued to occupy them during summer 1911.[145] De la Barra responded with a detachment of federal troops.[146] When these did not prove sufficient, he asked González to supplement the federal troops with state forces.[147] González responded with alacrity, saying that he had put thirty soldiers at Terrazas' disposal as he made the rounds of his properties, inspecting the damage inflicted during the revolution.[148]

The members of the progressive consensus, many of whom were persons of property, did not subscribe to the popular maderista notion that the insurrectionists could simply redistribute property as they saw fit. Like de la Barra, they endorsed the idea of due process for agrarian reform. Thus, because of the revolution's insistence on following legal process, Creel and his family were able, in part through their ability to manipulate the legal system, to retain or repurchase much of their lands even during the height of the agrarian reforms of the 1920s and 1930s.[149]

The government also attempted to impose a lawful solution to agrarian issues in the Yaqui Valley of Sonora. For about two centuries, the indigenous people had contested white incursions onto their lands. During the Porfiriato, the failure of the last of the Yaqui rebellions had resulted in vigorous repression; Sonora's governor shipped dissenters to the Yucatán by the hundreds.[150] The Yaquis saw Madero's triumph as an opportunity to redress their grievances and restore the balance of power in the Yaqui Valley that predated Díaz, although this goal ran counter to the desire of many Sonora landowners. The civilian maderista governor José María Maytorena, for example, needed Yaqui labor in order to make his haciendas operate profitably. He was willing to talk about the issue, however, and even conceded that some of the Yaqui Valley lands might be redistributed to the tribe while other properties remained in the hands of white settlers like him. Yaqui extremists would not long accept this compromise because they believed only Yaquis belonged in the valley and that intruders simply had to be driven off.[151] But in the atmosphere of optimism that prevailed in the aftermath of Díaz's fall, the Yaquis were willing to talk; like many others, they had great expectations of Madero, a man they believed to be as "just as God."[152]

The Yaquis appointed three commissioners and after some delays sent them to Mexico City in July. The schedule change meant that the commissioners did not meet Madero until September 1; he had already slipped away to the spa of Tehuacán, Puebla, on summer holiday when they arrived in the capital. In the meantime, the tribal leadership met with de la Barra.[153] As mentioned previously, while the two sides negotiated, the government provided provisions for the peaceful Yaquis in the sierras, who had agreed not to raid neighboring haciendas for food.[154] Yet the state government did not altogether trust the Yaquis. While the discussion went on in Mexico City, Maytorena halted further demobilization of the popular maderistas and posted troops in and near the Yaqui Valley to keep an eye on the disenchanted. Although, generally, the Yaquis kept the peace, occasional transgressors raided ranches and caused disorders.[155]

The negotiations reached fruition in late August when de la Barra announced that the government would redistribute 24,700 hectares to the Yaquis. But the treaty, which Madero signed with the Yaqui leaders on September 1, was considerably vaguer. It obligated the government to distribute national public lands in ejidos to certain villages, and if these allotments were insufficient, to acquire additional lands in the Yaqui Valley for redistribution. In the meantime, Yaquis working on these lands were to receive one peso a day in wages.[156] Not all the cabinet accepted the agreement happily; Alberto García Granados was said to have complained again about Madero's meddling.[157] Because the government never decided exactly how much land it intended to redistribute, the treaty's vagueness eventually proved its undoing.[158] Further, Governor Maytorena would not accept the total exclusion of whites from the Yaqui Valley, although he was willing to provide some land for the Yaquis.[159] Ultimately, the government's proposed compromise could not satisfy the Yaqui extremists. Some of the Yaquis, probably those inclined to moderation, settled on the land granted by the Madero government, but others remained hostile, raiding settlements and driving off cattle. By spring 1912, the treaty had no effect.[160] The Yaqui dissidents remained out of concert with the Mexican state until Alvaro Obregón recruited them for the constitutionalist revolt in 1913.

Discontent with the de la Barra government's policy of legalistic land reform found an echo with at least one expert on the issue.

Andrés Molina Enríquez, who became a reyista and an unsuccessful gubernatorial candidate in 1910 after publishing his great work on the agrarian problem, suddenly gave a call to revolution in late August 1911 and issued the Plan de Texcoco. The plan, had it been successful, would have established a dictatorship committed to land reform, parceling out large haciendas to individual, not communal, claimants. As a practical revolutionary, Molina Enríquez proved an abject failure. He had apparently discussed his revolution with some minor bureaucrats in the government of the state of Mexico but had failed to consult any of the nation's military figures on whom he counted for support. Apparently he hoped that the nonverbalized discontent with de la Barra's land policies would well up once citizens read the impassioned phrases of the Plan de Texcoco. But the popular maderistas did not respond. No military activity occurred in support of the revolution, and the government arrested Molina Enríquez on August 25. Manuel Bonilla, the minister of communications, reportedly stated that Molina Enríquez would be examined by brain specialists upon capture because his plan was so laughable.[161] Shortly after the arrest he was sentenced to a year in prison for the crime of treason.

De la Barra was willing to help the landless, under the appropriate circumstances, just as he agreed to help industrial workers. Many rural people hoped that de la Barra would listen to them, and they flooded him with petitions in summer 1911. Most petitions asked de la Barra to address the encroachments that haciendas had made on village lands nearly everywhere in the republic. From northeast to south central Mexico, villagers saw the demise of the Díaz dictatorship as an opportunity for justice.[162] Other villagers protested the loss of community woodlands and mountain grasslands traditionally used for raising fodder.[163] The written petition was precisely the type of rural demand that the de la Barra government hoped to trigger, and to which it would respond favorably.

Ideas for change abounded in 1911, just as they had at the end of the Porfiriato. Alberto García Granados published a tract advising that Mexico follow Friedrich W. Raiffeinsen's agrarian reform scheme that had modernized German agriculture in the mid-nineteenth century. With capital provided by philanthropic large farmers, Raiffeinsen established cooperative banks, about 1,729 by 1890, which lent money to the poor to enable them to purchase and improve their land.[164] Rafael Hernández, the minister of development, felt that a comprehensive agrarian reform scheme had to both increase production and distribute land more equitably. To accomplish the second goal, he advocated distributing public lands and property purchased from private owners to ejidos or individuals.[165] Even Porfirio Díaz in his April 1, 1911, speech had discussed redistributing lands in small parcels to the landless, the acreage depending on the size of the family needing to be fed.[166]

Faced with an abundance of suggestions, and rather than allowing villages to slug it out with their neighboring haciendas and the federal army or rurales, de la Barra decided to establish a commission to weigh the various proposals, adjudicate disputes, and determine after legal due process a final result on the status of conflicting titles. Specifically, de la Barra recommended that congress create a national agrarian commission comprised of three engineers, three attorneys, and three agricultural experts to work out solutions to rural problems. At the end of September 1911 congress enacted the recommendation into law. Part of the mission of the National Agrarian Commission was to "study the problems of the divisions of the lands to favor the poor workers."[167] Beyond that, the commission was also empowered to examine irrigation policy and colonization schemes.[168] De la Barra had given considerable thought to the creation of the National Agrarian Commission; almost six months earlier he had revealed to the U.S. ambassador that he intended to bring the issue of the division of great estates before congress.[169]

As with any new statutory creation, disputes arose over the procedures the National Agrarian Commission should follow to fulfill its mission. In Michoacán, for example, landlords and villagers agreed that the commission should suspend its activities pending a presidential review.[170] Other villagers also asked the president for help. They knew that the commission existed, but they did not understand the procedures required to bring claims before it to resolve old disputes with the neighboring hacienda.[171] At least one hacendado chafed over the slowness of the commission in reaching a judgment. Portions of his lands had been occupied early in the summer, and while the litigation was pending, the trespassers were still in possession, making it impossible for him to use the land.[172] In another case, an alleged bona fide purchaser (or so he claimed) feared that in the conspiracy-laden climate of these hearings, he would lose his case, and so he proposed to circumvent the process and reach a settlement, in keeping with Hernandez's ideas, by selling his land to the government, which could then divide it among the litigious villagers.[173] Given the relatively small budget of his department, Hernández and the commission recommended that redistribution efforts be concentrated in Morelos, Chihuahua, Puebla, and México, where the agrarian problems seemed most acute.

In addition to handling pending land disputes, the National Agrarian Commission also recommended the revival of the rural credit bank, the Caja de Préstamos. By selling bonds, the caja received enough capital to be able to reduce its mortgage rate from 9 to 6 percent for small farmers, thus making property more affordable. The caja also funded fifty artesian wells and some small irrigation projects.[174] But for most rural Mexicans, those steps were too insignificant and too hesitant. Further, the commission has come under considerable criticism in the literature for its failure to act swiftly to subdivide haciendas. It did not shift into high gear until 1912, and even then, its decisions remained fairly restrained. Nevertheless, the commission satisfied the civilian maderistas' intellectual and legalistic desires because it provided a quasi-judicial process for resolving conflicting land claims.

The other major thrust of de la Barra's land reform program, later endorsed by the commission, was to increase agricultural production, for export trade and national markets, by encouraging the settlement of land previously vacant. Whether the land was truly empty or simply occupied by invisible, voiceless people is difficult to detect. Colonization schemes have been tried in many Latin American republics, and most have failed. Ecologists point out that truly uninhabited lands in Latin America have been unoccupied for good reasons; the terrain is harsh, the soil is thin, or rainfall is irregular, making the likelihood of successful colonization slim. While colonization seems to be the perfect solution to agrarian ills because it avoids political conflict and the disruption of the status quo in settled areas, it has failed for these ecological reasons. Further, most rural peoples are attached to their lands and do not want to move. Peasants have simply rejected the idea of leaving their traditional lands for remote regions when they see neighboring haciendas, on which they once may have raised crops, as available for redistribution. Nor do local landlords want the rural poor to leave, because these people often make up the hacendado's necessary labor force.

In de la Barra's time, however, the government could look at several successful colonization schemes in Mexico and outside as models for development. For example, the Imperial Valley of California, as well as the opening of lands in southern Argentina and

Chile, provided persuasive examples of success. Proponents of colonization also cited the Protestant colonies in northern Mexico. Despite many practical hardships, these colonies had become fixtures by the time of the insurrection of 1911.[175] Although de la Barra's belief that colonization was a workable solution proved mistaken, particularly in the light of the limited resources that the government had available to further such a scheme, his suggestion was appropriate to the times and the nature of the agrarian problems of Mexico.

The progressive consensus did not comprehend that land hunger and the new xenophobic resentment in Mexico in 1911 made new colonization schemes, which in the past had largely benefited foreigners, politically unworkable. A good example occurred in the state of Sinaloa, where the Land Finance Company, backed by investors from North Dakota, encountered both xenophobia and a property intrusion. The corporation had purchased an estate in February 1911 and brought seventeen U.S. colonists to farm a portion of its land. The company rented the remainder of the property to Mexican workers. In the aftermath of the insurrection of 1911, "lawless elements" from the community tore down the colonists' fences, refused to pay rent, and occupied land belonging to the company. These squatters claimed that "the new government will take the land away from [the company] and give it to them."[176] The U.S. settlers were convinced that they were in the right because they believed that "private property cannot be made into Puebla [*sic*]."[177] According to the property manager, the best solution to the problem lay in "a liberal supply of rope" to be sent to the local authorities to help them deal with the squatters.[178]

The government persisted in entertaining colonization schemes throughout the country. Baja California was particularly popular, as noted in Chapter 3, in part because of fears of U.S. expansion southward. De la Barra sympathized with the nationalists; he wrote to an interested North American that his government preferred to colonize Baja California with Mexicans.[179] De la Barra liked Jorge Vera Estañol's colonization schemes, seeing in them a great opportunity for settling Baja California. The National Agrarian Commission endorsed the scheme, and some Mexicans read the news with enthusiasm and volunteered to settle.[180] Madero, too, thought colonization a good answer. He asked a friend of his in Yucatán to examine a land concession and suggested that Indians might be used to settle the vacant lands. If possible, Madero hoped vacant land everywhere could be colonized "with Mexicans and foreigners so as to exploit the immense wealth for the good of the nation."[181] The government also saw colonization as a means for placating troublesome revolutionaries who threatened peace in the countryside. For example, a state government negotiated a deal, which de la Barra approved, to offer land to Emilio Campa, a former magonista who had fought as a rural maderista in 1910, and four hundred of his men. Years later the Obregón government would propose an identical solution to pacify Francisco "Pancho" Villa. Campa agreed in principle to the offer although it apparently came to naught because an appropriate hacienda could not be found.[182] Elsewhere, private citizens offered to sell land to the government for colonizing or to redistribute the land to colonists privately, probably because they saw potential profits in the sale.[183]

The de la Barra government's emphasis on colonization has led at least one author to conclude that it did nothing more than continue past Porfirian practices. As evidence for his view, this author offers statistics from the ministry of development that confirm colonization schemes benefiting a few large landowners, and the distribution of paltry amounts of land to poor laborers during the interim regime.[184] Some mitigating circumstances need to be considered, however, before this conclusion condemning the de la Barra government's agrarian practices can be accepted. De la Barra's agrarian reform measure creating the National Agrarian Commission and establishing the machinery for implementing reforms passed the congress with only a month remaining in the interim government. Therefore, the agrarian commission had insufficient time during the de la Barra presidency to consider land petitions and divide property. Attributing a land reform "success" to the date when land petitions were finally granted distorts the historical record; a fairer conclusion would be drawn based on the date when the petition originated before the commission. Many of the claims that Madero resolved were first litigated during the de la Barra interim period. Again, the point is not to elevate de la Barra's historical reputation at the expense of Madero's but to indicate that they shared a vision, along with other members of the consensus, on the need for agrarian reform.

Members of the consensus had a limited vision. To them, restrictions on the power of the federal government and the executive branch specifically impeded the government's ability to confiscate and divide private property, even had either Madero or de la Barra been inclined to do so. As a result, both Madero and de la Barra focused their efforts on public lands that the federal government already owned rather than on private property. More important, property interests were inviolate, and, de la Barra believed, the government could only ask owners to sell land, not confiscate it. In the various states, the governors had considerable leeway in developing their own agrarian reform plans, a localized solution that the later revolution would find ineffectual. As a result, the constitution of 1917 would grant far greater authority to the president. The need for a stronger federal mechanism to implement reform was also apparent when the interim government considered issues of regulating water supplies and improving the working conditions of agricultural laborers.

The interim government clearly thought of its irrigation policy as a means to make previously uninhabitable lands available for settlement. A massive dam construction project could unlock wealth from the land and create work for the unemployed. The cost associated with such public works, however, inhibited a major construction program. Further, the de la Barra government's ideology, typical in the days before Keynesian economics, did not permit it to conceive of itself as a major employer of paid workers. Convict labor seemed logical and cost effective, especially to the "revolutionary" minister of the interior.[185] Although the government did not adopt Vázquez Gómez's proposal on the workforce, it nevertheless initiated some irrigation projects. For example, a project near San Juan del Río promised to benefit many families.[186] Entrepreneurs agreed with de la Barra that irrigation would help poor Mexicans. One developer suggested that the government buy up large estates, redistribute half of the land free to the poor in ten-acre parcels, and then sell the remainder to foreigners at a price sufficient to compensate the expropriated hacendado and pay for the necessary irrigation works. Such a scheme would provide work and land for the poor, but also the government would continue to earn tax revenues from the settlers for generations.[187] Although the government did not adopt this particular proposal, it did agree philosophically with the notion that irrigation could open up new lands to colonization and relieve some of the land shortage.

Irrigation projects, where they did occur, certainly increased land values and enhanced competition for its use. After Díaz's ouster, many Mexicans believed that the government would reevaluate its water usage policies, which favored the large landowner over the small farmer. One village asked de la Barra to investigate their plight. The village council had transferred the ownership of their irrigation system to the local hacendado in 1899 because of the high cost of maintaining the system, which the village could no longer afford. After a decade of problems, some citizens were rethinking that act and arguing that the council had originally lacked the authority to alienate the common property of the village.[188] The government's position remained constant in such cases. Parties seeking adjudication of water rights needed to go through the court system.[189] Nor did the type of new construction favored seem to evidence a change in philosophy from the Díaz period.

The government lacked the resources, just as the Díaz government did, to provide irrigation for all needy Mexicans and therefore had to maximize the benefit received for the money invested. In terms of GNP, Mexico was a poor land. Travelers often mistakenly referred to Mexico as a rich land because of its historical level of mineral production. But a comparison of its agricultural resources, particularly the quantity of land suitable for dry farming, with those of the United States and Europe shows otherwise. With resources limited the government had to concentrate its efforts on large projects in order to maximize its returns.

The de la Barra government also had to deal with the plight of agricultural workers, who saw the expulsion of Porfirio Díaz in 1911 as an opportunity to improve their status. Wages had declined during the last decade of the Porfiriato, and these workers hoped that trend would reverse with a more sympathetic government in power. Further, some agrarian reformers sought to improve the conditions of the most exploited of all Mexican workers, the *enganchados* or contract laborers, who voiced a legion of complaints. For example, a group of laborers had left their homes in Veracruz in 1897 to work in Campeche after being promised a wage of 1.5 pesos a day. The owner actually paid them 25 centavos a day, provided no health care, and refused to let any of the *enganchados* leave.[190] Other *enganchados* reported brutal treatment such as being suspended for hours by the wrist after making a complaint about work conditions.[191] *Enganchados* rarely had a chance to get even with those who abused them. One group did manage to imprison a labor recruiter, who complained mightily about his fate and argued that he had never harmed his charges.[192] Although undoubtedly some labor recruiters treated their men decently, in general that does not seem to have been the practice. All too often the plantation owners reneged on their promises of decent wages, leaving the laborers to suffer in penury. One group asked de la Barra to at least enforce the minimum wage provision of article 5 of the constitution of 1857, which had been ignored throughout the Porfiriato.[193]

Because of respect for states' rights under federalism, the issue of wages paid to rural workers may have seemed beyond the responsibility of the National Agrarian Commission. In at least one state, however, the "radical" governor, Antonio Hidalgo, decided that a state agrarian commission ought to investigate complaints about low wages with a mind to implementing reforms locally and reporting its work to the National Agrarian Commission. Responding to local government pressures, one hacendado did accept a workers' petition and agree to pay his men improved wages.[194] Nationally mandated wage increases may have seemed beyond the federal government's power to federalists such as Francisco León de la Barra. During the constitutionalist period from 1914 to 1920, the power to legislate such reforms would rest with the military governors, who often imposed minimum wage laws, albeit ineffectively. But in the de la Barra and Madero period, the federal government believed it lacked the constitutional authority to establish a national minimum wage.

De la Barra also believed that there was no federal solution to the food production problem of 1911. So many workers had left the rural areas to participate in the insurrection that the harvest was jeopardized. One farsighted civilian maderista suggested to de la Barra that he encourage a late planting, another called for returning to the farmers some of their local taxes as an incentive.[195] But the government did nothing along these lines. Food shortages do not seem to have occurred in winter 1911–1912 to the extent that they did later in the revolution. The fighting ended soon enough that farmers in at least some states returned to the land in summer 1911 to raise crops.

Imposing a federal solution to food shortages seemed unconstitutional, however, just as federal wage solutions and land redistribution schemes seemed impossible to the members of the progressive consensus. Thus, while the consensus recognized the need for change in the rural areas and agreed that the change must take place through some sort of legal process, it believed that there were clear limits to the federal government's authority to mandate such a change. This vision doomed the agrarian reform policy of the progressive consensus to failure. Leaving reforms to the states meant little would happen. Could agrarian reform have happened at the local level consistent with the rural peoples' desire to resist further intrusions of the central government? Probably not, for reasons suggested earlier. As it was, de la Barra's policies ultimately could not respond quickly enough or dramatically enough to satisfy the needs of the rural poor. Nevertheless, as the end of his presidential term approached, de la Barra felt proud of his social reforms, particularly the school lunch program and the progressive labor policy.

Conclusion

Even as the Chamber of Deputies confirmed the national election results and debated the progressive reforms, President de la Barra decided to tender his resignation early. Two cabinet members, Francisco Vázquez Gómez and José González Salas, had resigned at the end of October; and de la Barra believed it made sense for Madero, as the duly elected president, to take office and establish his own cabinet. De la Barra summarized the accomplishments and the failures of his presidency in a speech to the Chamber of Deputies on November 4. Stopping frequently for applause, he admitted at some length his failure to pacify the countryside, and not just Morelos. Always upbeat, he spent more time accentuating the successes: the free and democratic elections of 1911 and the progressive reforms for social change embodied in the department of labor and the National Agrarian Commission.[196] Ironically, de la Barra is most commonly remembered for the "evil" he did, trying to suppress Zapata and other rural maderistas; the "good," the elections and the reforms, have either been attributed to someone else or interred with his bones. At the time, however, de la Barra's contemporaries congratulated him on successfully bridging the gap between the old and new political regimes.[197] To them, de la Barra had displayed energy in restoring order, and so he received "a remarkable public ovation by all classes." His path on his last day in office was strewn with white flowers, the symbol of his administration.[198] De la Barra received loud applause in the chamber, and then retired to his home for a farewell tea. "Everyone seemed loath to depart. They acted as do people who are saying goodby to a place they have loved and may never see again."[199]

De la Barra's government legislated far more reform than has traditionally been credited to it. The participants in the progressive consensus recognized the deficiencies in the agrarian, labor, and education policies of the dictatorship and modified them. As a result, the interim government embarked on a new rural educational program in the territories, mediated industrial strikes, and elevated to new importance agrarian land redistribution and colonization projects. De la Barra himself regretted that he had been able only to begin the process of reform during his brief tenure; he could not develop a coherent policy fully in such a short time.[200] Yet in all these endeavors the government remained hampered by its own philosophical restraints and the limits of federal power set forth in the constitution of 1857, and thus in some ways the reforms discussed in this chapter represent intellectual history rather than actual deeds. Participants in the progressive consensus borrowed these ideas from foreign sources, including the United States, in the case of the congressman advocating a Mexican version of the Sherman Antitrust Act, and Germany, in the case of García Granados and the Raiffeinsen mutual credit banks. De la Barra drew mostly on European experiences, as he stated when he proposed the labor department. He may well have been influenced also by his friend Léon Bourgeois, the prime minister of France from 1895 to 1896 and author of *La Solidarité,* which tried to reconcile French liberalism with the demands of a just society by emphasizing mutual obligations of the well-to-do and poor, just as Catholic social action did.[201] But as nearly every writer of Mexico has noted, the reformism of 1911 failed.

Finally, we might ask how the progressive reformism of de la Barra and the progressive consensus differed from what eventually emerged from the decade of fighting in 1920. Clearly, the civilian consensus had a different vision of a state; they preferred a weak, federated system to the interventionist state created in the constitution of 1917. But did the new empowered and recreated post-1917 state deserve the credit for changing the face of Mexico? Did the Mexican government after 1917 fundamentally alter landholding patterns and end the enhanced role of the privileged? Recent studies suggest not. Hence the continuity between the de la Barra government and the post-1917 reformers probably is greater than most writers have suggested. The "revolution" of the progressive consensus was a reformism that maintained basic institutions and especially private property interests intact but gradually would have improved the conditions of the poor.

Yet the coming of the Mexican Revolution of 1910 did ultimately mean something, although perhaps not anything as tangible as the traditional prorevolutionary school of historiography would have us believe. Perhaps the most important differentiation was one of attitude—Mexicans of the lower class no longer walked with their faces pointed to the earth but stood upright as proud human beings. This change in self-esteem, the real Mexican Revolution of the popular maderistas, began as early as the de la Barra presidency. For example, in Torreón, people of lower-class origins were talking about equality and forcing "decent men and women to walk in the middle of the street" just as the poor once had been required to do. These ordinary folk would not return to the old ways of subservience; they demanded land and a better way of life.[202] This attitudinal change would ultimately be the legacy of the 1910 insurrection. It was nothing that the government did, or appeared to do, that stimulated it. Thus, the long-term "Mexican Revolution," the inarticulate mental transformation occurring without state support or interference, began during the de la Barra government. The question that remained was whether Francisco León de la Barra, Francisco Madero, and the rest of the progressive consensus could adjust to the new Mexico.

Francisco León de la Barra on his mission to Japan in 1913. *Courtesy of the Centro de Estudios de la Historia de México*

6

The Aftermath of the Presidency

There was no going back. It was as if I had jumped into a well.

—Joseph Conrad, *Lord Jim*

Seldom does a man of political prominence retire gracefully from public life. Instead, such a public person often feels the need to stay around, to serve in other ways, and to make certain that his deeds are not blemished by those who follow him. So it was with Francisco León de la Barra, who, although he had no desire to return to the presidency, still hoped that his achievements would be lasting and would provide the stable foundation on which the new Mexican state could be built. As a result, de la Barra participated in the Madero government as a diplomat, senator, and governor. Consistent with the notion of the progressive consensus, de la Barra generally concurred with the policy initiatives of the Madero government, until sometime in 1912.

Then he too, like millions of Mexicans, joined the ranks of the discontented. Concerns with Madero's bumblings enticed de la Barra to join the military strongman, Victoriano Huerta, who overthrew Madero and promised to restore order with the iron hand. This decision haunted Francisco León de la Barra for the remainder of his life, excluding him from the first denouement of the revolutionary family in 1920. In this sense, de la Barra's life symbolizes one of the tragedies of the Mexican Revolution; unlike the provincial elites who reached an accommodation with the revolution, many of Mexico's best-educated and best-trained middle-class intellectuals, statesmen, and politicians were excluded from the nation-building process in the 1920s because they made the same mistake as de la Barra. Yet in another sense de la Barra's passing from the national scene was quite fitting, as all over the western world the belle époque that de la Barra represented ended abruptly with the outbreak of World War I.

De la Barra never lost touch with his country and his friends after 1913 even though his primary interests migrated with him to the European continent. While the revolution raged from 1914 to 1919, he eagerly sought news of Mexico and lent moral encouragement to those who promised Mexico peace and stability. But unlike so many of the other exiled Porfirian politicians, de la Barra had the talent and the connections to start a new career in a foreign land. By renewing old acquaintances from his days as a diplomat, de la Barra became a professor of international law at the University of Paris at the Sorbonne and an important figure in the postwar mixed arbitration claims tribunals created by the Treaty of Versailles. During the 1920s and 1930s, he turned his attention away from his homeland more and more. His correspondence took place almost entirely in French, and he participated in the glittering social beau monde of the Third Republic, becoming, after Diego Rivera, the best-known Mexican of his day in European circles. Education, training, and his fortuitous marriage gave Francisco León de la Barra a second chance, which transcended his Mexican career.

Service to the Madero Government

Almost immediately after Madero's inauguration, Francisco León de la Barra and his family left for an extended stay in Europe. De la Barra had accepted a diplomatic assignment from Madero to go to Italy and thank the nation for participating in the centennial celebration of 1910. But it was also a chance for him and his new wife to take a delayed honeymoon. De la Barra had completed the chore that Porfirio Díaz had placed on his shoulders; now, he reasoned, he and his wife deserved a chance to see the sights of Europe. A crowd of well-wishers loudly applauded de la Barra and saw the family off from Veracruz.[1]

After a stormy ocean voyage, the de la Barras entrained for Paris, where the exile community turned out in full force to greet them. The family then visited Sra. de la Barra's French relatives while awaiting a formal interview with King Victor Emmanuel III of Italy, eventually scheduled for January 24 in Rome. En route, the family toured Lucerne, Milan, Venice, and Florence. De la Barra then enjoyed a warm interview with Victor Emmanuel, who presented him with a medal before the two men exchanged views on

Mexico's claim to Clipperton Isle, which Victor Emmanuel was supposed to arbitrate. Some contemporaries questioned whether these post-1910 diplomatic assignments to visit heads of state and thank them for their participation in the centennial celebration constituted any more than a convenient excuse to exile unwanted political rivals.[2] The clearest case to the contrary is that of Madero's favorite brother, Gustavo, who was scheduled to undertake a similar but lengthier mission to Japan. Probably mixed motives were behind de la Barra's appointment, coupled with his frequently stated personal desire to leave Mexico for a while to vacation.

The Mexican government's note of congratulations to de la Barra on his success with King Victor Emmanuel contained bittersweet news, an inkling of which had reached de la Barra days before. President Madero decided on a wholesale replacement of personnel in the foreign relations ministry, including many of the consuls assigned overseas. While the change in career diplomatic officers smelled strongly of the spoils system so often decried, the Madero government was concerned about the loyalty of some of the longtime Díaz appointees still in the service. As a result of the housecleaning, de la Barra's friend Gustavo A. Esteva, who had just made the arrangements for de la Barra's visit to Italy, lost his position as consul to Italy. So too did de la Barra's old friend and second-in-command at foreign relations, Luis Carvajal y Rosas, who was offered the ministry post in Russia as a consolation prize.

Foreign Minister Manuel Calero's better news was that the Madero government had conceived of a new role for Francisco León de la Barra, which was much to his liking and which would enable him to remain in Europe. Calero proposed that de la Barra be offered the title of minister plenipotentiary, which would enable him to maintain his ambassadorial rank. He would be assigned permanently to the French government, which had expressed some interest in having an ambassador, rather than a lower-ranking consul, from Mexico.[3] De la Barra responded with interest, but nothing came of the proposal for a permanent ambassadorship, the impetus for which may have been more Mexican than French in origin.[4] Was Madero's motive in trying to create the position to keep de la Barra, potentially a powerful critic, away from the Mexican scene? If de la Barra perceived a political ploy behind the offer, he did not mention it. Essentially, he drew the conclusion that Mexico's new disorders, beginning with the vazquista revolt of February 1912, and other European diplomatic concerns of greater weight turned the French government against the idea.[5] And so it was time to return home.

Foreign Minister Calero notified de la Barra on behalf of the government that his mission had concluded, although several prominent Mexican politicians from Madero's party begged him to stay abroad because his presence in Mexico might aggravate the political situation.[6] For such concerned critics de la Barra had a simple message. He was returning to Mexico as a private citizen without a governmental sinecure. His sole desire, he repeated to reporters on several occasions, was to assist in the pacification of Mexico.[7] (These two goals may have been contradictory.) The implicit criticism of Madero indicated to some that the rift between Madero and de la Barra was widening. One U.S. observer decried Madero's failure to take advantage of de la Barra's presence in Mexico by offering him a cabinet post and thereby creating a government with a broader appeal. Madero, he claimed, was extremely jealous of de la Barra.[8] For his part, de la Barra felt pessimistic about Mexico's future. In a private interview with the U.S. ambassador, de la Barra confessed that he did not believe that the Madero government would last, "though personally he hoped it might." U.S. Ambassador Henry Lane Wilson urged de la Barra to support Madero "to a point," at least until the government fell.[9]

Ambassador Wilson and de la Barra were pessimistic because of a spate of new revolts that shook Mexico in February and March 1912. This was the sort of violence that the Porfirians abhorred, uprisings by popular maderistas with vaguely focused agendas at best, which cost Mexico further prestige in the international business community. The aforementioned revolt led by Emilio Vázquez Gómez was as predictable in its occurrence as in its failure. Vázquez Gómez wrote and spoke tough words but never summoned the courage to set foot in Mexico and lead those foolish enough to rise to his rhetoric. As a result, Pascual Orozco's revolution in early March quickly subsumed the vazquista revolt. In the beginning, Orozco looked like a sure bet to topple Madero. Recruits flocked from their villages in support of their old jefe, and Orozco's untrained but basically sound military strategy stood him in good stead at the first battle of Rellano, where he defeated the federal army so badly that the despondent federal commander, Minister of War José González Salas, committed suicide. But Orozco hesitated to begin his drive to Mexico City: perhaps his men were reluctant to stray beyond the familiar sparse grasslands and mountains of Chihuahua and so urged him not to move, perhaps a more practical matter such as the shortage of ammunition delayed his advance. Whatever the reason for Orozco's hesitancy, the federal army took advantage of this opportunity to regroup and, now headed by the redoubtable Victoriano Huerta, pressed Orozco to a rematch at Rellano. With superior equipment and heavy reinforcements, Huerta reversed the prior loss and turned the campaign around against Orozco. Although Orozco remained a military threat for the remainder of 1912 and into 1913, his viability as a national figure had ended. Like Emiliano Zapata, Orozco remained an open irritant, a constant reminder that Madero could not contain the tiger that he had unleashed.[10]

Madero apparently consulted with de la Barra periodically during 1912, but all too frequently, de la Barra felt, rejected his advice. One diplomat noted the growing coolness between the two men and concluded that de la Barra's "great popularity rendered him more and more an object of suspicion to the Madero family and their adherents."[11] Tensions could only have heightened when de la Barra announced he was the senatorial candidate from the state of México for the opposition Catholic party. De la Barra won his election handily, in confirmation of Madero's commitment to democracy, but undoubtedly made bad feelings fester. Because of de la Barra's former position, he soon became one of the most visible figures in the senate, talking openly on the floor about the need to restore order in Mexico. But de la Barra remained a member of the loyal opposition. He did nothing to encourage the second conservative military revolt against Madero, by Porfirio Díaz's nephew Félix in October. A dearth of military skills and a general reluctance on the part of the Mexican population to conceive of Félix Díaz as the "iron hand" doomed the rebellion to quick failure.[12] Despite the military failure, Madero's opposition seemed to be increasing its following in congress, and so some of the civilian maderistas decided to strike back to regain lost political ground. For example, Benjamín Balderas Márquez launched a scurrilous attack on de la Barra in the Chamber of Deputies, alleging corruption during his term as president.

Balderas's first charge against de la Barra was that he had misappropriated public funds on two occasions, first as secretary of foreign relations and later during his mission to Italy. In the first instance, the total allegedly misused amounted to only 2,000 pesos, and on the second occasion, about twice that amount. In addition, Balderas Márquez charged that while dispersing treasury funds for demobilization de la Barra failed to observe the accounting formality of obtaining the signature of the minister of the interior, as required on all expenditures of this sort. The former president took the charges sufficiently seriously to engage as counsel the well-known lawyer and political writer Esteban Maqueo Castellanos. Maqueo Castellanos raised formal but persuasive defenses including presidential and legislative immunity from minor charges such as these, and a further defense that the one-year statute of limitations had expired months ago.

Given de la Barra's record of honesty, the allegations of minor corruption made no sense. Further, omitting the procedural formalities, as his lawyer argued, would have been a serious lapse only if either minister of the interior had disapproved philosophically of spending the money on pacification, which neither Vázquez Gómez nor García Granados did. Such attacks only hurt Madero's standing among the Porfirian members of congress. The motives for embarrassing de la Barra seemed blatantly political.[13] Thus, when the ultimate crisis of the Madero presidency broke out on Sunday morning, February 9, 1913, the opposition politicians, including de la Barra, did nothing to help Madero. Factional dissension clearly had rent the progressive consensus.

By now, nearly all the Porfirian members of the consensus, as well as the diplomatic corps, had concluded that Madero was incompetent.[14] Based on the criteria that a government must provide internal stability and promote a sense of social and economic wellbeing for its citizens, their conclusion seems reasonable. Only a small number of Madero's contemporaries, however, went so far as to plot a military coup against the president. Félix Díaz and Bernardo Reyes approved of the plan, and while several of their civilian friends took the lead in organizing it, they do not appear to have consulted with Francisco León de la Barra. His name does not appear on the "conspirator list" that Madero's brother Gustavo got his hands on just days before the revolt began.[15] And so, without support from de la Barra, the anti-Madero forces launched their revolt, with mixed success. They managed to liberate both generals and win over a couple of regiments, but loyal troops (led by a close friend of de la Barra's) killed General Reyes when he attempted to assault the National Palace. In the aftermath, the remaining rebels, under the command of Félix Díaz, holed up in the city arsenal, where they controlled most of the locally available supply of artillery ammunition. Thus, instead of a quick, bold coup, the revolt of February 9 turned into a protracted stalemate with each side hoping for the other to surrender.

Madero's response to the news of the revolt was typical. He and his escort mounted their horses and headed off downtown in the direction of the battle, waving courageously to passers-by who cheered him. At the same time, the Madero government reacted ruthlessly to the initial attack. Porfirian general Gregorio Ruiz, captured during the failed attack on the National Palace, was executed immediately without trial. This unusual event in Madero's Mexico, which may have occurred without the president's knowledge, would cost him dearly thirteen days later. Madero, who had been accused of being too soft on his enemies, in this instance was blamed for acting too harshly and without observing the due process of law. De la Barra feared for his own life because of his oppositionist role, and so he and one of his sons took refuge in the British legation, where he told newly appointed British Minister Frances Stronge (who had the strange habit of walking around with his pet parrot perched on his shoulder) that he, Alberto García Granados, and Jorge Vera Estañol were on a government hit list in the event the revolt failed. Stronge certainly seemed convinced of the truth of this story; he insisted that de la Barra remain in the legation except for those public moments when he must leave to pursue his role as peacemaker. Later, Stronge reported that a list of people to be killed had indeed been found, written in Gustavo Madero's handwriting, and that it included de la Barra's name.[16]

For ten bloody days the battle, which became known as the Decena Trágica, raged in the streets of Mexico City. Although most writers have assumed the military engagement to be a sham, probably because Huerta and Díaz ended up on the same side after ten days, the participants in the conflict and the denizens of the city certainly did not agree. Federal soldiers sent to attack the citadel died because, short of an artillery barrage, which could not take place because the rebels possessed a near monopoly of shells, the fortress was virtually impregnable.[17] In the interim, with heaps of putrefying bodies rotting in the city streets, and the foreign community increasingly alarmed by Mexico City's first taste of the revolution, many diplomats, influential Mexicans, and other individuals attempted to intercede.

Almost from the outset of the battle, de la Barra sought to mediate and restore peace. On the evening of the 10th he wrote a note to Madero offering to serve as an intermediary in negotiations between the government and the rebels. Madero did not respond directly until three days later, when he finally invited de la Barra to the National Palace for a meeting. The president asked de la Barra to negotiate an armistice, and so he and his brother Luis drove to the citadel. There, Mondragón and Félix Díaz refused to talk about anything other than Madero's resignation, the same stance they had taken with the Spanish ambassador just an hour before. Since Madero remained obdurate on that score, as he had a right to do (and as Porfirio Díaz was for much of 1911), the talks were stalemated. Certainly aggravating the situation for Madero was the fact that when de la Barra left the palace, he was greeted by enthusiastic applause from the assembled crowd.[18]

Although once rebuffed, de la Barra tried again. Two days later, he led a delegation of twenty-five senators who hoped to talk Madero into resignation. Madero was out but his uncle Ernesto met with them briefly and reiterated the president's refusal to quit. On Sunday the 16th, an armistice finally quieted the boom of the big guns, and people began to remove the bodies of family and friends from the streets.[19] Later de la Barra would gloss over the fact that these negotiations with Madero had ever taken place, as he attempted to distance himself from the Huerta government.[20] But at the time, he undoubtedly could see clear parallels to the events of early May 1911. The president stubbornly refused to give up his office, and this refusal promised to lead to more bloodshed when and if the fighting resumed. Whether de la Barra did anything beyond negotiate is sheer speculation, although it can be assumed that de la Barra believed that Madero should resign for the best interests of Mexico. De la Barra was rumored to have suggested to his long-time acquaintance, U.S. Ambassador Wilson, that the United States could threaten military intervention as a device to persuade Madero to resign, although in the light of de la Barra's feelings on U.S. intervention, this charge seems unlikely.[21]

Nothing worked. Madero refused all of these suggestions, and so in the end the military had to rely on trickery, subterfuge, and deception to capture him. The principal agents here, General Victoriano Huerta and his friend General Aureliano Blanquet, who were supposedly protecting Madero, took him prisoner after agreeing with Félix Díaz on the personnel of the future government, including the cabinet ministers. Many civilian Porfirians returned to the cabinet, including de la Barra, who took the position of secretary of foreign relations. The coup was over on the 19th, with General Díaz emerging from the citadel as the hero of the hour. All evidence suggests that for three days, the coup was popular all over Mexico, but particularly in the capital. The citizenry rejoiced that the fighting was over. But they also rejoiced in the belief that a new iron hand, whether it be interim president Victoriano Huerta or future President Félix Díaz, would restore peace to the land where Madero had failed.

From the perspective of de la Barra and many Porfirians and civilian maderistas, Madero's presidency was a failure. He had failed to provide the most important prerequisite of any good government, peace and stability. As a result, even though the GNP had held up, at least for the time being, foreign investors and businessmen had lost confidence in Mexico, and a period of significant economic downturn seemed about to begin.[22] Madero's inability to control his erstwhile popular followers baffled many of those who had criticized the de la Barra regime. Those critics had assumed that Madero, as the leader of the successful revolt, could control his men and return Mexico to its peaceful path, as José González Salas had told the congress in late October 1911. But prospects of lasting peace clearly diminished under Madero, a fact that most writers have been reluctant to acknowledge.

Madero's attempt to implement the progressive consensus for reform also failed. Whereas industrial workers and those concerned with education reform were initially pleased with their progress, those initiatives really belonged to the de la Barra period. Madero did little to enhance the original legislation, and in the eyes of many, the implementation of the reforms in 1912 was too slow and cautious. The popular maderistas were impatient with the legalistic sorts of reforms that the progressive consensus legislated, and even the congressional discussions of agrarian reform in December 1912 might not have satisfied them. Madero could have shown real leadership and advocated an accelerated pace of reform, but such a proposal would have been inconsistent with his intellectual predilections. Nor is it reasonable to excuse Madero for his dilatory reformism on the grounds that his regime was beset with political violence, as many apologists have tried to do; such violence was a symptom of the regime's failure rather than a cause of it.[23] Thus, all but the most partisan maderistas delighted in Madero's fall. For de la Barra, the coup of 1913 brought new hope that a successful government would be restored in Mexico.

Madero's Assassination: Troubled Times Worsen

Mexico's most famous historical "whodunit" took place on Saturday night, February 22, when the military murdered recently deposed President Francisco I. Madero and former Vice President José

María Pino Suárez. The triggermen eventually were identified as Captain Francisco Cárdenas and Corporal Rafael Pimienta of the rurales, who headed the military escort transferring the prisoners from the city jail to the penitentiary. The mystery involved the identity of the person or persons who authored the plot to assassinate Madero. The prime suspect has always been Provisional President Victoriano Huerta, who had opportunity, means, and motive but against whom only circumstantial evidence exists.[24]

Huerta certainly had the strongest motive because he intended to hang on to the presidency permanently, despite his promises to Félix Díaz. Alive, Madero represented a threat to Huerta's legitimacy and could have become the focal point of a rebellion to undo the coup. Huerta promoted Francisco Cárdenas after the assassination and kept him away from the official investigation as long as possible. In addition, he was deeply involved in the prisoners' transfer to the penitentiary, which provided the opportunity for the murders. He ordered the transfer, supposedly for security reasons. Huerta also took great pains just before the murders to replace the administrator in charge of the penitentiary with a friend, Luis Ballesteros, whom he told publicly that "he had a great responsibility." A cabinet member, who for subsequent reasons had no love for Huerta, overheard this statement and claimed that it made him uneasy.[25] Somebody at the penitentiary certainly knew about the assassination plot, because the spotlights that were usually on had been turned off when the military escort arrived with Madero, and the normally open entrance gates were shut. Finally, Huerta certainly did not shy away from other political murders during his tenure in office. Such evidence, while strongly inferential of Huerta's guilt, might not convince a jury in part because a competent defense attorney would point to other suspects. Hollywood, however, caught the popular image of the story when it portrayed Huerta grinning evilly in a darkened automobile outside the penitentiary while the shootings were taking place.[26]

Another possible suspect, Félix Díaz, also had a good motive for wanting Madero dead. Under the terms of his agreement with Huerta, Díaz had every expectation of becoming the permanent president. Further, close friends of Díaz's procured the two automobiles that conveyed Madero and Pino Suárez to their deaths. But committing cold-blooded murder was not consistent with Félix Díaz's character. In fact, that was one of the unspoken criticisms about his candidacy as the iron hand; he simply did not have the requisite toughness. Finally, another possible suspect was newly appointed Minister of the Interior Alberto García Granados, who seldom is mentioned as a possibility. García Granados had opportunity; he gave orders to the rurales. He had been a strong proponent of the iron hand and had been outspokenly critical of Madero's meddling in the Zapata affair in 1911, which permitted the "outlaw" to escape from federal troops, and had even said in 1911, "The bullet that kills Madero saves Mexico." But García Granados was an educated man who would never stoop to murder, and whose motive for revenge did not go so deep. Although he had been ousted from office at the end of the de la Barra period, because he had been outspokenly critical of Madero, he had no expectation of continuing in the cabinet. Thus, both Félix Díaz and García Granados seem to be less likely suspects.

The original Huerta cabinet, including de la Barra, has also been charged with responsibility for the crime, largely as a result of stories spread by huertista apologists in 1914 and taken up by the revolutionary victors in 1917.[27] Based on the testimony of an unnamed eyewitness, the allegations are that the cabinet met on February 21 to discuss Madero's fate and ultimately decided that he was more dangerous alive than dead. Based on that discussion, and an additional one the following day during which the practical details of the transfer to the penitentiary were allegedly worked out, the cabinet, rather than Huerta, made the decision to kill Madero and the tag-along victim, Pino Suárez.

The cabinet members uniformly and categorically denied these charges. De la Barra explained his actions on those two days at least four different times with utter consistency, and the other cabinet officers verified his version with the exception of two minor details. According to de la Barra, the cabinet met on February 21 from noon to 2:00 P.M. to discuss a variety of subjects. Among other matters, Minister of Foreign Affairs de la Barra, as ranking cabinet officer, asked Minister of Justice Rodolfo Reyes about the legal grounds for Madero's detention. The cabinet discussed the issue, with Reyes and others suggesting that Madero might be held responsible for the murder of Gregorio Ruiz, the Porfirian general shot preemptorily without a trial on the morning of February 9. De la Barra asked Reyes to study the matter and emphasized that whatever criminal proceeding took place must be legal and aboveboard. Several of the cabinet members agreed that Madero could be successfully charged with the murder. Huerta, perhaps disingenuously, stated that if Madero were sentenced to death he would commute the sentence to a five-year prison term, by which time the threat of a Madero countercoup presumably would have ended. Huerta then went on to dictate the prisoners' transfer to the penitentiary.[28]

Because these versions were written in private letters not intended for publication and were entirely consistent, the cabinet members' testimony seems very credible. The only cabinet member whose recollection differed from de la Barra's was Toribio Esquivel Obregón, and then on a very minor point. He believed, though his logic is questionable, that the issue of researching Madero's potential guilt had been given to Interior Minister Alberto García Granados.[29] In sum, according to the public and private testimony of all the cabinet members who have left written recollections of the events, the cabinet never discussed killing former president Madero on February 21.

A second meeting took place on the 22nd, but lasted only a few minutes because members of the government had to attend an official reception at the U.S. Embassy that afternoon. According to the cabinet members, the ministers said little about Francisco Madero and agreed to continue their prior discussion at a later date. All participants agree that de la Barra did not attend this particular cabinet meeting. De la Barra initially stated that he remained in his office working the entire day except for the two occasions when he met with the American ambassador. Later, however, he claimed that a family member's illness kept him at home except for the two official outings.[30] Although a prosecuting attorney would feast on two contradictory stories like these to impeach de la Barra's credibility at trial, the passage of time and faulty memory may help to explain the discrepancy.

The main weakness of the case against the cabinet is a lack of motive. Nobody in the cabinet had as much to gain from Madero's death as did Huerta. The cabinet functioned as a consultative body to advise the president, not as a policymaker. Further, the cabinet members were outstanding men, some of the most honorable civil servants, attorneys, and writers ever to serve their country. To assume that such a body of men would stoop to murder defies logic. A more likely scenario, assuming one makes the leap of faith that Huerta is innocent, is that several of his military sycophants carried out the murder, thinking to cleanse a corrupt society. Huerta no doubt was exasperated with Madero and might well have asked, to paraphrase Henry II's anguish of many years before, "Will no man rid me of this troublesome president?" Motive, means, and opportunity, however, all point to Huerta.

De la Barra and the cabinet members presented a credible case when the allegations of their guilt came forward in 1914 and again in 1917.[31] Four cabinet members independently confirmed identical sets of events, both in their private correspondence and in their published memoirs.[32] These men had distinguished records. Jorge Vera Estañol, Rodolfo Reyes, and Toribio Esquivel Obregón were all prominent lawyers, and Esquivel Obregón had been among the first to speak out against Díaz's reelection in 1910. To such men the charges were horrifying, and, like de la Barra, they could not allow the allegations to go unchallenged. To de la Barra, his good name and reputation were all-important.[33]

Certainly the cabinet enjoyed great credibility among their foreign contemporaries. Speaking of de la Barra, the British minister stated, "His presence in the chief post of the cabinet is a very strong guarantee for honesty and activity."[34] In fact, it was de la Barra's presence in the cabinet that persuaded many of the diplomatic corps to accept the government's rather implausible explanation of the assassinations. (There were no government or attacker casualties in the exchange of gunfire; only Madero and Pino Suárez were hit by bullets.) The diplomats fully expected de la Barra to resign as promised if the investigation did not prove Huerta innocent.[35] Further, de la Barra insisted he had no real ambition to join the government, and initially he turned down Díaz's offer of a cabinet position in foreign relations.[36] Only when members of the diplomatic corps and friends implored him did he agree to join Huerta's ministry.

De la Barra claimed that he first heard from Huerta about the murders at 11:45 P.M. on the 22nd when the president asked him to come immediately to the palace on an urgent matter. García Granados, who had received an identical message, appeared at de la Barra's door to share a ride. When they and the other cabinet members assembled shortly after midnight, Huerta told them that Madero and Pino Suárez had been gunned down during a shootout with a squad of men who were apparently trying to rescue them. Huerta's rendition became the "official" version of the murders that he released to the press and to the world. The cabinet immediately demanded an investigation into the killings, and de la Barra suggested that the military prosecutor, José Vázquez Tagle, an impartial person whose brother had temporarily served in Madero's cabinet, be appointed as investigator. Vázquez Tagle declined, claiming his schedule did not permit him to get involved quickly, and so Huerta appointed another prosecutor in his stead.[37]

Did de la Barra's refusal to resign over the suspicious assassinations and his willingness to accept other appointments from Huerta evidence the "coarsening of his moral fibre," as one historian has argued? De la Barra sought to excuse himself by asserting that, lacking evidence of Huerta's guilt, he gave the dictator the presumption of innocence.[38] But this legalistic argument was not enough. Ultimately, the Madero assassination and de la Barra's continued presence in the Huerta government raised a shadow so dark over de la Barra's reputation that he would never be able to return to Mexico. The murders provided an excuse for Venustiano Carranza, in the name of the revolution, to confiscate de la Barra's property, which was not very extensive, and to paint him a villain. While the facts surrounding Madero's murder suggest strongly that de la Barra was innocent of complicity, the official party historiography would never forgive him. Like Lord Jim in Conrad's novel, he could not dodge the reputation that haunted him as he moved from place to place. For many contemporaries, de la Barra compounded his guilt by failing to question more thoroughly the official version of the assassination and by continuing to associate himself with Victoriano Huerta.

Further Service with the Huerta Government

De la Barra's confidence that the Huerta government would restore order in Mexico was misplaced. The opprobrium that many Mexicans felt for the new provisional president, and particularly the deeds of February 22 popularly attributed to him, vitiated any potential virtues Huerta might have had as the most recent personification of the iron hand. Militarily, those who opposed him, under the titular leadership of Coahuila's governor Venustiano Carranza and including in their ranks Francisco "Pancho" Villa and Emiliano Zapata, made little headway at first. In April and May, their numbers small, they attacked guerrilla style and captured smaller communities in the north and in Morelos. By fall, the rebels enjoyed larger successes, particularly as many who initially had been indifferent to Huerta joined the ranks of the disenchanted. In addition to an increase in the number of political murders, Huerta also disappointed many of his initial supporters by reneging on his promise for early, free elections and instituting dictatorial rule. Dismissing the congress in October and effectively eliminating all other candidates from the presidential ballot by coercion, he transformed the government into a new dictatorship that lacked the redeeming merit of the Porfiriato. To make matters worse, Huerta was a moral reprobate, clearly a drunkard, possibly a drug addict; he never enjoyed the respect that a president should engender in his people. The iron hand never really had a chance in 1913 because the civilian leadership that might have established a moral, decent, thoughtful government based on the progressive consensus never took power.

The murders of Madero and Pino Suárez also offended the ethical sensibilities of the president-elect of the United States, Woodrow Wilson. The son of a Presbyterian minister, Wilson believed in certain moralistic principles and values, and as a former university professor, was wont to lecture others and expect obedience. To Wilson, the Huerta dictatorship represented everything detestable about Latin American politics, the utter rejection of democracy, and the use of physical force to subvert the popular will. And because the outgoing Taft administration decided to leave the Mexican question for Wilson to decide, he had the opportunity to impose his views on Mexico. Thus, the stage was set for a confrontation between Huerta and Wilson with Francisco León de la Barra as minister of foreign relations and Ambassador Henry Lane Wilson caught in between.

What Huerta wanted, and what Wilson refused to give him, was an intangible legal abstraction called "recognition." In international law, the recognition of a government had been traditionally granted if the government seeking recognition met three tests: Did the government have the consent of the people? Did it effectively control the machinery of the state? Did it agree to meet all of its international obligations? Under traditional public international law, the Huerta government clearly qualified for recognition, as Taft's and Wilson's legal advisors in the State Department suggested. Further proof that the Huerta government met the traditional tests was demonstrated by the fact that in May, Great Britain, France, and virtually all of the rest of the world extended recognition to Huerta. Having acted before the United States, the Europeans believed their citizens would have their claims against Mexico settled promptly, while Huerta anticipated closing loans that would enable him to purchase military hardware.[39]

Meanwhile, the dialogue about recognition between the United States and Mexico continued. Ambassador Wilson initially labored under the misapprehension that the traditional precepts governed the discussions, and that President Wilson, like his Republican predecessor, was simply trying to secure some additional advantages for the United States. The tactic was nothing new; Rutherford B. Hayes delayed the recognition of Porfirio Díaz for two years seeking diplomatic advantages. Knowing the importance of the recognition issue for Huerta, Ambassador Wilson pressed the dictator to accept the U.S. position on the Chamizal border dispute—that contested little dot of land caused by the shifting of the banks of the Río Grande near El Paso, Texas—and to agree to satisfy the Tlahualilo Company claims, which involved possessory rights over the waters of the Nazas River in the Laguna region, as well as to resolve favorably U.S. citizens' claims for damages arising out of revolutionary violence in Mexico.[40] President Wilson, however, had mentally concocted a fourth criterion for recognition, one based on morality, which Huerta could not meet in the light of the Madero assassination.[41]

As a result, Wilson procrastinated. An embarrassed State Department tried to explain to the British that Wilson "was so busy with other matters he hadn't gotten around to Mexico."[42] De la Barra tried to leverage the situation by making a fuss about U.S. warships in Mexican waters (it had worked in March 1911) and by pointing out that the European powers had recognized Huerta.[43] But by May 1913, nothing short of Huerta's resignation would satisfy President Wilson, while Huerta was equally determined to remain as president. Thus, the two governments had reached an impasse. De la Barra regretfully told Ambassador Wilson that from this point forward, only routine matters would be brought to the embassy's attention, and that nothing substantive would be discussed until Washington accorded recognition.[44] Because of the deadlock, and also because President Wilson did not trust his ambassador, the latter was soon packing his bags, leaving Chargé d'Affaires Nelson O'Shaughnessy as head of the embassy.

The diplomatic stalemate also offered Huerta a convenient excuse for terminating Francisco León de la Barra's services as minister for foreign relations. De la Barra had accepted the position provisionally with the understanding that he would solve some of the pending diplomatic disputes with the United States and then resign. With no solutions possible because of nonrecognition, de la Barra could not deliver on his promise. In addition, Huerta had political motives for getting rid of any cabinet member who might be friendlier to Félix Díaz than he was to Huerta (as were all the original cabinet members, each of whom had left government service by the summer of 1913). Still Huerta had to act circumspectly in de la Barra's case for a number of reasons, not the least of which was that his brother Luis was negotiating a loan Huerta desperately needed with French bankers.

Huerta therefore did not simply fire de la Barra, as he did the rest of the cabinet. Instead, he appointed de la Barra to two positions that required him to leave Mexico. The first was to arrange a navigation treaty with Great Britain about disputed waters off Quintana Roo, and the second was to serve as his special envoy to France. Huerta also gave de la Barra a specific, special mission to travel through the United States en route to Paris, where he might use the opportunity to discuss, if possible, the recognition question with high-ranking U.S. officials.[45] The dictator had not altogether given up hope of winning U.S. recognition, partly because he clearly held the upper hand militarily in summer 1913. President Wilson had publicly adopted the policy of "watchful waiting" to see which side would win the civil war and had implied that the spoils of recognition would go to the victor. With the official U.S. position articulated, Huerta hoped to learn precisely what Wilson was watching and waiting for before bestowing recognition.

Responding to informal feelers from Mexico City, President Wilson sent Undersecretary of State Boaz Long to meet with de la Barra at the Hotel Astor in New York on August 10, 1913. Long stated once again the Wilson government's premises, which de la Barra understood all too well—that despite the fact that President Wilson's position on recognition was contrary to traditional public international law, and against the best interests of the U.S. business community, he intended to persist in his nonrecognition policy. De la Barra debated the traditional law of recognition and its three requirements with Long, and in his own mind at least made a convincing case. Long seemed somewhat persuaded and finally suggested that de la Barra meet with President Wilson and Secretary of State William Jennings Bryan.[46]

Although intrigued with the idea of meeting the president himself, de la Barra had strict instructions to accept nothing less than a public invitation to Washington.[47] The White House rejected that idea, however, wanting the meeting kept secret. Probably Huerta hoped to trick the U.S. government into de facto recognition by insisting on a public forum, but if so, President Wilson saw through the ploy and rejected Huerta's demands. De la Barra had no choice but to decline the U.S. government's offer. In his public interview, however, he warned the United States against any form of intervention, formal or informal.[48]

De la Barra intermittently tried to influence President Wilson to change his mind on the recognition question even while serving Huerta in Europe. During a luncheon engagement with an old friend who served as the U.S. ambassador to Germany, de la Barra lobbied for a change in U.S. policy, arguing that nonrecognition was creating chaos in Mexico.[49] Many agreed with de la Barra. Former President William Howard Taft sent de la Barra a note of deep regret, stating that "some things have been done which have been less than helpful for Mexico."[50] But by the end of 1913 almost everybody realized that President Wilson had won the battle with Huerta. The latter's second coup in October, his arresting the majority of the legitimate, freely elected congress, and his governing with only a sycophantic rump proved too much for even his apologists to accept. Military victories occurred less frequently, and although the regime would hang on until July 1914, the end could be predicted. Thus de la Barra failed in his diplomatic services for Huerta, although in all fairness de la Barra did face an unforeseeable obstacle, President Wilson's new criteria for recognition. But beyond the failure of his specific objective, de la Barra made the moral blunder of continuing to work for Huerta, even in a limited capacity, that would blemish his reputation forever. An idealist would have severed all ties with Huerta in summer 1913, but de la Barra was not one.

De la Barra also flirted with domestic politics twice during the Huerta period, first as the governor of the state of México and then briefly as the vice presidential candidate on Félix Díaz's ticket. His gubernatorial electoral victory actually occurred at the end of the Madero presidency, and it was a landslide win by all accounts. As mentioned previously the ability of an opposition candidate to win elected office speaks well for Madero's democratic guarantees. But de la Barra was fated to spend only a few days in the gubernatorial mansion in Toluca. Inaugurated in late March, he almost immediately took a leave of absence to return to his duties in foreign relations. In early July, at Huerta's request, de la Barra took another furlough, this time to take his new overseas assignment. As matters turned out, he would never return to Mexico, and when this became evident a little less than a year later, he formally resigned his governorship.[51] De la Barra could not have spent more than a week or two as governor; statistically he joined the parade of civilian administrators Huerta ousted in favor of military figures.[52] Moreover, his term of office was so brief that his impact on state government was negligible.[53]

To Huerta, de la Barra's running as Félix Díaz's vice presidential candidate constituted dangerous political activity. His name on the ticket greatly strengthened Díaz's chances of winning and directly contravened Huerta's plan to continue in office. The candidate presumed that the elections would be held promptly; April 1913 was the date he had in mind. Early in March, de la Barra accepted the nomination for vice president as a compromise; the felicistas had divided between Rodolfo Reyes and General Mondragón. De la Barra's popularity and his eminent role in the Catholic party brought important electoral support to the ticket. The felicista party organized many political clubs at the local level and, having no opposition, probably would have swept to a landslide victory had Huerta permitted an April election to occur.[54]

Huerta determined, however, to foil Díaz's candidacy. When congress met to set the election date, presumably in accordance with the Pact of the Ciudadela, some of Huerta's friends in the congress known as the *cuadrilátero* joined with the remaining maderista opposition to postpone the election indefinitely on the grounds that pacification needed to precede elections. The bold stance in the short run benefited Huerta, and in the long run the constitutionalists, who billed themselves as Francisco Madero's legitimate successors.

In response to this congressional action, Francisco León de la Barra resigned his candidacy for the vice presidency. He told the British minister that delaying the elections caused him to make this decision. Others suspected that de la Barra decided not to run so he would be untainted for the 1916 presidential elections.[55] Félix Díaz attempted to rally his partisans after de la Barra's announcement when some of the more astute asked for an explanation. Díaz offered none but claimed complete indifference about the vice presidential nominee and declared that the party convention could make the selection.[56] Clearly, Díaz's political campaign was in a chaotic state that even the selection of a new running mate could not resolve.

Huerta purposefully kept the political waters churning for the next few months, exiling viable rivals and encouraging nonentities who posed no threat to run and create the illusion of a democratic contest. De la Barra formed the Civil Political League to work for fair elections. But fair elections were not part of Huerta's self-serving scheme for Mexico. Because of his manipulations, the

Catholic party, the most important conservative party in the country, ultimately decided not to field a candidate.[57] Huerta's ploy succeeded temporarily. In October, with no recognizable candidates running, and with military henchmen in charge of the polling places, he won a "popular victory" at the polls. Nobody was fooled by the charade, least of all President Wilson. Huerta's unrealistic ambitions caused him to stoop to tactics that alienated many of his earlier supporters.

Huerta thought de la Barra might have some value in Europe. De la Barra's new instructions were to persuade the French to maintain the diplomatic status quo, continue diplomatic relations with Mexico, and provide the next installment on the loan. But some of the members of the French Chamber of Deputies had misgivings about Huerta's credit rating. De la Barra tried to head off the chamber's concerns and spoke to an important French senator. But by December the French government had urged the bankers not to extend more money, and early in 1914 they complied.[58]

By this time Huerta had already dispatched de la Barra to Japan as a special envoy to thank the emperor for participating in the centennial celebration of Mexico's independence in 1910. Three other politicians had been given this assignment but for various reasons had failed to complete it. In the era before transcontinental air flights, the trip required many weeks of travel. Further, because of delicate relations between Japan and the United States, particularly their Pacific rivalry and the treatment of Japanese nationals in California, the envoy had to employ caution and diplomacy. Yet de la Barra also hoped to accomplish something beyond the mere ceremonial exchange of formalities. Huerta, too, probably wanted something more concrete from the Japanese.

De la Barra traveled overland through Russia and Siberia to avoid two long ocean voyages. His wife remained in Paris, caring for one of their sick children.[59] The trip took de la Barra from Moscow on the Trans-Siberian Railroad nine full days to its termination point in Asia at Fuson. Finally, on December 21, 1913, de la Barra arrived on Japanese soil in Korea. There, he observed what he later described as a symbolic contradiction in Japanese society; men still wore traditional kimonos but had already adopted European hats. While westernization was clearly under way, traditions remained strong.[60]

Much of de la Barra's visit was consumed with diplomatic showmanship—the type of ceremony where his polished skills shone. When he arrived in Tokyo, a procession met him carrying paper lanterns and shouting, "Banzai." Japanese businessmen feted him with a banquet and a show staged by thirty actresses. He went duck hunting on the imperial hunting grounds and received a gift of one thousand cherry trees for Chapultepec Park. The emperor personally bestowed on de la Barra the Order of the Rising Sun.[61] Private meetings had more substance. De la Barra talked on four occasions with Baron Makino, the minister for foreign business, who initially appeared very cool toward de la Barra and Mexico in general. Makino told de la Barra candidly that the press had blown the importance of de la Barra's visit way out of proportion. The Japanese media (and some constitutionalists back home) surmised that Mexico hoped to capitalize on the tense relations between Japan and the United States to fashion a weapons deal for the Huerta regime. But de la Barra reassured the minister that he had no ulterior motives and that the purpose of his visit was limited to expressing the warm feelings and goodwill that the Mexican people had for the Japanese. De la Barra reported home that his gracious approach had laid the groundwork for better relations in the future.[62] The Japanese apparently concurred with this assessment.[63]

Despite de la Barra's subtle successes, Huerta considered firing him from his foreign service position because he no longer was useful. But the minister of foreign relations, Querido Moheno, allegedly interceded by asserting that de la Barra was one of two Mexican diplomats doing an effective job.[64] In the long run, de la Barra probably would have been better off had Huerta terminated him, even at this late stage. But de la Barra did not have long to serve because the military picture had suddenly turned quite bleak from Huerta's perspective. The constitutionalist armies made major inroads with three great thrusts from the north, while Zapata's troops managed to keep much of the south in turmoil. The United States added further pressure, seizing the port of Veracruz in April 1914, although as a military tactic the invasion probably backfired.[65] By July, Huerta finally admitted that his situation was hopeless and left for European exile. De la Barra, like all governmental employees, offered his resignation to the victorious constitutionalists, and by August, when the government began to reorganize its foreign service, he was replaced.[66] De la Barra's career in the Mexican government had ended.

From the perspective of many, de la Barra's service to the Huerta government had been a terrible blunder, showing poor judgment at best.[67] De la Barra should have refused any assignment for the dictatorship after February 1913 and instead taken the high moral ground by resigning his cabinet post and going into exile. One of President Wilson's special envoys stated it well when he said that de la Barra was probably the most qualified politician Mexico had but one who was flawed because "he lacks positiveness of conviction and that complete sincerity which would so well adorn an otherwise fine figure."[68] In his defense, de la Barra persisted with Huerta to the end because, although he must have recognized Huerta for the drunken, villainous lout that he was, he believed in Huerta's mission of pacification. Like many Mexicans in 1913 after the tumult of the Madero period, de la Barra dreamed of the iron hand. Huerta ultimately was not the man for the role. Maybe nobody could have been in 1913; maybe the country needed a period of expiation before the next successful iron hand, Alvaro Obregón, one of the authors of a whole new consensus, could successfully manipulate power and reconstitute a relatively orderly society. Later, de la Barra tacitly admitted the error of his ways and tried to distance himself from Huerta and his role in the dictator's government, just as he did with Madero's murder. He claimed in a letter to the *New York Times* that he really served Huerta as foreign minister for only "a few days" and that his diplomatic missions were on behalf of the nation and not the dictatorship, a fine point that presumably few readers found convincing.[69] But the damage had been done. De la Barra could not regain the moral status he lost because of his participation in Huerta's regime.

Exile and the Political Aspirations of Others

Even though the constitutionalists had eliminated the dictator, theoretically ending the civil war, conditions in Mexico worsened, at least from the perspective of proponents of law and order. To borrow famed historian Crane Brinton's metaphor about the French Revolution, the malaise of Mexico now erupted into a fever. Factions within the constitutionalist ranks turned on one another, and a whole new series of civil wars ensued. Historians have been hard pressed to draw a thread of coherence from the confusion; ideological differences, personal differences, regional quarrels, cultural differences, and sheer love of violence led a generation of Mexicans as far from the Porfiriato's peace as imaginable.[70] Men danced to primordial drums that observers often could not understand.

To those who dreamed still of the iron hand, the only answer (and it was not much of one) entailed more violence, a revolution of their own to install as president somebody who would guarantee peace. And so Félix Díaz, by default as much as anything else, came to lead the Porfirian forces. De la Barra now had two paths open to him: he could live in the past like so many of his fellow exiles and try to restore past glories and the presidency of Félix Díaz, or, he could begin another new career for himself. To his credit, de la Barra chose the second alternative, partly because he had neither the time nor the stomach for the fight. His goods forfeited and his lands appropriated, de la Barra found himself in straitened financial circumstances in September 1914.

Without a government paycheck or his modest investment income, he had to rely on his wits and his professional training to provide for himself, his wife, and their children. He started a private law practice, serving clients, particularly banks with international business transactions, and teaching international law at the University of Paris at the Sorbonne. The family moved into a comfortable six-story residence at 109 Malesherbes in the eighth arrondissement on the right bank of the Seine. The de la Barras stayed aloof from the monied Mexican colony in Paris, although they attended important functions such as weddings and Porfirio Díaz's funeral.[71] Although de la Barra described their quarters as modest, the neighborhood was very pleasant and the family sitting room looked out over the picturesque Parc Monceau with its many flowers and amusements. His family would remain at this address until de la Barra's death in 1939.

As de la Barra told his former political colleagues, he was simply too busy supporting his family to take an active role in the campaigns against Venustiano Carranza. De la Barra expressed an occasional interest in mediating disputes such as the diplomatic problems caused by the Columbus raid, but generally he kept his hands out of exile politics.[72] No doubt de la Barra resented the Carranza government because of his confiscated property; certainly he disagreed with them philosophically, especially after they promulgated a new constitution in 1917. The constitutionalists, for their part, harbored deep suspicions about de la Barra. Every business trip he took resulted in a multitude of rumors circulating in the Mexican press that his well-connected friends were about to assist the anti-Carranza forces in a campaign to unseat the new government. For example, when he visited New York in 1916 on behalf of one of his French bank clients, Carranza's diplomatic service assumed that he was raising funds for a new revolution.[73] De la Barra denied any political activity at all and in an interview with the press underscored the purely business nature of his trip.[74] Yet circumstantial evidence could have led paranoid constitutionalists to a different conclusion. If de la Barra's trip were entirely for business, why did he meet with former President Taft and former Attorney General George Wickersham? Was he merely exchanging pleasantries, as he claimed, or was he discussing more devious political schemes involving Mexico?[75] Since Taft and Wickersham were both outside the government practicing law on Wall Street, and neither had an interest in returning to political life, logic suggests that business prompted the meetings.

De la Barra admitted being mildly interested in the anti-Carranza activities of his former colleagues. For their part, the felicista exiles (those supporting Félix Díaz's rebellion from 1916 to 1920 in Veracruz and the south of Mexico) hoped to recruit de la Barra because of his prestige as a former president and because of his important diplomatic connections. What began harmlessly as a request for de la Barra to contribute an article to the felicista newspaper led to the exiles' hope that de la Barra would serve as Díaz's European representative.[76] Other exiles aspired to have de la Barra persuade the United States to recognize Díaz as a belligerent, a legal status that would have assisted his army in acquiring weaponry. But de la Barra never succumbed to the felicistas' blandishments.[77] Whether he simply pegged Díaz as a loser, or whether he sincerely believed in a broader alliance of anti-Carranza exiles, as he stated publicly, is hard to tell. Instead, he focused his minimal efforts in exile politics on getting the exile community to cooperate and unify against Carranza, thereby enhancing their chances for victory.

De la Barra had correctly identified one of the major problems facing the rebels attempting to unseat the first chief. Personal squabbles and factionalism lessened chances of victory. Therefore, even back in 1916, de la Barra proposed that the anti-Carranza forces enter into a league to pool their military efforts in the name of a cause greater than a personal one—that of rebuilding Mexico.[78] De la Barra posed this pragmatic solution consistently for three years, asking his former colleagues for their thoughts on the matter.[79] His friends acknowledged the problem of disunity and agreed that a house united would enjoy better prospects. Unfortunately, the deep antagonisms that divided people such as Félix Díaz and Pancho Villa made accommodation impossible.[80] As a result of the heightened factionalism and personalism that a decade of violence caused, de la Barra's dream of government by conciliation was simply not feasible.

But did de la Barra's steadfast opposition to Carranza make him a "reactionary" as the constitutionalists' charged? That epithet first appeared in summer 1911, used occasionally to describe some of the former supporters of Porfirio Díaz. Particularly after 1914, the frequency of the use of the term mushroomed, as did the number of people to whom it was applied. As with any pejorative term or profanity, frequency of repetition tended to deprive it of real meaning. Carranza's friends used it to describe Félix Díaz, Pancho Villa (after he broke with Carranza, but not before), and Emiliano Zapata, the prototypical agrarian reformer who has come to personify the goals of the revolution. With such a diverse group of men and ideologies lumped together under the identical invective, the term "reactionary" had no real meaning other than a person who opposed Carranza. The revolutionary school of historians, and unfortunately some of their more professional brethren, lacked the acuity to see that the word was nothing but propaganda.[81] Thus, simply because Francisco León de la Barra opposed Carranza did not make him a reactionary. To determine whether a given figure was reactionary, one must examine his stance on social issues, particularly labor reform, education, and agrarian reform. There, the record for de la Barra is clear. He continued to believe in the tenets of the progressive consensus, which included provisions for social change in each of these categories. Carranza's reforms offered no more (and, after 1917, less) than de la Barra's ideas.

Carranza's early populism embraced agrarian reform. His 6th of January (1915) decree promised land redistribution, and his government quickly began confiscating properties owned by the "enemies" of the revolution. Where labor was concerned Carranza forged an alliance with the radical Casa del Obrero Mundial and promised a political alliance and improved conditions in exchange for several worker battalions to fight against his enemies. But with the defeat of the conventionalists in 1916 (the Villa-Zapata alliance), Carranza's reforms halted. He returned property to the Porfirian elite (with the exception of property belonging to his very visible enemies such as Huerta's widow, Félix Díaz, and de la Barra) and began the process of rebuilding a centralized Mexican state. He crushed strikes and allowed reforms to endure only in those states where governors committed themselves to agrarian reform policies, certainly a tiny minority nationwide. By the end of his term in

1919, Carranza evinced more interest in a restoration of the Mexican economy than in a radical transformation of society. Nationalism and mild anticlericalism served as his substitute for social change.[82]

Merely opposing Carranza did not make de la Barra a reactionary, but did opposition to the new constitution of 1917 make him a conservative, or worse, an enemy of the new Mexico? The constitution of 1917 marked the most significant legal change that occurred during the decade of violence, even though it would remain a dead letter for years to come. For traditional historians, the constitution blueprinted the program of twentieth-century liberalism that would be partially implemented during the 1920s and 1930s. But Carranza himself was no supporter of the constitution; he accepted it, under duress, only because many of his most powerful generals lined up behind it.[83]

De la Barra believed that the reforms necessary to insure social justice in Mexico could have been enacted under Mexico's longstanding constitution of 1857. Certainly the most important influence on that document, the U.S. Constitution, has retained sufficient flexibility to remain viable for more than two centuries despite the changes that transformed the United States from the land of Jefferson's agrarian vision to the modern post-industrial state of the twenty-first century. But de la Barra and the progressive consensus also claimed that the federalist principles of the 1857 constitution provided the reasons why his government could not extend progressive social programs to the states. The irony is that the popular forces, the supposed beneficiaries of the constitution of 1917, were the most adamant about limiting federal intrusions into local concerns. Thus, was the constitution of 1857 compatible with ideas such as economic nationalism, embodied in article 27, which potentially changed dramatically the state's role with regard to private property? Probably not, because the constitution of 1857 held private property to be inviolable, except under very limited circumstances. In short, de la Barra's opposition to the constitution of 1917 rendered him technically a conservative, although whether the revolutionaries themselves paid more than lip service to the new constitution is debatable. Even now, the larger issue about whether a strong state can create social justice remains unanswered.

As World War I drew to a conclusion in 1918, de la Barra's thoughts turned more frequently to Mexico. For one thing, his professional career was now on solid footing, and he worried less about meeting the immediate needs of his family. Also, the lurid charges that he and the other cabinet members had participated in the Madero assassinations were renewed in the Mexico City press, as the new revolutionary state sought to rally public opinion on its behalf by vilifying old enemies. These are the revived charges that stimulated a flurry of correspondence between the former cabinet members and moved de la Barra to a rebuttal to preserve his good name.[84] The journalistic attack was also a response to a perceived threat, stirred up by Carranza's agents, who wrongly placed de la Barra in the midst of innumerable conspiracies.[85] Finally, the end of the war raised fears within Carranza's government that Woodrow Wilson would now turn his full attention to Mexico and intervene on behalf of U.S. property owners. De la Barra also believed this intervention was possible and saw an opportunity to prevent it from happening. The Versailles Conference of 1919 was precisely the milieu in which he best operated, a formal diplomatic setting where gentlemen negotiated behind closed doors and resolved problems rationally (at least in theory).

De la Barra's assumptions that the peace negotiations would follow the traditional European way of doing business ran headlong into Woodrow Wilson's idealism. World War I was the war to end all wars, and therefore the Peace of Versailles, President Wilson proclaimed, would open a new vista to the millennium. No longer would deals be conjured in secret; instead, agreements would be brokered openly and freely. Secret treaties for territorial acquisition, the norm of traditional European diplomacy, would no longer be tolerated nor would past arrangements of this ilk be respected. In reality, of course, Wilson could not keep his idealistic promises, nor did his character permit him to do so; he, above all others, favored the personal touch in diplomacy. But the people of western Europe responded enthusiastically to Wilson's rhetoric and his Fourteen Points. The man whose armies had liberated Europe from the most fearful destruction and loss of life in absolute numbers up to that time in human history enjoyed immeasurable prestige. To those who vowed never to witness a repetition of the Great War, Wilson pledged his support for a League of Nations, a world organization that would help nations involved in controversies resolve their differences peacefully and rationally.

Some observers believed that the Versailles Conference would review all world problems and include the "Mexican question" in its agenda. Francisco León de la Barra certainly hoped so. He saw an opportunity to use his position at the Versailles meeting to forward the anti-Carranza program. In an irony not lost on Mexico City, de la Barra, unlike any representative of the Carranza government, was an official part of the Versailles meeting. Because of his expertise as an international law scholar, the French government asked him to serve on the Committee for International Law, and that position gave him entry into official circles. In contrast, because Carranza had maintained Mexico's neutrality during the war, its representative, Alberto Pani, was excluded from all sessions and not formally received until May 1919. This treatment made the Carranza government irritable and nervous.

Perhaps the fear that the victorious allies would display their armed might and straighten out the Mexican imbroglio prompted Pani to try to set up a meeting with de la Barra. An intermediary opened the door to this possibility in late January 1919, much to the astonishment of de la Barra, who imposed tough conditions for the meeting. The interview, he said, could occur either at his house on Malesherbes, making Pani a true supplicant, or else in a Latin American legation, which would have lent an official character to the proceedings.[86] Pani refused both offers. His refusal raises the question, Did de la Barra sacrifice the possibility of an accommodation with Carranza because of a confrontation over formalities? Undoubtedly he did not. The exiles probably would not have reconciled with the government in 1919, especially since de la Barra did not speak for them. De la Barra probably enjoyed Pani's frustration, as the Mexican envoy continued to cool his heels for months. But the government's pique may have been behind the new series of attacks that the Mexico City press launched on de la Barra, this time raising allegations, which de la Barra furiously refuted, that he was living abroad in luxury on monies that he had gained from political bargainings.[87]

De la Barra's access to the inner circle at the Versailles meeting permitted him to confer with two very important U.S. delegates, Wilson's close personal adviser, Colonel Edward House, and Secretary of State Robert Lansing. De la Barra seems to have had little interest in cultivating the British, since he never made any serious contacts with their delegation during the conference. Perhaps he realized that the U.S. delegates would indeed be calling the shots at Versailles. The specifics of the talks that he had with House and Lansing, however, are pretty much shrouded in mystery, although some general outlines have been preserved. In early December, through the U.S. ambassador to France, Leland Sharp, de la Barra met with House and later claimed that he persuaded House to arrange subsequent talks with Lansing and President Wilson.[88] House's memory of the December meeting was more succinct. According to him, de la Barra "expressed the hope that the Peace Conference would bring about some world settlement which would be of advantage to Mexico, and settle her troubles along with the rest."[89] The two men, under Ambassador Sharp's auspices, had several follow-up meetings over the next two months. De la Barra explained the need for foreign nations, particularly the United States, to respect Mexico's sovereignty and to indicate by example "the principles of true democracy and justice."[90] Although lacking any specifics, the conversations with House and Sharp encouraged de la Barra. Little did he know, however, that for various reasons, House's influence with President Wilson was waning and that House would be unable to make the informal introduction to the U.S. president.

When de la Barra met with Secretary of State Lansing, he spent some time educating Lansing about the realities of the Mexican situation, to use de la Barra's own phrase. De la Barra again emphasized the importance of nonintervention and respect for Mexico's sovereignty. He went on to talk about the need for a new regime in Mexico that respected liberty, freedom of conscience, and a free press. De la Barra believed that his words made an impact on Lansing, and that because of these discussions, the United States did not intervene in Mexico.[91] Lansing and de la Barra continued to meet occasionally over the next few months, having tea and attending formal dinners together at the secretary's request. But de la Barra could never gain access to President Wilson. He did not know that Lansing was about to be frozen out just as Colonel House had been. One of Wilson's most grievous character flaws was his insistence on playing a lone hand at Versailles because he believed nobody else could meet his high moral standards and nobody else could be trusted completely to carry out his dictated wishes. For this reason, Wilson quickly shut out all of the other U.S. delegates from meaningful consultations, even though the delegation was made up of handpicked Democrats and close friends. Thus, de la Barra's skillful politicking with the U.S. delegation came to naught. In addition, by the time Wilson completed his triumphal tour around Europe and settled down to the business of writing the peace treaty, he had no time for Mexico, only for the job at hand. Thus, de la Barra finally realized by summer 1919 that any discussion of the Mexican matter would be postponed to a later date, if it occurred at all.[92]

Meanwhile, the anti-Carranza exiles in the United States must have found de la Barra's negotiations baffling. By 1919, the Carranza government had consolidated itself fairly effectively. At least some of the exiles decided at this point that their only hope for victory lay with U.S. intervention. They cultivated U.S. businessmen and influential senators such as Albert Bacon Fall, hoping to precipitate an intervention that would unseat Carranza. That policy of course contradicted de la Barra's insistence on nonintervention in his talks with Lansing and House. Likewise, the Mexican Catholic Church also hoped to advance its agenda at the Versailles meeting, and the hierarchy hoped that de la Barra, as the leading Catholic party politician from the previous decade, would speak on their behalf to his influential friends at the meeting. De la Barra responded politely and told several high-ranking clergy that he had made some contacts at the meeting. Eventually, though, he candidly informed them that he doubted that the conference would endorse the church's views on Mexico.[93]

De la Barra held firm to his idea that the exiles needed to form a common front against Carranza. As in the past, however, he lacked specifics about how this objective might be accomplished. He emphasized the potential unifying effect of the constitution of 1857, one of the few principles on which the anti-Carranza forces could generally agree.[94] The Porfirian intellectual Jorge Vera Estañol discussed the need to develop the economy and provide universal education for the masses as a means of rebuilding the country.[95] De la Barra in turn advocated the fulfillment of the progressive consensus, that is, providing protection for labor under the labor code his administration had passed and permitting a legal method of agrarian reform, the basis for which had been legislated in 1911. Before social reforms could take place, however, de la Barra believed that the individual's right to person and property must be protected.[96] Not much had changed philosophically with the consensus since 1911.

After the Versailles conference ended without a discussion of the "Mexican problem," de la Barra's momentary influence evaporated. He briefly considered traveling to the United States to become actively involved in exile politics, or so he told the community, but then he more sensibly decided to remain in France, pleading that his work with the Union Juridique International, the international law organization centered at the University of Paris, kept him too busy.[97] Within five months, major developments did take place in Mexico, focused once again on a contested presidential election. Carranza, over the protests of his most powerful general, Alvaro Obregón, tried to retain control by imposing a puppet president.

In April 1920, Obregón escaped Carranza's clutches in Mexico City, where he had been under house arrest, and made his way to the countryside where virtually the entire nation flocked to his cause. Within two months, Obregón had returned to Mexico City in triumph, and Carranza lay dead in an obscure village. Ironically, neither the public nor Woodrow Wilson made a great hue and cry over the assassination of this democratically elected Mexican president. Obregón's victory provided the possibility of ending factionalism and restoring de la Barra's cherished order and unity. Zapata's men accepted the new president (Zapata himself had been assassinated in 1919), as did Félix Díaz and Pancho Villa. But Díaz and his "reactionary" ilk were still persona non grata in Mexico; as a condition for his surrender and adherence Obregón informed him that he would have to leave Mexico permanently. Thus, the stigma from the Huerta years remained attached to the principal Porfirian political leadership. Francisco León de la Barra, like Félix Díaz, could not come home.[98]

Partly as a means of unifying the nation, the government's persecutions of high-profile Porfirian politicians continued. Although Obregón returned de la Barra's confiscated properties in the wave of good feeling after the revolt of 1920, the government later revoked his Mexican citizenship.[99] Undersecretary of State Aaron Sáenz charged that de la Barra had accepted employment from the French government without soliciting prior approval of congress as the constitution required. Sáenz referred specifically to de la Barra's recent appointment as a judge on the Franco-Austrian Mixed Arbitration Tribunal set up under the provisions of the Treaty of Versailles. (See the next section.) Had de la Barra accepted employment from the French government, Sáenz would have made a reasonable, if technical, case. All of the presiding judges of these tribunals, however, were chosen specifically because their nations had been neutral during World War I. No other judge lost his citizenship.[100] De la Barra offered a rebuttal, pointing out that as judge, he acted independently and did not serve one particular country. Second, he argued that his work served humanity and not a particular government. Finally, de la Barra pointed out that the prosecution was pointless and mean-spirited because he never intended to return to Mexico.[101] Obregón may have been so contentious because the government feared de la Barra's lingering political popularity.

Rumors in the press had him returning to Mexico to run on a Fascist ticket in 1924. To make matters worse, in *El Universal*'s presidential poll, de la Barra finished well (ninth) with about half as many votes as those favoring Obregón's chosen successor, Plutarco Elías Calles.[102]

The spiteful attacks continued sporadically into the 1930s. Isidro Fabela, de la Barra's former pupil, accused him of paying foreign claims improperly and in violation of Mexican law in fall 1911. De la Barra rejoined that the charges were nonsense. The claims arose, he pointed out, over the slaughter of foreign nationals in Torreón (Chinese) and Covadonga (German and Spanish). International law recognized the host nation's liability for monetary damages paid to the families of the victims. Further, de la Barra pointed out, both the congress and Madero himself had investigated the claims and found them to be meritorious before the congress ultimately appropriated the money to pay them.[103] The schoolmaster won the battle of words, it appears, but the attacks continued. For example, the government began a quiet investigation to ascertain whether de la Barra had ever earned his law degree. Of course he had, and so this line of attack dissipated quickly.[104] Probably the government continued to criticize de la Barra because of his symbolic value as an enemy.

While the new state persecuted de la Barra in the 1920s and 1930s, other Porfirians made successful comebacks in these decades, among them the Terrazas family of Chihuahua, once the greatest landowners in all of Latin America.[105] De la Barra's former boss, Enrique Creel, the son-in-law of General Luis Terrazas, reentered the banking business in Chihuahua and generally made peace with the revolutionary regime, although he had some concerns about the rhetoric of the agrarian reform program.[106] Rodolfo Reyes decided that he wanted his children to grow up in their homeland, and so he returned to Mexico from Spain for a while, even though he had some trepidations at first. Reyes intended to make a living defending Spanish citizens from expropriations of their properties and asked de la Barra to refer any of his French clients who faced similar problems.[107]

De la Barra, however, genuinely had no desire to follow his colleagues home, even if the Mexican government had been willing to repatriate him. Reconciliation seems to have been more palatable for the provincial elites, where Porfirians formed common cause with the better-educated, more middle-class elements of the revolutionary army to share economic opportunities.[108] But for the

Mexico City professional elite like de la Barra, who had nothing to offer but know-how (and a lot more political baggage) reconciliation was not feasible. Nor was de la Barra particularly interested. First, his career had blossomed in the 1920s, and he enjoyed his work as a judge. Second, his wife's family lived in France, and his brothers lived elsewhere in Europe. And so de la Barra grew farther away from Mexico, a true man without a country. Yet he retained a deep feeling for his birthplace, which he demonstrated when he offered to help the Mexican government, despite all its acts of persecution, with its problematic oil policies in the mid-1930s.

De la Barra's offer was in response to another challenge that Mexico faced in the late 1920s, the worldwide economic depression. And although that depression began earlier, ended sooner, and generally was shallower in Mexico than in the developed world, it nevertheless severely affected the lives of many people.[109] Rather generously, de la Barra discussed Mexico's economic future and investment prospects with his French friends. One of his writings, which appeared in the Paris "Latin American Newsletter," was an outright public relations piece in which he praised the richness of Mexico's resources and the industriousness of its workers. In another interview, de la Barra continued to advocate investment capitalism. He asserted that Mexico needed to pay its foreign debts and to offer appropriate assurances to foreign capitalists, particularly the French. Apparently French business had built up a significant reserve of gold in the 1920s and were looking for an attractive locale in which to invest it. Thus, de la Barra's economic views never changed from the Porfiriato until the 1930s. He believed that the blessings of foreign capital could help build the infrastructure that Mexico needed in order to modernize and achieve greatness.[110]

De la Barra stuck consistently to this philosophy throughout the 1930s, even when it became apparent that Lázaro Cárdenas's government favored the alternative scheme of economic nationalism. Mexico's foreign-dominated petroleum industry had long been a sore point with nationalists. Owned largely by British and U.S. corporations, the companies pumped vast quantities of oil and profits back home. To make matters worse, the companies resisted paying taxes and caused endless headaches with Washington by complaining about the confiscatory nature of article 27 of the constitution of 1917, which theoretically permitted the Mexican government to expropriate foreign-owned property under certain circumstances. Guarantees and treaties did not seem to satisfy the oil companies. With their doomsday mentality, investment in Mexican oil fields plummeted in the 1920s.[111] In response, the Mexican government in the 1930s sought alternative sources of capital development, with appropriate restrictions, and so looked toward the French. Because of de la Barra's political connections in Paris, the Cárdenas government offered to let de la Barra investigate the possibilities.

Specifically, the Mexican consul in France asked de la Barra to negotiate a joint venture agreement between Petromex, the state-owned oil company (as it was called then), and the French Petroleum Company.[112] The Mexican plan called for the joint exploration of known reserves, the sale of Mexican oil to France, and the receipt of drilling equipment as payment for the oil the French company found. France, for its part, wanted some assurances about the security of its investment in light of article 27. The French hoped to make a deal with the Mexicans or some other transatlantic supplier of oil because, with World War II looming and no oil reserves in their own country, they needed to guarantee France's supply of the strategic resource. The Iraqi pipeline, which supplied most of France's oil, looked particularly vulnerable, as did France's second major source, Morocco, which the Italian and German navies could blockade. Therefore, French policy was predicated on the need to find a reliable and secure source of oil, and Mexico seemed to fill the bill.[113]

Despite the mutual interest, the joint venture never developed, partly because of an economic downturn in France that made investors more conservative and partly because of the 1938 crisis with the U.S. oil companies.[114] The Mexican oil workers union and the U.S. companies had been locked in a wage dispute for two years that ultimately had gone to the Mexican supreme court for final adjudication. When the U.S. oil companies refused to abide by the court's decision, President Cárdenas expropriated their holdings on March 18, 1938. The resulting wave of nationalistic sentiment made petroleum a highly politically sensitive subject in Mexico and eliminated the likelihood of further foreign investment in the sector. Instead, Mexico now wanted a deal for someone to purchase their product, not invest in new fields. Although Germany expressed an interest, in the long run it valued its relationship with British and U.S. oil companies too much to risk losing the oil companies' friendship over a potential new supply in Mexico. Eventually, France identified Venezuela as its alternative oil source.[115] But the oil episode did accomplish one thing for Francisco León de la

Barra personally. Officials in the Mexican government noted the efforts he had made to help Mexico. Persecutions of de la Barra stopped after 1936, in keeping with Cárdenas's policy of reconciliation with all former presidents of Mexico living in exile, as well as with other former enemies of the revolution. Nevertheless, the denouement with the Mexican government must have accorded de la Barra great satisfaction as he entered the last years of his life. True to his word, he never returned to Mexico, but at last he had made peace with his country.

De la Barra's New Career

Francisco León de la Barra spent the majority of his time in exile after 1914 pursuing a new career. In fact, his ventures into politics described in the previous section occupied limited portions of his life. Like many of his generation, de la Barra hoped that the Great War, with its horrors and destruction far beyond anything the Mexican Revolution ever imagined, would never be repeated. As a result, he expended considerable efforts working for the cause of lasting peace. In a sense, the postwar idealism recapitulated the prewar peace movement and some of the ideas of the Hague Peace Conferences. Consistent with his past experiences, de la Barra believed that arbitration and the principles of international law, rather than the carnage of warfare, should resolve problems between nations. De la Barra had the legal training necessary to assist in the peace movement, and his connections in France provided him the opportunity. Thus, during the 1920s, the former president of Mexico became involved with the International Court of Justice and with special courts created by the Treaty of Versailles and related agreements.

At the same time, de la Barra continued the private practice of law, building a client base apparently consisting primarily of banks engaged in international business transactions such as J. P. Morgan.[116] He also taught courses in international law at the University of Paris. In 1917, de la Barra organized a conference at the university to address the issue of the rights of neutrals during the war, an issue on which the Spanish government had consulted him and about which he had published in the past. In sum, de la Barra built a reputation as a leading practitioner in his field and in the process made the acquaintance of other scholars and influential individuals. His professional successes, along with his status as a former president, gave him entry into what remained of the social world of Europe, which included important men of affairs such as President Raymond Poincaré of France and Spain's King Alfonso XIII, who would continue to exercise influence in the post-war world. De la Barra's professional work, his practice, and his teaching kept him very busy and enabled him to provide for his family in a modest way.[117]

De la Barra used his connections in France and Spain to facilitate a deal to help his adopted homeland in its darkest hour. At the end of 1917 a new offensive by the Germans brought them to within one hundred miles of Paris; de la Barra reported he could hear guns in the distance and sent his family south to Biarritz, where many of the socialite Mexican exiles spent the summer. Nobody knew that this offensive was Kaiser Wilhelm's last desperate attempt to stave off defeat and that the end of the war was less than a year away. The French government felt desperate and knew that it needed help, financial as well as military. Apparently, some cabinet members asked de la Barra to use his influence with his Spanish bank clients to secure a 300-million-peseta line of credit for France. De la Barra spent two months in Madrid fine-tuning the deal, and eventually France did receive the line of credit.[118] Thus, in a small way, de la Barra contributed to the victory of the Triple Entente in November 1918.

As an international law expert, de la Barra joined traditional and well-established professional organizations such as the Institute of International Rights, as well as a newer organization, the Union Juridique International, a select group of forty practitioners that included former U.S. Secretary of State Elihu Root and the international law faculty at the Sorbonne. Woodrow Wilson, Ruy Barbosa, the former Brazilian president and a member of the International Court of Justice, and former Premier Léon Bourgeois of France served as its honorary presidents.[119] Founded to work for the scientific progress of international law, the Union Juridique after the Versailles Conference took on an additional responsibility, the codification of international law principles (a challenging task because of the differences between Anglo-Saxon and continental jurisprudence).[120] The value of codification has long been debated in Anglo-American jurisprudence, and so the Union Juridique's failure to complete its self-appointed task may not have had a measurable effect on world peace.

Otherwise, de la Barra performed the typical duties of an academic. He commented frequently on the writings of other international law scholars, emphasizing his personal interest in human rights and in arbitration as a means of dispute resolution.[121] Like all good scholars, he gave formal presentations and had at least one of his talks on the role of international mediation published.[122] The lecture circuit occasionally took him abroad. For example, in 1920 he delivered a series of lectures at Cambridge University on colonial New Spain, a safer subject for him than Mexico's more recent history. In that talk, de la Barra contrasted the violent behavior of the conquistadors with the peaceful conversion efforts of the missionaries and then discussed the process of mestizaje that had occurred after 1521.[123] De la Barra also participated in the Latin Union, an organization whose purpose was to forge closer ties between European Latins and the peoples south of the Rio Grande.[124] Speculation about reviving the Pan-American Union also piqued his curiosity, prompting his suggestion that the Latin American states ought to begin to examine the efficacy of compulsory mediation as a mechanism for dispute resolution. De la Barra believed that the United States had to relinquish the idea of military intervention, a process that was ongoing in Central America (particularly Nicaragua) and that de la Barra decried.[125] Because he had just been asked to help arbitrate the longstanding Leticia dispute between Colombia and Peru, de la Barra believed his ideas on mediation were particularly current. In short, de la Barra's academic career echoed his important work as a practitioner in the field of arbitration.

De la Barra's most important activity during the 1920s, however, was as the president of several of the mixed tribunals created under Article 10 of the Treaty of Versailles and corresponding treaties, including the treaties of St. Germain, Trianon, Lausanne, and Neuilly. The victors claimed that the Central Powers had violated the traditional rules of war by their "exceptional war measures"; specifically, they, or individual citizens of their state, had confiscated the assets of individual citizens of the Triple Entente within their jurisdiction. In all prior conflicts, the Entente claimed, foreign citizens' assets were inviolable private property. Seized goods included everything from ordinary household furniture to bank accounts worth millions of dollars. In the same spirit as the philosophy of reparation for war damages, the Entente believed that its citizens ought to be compensated for the losses that they had suffered, and the mixed tribunals were established to accomplish that end. Each tribunal consisted of three members, one from each of the contending countries and one independent member from a neutral state who automatically served as the president. In the event that the two suitor nations could not agree on the identity of the impartial third judge, the International Court of Justice appointed him. De la Barra eventually served as the president of five of these mixed tribunals, beginning with the French-Austrian one and later the French-Bulgarian, Greek-Bulgarian, Greek-Austrian, and French-Hungarian. All five of these courts had plenty of business during the 1920s, and so de la Barra spent his days as a full-time judge.[126] But he did not serve on the most important and the most controversial of all the tribunals, the French-German, an indication that he remained a secondary figure in the peace process.

The jurisprudence behind the mixed tribunals and the procedures employed merit some attention. Initially, claimants presented their case to a clearing office in the host country. If the clearing office could not resolve the claim, the litigant went to the mixed tribunal, whose decisions, according to the treaties, were final. The tribunals, deciding the rights of private individuals, really did not create law of great international importance. They dispensed justice equitably and with little expense to the litigants, about six dollars in court fees (although of course attorney's fees added significantly to costs). More to the point, arbitration provided a government a means of redressing a grievance on behalf of one of its citizens without having to resort to the costly option of war in the manner of Don Pacifico (an incident that involved Lord Palmerston's deploying the British Navy to Greece to recover damages on behalf of a British street peddler whose vegetable cart was damaged during a riot in Athens).[127] Some pragmatic problems with the tribunals did continue to exist, however. Many defendants claimed, sometimes successfully, that the tribunals lacked jurisdiction over them for a variety of reasons.[128] Further, since international law is essentially voluntary in terms of compliance, no formal mechanism existed for the execution of the tribunal's judgment. That problem heightened in the 1930s when memories of the horrors of the Great War had somewhat faded. In the 1920s, the decisions of the tribunal were complied with voluntarily.[129]

Contemporaries also applauded the tribunals because the idea of arbitration soon spread into more traditional diplomatic disputes. For example, the Bulgarian and Greek governments asked de la Barra to help them resolve the issue of Bulgaria's legal claim of access to the Aegean Sea. The resulting decision, according to some observers, averted another Balkan War.[130] These judicial successes earned de la Barra the French Legion of Honor Medal.[131] Also, he was twice nominated for a permanent seat on the International

Court of Justice, first by Bulgaria and then by Hungary, and served at least once as an ad hoc judge on the International Court of Justice.[132] Although the mixed tribunals finished their work by 1930, all claimants having been satisfied or dismissed, many legal scholars and European politicians hoped that arbitration would be used even more frequently in the future.[133] But the presence of arbitration panels depended on the climate of public opinion, and an agreement on a rational world of diplomacy and compromise. The generation in power in the 1920s believed in such a world. The totalitarians of the 1930s, however, did not, and the weakness of the rationalists' position became all too apparent with the onset of the crises that would ultimately lead to World War II.

One conflict, for example, that briefly disrupted European peace and prefigured the war to come was the Italo-Ethiopian conflict of 1935. The Italians, under their fascist dictator, Benito Mussolini, sought military revenge for the humiliating defeat that Italian troops had suffered at the hands of poorly equipped tribesmen at the battle of Adowa in 1896. As Italy began to manufacture an excuse for military intervention in Ethiopia, de la Barra met with members of the French and the British governments in an attempt to arbitrate the quarrel. All favored such a step except the Italians. As de la Barra pointed out to a reporter, arbitration might have provided a compromise solution, but Italy had no desire to compromise.[134] Thus, the crises of the 1930s revealed an inherent weakness of mediation; all the parties had to want to dance or else the ball was off.

The other precursor of World War II, the Spanish Civil War, also saw combatants who preferred fighting to compromise. Here, de la Barra had more at stake personally: his stepson, Alfonso Alamán, had enlisted in the Falange. But as the Republicans grew desperate in 1938 and began finally to speak of compromise, Franco and the Falange would accept nothing less than total victory. Franco rejected de la Barra's offer to negotiate. A disappointed de la Barra stated that the victory of the Falange did not bode well for France.[135] Compromise and international dispute resolution were simply not possible because of the totalitarian mindset. Yet in his last interview de la Barra remained hopeful that the will for peace manifested by England and France (he undoubtedly supported Neville Chamberlain's compromise at Munich) would preserve the peace.[136] Unfortunately for the world, both Chamberlain and de la Barra were wrong.

As World War II approached, de la Barra began to falter physically. He had already lived through a serious operation five years earlier and began to look his age. He experienced the tragedy of having his sons predecease him, although his first grandchild was born in 1937.[137] On each occasion when illness threatened a family member, the de la Barras moved south for the warm climate of Pau or the glitzy resort of Biarritz on the southwestern coast of France in traditional Basque country, where many Mexican exiles, including Porfirio Díaz, spent time.[138] Apparently de la Barra began to decline seriously in summer 1939, and so the family made its last journey to Biarritz. De la Barra still had one final project in which he expressed an interest, an ecclesiastical ceremony at Notre Dame in Paris for the Virgin of Guadalupe that was scheduled for October. But de la Barra never lived to participate in the festivities. He died on September 22, 1939, while at Biarritz and is buried in the Sabou Cemetery there.[139]

Conclusion

Like the years spent abroad by many other exiles who unwillingly left their homelands behind, Francisco León de la Barra's twenty-five years abroad were filled with accomplishments as well as disappointments. The European counterpart of the Mexican world in which he had flourished, the Victorian beau monde of the Porfiriato, vanished. The two years following his presidency had begun promisingly enough with the resumption of his diplomatic career and his participatory role in the nation's political life, albeit as a member of the political "outs." But the murder of Francisco Madero proved to be a turning point in his life. The incident set Mexico on a new course that made de la Barra unacceptable to the new consensus. De la Barra's role in Madero's assassination, which amounted to no more than blind acquiescence to it as a fact of life, marked him with a blemish that he could never remove. With his Mexican political and diplomatic career seemingly at an end, he reached a personal crossroads in 1914.

Most Porfirian political exiles initially chose the path of resistance, attempting to return to power in Mexico through violent revolution under such champions as Félix Díaz. Thereafter, they tried to make accommodations with the victors and return home forgiven and forgotten, as many lesser regional figures such as Enrique Creel and Diego Redo did. De la Barra's interests in following this path rapidly waned as he became increasingly successful professionally. Furthermore, de la Barra was too important for the victors to forgive and too visible to forget. So the government tarnished his image whenever possible in the 1920s and 1930s, before Cárdenas finally called off the anti-Porfirian propaganda campaign. Had de la Barra lived another few months, the Cárdenas regime probably would have included his name among those officially forgiven and asked him to return home in the same grand gesture of reconciliation that brought other past presidents back. De la Barra probably would have resisted the temptation; he had been gone so long that his family and interests were deeply rooted in Europe. But the European world in which he played a minor role also had changed beyond recognition; de la Barra's rational world where international disputes were settled through arbitration and compromise no longer existed. His vision proved too idealistic for the tough European totalitarian world of the 1930s. This, then, was the tragic side of the Mexican Revolution as well. Men of talent and ability such as de la Barra and other educated Porfirians, particularly those from Mexico City, were forced out of the system when in other times they might have rendered great service to Mexico. Such is the judgment of revolution, however, to sweep out the old and bring in the new.

Francisco León de la Barra late in his career. *Courtesy of the Centro de Estudios de la Historia de México*

Conclusion

The answer to the question of whether the Mexican Revolution was the first major social revolution of twentieth-century Latin America or merely an elite replacement resulting in little significant socioeconomic change remains complex. The evidence suggests that the best answer lies between these two extremes and that two "revolutions" occurred simultaneously.

The first revolution—the spontaneous labor strikes and land seizures, the violence and opportunism of the popular maderistas responding to regional issues—was a social revolution, a popular uprising without ideology or national leadership. In the long haul of Mexican history it accomplished little in pragmatic terms such as any permanent redistribution of acreage or workers' ownership or management of privately held enterprises. But the popular revolution did alter attitudes and allow previously subjugated peoples to hold their heads high, completing a process that had clearly begun during the de la Barra presidency. As one of Porfirio Díaz's close friends lamented to the former dictator, the people had lost respect for property. Another former insider spoke of popular "insolence," a complaint echoed by the United States ambassador.[1] As early as 1911, the popular revolution had changed *los de abajo*'s view of themselves.

The second revolution, that of the progressive consensus, closely resembled the reform movement taking place simultaneously in the United States. Calling for political enfranchisement, order, economic development, and modest social change through nonviolent and legal processes, the progressive consensus resembled in many ways the "revolutionary" reformism that eventually triumphed, expanding the middle class and empowering a whole new group of "haves." This new (or in some cases reborn) national elite created a more equitable system, recruiting its membership on a much wider basis than had Porfirio Díaz.[2] Yet the continuity between the Porfiriato and the post-1920 "revolutionary" government, which had much in common with the progressive consensus, seems to outweigh the discontinuities. The state reemerged larger than ever, and capitalism reinvigorated itself.[3]

Perhaps this continuity occurred because the two principal goals of the popular classes were antithetical. On one hand, many popular revolutionaries wanted a redistribution of the land that only the state could accomplish since it was the sole institution with jurisdiction to decide the ownership of the land in question. Yet at the same time the popular classes also called for the diminution of the state, which they regarded as tyrannical. This fundamental contradiction underscores again the regional nature of the Mexican Revolution of 1910.[4] Other continuities with the Porfiriato are equally striking. Over the ensuing decades Mexico has reemphasized economic development and the role of technically trained intellectuals to guide the destiny of the state. At the same time, the government has periodically promoted reform and laid claim to being democratic. All of these trends can be traced back to the late Porfiriato and the de la Barra presidency in 1911.

The outcome of these two revolutions was not clear to the people living in 1911. Few suspected that they stood at the brink of a cataclysmic struggle that would convulse the country for a decade. Policymakers clearly remembered the strengths and failings of the Díaz dictatorship and recognized that in Díaz's absence Mexico would have to allow more opportunities for all Mexicans. (Not that the Porfiriato was an entirely closed society.) Francisco León de la Barra's career during the Porfiriato demonstrated that the dictatorship permitted some merit-based advancement, particularly for the well-educated who succeeded in Mexico City. Díaz's elite included not only the socially privileged who remained influential generation after generation but a whole group of newcomers who advanced because of their talent. The opportunity that had always existed clearly expanded along with the economy of the Porfiriato. In this setting de la Barra's money and lineage meant that he had less to overcome than most of his countrymen. Further, his academic brilliance brought him praise from powerful people and paved his way into the diplomatic service, where he rose to the top as ambassador to the United States.

By the time de la Barra went to Washington, the dictatorship was showing signs of aging, and members of the provincial elite and the middle class were leading the demands for change. In 1910 and 1911 Porfirians and civilian maderistas quarreled over the identity of the persons who would serve as state governors and president. When the electoral process broke down in 1910 in an orgy of fraud, the civilian maderistas resorted to insurrection. But they tempered the violence, realizing that it threatened the peace and order that had elevated Porfirian Mexico's stature in the eyes of the world leaders. Thus, the insurgents consciously used only enough force to persuade the dictator to step down. The process of battle and negotiation escalated for six months and culminated in a treaty that placed Francisco León de Barra in the presidential palace. De la Barra's long absence from Mexico and his distance from the political activities of 1910 made him the perfect candidate for the interim presidency. His neutrality recommended him to both Madero and Porfirio Díaz and their followers.

In the absence of Porfirio Díaz, de la Barra had three objectives: peace, democracy, and progressive social change. Of the three, the one with the most immediacy was the need to restore order before the physical achievements of the Porfiriato, the visible signs of material progress, were destroyed and foreign investors frightened away. The interim government responded to property seizures, jail breaks, destruction, and violence by demobilizing the perpetrators, the popular maderistas. By the end of July, de la Barra felt, the celebratory mood had gone on too long. The budget could not withstand the expense of keeping the insurgents on the payroll for no apparent purpose. Repression seemed to offer the only solution, which meant using the federal army to put down troublemakers and demilitarizing the countryside by quickly mustering out the remaining troublesome popular maderistas. The zapatistas posed the most serious problem, refusing to follow the president's directives and doing everything in their power to retain their arms. Of all the de la Barra government's initiatives, the quest for order proved the least successful. Popular maderistas like the zapatistas had no patience for the time-consuming legalities of progressive reformism; they wanted land immediately. For many popular maderistas, the de la Barra government (and its successors through 1920) lacked legitimacy. De la Barra (like Madero after him) would never win the respect of the popular revolutionaries; he was too much of a lawyer, a dandy, and a compromiser. As a result, even though in many regions the violence temporarily diminished, Mexico never returned to its Porfirian quiescence during his presidency.

De la Barra had considerably more success with political reforms, though he is seldom credited with restoring individual civil liberties and holding reasonably fair elections. The members of the progressive consensus clearly disliked the old dictatorial system. With Porfirio Díaz, the *científico* clique, and tyrannical local jefes politicos eliminated, the country was ripe for political change, including an assertion of greater local autonomy. State and local elections seemed more autonomous. These regional votes brought new participants into politics and did not always result in the election of Madero's (or de la Barra's) candidate. The elections for the presidency and the vice presidency also seemed more honest than earlier, though again critics and disgruntled candidates spread innuendo about their fairness. These incidents demonstrated more than anything else that Mexico lacked the political culture for western European-style democracy, not surprising since the process was so new. Nevertheless, observers from all over the world concluded that the elections were better than what had occurred previously and commended de la Barra for his efforts.

Finally de la Barra suggested progressive reforms in the areas of education, labor, civic morality, and land ownership. These reforms were at the heart of the progressive consensus, which is not to assert that all of the civilian leadership agreed unanimously on the precise proposals, but to suggest that a vast majority at least recognized that these specific social problems needed prompt resolution. Education had to be provided to the rural as well as the urban peoples of Mexico if the country hoped to modernize and inculcate democratic capitalistic values in its citizenry. Industrial workers needed the opportunity to earn a fair wage and be protected from exploitation and injury. Workers needed the moral uplift of a prohibition on alcohol and gambling if they hoped to prosper. Most of the population, which still toiled on the land, needed reformist policies that would oversee the redistribution of property from both public and private sources. The government had to expand irrigation projects and improve land use if it were to feed the growing population.

Eventually, the post-1940 government implemented many of these reforms, prompting commentators to note the growing resemblance between the Porfiriato and contemporary Mexico. This denouement, however, arrived too late to comfort de la Barra and many of his fellow travelers. For them, the false steps they took in 1913 forever darkened their historical reputation. Like many other Porfirians, Francisco León de la Barra drifted from serving as the loyal opposition to supporting Victoriano Huerta, the man who unseated Madero. When responsibility for Madero's assassination pointed to Huerta's accomplices, de la Barra's reluctance to distance himself from the general marked the "coarsening" of his moral fiber, in the words of at least one commentator. That decision trapped de la Barra and the other Porfirians from 1914 to 1920, limiting their options.

De la Barra's personal political choices coupled with his retention of the ideas of the progressive consensus made him a reactionary to the leaders of the newly emergent Mexican state, and it meant that his counsel would not be heeded. And so for the remainder of his life, de la Barra returned to the precepts of his youth, preaching arbitration instead of war as a means of dispute resolution. His writings and labors as a judge justly earned him the respect of his European colleagues. Even in the 1930s, however, he proved shortsighted, unable to see that Adolf Hitler, like Emiliano Zapata in a very different way, did not accept the Victorian rational paradigm in his dealings with other powers. In sum, Francisco León de la Barra was a talented and generally astute man who lacked the perception to notice that his world had changed. The circumstances of the civil war caused him, like many other able men of the Porfiriato, to spend much of his productive life abroad and not in the service of his country. That was the real tragedy of the life of Francisco León de la Barra and, in some respects, of Mexico itself.

Appendix A

The Treaty of Ciudad Juárez May 21, 1911

In the city of Juárez, on the 21st day of May, 1911, in the customs house, Francisco S. Carvajal, representing the government of Porfirio Díaz, Dr. Francisco Vázquez Gómez, Francisco Madero, and José María Pino Suárez, as the representatives of the revolutionary forces, have gathered to treat about the method of effecting a cessation of hostilities in the entire national territory, wherefore considering:

1) that General Porfirio Díaz has manifested his resolution to resign the presidency of the republic before the end of the present month; and

2) that bona fide news is at hand that Ramón Corral will resign the vice-presidency of the republic within the same time period; and

3) that by administration of law, Francisco León de la Barra, at present minister of foreign relations, will assume for the interim the power of executive of the nation and will call the general election according to the terms of the Constitution; and

4) that the national government will study the conditions of public opinion within the provisions of the Constitution and will come to an agreement to indemnify the losses directly caused by the revolution;

Therefore, the two parties in this conference, in view of the previous considerations, have agreed to formulate the following agreement:

From today on, hostilities which have existed in the entire national territory of the republic shall cease between the forces of the government and the forces of the revolution, those forces to be dismissed in proportion in each state so that the necessary steps are taken to guarantee tranquility and public order.

Transitory provision:

As soon as possible, reconstruction and repair of the National Railway lines hitherto interrupted shall be begun.

Agreed and signed in duplicate by Francisco Carvajal, Francisco Vázquez Gómez, Francisco I. Madero, and José María Pino Suárez.

Appendix B

De la Barra's Inaugural Address May 25, 1911

Mexicans: Upon taking possession in compliance with the supreme law of the republic, of the office of interim president of the United States of Mexico, I fulfill a pleasing duty by addressing myself to you for the purpose of making you a solemn promise and an earnest appeal.

The gravity and the delicate character of the political problems that have to be resolved in consonance with the broad interests of the country would ordinarily have made me hesitate before deciding to assume the heavy responsibility of the presidency. However, my strong feeling of duty and my profound love of our country, as well as my knowledge of the qualities of the Mexican people and my conviction that my sincere and precise words will not be addressed to the people in vain, require that I take office.

Being without political ambition and desiring only the good of my country, I will in the position in which I occupy provisionally be a zealous defender of the law, especially the electoral law, so that the will of the people can manifest itself freely in the forthcoming federal and local elections.

Although the constitutional reform relative to "no reelection" has not been approved by the state or federal legislature, I consider it my duty to declare, as a guarantee of the purity of my intentions (as if the antecedents of my public life were not enough), that in no case will I accept the candidacy for the presidency or vice presidency of Mexico in the upcoming election. I realize that in conforming to the precepts as contained in the proposed amendment approved by Congress, I am acting in accordance with the dictates of an enlightened public opinion.

The happiest day of my public life will be that on which, within the shortest time compatible with the electoral law and the welfare of the country, I can deliver up the power that today I receive to the citizen elected by the republic. I will then return to my private life with the tranquility provided by duty accomplished and with the satisfaction of seeing my native country developing once more its resources through assiduous industry under the aegis of peace.

Under the jurisdiction of the laws and in obedience to its mandates, political parties will find the widest scope for their efforts on behalf of their principles. Their rights will be respected scrupulously as long as they keep within the limits imposed by law, but any transgression of legal bounds will be energetically repressed.

Although the cordiality of the relations with foreign countries to which we are bound by ties of affection and interest ought to relieve me from the need to make a declaration about the foreign policy that I will follow in my brief presidency, I desire, nevertheless, to say that the government, respectful of the rights of all the other nations and zealously defending our own, will endeavor, as it has in the past, by its frank and straightforward attitude, to enhance those relations every day to the mutual benefit of all powers and to the honor of the principles of established international law.

In order to carry out the political program that briefly I have outlined, the country must realize the gravity of the situation that jeopardizes our national existence. Doing justice to the sincerity and vehemence of my love of country, a sentiment that will compensate for my deficiencies, I must repeat my appeal that all of us unite in a common spirit of peace and progress. The circumstances demand it.

Recent events permit me to remind you again of the great and solid qualities of our heroic army, which has shown itself worthy of its glorious traditions and capable of loyally and resolutely upholding them.

The present stormy time, in which I have succeeded provisionally the statesman who has written pages of glory for our country, will be followed by another tranquil and serene epoch during which the republic will undertake anew its march along the true road of progress, developing in an orderly and systematic manner toward the ideal of a healthy and strong democracy.

Let us strive for the realization of this beautiful ideal that is within our reach if we all subordinate our personal interests to the paramount vital interests of our native country, which though today ruined, will tomorrow be happy again, through the elevated and effective efforts of our good citizens.

Appendix C

List of Governors, 1910–1911

State	*Porfirian Governor*	*Interim*	*Elected*
Aguascalientes	Alejandro Vázquez del Mercado	Alberto Fuentes D.	Alberto Fuentes D.
Campeche	José García Gual	J. Suzarte Campos	Manuel Castillo Brito
Coahuila	Jesús del Valle	Venustiano Carranza	Venustiano Carranza
Colima	Enrique C. de la Madrid	Miguel García Topete	José Trinidad Alamillo
Chiapas	Ramón Rabasa	Manuel de Trejo	Manuel Robello Arguella
Chihuahua	Miguel Ahumada	Abraham González	Abraham González
Durango	Esteban Fernández	Luis Alonso y Patiño	Carlos Patoni
Guanajuato	Joaquín Obregón González	Juan B. Castelazo	Juan B. Castelazo
Guerrero	Damian Flores	Francisco Figueroa	José Lugo
Hidalgo	Pedro L. Rodríguez	Jesús Silva	Ramón Rosales
Jalisco	Manuel Cuesta Gallardo	David Gutiérrez Allende	José López Portillo y Rojas
México	Fernando González	Rafael Hidalgo	Manuel Gaduño
Michoacán	Aristeo Mercado	Miguel Silva	Miguel Silva
Morelos	Pablo Escandón	Juan N. Carreón	Ambrosio Figueroa

Nuevo León	José María Mier	Leonardo Chapa	Bibiano L. Villarreal
Oaxaca	Félix Díaz	Heliodoro Díaz Quintas	Benito Juárez Maza
Puebla	Mucio P. Martínez	Rafael P. Cañete	Nicolás Meléndez
Querétaro	Francisco G. Cosió	José Antonio Septién	Carlos M. Loyola
San Luis Potosí	J. M. Espinosa y Cuevas	Rafael Cepeda	Rafael Cepeda
Sinaloa	Diego Redo	Celso Gaxiola-Rojo	José Rentería
Sonora	Alberto Cubillas	José María Maytorena	José María Maytorena
Tabasco	Policarpo Valenzuela	Manuel Mestre Ghiglliazza	Manuel M. Ghiglliazza
Tamaulipas	Juan B. Castelló	Espiridión Lara	Matías Guerra
Tlaxcala	Próspero Cahuantizi	Agustin Sánchez	Antonio Hidalgo
Veracruz	Teodoro Dehesa	Eliezar Espinosa	Francisco Lagos Cházaro
Yucatán	Luis C. Curiel	José María Pino Suárez	José María Pino Suárez
Zacatecas	Francisco de P. Zarate	J. Guadalupe González	Guadalupe González

Note: Several states and territories had more than one provisional governor and several had more than one elected governor in this period. The purpose of this table is to show that the turnover at the top was quite thorough.

Appendix D

The Vice Presidential Election
October 1, 1911

State	*Candidate*				
	Pino Suárez	*De La Barra*	*Vázquez Gómez*	*Iglesias Calderón*	*Others*
Aguascalientes	142	45	0	0	0
Campeche	No returns				
Coahuila	268	0	179	0	0
Colima	92	21	0	1	0
Chiapas	266	61	99	0	0
Chihuahua	206	0	151	24	1
Durango	427	84	13	1	0
Guanajuato	353	710	40	2	11
Guerrero	No returns				
Hidalgo	328	96	76	51	2
Jalisco	190	1,265	96	0	0
México	404	732	135	4	4
Michoacán	195	674	354	11	0

Morelos	109	6	134	0	0
Nuevo León	525	6	134	0	2
Oaxaca	350	148	488	1	92
Puebla	450	189	132	0	0
Querétaro	205	156	4	0	0
San Luis Potosí	361	58	32	0	0
Sinaloa	218	3	16	0	0
Sonora	194	8	31	0	0
Tabasco	169	3	5	32	0
Tamaulipas	187	0	153	0	0
Tlaxcala	177	67	32	0	0
Veracruz	917	65	301	8	2
Yucatán	561	0	1	0	0
Zacatecas	226	314	104	1	0
Federal District	859	247	79	1	0
Tepic	108	92	3	0	0
Baja California N.	No returns				
Baja California S.	No returns				
Total	*8,566*	*5,052*	*2,680*	*145*	*114*

Appendix E

De la Barra's Farewell Address November 4, 1911

I have been motivated in rendering this report by my desire to assume full responsibility for my acts and the results of my provisional administration at the bar of public opinion.

I have been out of touch for many years with the politics of our country, years when my services to the nation were of a different order. I was called upon to assume the direction of national affairs at a moment of extraordinary difficulty, when a government which had been thought to be impregnable had suddenly fallen and when the new regime had not yet acquired the cohesion and strength necessary for the establishment of tranquility and social order.

I am not affiliated with any party but have been in accord with the two main principles of the revolution—namely, the single-term constitutional reform and the effectiveness of the popular suffrage. The latter is an essential condition in a nation living under democratic institutions, and the former is a necessary safeguard against the perpetuation of personal regimes. I encountered grave difficulties in mustering out the revolutionary forces. In the state of Morelos the problem of the disarmament and the dispersal of the revolutionary forces met from the start with more serious and perplexing difficulties than in most of the other states in the federation. For, although the men in arms seemed disposed to return peacefully to their homes, they at first began to adopt covertly and then afterwards openly an attitude of defiance which soon degenerated into a formidable movement of brigandage. Confronted with this movement and giving heed to the urgent requests of a large group of prominent residents of the state of Morelos, I decided to send to that state a body of troops with clear and categorical instructions to proceed vigorously against the marauders.

In these circumstances, Señor Francisco I. Madero, influenced by a sentiment with which no one certainly would reproach him, offered spontaneously to exercise his personal good offices in the conflict, in the hope that his ascendancy as chief of the revolution might obviate further bloodshed. This proposal no humane person would have rejected but, unfortunately, his laudable efforts did not produce the desired result; and as the rebels not only did not make their submission but continued to commit excesses of every kind, I, on the expiration of the period of forty-eight hours allowed them for unconditional surrender, gave orders for the initiation of an immediate and vigorous campaign against them.

This campaign was started at once. I can assure you that the orders transmitted to the officer in command of the operations all passed through the proper channels and that no important decision was reached without having been previously discussed at a cabinet council.

As to the results of these operations, the report of the commander in chief will inform you of the difficulties which have prevented the subjugation or extermination of the marauding bands. Moving in small groups, the outlaws rarely venture on a serious engagement with the regular troops, but avail themselves of the character of the country with which they are perfectly familiar, to scatter when pursued only to assemble again a little while later. Thus the campaign has become one requiring the services of the rural police and must be finished by them.

The question has been asked: How is it that a campaign which seems simple has lasted so long?

The government placed in command of the expedition an officer of repute and gave him the forces which he considered necessary. The instructions communicated to him were clear and categorical, and the events which have transpired to this day prove conclusively that a policy of repression was necessary for the extirpation of lawlessness and the establishment of a definite peace. The leader of the seditious movement made himself popular among the rude inhabitants of the state by promises of the distribution of land, regardless of the rights of property; and by these and other means he worked on the passions of the humbler classes, who do not understand that the economic situation of their state, like that of other states, can not and must not be transformed by deeds of violence and methods contrary to the law.

The promises made by the revolution with respect to the agrarian question have aroused great expectations among the peasant class, who supposed that on the inauguration of the new government they would enter into possession of the promised lands, without understanding that this is a problem that must be solved in accordance with the law and subject to a carefully matured plan. It is probable, also, that many of the individuals who are in arms against the government have been unwilling to lay them down in the hope, which I am sure is unwarranted (for I am well acquainted with the sense of justice of the president elect), that when the new administration comes in, they will not have to answer to the judicial authorities for crimes of the common order which they know they have committed.

But as you will see, the government has acted with firmness, in accordance with its rational plan. It has always kept in mind its duty to avoid, so far as possible and as is consistent with acclaims of justice and the principle of authority, the shedding of blood and fratricidal encounters. In the case of the state of Morelos, however, more blood has been shed by the rebels in their raids and marauding excursions than by the federales in repelling the attacks of the outlaws.

The facts which I have just narrated are borne out by the documents accompanying this report. I have only to add that public tranquility is virtually reestablished in the state of Morelos, according to recent reports from the provisional governor.

Our government has also intervened in the affairs of other states such as Sinaloa, Aguascalientes, and Chiapas. In all instances, I proceeded on the principle of respecting as far as possible the sovereignty of the states, using my good offices to bring the contending parties together and only taking overt action when it was imperatively demanded by the paramount necessity of maintaining or restoring public order.

The agrarian problem has been at the bottom of all of Mexico's great political upheavals. I cannot flatter myself that, during the short period of my provisional administration, I was able to settle so momentous and complex a question. But I have made a start in that direction by the creation of the agrarian commission; and some day, when the great desideratum has been attained and each square foot of the national territory capable of tillage yields its wealth of golden grain for the sustenance of its inhabitants, perhaps the modest start which I have given to the great transformation of agricultural ownership will be remembered with appreciation.

The labor problem was the result of the industrial evolution of the country in recent years, and to solve it I sent to congress a bill for the establishment of a labor bureau. The object is to bring about due equilibrium between the supply of labor and the demand, to put a stop to abuses committed by contractors of labor, to put factories under official supervision so that the health and lives of the operators shall be protected, to regulate the employment of women and children, to bring about the establishment of arbitral boards which will endeavor to adjust disputes between capital and labor, and, in fine, to do everything possible to harmonize the interest and views of those two essential factors of human progress.

The recent elections were conducted without the slightest pressure from the federal government, and if any frauds and irregularities took place they were due to circumstances beyond my control. It is up to congress and the courts to pass on these frauds and irregularities according to the dictates of conscience and patriotism.

I have faithfully adhered to the declaration which I made upon assuming the provisional presidency, viz.: that I would on no account be a candidate for the presidency or the vice presidency for the next term. I withstood open solicitations as well as covert insinuations to which it is very hard for any man who even for a day is elevated to a position of great power not to lend a willing ear. But to all I have returned the same answer, resolutely refusing to depart from duty and set forth by my declarations to the nation and by my own self-respect, the duty namely of turning over the presidency to the candidate designated by the popular will.

The financial situation of the country is satisfactory. In the first three months of the current fiscal year, import duties and the proceeds of the stamp tax show only a falling off of little more than 2 million pesos as compared with the corresponding year 1910 to 1911, when the receipts from those sources were exceptionally high owing to the activity consequent to the centennial celebration. As compared with the corresponding period of 1909 to 1910, the falling off is only 600,000 pesos. It may therefore be hoped that as soon as business resumes its natural development, the slight reduction will be recovered.

In view of these considerations, I have sent to congress a bill proposing additions of 3 million pesos for the current budget of expenditures, feeling assured that these new disbursements will not affect the nation's financial stability.

I have also sent to congress a bill empowering the president to take from the reserves the sum of 12 million pesos for indispensable expenditures such as the increase of pay to the army, the creation of new corps of rurales, and the mustering out of the remaining revolutionary forces. But as some items of expenditure already voted are about to be canceled, in case congress acts favorably on my suggestion, the net amount to be taken from the reserves will only be 5,800,000 pesos.

The treasury reserves now amount to 48 million.

I conclude by saying that in the difficult circumstances which followed after the revolution, I regret that the executive power had not come into the hands of one better qualified to exercise it than I. I have endeavored, however, to enlist the cooperation of all good citizens and to give ear to all wise counsel.

Convinced as I am that the best guide of a ruler who aspires to fulfill his duty is the free discussion of his acts, I have afforded the widest scope to criticism and censure without seeking the interested support of any organ of the press, and toward the press as a whole I have acted with the consideration to which this important factor in the formation of public opinion is entitled. I consider that one of the needs of the present time is a new free press which affords ample guarantees for the expression of opinion within the limits marked by public order and respect for public life.

Some have accused me of a lack of firmness, but I can assure you that I have never lacked firmness when it has been a question of obeying the law and causing it to be obeyed. As for those who advocate the immoderate use of radical measures, I can tell them that a greater amount of firmness is needed in restraining oneself when circumstances seem to warrant extreme action than in having recourse to such action for the sake of an immediate result. I will say openly that I am opposed to the undue and unnecessary shedding of blood, and that if this be a fault I unhesitatingly submit myself to your verdict and to the verdict of history. I believe in the law and am convinced that every violation of the law, whatever may be the motives invoked to justify it, is fraught with perilous consequences for the future. I have never allowed any pretext to betray me into transgressing its precepts.

My government has labored under the disadvantage of being a transitory one and a government of compromise. I felt it incumbent upon myself to avoid adding to the elements of dissension and conflict. Professing the liberal creed as I understand it—namely, a respect for the rights of all—I still believe that the principles of freedom must be limited by the paramount necessities of national safety and social conservation.

I conclude with the earnest desire and the consoling hope that we may all be united in one sentiment and one sense of duty, that we may rise above dissensions and animosities, and that we may harmonize our efforts and our wills and at last rest our throbbing brows on the loving bosom of la Patria, our mother.

Abbreviations

AARD	Archivo Alfredo Robles Domínguez
ABR	Archivo de Bernardo Reyes
AdlB	Archivo Francisco León de la Barra
ADRF	Archives du Ministère des Affaires Etrangères
AFGG	Archivo de Federico González Garza
AFIM	Archivo de Francisco I. Madero
AFVG	Archivo de Francisco Vázquez Gómez
AGA	Archivo Particular de Genaro Amezcua
AGM	Archivo Particular de Gildardo Magaña
AHDN	Archivo Histórico de la Defensa Nacional
AJYL	Archivo de José Yves Limantour
ARE	Archivo Particular de Roque Estrada
AREM	Archivo de la Secretaría de Relaciones Exteriores de México
BNAM	Biblioteca Nacional, Archivo Madero
CPD	Colección Porfirio Díaz
DHRM	Isidro Fabela, ed., *Documentos históricos de la revolución mexicana*
FCP	Francisco Carvajal Papers
FIM	Francisco I. Madero
FLdlB	Francisco León de la Barra
FO	Foreign Office Reports, Great Britain
HAHR	*Hispanic American Historical Review*
JMMP	José María Maytorena Papers
JVEP	Jorge Vera Estañol Papers
OC	Fausto Orozco Archive
RDS	Records of the Department of State
UNAM	Universidad Nacional Autónoma de México

Notes

Introduction

1. Gregorio Ponce de León, *El interinato presidencial de 1911* (Mexico: Imprenta y Fototipia de la Secretaría de Fomento, 1912). There are four studies of de la Barra, none of them recent. Ponce de León volunteered to write an official history for pay, although he never received his money from the Madero government. Three graduate students have written about portions of de la Barra's life: Amaya Garritz Ruiz, "La presidencia interina de Francisco León de la Barra: Política interina" (master's thesis, Universidad Nacional Autónoma de México [UNAM], 1965); James Planck, "The Ad Interim Regime of Francisco León de la Barra" (master's thesis, University of the Americas, 1966); Virginia Hernández-González, "Guia comentada del archivo documental Francisco León de la Barra, fondo condumex" (master's thesis, UNAM, 1978). Properly, de la Barra should be referred to as León de la Barra. Almost all sources, both English and Spanish, use the form de la Barra, and so I have adopted it. Hereafter in the notes, he is referred to as FLdlB.

2. Penelope Lively, *According to Mark* (Harmondsworth, England: Penguin Books, 1984), 212.

Chapter 1

1. *Mexican Herald*, July 3, 1911; Edith O'Shaughnessy, *Intimate Pages of Mexican History* (New York: George H. Doran Company, 1920), 105.

2. Richard J. Salvucci, *Textiles and Capitalism in Mexico: An Economic History of the Obrajes, 1539–1840* (Princeton: Princeton University Press, 1987), 89–93; John C. Super, "Querétaro Obrajes: Industry and Society in Provincial Mexico, 1600–1810," *Hispanic American Historical Review* (hereafter cited as *HAHR*) 56 (May 1976): 197–216; Robert Potash, *The Mexican Government and Industrial Development in the Early Republic: The Banco de Avío* (Amherst: University of Massachusetts Press, 1983).

3. Hugh Hamill, *The Hidalgo Revolt: Prelude to Mexican Independence* (Gainesville: University of Florida Press, 1966).

4. William H. Beezley, *Judas at the Jockey Club and Other Episodes of Porfirian Mexico* (Lincoln: University of Nebraska Press, 1987); Jeffrey D. Needell, *A Tropical Belle Epoque: Elite Culture and Society in Turn-of-the-Century Río de Janeiro* (New York: Cambridge University Press, 1987).

5. Luis León de la Barra, *Memorias de la Academia Mexicana de Genealogía y Heráldica*, vol. 1, no. 1 (Mexico: Private Printing, 1945), 87–109. See also idem, *Historia de un linaje* (Mexico: Editorial Luis Foja, 1958).

6. Luis León de la Barra, *Genealogía y Heráldica*, 109–11; Diane Balmori and Stuart Voss, *Notable Family Networks in Latin America* (Chicago: University of Chicago Press, 1984), 43.

7. Bernabé León de la Barra to an unnamed brother, February 13, 1841, and July 5, 1841, Archivo Francisco León de la Barra, Centro de Estudios de la Historia de México, Mexico City, folder 1, #1and #2. Hereafter, this archive, which contains de la Barra's personal papers, is cited as AdlB, followed by the number of the folder and the document number within the folder. Emilio Lynch Zaldívar (Francisco León de la Barra's uncle) to FLdlB, January 2, 1894, AdlB, 1, #17; Leslie Bethel, ed., *Chile since Independence* (New York: Cambridge University Press, 1993).

8. Bernabé León de la Barra to Juan Francisco León de la Barra, October 7, 1861, AdlB, 1, #4.

9. Emilio Lynch Zaldívar to FLdlB, January 2, 1894, AdlB, 1, #17.

10. Albert H. Carr, *The World and William Walker* (New York: Harper and Row, 1963).

11. Jaime Rodríguez O., *The Emergence of Spanish America: Vicente Rocafuerte and Spanish Americanism, 1808–1835* (Berkeley and Los Angeles: University of California Press, 1975).

12. Emilio Lynch Zaldívar to FLdlB, January 2, 1894, AdlB, 1, #17.

13. Laurens B. Perry, *Juárez and Díaz: Machine Politics in Mexico* (De Kalb: Northern Illinois University Press, 1978), 415–21; Daniel Cosío Villegas, ed., *Historia moderna de México: La república restaurada*, 9 vols. (Mexico: Editorial Hermes, 1955), 865–70.

14. Manuel de la Barra Lira (another uncle) to FLdlB, June 1, 1911, Archivo Particular de Gildardo Magaña, UNAM, Mexico City, box 31, Exp. B-3, 237. Hereafter, this archive, which mostly contains de la Barra's presidential papers, is cited as AGM, followed by the box number, the number, and the document number. Cuahtémoc González Pacheco, *Capital extranjero en la selva de Chiapas, 1863–1982* (Mexico City: UNAM, 1983), 120; François-Xavier Guerra, *Le Mexique: De l'ancien régime à la révolution*, 2 vols. (Paris: Editions L'Harmattan, 1985).

15. Roderic Ai Camp, *Political Recruitment across Two Centuries: Mexico, 1884–1991* (Austin: University of Texas Press, 1995), 45–52, 164.

16. Charles Hale, *The Transformation of Liberalism in Late Nineteenth-Century Mexico* (Princeton: Princeton University Press, 1989), 140–203; Mílada Bazant, *Historia de la educación durante el Porfiriato* (Mexico: El Colegio de México, 1993), 166–71.

17. Daniel Cosío Villegas, ed., *Historia moderna de México: El Porfiriato: La vida social* (Mexico: Editorial Hermes, 1965), 4:607–26; Clementina Díaz y Ovando, *La Escuela Nacional Preparatoria*, 2 vols. (Mexico City: UNAM, 1972), 1:200, 2:365.

18. Isidro Fabela to FLdlB, July 10, 1911, AGM, 9, Exp. F-1, #10; Francisco R. Pradillo to FLdlB, September 30, 1911, AGM, 8, Exp. P–5, #31; Domingo Palacio to FLdlB, December 3, 1911, AdlB, 3, #258; Isidro Fabela to FLdlB, July 11, 1911, AGM, 9, Exp. F-1, #14.

19. Manuel Castilla Echánove, *Apuntes para la biografía del Sr. Don Francisco León de la Barra y Quijano, presidente interino de la república* (Mexico City: Imprenta Universal, 1911), 6.

20. FLdlB, *El sistema de reciprocidad en el derecho civil mexicano* (Mexico: Oficina de la Secretaría de Fomento, 1887).

21. FLdlB, *Estudio sobre la ley mexicano de extradición* (Mexico: Imprenta del Gobierno Federal, 1897).

22. FLdlB, *La neutralidad: Derechos y obligaciones de las naciones neutrales* (Mexico: Tipografía T. González Sucesores, 1898). This volume was revised, translated, and reprinted as *Les neutres et le droit international* (Paris: Librairie de la Société du Recueil Sirey, 1918).

23. See Castilla Echánove, *Biografía*, 6. De la Barra mentions his original appointment in his unpublished memoirs, "Algunas páginas de la historia de México," AdlB, 25, #2923, p. 19. See also Percy N. Furber, *I Took Chances, from Windjammers to Jets* (Leicester: E. Backus, 1953), 94–109; *Mexican Herald*, November 14, 1908.

24. Garritz Ruiz, "La presidencia interina," 1. Daniel Cosío Villegas, *Historia Moderna de México: El Porfiriato: La vida política interior*, vol. 9, pt. 2, 842–61.

25. Walter N. Breymann, "The Científicos: Critics of the Díaz Regime, 1892–1903," *Proceedings of the Arkansas Academy of Science* 7 (1954): 91–97.

26. Charles A. Hale, "Scientific Politics and the Continuity of Liberalism in Mexico, 1867–1910," in *Proceedings of the Fifth International Conference of Mexicanists* (Austin: University of Texas Press, 1982), 139–52. FLdlB, *La Inmigración en la República Argentina* (Buenos Aires: Companía Sud-Americana de Billetes de Banco, 1904); Jeffrey M. Pilcher, *Que Vivan los tamales: Food and the Making of Mexican Identity* (Albuquerque: University of New Mexico Press, 1998), 84–86.

27. Peter V. N. Henderson, *Félix Díaz, the Porfirians, and the Mexican Revolution* (Lincoln: University of Nebraska Press, 1981), 19.

28. Pierre Py, *Francia y la revolución mexicana* (Mexico: Fondo de Cultura Económica, 1991), 23–31. See also Stephen Haber, *Industry and Underdevelopment: The Industrialization of Mexico, 1890–1940* (Stanford: Stanford University Press, 1989).

29. *Mexican Herald*, February 14, 1911, and March 26, 1911. See also FLdlB to Porfirio Díaz, February 12, 1911, Colección General Porfirio Díaz, hereafter cited as CPD, reel 368, Leg. 70, #3110, University of the Americas, microfilm, Cholula, Mexico. Balmori and Voss, *Notable Family Networks*, 17; Michael Johns, *The City of Mexico in the Age of Díaz* (Austin: University of Texas Press, 1997), 17–21, 102–3.

30. Luis León de la Barra, *Genealógia y Heráldica*, 114. One stepson, noted writer Alfonso Alamán, as well as one stepdaughter survived.

31. FLdlB, "Algunas páginas," AdlB 25, #2923, pp. 26–34. *Le Petit Marseillaise*, March 15, 1923, in AdlB, 4, #390. The quotation is from Hale, *Transformation of Liberalism*, 152.

32. FLdlB, "Algunas páginas," AdlB 25, #2923, pp. 22–24. Certificates for the Imperial Order of the Double Dragon from China and the Cavalieri di Gran Croce (Italy) are in AdlB, 1, #14, #23, #46, and #63.

33. Calvin DeArmond Davis, *The United States and the First Hague Peace Conference* (Ithaca: Cornell University Press, 1962), 95; David Zook, *Zarumilla-Marañón: The Ecuador-Peru Dispute* (New York: Bookman Associates, 1964).

34. Calvin DeArmond Davis, *The United States and the Second Hague Peace Conference: American Diplomacy and International Organization, 1899–1914* (Durham, NC: Duke University Press, 1975), 271–75; FLdlB, *La*

igualdad jurídica de los estados, base del derecho internacional moderno (Mexico: Eusebio Gómez de la Puente, 1912).

35. FLdlB, *La igualdad jurídica.* See also de la Barra's speech to the American Peace and Arbitration League, March 22, 1910, Archivo Histórico de la Secretaría de Relaciones Exteriores de México, Mexico City (hereafter cited as AREM), FLdlB, Su Expediente Personal, 5 vols., L-E 419, 161–65.

36. *Second International Conference of American States* (The Report) (Washington, DC: Government Printing Office, 1902); *Report of the Delegates of the United States to the Third International Conference of American States* (Washington, DC: Government Printing Office, 1907).

37. Ignacio Mariscal to FLdlB, July 10, 1902, AREM, L-E 418, 9. See also Mariscal to FLdlB, May 30, 1902, AdlB, 1, #29; Ingrid E. Fey, "First Tango in Paris: Latin Americans in Turn-of-the-Century France, 1880–1920" (Ph.D. diss., UCLA, 1996), 307–8.

38. James T. Scobie, *Buenos Aires: Plaza to Suburb, 1870–1910* (Oxford: Oxford University Press, 1974); idem, *Revolution on the Pampas: A Social History of Argentine Wheat* (Austin: University of Texas Press, 1964); Douglas W. Richmond, *Carlos Pellegrini and the Crisis of Argentine Elites, 1880–1916* (New York: Praeger, 1989).

39. FLdlB, "Algunas páginas," AdlB 25, #2923, p. 39; FLdlB to Ignacio Mariscal, May 27, 1904, AREM, L-E 418, 86.

40. FLdlB to Ignacio Mariscal, April 7, 1905, AREM, L-E 418, 149; FLdlB to Ignacio Mariscal, June 26, 1905, AREM, L-E 418, 163; FLdlB to Manuel Zamacona é Inclán, April 17, 1911, AGM, 25, exp. 4, #210–13; Henry Lane Wilson, *Diplomatic Episodes in Mexico, Belgium, and Chile* (New York: Doubleday and Page, 1927).

41. FLdlB, "Algunas páginas," AdlB 25, #2923, pp. 40–45.

42. Porfirio Díaz to FLdlB, December 8, 1908, AdlB, 1, #55; Ignacio Mariscal to FLdlB, November 1908, AdlB, 1, #49. Creel served as governor of Chihuahua simultaneously and, as a consequence, spent only one month in Washington during his two-year ambassadorship. W. Dirk Raat, *Revoltosos: Mexico's Rebels in the United States, 1903–1923* (College Station: Texas A&M University Press, 1981), 178.

43. FLdlB, "Un situacíon dramática en mi carrera diplomática," unpublished manuscript, AdlB, 25, #2978.

44. Elihu Root to Ignacio Mariscal, November 14, 1908, AREM, L-E 418, 195.

45. FLdlB, "Mi labor como embajador en Washington, 1908–1911," unpublished manuscript, AdlB, 1, #89; idem, "Un situacíon dramática."

46. Sheldon Liss, *A Century of Disagreement: The Chamizal Conflict, 1864–1964* (Washington, DC: American University Press, 1965), 21–22; Norris Hundley, *Dividing the Waters: A Century of Controversy between the United States and Mexico* (Berkeley and Los Angeles: University of California Press, 1966); *Mexican Herald,* January 26, 1911; FLdlB to José Yves Limantour, April 8, 1911, AGM, 25, Exp. 4, #80–83.

47. James Morton Callahan, *American Foreign Policy in Mexican Relations* (New York: Macmillan Company, 1932), 465.

48. Cosío Villegas, *Historia moderna de México: El Porfiriato: La vida política exterior,* vol. 5, pt. 1, 699–700, 726–28; pt. 2, 311–14. FLdlB to Porfirio Díaz, January 12, 1910, CPD, legajo 34, reel 266, #019968; FLdlB to Porfirio Díaz, November 5, 1910, CPD, Leg. 25, reel 276, #017073; FLdlB to José

Yves Limantour, January 5, 1910, Archivo José Yves Limantour, Centro de Estudios de la Historia de México, Mexico City, folder 2, reel 65 (hereafter cited as AJYL).

49. FLdlB, "Mi labor como embajador," AdlB, 1, #89; Victoriano Salado Alvarez, *Memorias*, 2 vols. (Mexico: E.d.i.a.p. S.A., 1946), 2:197–206; FLdlB to Porfirio Díaz, August 24, 1909, CPD, Leg. 34, reel 263, #014844.

50. FLdlB to Manuel Zamacona e Inclán, April 17, 1911, AGM, 25, exp. 4, 210–13; FLdlB to José Yves Limantour, January 24, 1910, AJYL, folder 2, reel 65.

51. Frances M. Huntington-Wilson, *Memoirs of an Ex-Diplomat* (Boston: Bruce Humphreys, 1945).

52. *Mexican Herald*, January 8, 1911; FLdlB to Ignacio Mariscal and Enrique Creel, AREM, L-E 419, 143–145, 155; FLdlB to Porfirio Díaz, December 12, 1910, CPD, Leg. 35, reel 277, #019425; FLdlB to José Yves Limantour, February 7, 1910, AJYL, folder 2, reel 65.

53. Camp, *Political Recruitment*, 43.

54. Cosío Villegas, *Vida politica exterior*, vol. 5, pt. 2, xxix.

55. FLdlB to W. L. Milner, August 25, 1909, AREM, L-E 419, 106; FLdlB to Ignacio Mariscal, August 27, 1909, AREM, L-E 419, 105.

56. O'Shaughnessy, *Intimate Pages*, 91–92.

Chapter 2

1. Adrián Aguirre Benavides, *Errores de Madero* (Mexico City: Editorial Jus, 1980), 42; Jesús Romero Flores, *Anales históricos de la revolución mexicana* (Mexico: Ediciones Encuadernables, 1939), 202; Stanley R. Ross, *Francisco I. Madero: Apostle of Mexican Democracy* (New York: Columbia University Press, 1955), 155, 159, 170–71.

2. Alan Knight, *The Mexican Revolution*, 2 vols. (New York: Cambridge University Press, 1986), 1:202; William Weber Johnson, *Heroic Mexico* (New York: Doubleday, 1968), 56–58.

3. Ronald Atkin, *Revolution: Mexico, 1910–1920* (New York: The John Day Company, 1970), 43.

4. Charles C. Cumberland, *The Mexican Revolution: Genesis under Madero* (Austin: University of Texas Press, 1952), 47–48.

5. *Mexican Herald*, January 15, 1911.

6. Ross, *Francisco I. Madero*, 74–109; Cumberland, *Mexican Revolution*, 69–113; and José C. Valadés, *Imaginación y realidad de Francisco I. Madero*, 2 vols. (Mexico: Antiguo Librería Robredo, 1960), 1:213–75.

7. Cole Blasier, "Studies of Social Revolution: Origins in Mexico, Bolivia, and Cuba," *Latin American Research Review* 2, no. 3 (1967): 28–64, 31, 37–38.

8. *Palsgraaf v. Long Island R.R. Co.*, 248 NY 339 (1928).

9. Jerry Knudsen, "When Did Francisco I. Madero Decide on Revolution?" *The Americas* 30 (April 1974): 529–34.

10. Ross, *Francisco I. Madero*, 125–27. Michael C. Meyer, *Mexican Rebel: Pascual Orozco and the Mexican Revolution, 1910–1915* (Lincoln: University of Nebraska Press, 1967); Friedrich Katz, *The Life and Times of Pancho Villa* (Stanford: Stanford University Press, 1998), 60–61, 76–77.

11. *Arizona Republican*, December 7, 1910, in AREM, L-E 617R, Leg. 13, 474, 479; *Washington Post*, December 4, 1911, in AREM, L-E 617, Leg. 13,

503; Francisco Vázquez Gómez's interview in *El Tiempo*, February 26, 1911; Juan Sánchez Azcona to Federico González Garza, December 3, 1910, Archivo Federico González Garza, Centro de Estudios de la Historia de México (hereafter cited as AFGG), 12, #1158; Gustavo Madero to his wife, February 22, 1911, in Gustavo Madero, *Gustavo A. Madero: Epistolario* (Mexico: Editorial Diana, 1991), 133–35; Katz, *Villa*, 78.

12. Paul Vanderwood, "Response to Revolt: The Counter-Guerrilla Strategy of Porfirio Díaz," *HAHR* 56 (November 1976): 551–79; Robert Alexius, "The Army and Politics in Porfirian Mexico" (Ph.D. diss., University of Texas-Austin, 1976), 307–21.

13. Cumberland, *Mexican Revolution*, 137. Ambassador Wilson to Philander Knox, October 31, 1910, Records of the Department of State Relating to the Internal Affairs of Mexico, 1910–1929, microcopy no. 274, National Archives, Washington, DC (hereafter cited as RDS), reel 10, 812.00/355; British Minister T. B. Hohler to Sir Edward Grey, February 16, 1911, Foreign Office Reports, 1911, British Public Record Office, microfilm, Bancroft Library, University of California-Berkeley (hereafter cited as FO), reel 14, 371.1146/8189.

14. Juan Sánchez Azcona to Federico González Garza, December 3, 1910, AFGG, 12, #1158.

15. Francisco Vázquez Gómez to Alfonso Madero, February 25, 1911, Archivo Francisco Vázquez Gómez, Morris Library, Southern Illinois University, Carbondale, Illinois (hereafter cited as AFVG), box 4, #388. This letter can also be found in Archivo Madero, Biblioteca Nacional, University of Texas, Austin, microfilm (hereafter cited as BNAM), box 4, #2100. The document also appears in AFGG, 14, #1316. Venustiano Carranza to Francisco Vázquez Gómez, April 16, 1911, AFVG, box 8, #454.

16. Ricardo García Granados, *Por qué y como cayó Porfirio Díaz* (Mexico: Andrés Botas e Hijos, 1928), 172–73; Iñigo Noriega to Porfirio Díaz, February 25, 1911, CPD, Leg. 36, reel 280, #3903–3910. Francisco Vázquez Gómez, *Memorias políticas, 1909–1913* (Mexico: Imprenta Mundial, 1933), 79–83.

17. John Mason Hart, *Revolutionary Mexico: The Coming and the Process of the Mexican Revolution* (Berkeley and Los Angeles: University of California Press, 1987), 247–49. For a contemporary who agreed, see Luis Lara Pardo, *De Porfirio Díaz a Francisco I. Madero: La sucesión dictatorial de 1911* (New York: Polyglot Publishing and Commercial Company, 1912), 181–94.

18. FLdlB to Department of State, November 19, 1910, RDS, reel 10, 812.00/476; Louis James Secrest, "The End of the Porfiriato: The Collapse of the Díaz Government, 1910–1911" (Ph.D. diss., University of New Mexico, 1970), 96–127.

19. Philander C. Knox to FLdlB, December 1, 1910, RDS, reel 10, 812.00/499; State Department to FLdlB, January 24, 1911, RDS, reel 10, 812.00/633.

20. Philander C. Knox to FLdlB, December 29, 1910, AREM, L-E 625, 1 Leg., 118–20; FLdlB to Gonzalo Fernández, Mexican consul in St. Louis, April 27, 1911, AGM, 25, Exp. 4, #280, and FLdlB to Enrique Creel, April 18, 1911, AGM, 25, Exp. 4, #217; Raat, *Revoltosos*, 228–40.

21. Philander Knox to William Howard Taft, March 15, 1911, Philander Knox Papers, Library of Congress, Manuscript Division, Washington, DC (hereafter cited as Knox Papers), container 13.

22. FLdlB to Enrique Creel, January 22, 1911, in Isidro Fabela, ed., *Documentos históricos de la revolución mexicana,* 27 vols. (hereafter cited as DHRM) vol. 5, #115; Joaquín Casasús to Enrique Creel, January 28, 1911, DHRM, vol. 5, #128.

23. Knight, *Mexican Revolution,* 1:151.

24. Edward Berbusse, "Neutrality Diplomacy of the United States and Mexico, 1910–1911," *The Americas* 12 (January 1956): 265–83.

25. Berta Ulloa, "Las relaciones Méxicanos-Norteamericanas, 1910–1911," *Historia Mexicana* 15 (July 1965): 25–46; idem, *La revolución intervenida: Relaciones diplomáticas entre México y los Estados Unidos, 1910–1914* (Mexico: El Colegio de México, 1971); Guerra, *Le Mexique,* 2:275–76.

26. Peter V. N. Henderson, *Mexican Exiles in the Borderlands, 1910–1913,* Southwestern Studies (El Paso: Texas Western Press, 1979).

27. José Yves Limantour to Porfirio Díaz, December 27, 1911, CPD, Leg. 35, reel 277, #018992-96.

28. Francisco Vázquez Gómez to Gustavo Madero, March 9, 1911, AFVG, box 4, #459.

29. Bernardo Reyes to Alberto Guajardo, March 5, 1911, AFVG, box 4, #413.

30. *Mexican Herald,* February 21, 1911; Atkin, *Revolution,* 59. See Wilson to William Taft, March 24, 1911, William H. Taft Papers, Library of Congress, Manuscript Division, Washington, DC (hereafter cited as Taft Papers), reel 125, series 3, no number.

31. William Howard Taft to Philander C. Knox, March 11, 1911, Knox Papers, container 13; W. H. Taft to Hart Lyman, March 27, 1911, Taft Papers, reel 506, series 8, vol. 24, #416; W. H. Taft to Theodore Roosevelt, March 27, 1911, Taft Papers, reel 506, series 8, vol. 24, #208; and W. H. Taft to General Leonard Wood, March 12, 1911, Taft Papers, reel 506, series 8, vol. 24, #142.

32. William Howard Taft to General Wood, March 12, 1911, RDS, reel 11, 812.00/963A; FLdlB to Philander Knox, March 14, 1911, RDS, reel 11, 812.00/965; *Mexican Herald,* March 21, 1911; Walter Scholes and Marie Scholes, *The Foreign Policy of the Taft Administration* (Columbia: University of Missouri Press, 1966), 85–86; W. H. Taft to Will Worthington, March 20, 1911, Taft Papers, reel 506, series 8, vol. 24, #169; W. H. Taft to Alvee Adee, March 12, 1911, Taft Papers, reel 506, series 8, vol. 24, #216; FLdlB to Porfirio Díaz, March 9, 1911, CPD, Leg. 36, reel 281, #004761; FLdlB to José Yves Limantour, March 9, 1911 and March 11, 1911, AJYL, Folder 2, reel 65.

33. FLdlB to Manuel Zamacona é Inclán, AGM, 25, Exp. 4, #49–50, repeated in his letter on April 17, 1911, AGM, 25 Exp. 4, 210–13; FLdlB to José Yves Limantour, February 19, 1917, AdlB, 7, #695; Alvey Adee to FLdlB, March 13, 1911, Knox Papers, container 13; José R. del Castillo, *Historia de la revolución social de México: Primera etapa* (Mexico: Private Printing, 1915), 282–84.

34. Francisco Vázquez Gómez to Federico González Garza, April 14, 1911, AFGG, 16, #1525; FLdlB to Manuel Zamacona é Inclán, April 12, 1911, AGM, 25, Exp. 4, #196–198; Jorge Fernando Iturribarría, "Limantour y la caída de Porfirio Díaz," *Historia Mexicana* 10 (October–December 1960): 243–81; idem, "La versión de Limantour," *Historia Mexicana* 16 (January–March 1967): 382–418; Limantour to Francisco Vázquez Gómez, October 26, 1911, AFVG, box 23, #363; Manuel Amieva to Francisco Vázquez Gómez, April 14, 1933, AFVG, box 47, folder 6, #3835.

35. Juan Sánchez Azcona, *La etapa maderista de la revolución mexicana* (Mexico: Biblioteca del Instituto Nacional de Estudios Históricos de la Revolución Mexicana, 1960), 43, 45.

36. José Yves Limantour, *Apuntes sobre mi vida pública* (Mexico: Editorial Porrúa, 1965), 243; FLdlB to Victoriano Salado Alvarez, August 14, 1931, AdlB, 19, #2333; Salado Alvarez, *Memorias,* 2:307–9.

37. See interview with FLdlB in *Independent,* March 16, 1911, in AFVG, box 5, folder 1, no number; Jorge Vera Estañol to FLdlB, April 29, 1911, AFM 23, Exp. 7, #47; FLdlB to Vera Estañol, May 1, 1911, AGM, 25, Exp. 4, #372.

38. "Desde Tierras de Francia," in AdlB, 8, #748; Emeterio de la Garza to FLdlB, April 3, 1911, AGM, 32, Exp. 1, BIS, #153; O'Shaughnessy, *Intimate Pages,* 94–97; James Bryce to Sir Edward Grey, March 28, 1911, FO, file 1573, reel 14, 371.1146 / 12632.

39. Limantour, *Apuntes,* 213–15.

40. Francisco Vázquez Gómez's notes, undated, AFVG, box 4, #00490. See also idem, *Memorias políticas,* 96–101.

41. *Mexican Herald,* April 2, 1911, and March 16, 1911; Atkin, *Revolution,* 61; Knight, *Mexican Revolution,* 1:202; Henry Lane Wilson to Philander C. Knox, April 26, 1911, RDS, reel 12, 812.00 / 1543; Venustiano Carranza to Francisco Vázquez Gómez, March 9, 1911, AFVG, box 4, #457; FLdlB to José Yves Limantour, April 8, 1913, AJYL, Folder 2, reel 65.

42. Federico González Garza to Juan Sánchez Azcona, April 3, 1911, AFGG, 15, #1461; Limantour to British Minister T. B. Hohler and Hohler to Sir Edward Grey, March 28, 1911, FO, reel 14, 371 / 1573 / 1146, no. 13582.

43. Federico González Garza to Francisco Madero, March 30, 1911, AFGG, 15, #1440 and April 7, 1911, AFGG, 15, #1483; Federico González Garza to Francisco Vázquez Gómez, April 8, 1911, AFGG, 15, #1490; Federico González Garza, *La revolución mexicana: Mi contribución político-literaria* (Mexico: A. del Bosque, 1936); Ross, *Francisco Madero,* 155–57; Carranza to Francisco Vázquez Gómez, April 8, 1911, AFVG, box 7, #431.

44. FLdlB to Henry Lane Wilson, April 8, 1911, AGM, 34, Exp. 3-BIS, #237.

45. FLdlB to Carlos Pereyra, April 4, 1911, AGM, 25, Exp. 4, #45–47; FLdlB to Henry Lane Wilson, April 8, 1911, AGM, 34, Exp. 3-BIS, #237 and 25, 4, #84–86; Carlos Pereyra to FLdlB, April 5, 1911, AREM, L-E 682, Leg. 4, 5; Manuel Zamacona to FLdlB, April 17, 1911, AREM, L-E 676, Leg. 1, 3, and a second note dated April 23, 1911, AREM, L-E 682, Leg. 5, 104–5. David Lawrence to E. M. Hood, March 31, 1911, RDS, reel 26, 812.00 / 1419; *Mexican Herald,* April 12, 1911, and April 21, 1911.

46. Ana Perches Terrazas to Carmen Romero Rubio, January 21, 1911, Silvestre Terrazas Papers, Bancroft Library, University of California-Berkeley (hereafter cited as Terrazas Papers), part 1, box 72, file Ana Perches Terrazas; Porfirio Díaz to Silvestre Terrazas, March 28, 1911, Terrazas Papers, box 19, file Porfirio Díaz; FLdlB to Miguel Ahumada, April 10, 1911, AREM, L-E 681, Leg. 4, 25; Miguel Ahumada to Porfirio Díaz, March 22, 1911, CPD, Leg. 36; reel 281, #4820; Silvestre Terrazas to Porfirio Díaz, March 23, 1911, CPD, Leg. 36, reel 281, #4339; Vázquez Gómez, *Memorias políticas,* 119–26; Katz, *Villa,* 86.

47. Oscar Braniff to Francisco Madero (FIM), May 16, 1911, in T. B. Hohler to Sir Edward Grey, May 24, 1911, FO, reel 15, 371.1148, #22767.

48. Toribio Esquivel Obregón, *Democracia y personalismo* (Mexico: Imprenta de A. Carranza, 1911); Héctor Ribot, *Las últimas revoluciónes* (Mexico: Imprenta de Humboldt, 1912), 170. See Oscar Braniff to C. A. Coltin, April 18, 1911, RDS, reel 12, 812.00/1589.

49. Braniff's statement, May 4, 1911, AFGG 18, #1817; *El Imparcial*, April 21, 1911, in AFVG, box 8, folder 6, no number. Cumberland, *Mexican Revolution*, 146; Esquival Obregón, *Democracia*, 27–29.

50. See interviews with Madero in *Mexican Herald*, April 22, 1911; Secrest, "The Collapse," 223–33.

51. Federico González Garza to Francisco Vázquez Gómez, April 22, 1911, AFGG 16, #1597 (the same document can be located in AFVG, box 8, #530–31); Juan Navarro to FIM, April 24, 1911, AFVG, box 9, #549.

52. Toribio Esquivel Obregón to Limantour, April 27, 1911, AFVG, box 9, #581; Juan J. Navarro to FIM, April 25, 1911, AFVG, box 9, #558; instructions to Francisco Carvajal, Francisco Carvajal Papers, Bancroft Library, University of California-Berkeley (hereafter cited as FCP), file no. 83/164m, undated, folder 1, #3. See also Ross, *Francisco I. Madero*, 156–61; Katz, *Villa*, 108–9.

53. Federico González Garza to Francisco I. Madero, April 21, 1911, AFGG 16, #1588; Ross, *Francisco I. Madero*, 159.

54. Francisco Carvajal to José Yves Limantour, May 4, 1911, FCP, folder 1, #6; Limantour's instructions to Carvajal, FCP, folder 1, #10; José Yves Limantour to Francisco Carvajal, May 7, 1911, FCP, folder 1, #12.

55. Francisco Madero and the other chiefs of the revolution, Proclamation, May 1, 1911, AFVG, box 10, #597; Madero's demands, May 4, 1911, AFVG, box 10, #638; Jorge Vera Estañol, *La revolución mexicana: Origenes y resultados* (Mexico City: Editorial Porrúa, 1957), 162–65.

56. Francisco Carvajal to José Yves Limantour, May 7, 1911, FCP, folder 1, #13; Henry Lane Wilson to Philander Knox, May 8, 1911, RDS, reel 13, 812.00/1664.

57. Francisco Carvajal to Francisco Vázquez Gómez, May 6, 1911, AFVG, box 10, #664.

58. Carlos Fuentes, *The Old Gringo* (New York: Harper and Row, 1985); Giuseppe Garibaldi, *A Toast to Rebellion* (Indianapolis: Bobbs-Merrill, 1935), 284; Rafael Aguilar, *Madero sin máscara* (Mexico: Imprenta Popular, 1911), 79–80.

59. Francisco Vázquez Gómez to Federico González Garza, April 22, 1911, AFVG, box 8, #520 and #510; Francisco Vázquez Gómez to Francisco Madero, May 3, 1911, AFVG, box 10, #622; Colonel Steever's circular, April 19, 1911, in Federico González Garza to Francisco Madero, April 20, 1911, AFGG, 16, #1575; Francisco Madero, "Al Ejérito Libertador," May 7, 1911, Archivo Particular de Genaro Amezcua, Centro de Estudios de la Historia de México, Mexico City (hereafter cited as AGA), 1, #20.

60. Lara Pardo, *De Porfirio Díaz*, 248; Meyer, *Mexican Rebel*, 36–37; Cumberland, *Mexican Revolution*, 143–44; Ira Bush, *Gringo Doctor* (Caldwell, Idaho: Caxton Printers, 1939), 181–184.

61. M. Chausson, Consul at Veracruz, to Minister of Foreign Affairs, April 13, 1911, Archives du Ministère des Affaires Etrangères, Politique Intérieure, Mexique, new series B-25-1 (hereafter cited as ADRF), vol. 2, 180–81. See also Ellen Bose, *Farewell to Durango* (New York: Doubleday and Company, 1927), 48.

62. Francisco Vázquez Gómez to Federico González Garza, April 7, 1911, AFGG, 15, #1485; Federico González Garza to Madero, April 22, 1911, AFGG, 16, #1612.

63. Federico González Garza to Francisco Madero, April 18, 1911, AFGG, 16, #1554.

64. Venustiano Carranza to Francisco Vázquez Gómez, April 22, 1911, AFGG, box 8, #527–28; Francisco Carvajal to José Yves Limantour, May 9, 1911, FCP, folder 1, #17; Rodolfo Reyes, *Demi Vida: Memorias Políticas*, 3 vols. (Madrid: Biblioteca Nueva, 1929), I: 150.

65. Jorge Vera Estañol and José Yves Limantour to Francisco Carvajal, May 14, 1911, Jorge Vera Estañol Papers, Bancroft Library, University of California-Berkeley (hereafter cited as JVEP), 2 folders, file 78/76, folder 2. The same document is in FCP, folder 1, #21.

66. FIM to Porfirio Díaz, May 17, 1911, BNAM, box 1, #513.

67. Jorge Vera Estañol and José Yves Limantour to Francisco Carvajal, May 16, 1911, FCP, folder 1, #29.

68. Francisco Carvajal to Jorge Vera Estañol and José Yves Limantour, May 17, 1911, FCP, folder 1, #32; Francisco Vázquez Gómez to Rafael Arellano, May 19, 1911, AFVG, box 11, #918; Juan Carreón to Francisco Vázquez Gómez, regarding Zapata, May 20, 1911, AFVG, box 11, #942.

69. Jorge Vera Estañol and José Yves Limantour to Francisco Carvajal, May 20, 1911, FCP, folder 1, #39; Jorge Vera Estañol to Francisco Madero, May 25, 1911, JVEP, folder 2, no number; Knight, *Mexican Revolution*, 1:229.

70. T. B. Hohler to Sir Edward Grey, April 17, 1911, FO, reel 15, 371.1148, #16688. Lara Pardo, *De Porfirio Díaz*, 249–50; Javier Garciadiego Dantan, "Movimientos estudiantiles durante la revolución mexicana," in Jaime Rodríguez O, ed., *The Revolutionary Process in Mexico: Essays on Political and Social Change, 1880–1940* (Los Angeles: UCLA Latin American Center Publications, 1990), 115–60, at 117–28.

71. Manuel Rivero Amieva to Francisco Vázquez Gómez, May 18, 1911, AFVG, box 11, #887; Ribot, *Últimas revoluciónes*, 173; Jorge Vera Estañol and José Yves Limantour to Francisco Carvajal, May 18, 1911, FCP, folder 1, #35. See also FIM to Porfirio Díaz, May 17, 1911, AFVG, box 11, #858; FIM to Díaz, May 19, 1911, AFVG, box 11, #904.

72. José Yves Limantour and Jorge Vera Estañol to Francisco Carvajal, May 17, 1911, FCP, folder 1, #30; Limantour, *Apuntes*, 189–91.

73. For the text of the Treaty of Ciudad Juárez, see Appendix A. Francisco Carvajal to José Yves Limantour and Jorge Vera Estañol, May 22, 1911, FCP, folder 1, #43; Francisco Carvajal to FLdlB, May 22, 1911, AGM, 21, Exp. 1, #1; Henry Lane Wilson to Philander Knox, May 17, 1911, RDS, reel 13, 812.00/1830.

74. Eugenia Meyer, ed., *Obra politica de Luis Cabrera*, 3 vols. (Mexico: UNAM, 1992), 1:229–49; José María Pino Suárez to Francisco Vázquez Gómez, April 4, 1911, AFVG, box 7, #420–23; Emilio Vázquez Gómez to José Vasconcelos, May 15, 1911, AREM, L-E 665, Leg. 99, 10; Rogelio Fernández Güell, *La revolución mexicana: Episodios* (San José: Editorial Costa Rica, 1973), 86.

75. Perry, *Juárez and Díaz*, 415–20. José Maytorena to Francisco Madero, May 4, 1911, José María Maytorena Papers, Claremont College Library, Claremont, California (hereafter cited as JMMP), box 1, folder 10, #1.

76. *Mexican Herald*, May 27, 1911.

77. Presidential Manifesto, contained in FO, reel 15, 371/1148, #23268; Santos S. Rojas to FLdlB, May 26, 1911, AGM, 1, Exp. R-1, #5. See also de la Barra's letter to the *London Daily Chronicle,* May 29, 1911, AGM, 17, Exp. 3, #26.

78. FLdlB to FIM, May 27, 1911, AGM, 17, 3, #9.

79. FIM to FLdlB, May 27, 1911, AGM, 17, 3, #8, #24; FLdlB to FIM, May 28, 1911, AGM, 17, 2, #23, FIM to FLdlB, regarding Coahuila, May 26, 1911, AGM, 17, Exp. 3, #11.

80. Victoriano Huerta to FLdlB, May 28, 1911, AGM, 12, Exp. 1, #5; Hilario G. Márquez to Alfredo Robles Domínguez, May 27, 1911, Archivo Alfredo Robles Domínguez, Archivo General de la Nación, Mexico City (hereafter cited as AARD), vol. 5, exp. 25, #86; FLdlB to Joaquín Maass, June 2, 1911, AGM, 18, Exp. 1, #29; Hugh B. C. Pollard, *A Busy Time in Mexico* (New York: Duffield and Company, 1913), 226.

81. Porfirio Díaz to FLdlB, May 30, 1911, AdlB 1, #88; FLdlB to Díaz, October 5, 1911, AGM, 19, Exp. 5, #4; FLdlB to Díaz, June 1, 1911, AGM, 18, Exp. 1, #33; John Body to Lord Cowdray, May 27, 1911, Weetman Pearson Papers, University of Texas, Austin, microfilm (hereafter cited as Pearson Papers), box 161, Box A-3; Porfirio Díaz to Lord Cowdray, June 1911, Pearson Papers, box 161. Carlos Tello Díaz, *El exilio: Un relato de familia* (Mexico: Cal y Arena, 1993), tells the story of Díaz and his family in exile.

82. T. B. Hohler to Sir Edward Grey, April 22, 1911, FO, reel 15, 371.1148, #17284; Hohler to Grey, May 18, 1911, FO, reel 15, 371.1147/20782; H. L. Wilson to Philander Knox, May 23, 1911, RDS, reel 13, 812.00/1981.

83. Limantour, *Apuntes,* 301–2; Fernández Güell, *Revolución mexicana,* 111–12. De la Barra described his reluctance in another handwritten section of his unpublished memoirs, AdlB, 6, #593.

84. T. B. Hohler to Sir Edward Grey, May 27, 1911, FO, reel 15, 371.1148/23269; Thomas Beaumont Hohler, *Diplomatic Petrel* (London: John Murray, 1942), 175; O'Shaughnessy, *Intimate Pages,* 90–91.

85. T. B. Hohler to Sir Edward Grey, May 18, 1911, FO, reel 15, 371.1148/20782; Vera Estañol, *Revolución mexicana,* 194–95; H. L. Wilson to Philander Knox, May 5, 1911, RDS, reel 13, 812.00/1726.

Chapter 3

1. Luis Cabrera, *The Mexican Situation from a Mexican Point of View* (Washington: The Norris-Peters Company, 1913); Valadés, *Imaginación y realidad,* 2:189.

2. For the first view, see Knight, *Mexican Revolution,* and for the most extreme statement of the revisionists' interpretation, see Ramón Ruiz, *The Great Rebellion, Mexico, 1905–1924* (New York: W. W. Norton, 1980), and Hans Werner Tobler, *La revolución mexicana: Transformación social y cambio político, 1876–1940* (Mexico: Editorial Alianza, 1994).

3. Ross, *Francisco I. Madero,* 180; Sánchez Azcona, *La etapa maderista 45–46;* Hart, *Revolutionary Mexico,* 251.

4. Vera Estañol, *Revolución mexicana,* 208; Ross, *Francisco I. Madero,* 180. Knight, *Mexican Revolution,* 1:234, claims that the last minute revolutionaries were conservatives hoping to restore the Porfirian past. I disagree.

Manuel Rincón Gallardo to Alfredo Robles Domínguez, May 29, 1911, AARD, vol. 2, Exp. 9, #3–4.

5. Diary of Harriet Freeman (the U.S. consul's daughter), June 5, 1911, Harriet Freeman Papers, Harry Ransom Humanities Research Center, University of Texas-Austin, 16.

6. Charles Freeman to Philander Knox, May 31, 1911, RDS, reel 14, 812.00/2106; Bose, *Farewell to Durango*, 72–73; Pastor Rouaix, *La revolución maderista y constitucionalista en Durango* (Mexico: Editorial Cultura, 1931), 16–17.

7. General Luis Valle to Secretary of War Eugenio Rascón, May 29, 1911, Archivo Histórico de la Defensa Nacional (hereafter cited as AHDN), 481.5/217 114, #353; Rascón to General Valle, May 30, 1911, AHDN, 481.5/217, 114, #301.

8. J. R. Isunza to Eugenio Rascón, May 31, 1911, AHDN, 481.5/217, 114, #360; Pascual Ortiz Rubio, *La revolución de 1910* (Mexico: Ediciones Botas, 1937), 372–73.

9. For other examples see maderista jefe P. A. Carvajal to Eugenio Rascón, May 30, 1911, AHDN, 481.5/311, 144, 180–82; Vicente García to FLdlB, May 31, 1911, AGM, 4, Exp. G–1, #41; Amado Aguirre, *Mis memorias de campaña: Apuntes para la historia* (Mexico: Private Printing, 1985), 13–14; Knight, *Mexican Revolution*, 1:208–10; Victor Obe Story, "The Genesis of Revolution in the Tamaulipas Sierra: Campesinos or Shopkeepers in the Carrera Torres Uprising, 1907–1911" (Ph.D. diss., University of North Carolina, 1911), 226–68.

10. Miguel Ahumada to FLdlB, May 29, 1911, AGM, 5, Exp. A–1, #65; Emilio Vázquez Gómez to FLdlB, June 17, 1911, AGM, 22, Exp. 1, #13; Marcelo Caraveo, *Crónica de la revolución, 1910–1929* (Mexico: Editorial Trillas, 1992), 59; Clement Edwards to Philander C. Knox, July 15, 1911, RDS, reel 14, 812.00/2242.

11. Beezley, *Insurgent Governor*, 67.

12. Fernando González Roa, *El aspecto agrario de la revolución mexicana* (Mexico: Departmento de Aprovisionamientos Generales, 1919); Knight, *Mexican Revolution*, 1:80–86.

13. George Cummins to T. B. Hohler, July 5, 1911, FO, reel 16, 371.1148/30407; Charles D. Rhodes, "Diary of a Special Mission to Mexico," unpublished manuscript, Hoover Institution, Stanford University, Palo Alto, California (hereafter cited as Rhodes Diary), 11; Vera Estañol, *Revolución mexicana*, 226; Henry Lane Wilson to Philander Knox, July 11, 1911, RDS, reel 14, 812.00/2219.

14. Carlos AllenVallejo to FLdlB, August 24, 1911, AGM, 5, Exp. A–3, #47, and José M. Dávila to FLdlB, September 12, 1911, AGM, 24, Exp. D-5, #3; Katz, *Villa*, 49, 59.

15. Colonel Francisco Javier Llanas et al. to Alberto García Granados, August 28, 1911, AGM, 8, Exp. V-5, #60; Trinidad Rojas to FIM, August 31, 1911, Archivo Francisco I. Madero, Love Memorial Library, University of Nebraska-Lincoln, microfilm (hereafter cited as AFIM), reel 21, #3282.

16. Governor Castelazo of Guanajuato to Emilio Vázquez Gómez, June 7, 1911, AARD, vol. 3, Exp. 11, #90; Abraham González to FLdlB, October 18, 1911, AGM, 18, Exp. 2, #44, Governor Venustiano Carranza to Pablo González, June 1, 1911, Archivo de Manuel González, Centro de Estudios de la Historia de México, Condumex, S.A., Mexico City (hereafter cited as

Arch. M. González), 2, #26; Alfredo García to Emilio Vázquez Gómez, June 4, 1911, AGM, 19, Exp. 3, #29.

17. Knight, *Mexican Revolution*, 1:333–34; Enrique Sediama to Carlos G. de Cosío, May 27, 1911, AARD, vol. 4, Exp. 10, #33; Juan D. Hernández to FIM, July 7, 1911, AFIM, reel 20, #2466. See also Adolfo Gilly, *The Mexican Revolution* (London: Thetford Press, 1983).

18. FIM to Roque Estrada, undated, BNAM, box 2, #571; Abraham González to José María Lujan, July 5, 1911, Fausto Orozco Collection, University of Texas–El Paso, microfilm (hereafter cited as OC), reel 2, #209.

19. Ernesto Madero to Alfredo Robles Domínguez, June 5, 1911, AARD, vol. 2, Exp. 7, #56; Alfredo Robles Domínguez to Rafael Tapia, May 25, 1911, AARD, vol. 4, Exp. 17, #18; FIM to F. A. Betancourt, May 24, 1911, BNAM, box 1, #211. See also Ortiz Rubio, *La revolución de 1910*, 384.

20. Ross, *Francisco I. Madero*, 175–76.

21. For the policy, see the interview of Emilio Vázquez Gómez in *El Tiempo*, June 6, 1911. For the villagers' complaint, see Adriano Carpizo to Governor of Campeche, May 23, 1911, AARD, vol. 3, Exp. 10, #1.

22. Acayuqueños to FLdlB, June 15, 1911, AGM, 22, 7, #53; M. San Vicente to Alfredo Robles Domínguez, June 15, 1911, AARD, vol. 3, Exp. 15, #135; Varios vecinos to Rafael Amezcua, June 14, 1911, AFIM, reel 20, #1911.

23. Eric J. Hobsbawm, *Bandits* (London: Penguin Press, 1972).

24. Baron de Vaux to Baron Cruppi, May 26, 1911, ADRF, vol. 2, 219–22.

25. José María Maytorena to FIM, July 21, 1911, JMMP, box 1, folder 13, #6; Ricardo Gúzman to FLdlB, June 22, 1911, AGM, 35, Exp. 3, #138; Francisco Rodríguez to Manuel Llamosa, May 31, 1911, AARD, vol. 1, Exp. 6, #135–38. De la Barra had agreed, in accordance with the treaty, to issue orders to free political prisoners; see FLdlB to FIM, May 28, 1911, AGM, 17, Exp. 3, #23.

26. Alexius, "The Army," 14–20; Emilio Madero to Ernesto Madero, June 15, 1911, AFIM, reel 19, #720

27. Cándido Navarro to Alfredo Robles Domínguez, May 29, 1911, AARD, vol. 5, Exp. 21, #9; Subsecretary of the Treasury to Robles Domínguez, June 13, 1911, AARD, vol. 4, Exp. 18, #76; Angel Arch to FIM, June 1, 1911, AARD, vol. 3, Exp. 14, #31; Vicente Mejía Galindo to Robles Domínguez, June 12, 1911, AARD, vol. 2, Exp. 7, #127; and Ireneo Contreras to FLdlB, June 3, 1911, AGM, 2, Exp. C-1, #83.

28. Gabriel Ferrer de Mendiolea, *Presencia de Don Francisco I Madero* (Mexico: Colección Metropolitano, 1973), 57–59; *El Diario*, October 14, 1911.

29. Mariano Ruiz to FLdlB, July 7, 1911, AGM, 1, Exp. R-2, #50; Ernesto Madero to FLdlB, June 25, 1911, AGM, 21, Exp. 7, #87.

30. Agapito Silva to FLdlB, October 1, 1911, AGM, 21, Exp. 3, #10; La Comisión (de Celaya) to FLdlB, August 25, 1911, AGM, 8, Exp. V-5, #26.

31. Manuel Cuesta Gallardo to FLdlB, June 5, 1911, AGM, 2, Exp. C-1, #57. The government budgeted 8 million pesos for demobilization and claims settlements; see Ernesto Madero to FIM, May 27, 1911, BNAM, 3-1253.

32. FIM to Pascual Orozco, July 5, 1911, AFIM, reel 18, #0304; Katz, *Villa*, 115.

33. José María Maytorena to FIM, October 5, 1911, AFIM, reel 19, #759.

34. Memo of the Peace Delegate (Robles Domínguez) to the Chiefs of the Revolutionary Army, May 24, 1911, AARD, vol. 6, Exp. 30, #98; Memorandum to Robles Domínguez, June 12, 1911, AARD, vol. 1, Exp. 5, #45; and Emilio Vázquez Gómez to FIM, June 14, 1911, AARD, vol. 1, Exp. 5, #81. Emilio Vázquez Gómez interview in *El Tiempo*, June 6, 1911.

35. FIM to Alfredo Robles Domínguez, June 26, 1911, AARD, vol. 1, Exp. 5, #84. Chávez, undersecretary of the interior, to Roque Estrada, June 22, 1911, Archivo Roque Estrada, UNAM (hereafter cited as ARE) 2, folio 11, #640; Planck, "The Ad Interim Regime," 21–22.

36. David LaFrance, *The Mexican Revolution in Puebla, 1908–1913: The Maderista Movement and the Failure of Liberal Reform* (Wilmington, DE: Scholarly Resources, 1989), 1–102.

37. Porfirio del Castillo, *Puebla y Tlaxcala en los días de la Revolución* (Mexico: Zavala, 1953), 67.

38. Eduardo Reyes to Agustín del Pozo, June 2, 1911, AGM, 28, Exp. 15, #3.

39. Alfredo Robles Domínguez to Agustín del Pozo, June 8, 1911, AARD, vol. 4, Exp. 19, #115.

40. Emilio Vázquez Gómez to Camerino Z. Mendoza, June 10, 1911, AGM, 10, Emilio Vázquez Gómez letterbook, #194; Emilio Vázquez Gómez to Agustín del Pozo, June 30, 1911, AGM, 10, Emilio Vázquez Gómez letterbook, #62.

41. FLdlB to FIM, July 13, 1911, AGM, 17, Exp. 5, #2.

42. Emilio Téllez Herrero to FLdlB, August 10, 1911, AGM, 5, Exp. T-3, #36. FLdlB to Emiliano G. Saravia, Governor of Durango, September 27, 1911, AGM, 11, book 1, #416; and Francisco Gómez Palacio to Laureano López Negrete, September 15, 1911, AGM, 24, unnumbered expediente, #32.

43. LaFrance, *Puebla, 1908–1913*, 109–13.

44. Ibid., 114–15; Emilio Vázquez Gómez to Rafael Cañete, July 9, 1911, AGM, 22, Exp. 1, #66.

45. Eduardo Reyes to Agustín del Pozo, July 15, 1911, AGM, 28, Exp. 15, #9; Francisco Madero to FLdlB, July 13, 1911, AGM, 17, Exp. 10, #5; Aureliano Blanquet to FLdlB, July 22, 1911, AGM, 31, Exp. B-3, #286; General Luis Valle to Eugenio Rascón, July 19, 1911, AHDN, 481.5/217, 114, #413; Eugenio Rascón to Luis Valle, July 13, 1911, AHDN, 481.5/217, #421; Ricardo Luna Morales, *Mi vida revolucionaria* (Mexico: Private Printing, 1943), 30–33.

46. LaFrance, *Puebla, 1908–1913*, 117–18; FIM to FLdlB, July 15, 1911, AGM, 17, Exp. 5, #4; de la Barra to FIM, July 14, 1911, AGM, 17, Exp. 5, #3; Baron de Vaux to Minister of Foreign Relations, August 10, 1911, ADRF, vol. 3, 6–10; T. B. Hohler to Sir Edward Grey, July 15, 1911, FO, reel 18, 371.1148/30080. Within a week, one thousand soldiers in Puebla did muster out; see *El Diario*, July 18, 1911.

47. Gabriel Soto to FLdlB, July 24, 1911, AGM, 9, Exp. S-2, #54; Carmen Toscano, "Memorias de un Mexicano," *El Tiempo*, July 18, 1911.

48. Vázquez Gómez, *Memorias políticas*, 336–39.

49. FLdlB to Rafael Cañete, July 20, 1911, AGM, 17, Exp. 10, #12; FLdlB to Cañete, July 21, 1911, AGM, 17, Exp. 10, #15; Cañete to FLdlB, July 20, 1911, AGM, 17, Exp. 10, #13; FLdlB to Emilio Vázquez Gómez, July 21, 1911, AGM, 13, book 5, #184; "Sucesos de la Covadonga," n.d., AFGG, 20, #2005.

50. David LaFrance, "Germany, Revolutionary Nationalism, and the Downfall of President Francisco I. Madero: The Covadonga Killings," *Mexican Studies, Estudios Mexicanos* 2, no. 1 (winter 1986): 59–82.

51. LaFrance, *Puebla, 1908–1913,* 119–20; FIM to Martín Vicario, August 18, 1911, AFIM, reel 19, #1268; Martín Vicario to FLdlB, September 1, 1911, AGM, 21, Exp. 2, #120.

52. Rafael Cañete to FLdlB, August 6, 1911, AGM, 2, Exp. C-3, #64; FLdlB to Rafael Cañete, August 23, 1911, AGM, 12, book 8, #118.

53. Rafael Martínez Carrillo to FLdlB, September 14, 1911, AGM, 22, Exp. 8, #6; Martinez to FLdlB, September 30, 1911 and October 19, 1911, AGM, 22, Exp. 8, #3, #4. De la Barra responded that Martínez "must not suppose he would put pressure on a judicial department." See FLdlB to Mucio Martínez, October 9, 1911, AGM, 11, book 2, #467.

54. Luis Valle to José González Salas, July 25, 1911, AHDN, 481.5/217, 114, #447; Federico Lázaro to José González Salas, October 11, 1911, AHDN, 481.5/217, 114, #483.

55. Benjamín Arredendo Muñozledo, *Historia de la revolución mexicana* (Mexico City: Librería de Porrúa, 1971), 11; Jesús Silva Herzog, *Breve historia de la revolución mexicana* (Mexico: Fondo de Cultura Económica, 1960); Hart, *Revolutionary Mexico,* 251.

56. Leonardo Ballesteros, *Apuntes biográficos de las Señores Lic. Emilio Vázquez Gómez y Doctor Francisco Vázquez Gómez* (Mexico: Talleres Tipográficos de El Tiempo, 1911). The cabinet members who left memoirs are Francisco Vázquez Gómez, FLdlB (unpublished), Manuel Calero (*Un decenio de politica mexicana* [New York: L. Middleditch Company, 1920]), and Subsecretary Federico González Garza.

57. Garritz, "La presidencia interina," 99; John A. Caleca, "The Vázquez Gómez Brothers and Francisco I. Madero: Conflict within the Mexican Revolution, 1909–1913" (Master's thesis, University of Nebraska-Lincoln, 1970); Ballesteros, *Apuntes biográficos.*

58. William Weber Johnson, *Heroic Mexico* (Garden City, NY: Doubleday, 1968), 76.

59. Ross, *Francisco I. Madero,* 203.

60. Emilio Vázquez Gómez to FLdlB, June 16, 1911, AGM, 22, Exp. 1, #12; José E. Ipiña, Governor of San Luis Potosí, to FLdlB, June 9, 1911, AGM, 1, Exp. Y-2, #11. For Puebla, see LaFrance, *Puebla, 1908–1913,* 102.

61. Ramón Prida, *De la dictadura a la anarquía* (Mexico: Ediciones Botas, 1958), 313–14.

62. Vera Estañol, *Revolución mexicana,* 200; Bonilla, *Diez años,* 258; Manuel González Ramírez, *La revolución social de México* (Mexico: Fondo de Cultura Económica, 1960), 288–93.

63. Emilio Vázquez Gómez to Domingo Magaña, July 5, 1911, Emilio Vázquez Gómez letterbook. AGM, 10, #389; Emilio Vázquez Gómez to Estanislao Mayorga, July 1, 1911, AGM, Vázquez Gómez letterbook, 10, #175. See also Emilio Vázquez Gómez Circular, July 26, 1911, 21, AFGG, #2076.

64. Julio Ibáñez to FLdlB, August 7, 1911, AGM, 1, Exp. Y-1, #7.

65. Emilio Vázquez Gómez to General Eugenio Rascón, Minister of War, June 30, 1911, AGM, 10, #52; Consul Clement Edwards to Philander Knox, July 15, 1911, RDS, reel 14, 812.00/2242; Emilio Vázquez Gómez to Alfredo Robles Domínguez, July 2, 1911, AARD, vol. 2, Exp. 8, #5.

66. Emilio Vázquez Gómez to Alfredo Robles Domínguez, July 2, 1911, AARD, vol. 2, Exp. 8, #5–6; Circular of Emilio Vázquez Gómez to Revolutionary Chiefs, July 2, 1911, AGM, 10, Vázquez Gómez letterbook, #211–14.

67. Vázquez Gómez, *Memorias políticas*, 302–4.

68. FIM to FLdlB, July 14, 1911, AdlB, 2, #101, and de la Barra's reply, July 14, 1911, AGM, 13, book 4, #420. See also Bernardino Villaseñor to FIM, June 12, 1911, AFIM, reel 20, #2208.

69. FLdlB, "Algunas páginas," AdlB, 24, #2919; FIM to Emilio Vázquez Gómez, July 15, 1911, AdlB, 2, #103.

70. FLdlB to Emilio Vázquez Gómez, July 21, 1911, AGM, 13, book 5, #188–89.

71. T. B. Hohler to Sir Edward Grey, July 14, 1911, FO, reel 17, 371.1150/30078; U.S. Ambassador Wilson to Philander Knox, July 18, 1911, RDS, reel 14, 812.00/2230. Of course, de la Barra did not really have a "free hand" as he continued to consult with Madero (nor did Madero have a "free hand") throughout the presidency and even after their open tiff on August 25.

72. Francisco Vázquez Gómez to FIM, July 22, 1911, AFVG, box 15, #1556; Francisco Vázquez Gómez to FIM, July 29, 1911, AFVG, box 15, #1641, and the second letter of July 31, 1911, AFVG, box 15, #1688; Vázquez Gómez, *Memorias políticas*, 365–69; T. B. Hohler to Sir Edward Grey, August 3, 1911, FO, reel 17, 371.1150/32135.

73. FIM to Francisco Vázquez Gómez, July 22, 1911, AFVG, box 15, #1563; FIM to Francisco Vázquez Gómez, July 31, 1911, AFVG, box 15, #1682; FIM to Emilio Vázquez Gómez, July 26, 1911, AdlB, 2, #116. Madero told de la Barra, "I am completely with you." See his telegram to FLdlB, July 26, 1911, AGM, 17, Exp. 5, #6.

74. FIM to Gustavo Madero, July 25, 1911, AGM, 17, Exp. 5, #9. Revolutionary Chiefs' open letter, AGA, 1, #29, and AFVG, box 15, #1548; Guillermo García Aragón to Editors of the "Nueva Era," August 7, 1911, AGM, 4, Exp. G-3. #68.

75. Emilio Vázquez Gómez to Cabino Gavira, August 3, 1911, Archivo Venustiano Carranza, Centro de Estudios de la Historia de México, Condumex, S.A., Mexico City (hereafter cited as Arch. Carranza), 1, #39; Matías Chávez to de la Barra, August 2, 1911, AGM, 3, Exp. C-3, #27.

76. FIM to FLdlB, July 24, 1911, AdlB, 2, #111; FIM to FLdlB, July 26, 1911, AdlB, 2, #115; Luis Cabrera to FLdlB, July 28, 1911, AGM, 3, Exp. C-4, #132; FLdlB to Madero, July 21, 1911, AGM, 13, book 5, #186–87; FIM to FLdlB, July 27, 1911, AGM, 18, Exp. 3, #1.

77. FIM to Francisco Vázquez Gómez, August 1, 1911, AFVG, box 16, folder 1, #5; Baron de Vaux to Minister of Foreign Relations Crippi, June 8, 1911, ADRF, II, vol. 2, 244–47.

78. Ross, *Francisco I. Madero*, 190.

79. FLdlB to FIM, July [sic] [August] 1, 1911, AGM, 13, book 5, #79–82; José Romero to FLdlB, August 3, 1911, AGM, 1, Exp. R–3, #23; Lauro Landero to FLdlB, August 5, 1911, AGM, 21, Exp. 1, #72. See FIM to Federico González Garza, July 30, 1911, AFGG, 21 #2094.

80. D. Ramos to FLdlB, August 23, 1911, AGM, 1, Exp. R–3, #102; Rafael López Portillo to FLdlB , June 29, 1911, AGM, 3, Exp. L–2, #27; C. C. Mengel to FLdlB, July 6, 1911, AGM, 7, Exp. M-2, #45; Justo Tirado to FLdlB, September 6, 1911, AGM, 5, Exp. T-4, #20. Bonilla did want to regulate the

railroads to some degree (a progressive reform in the United States) and de la Barra apparently agreed; see Bonilla to FLdlB, September 19, 1911, AGM, 31, Exp. B-4, #351.

81. FLdlB to FIM, July 27, 1911, AGM, 17, Exp. 5, #12; FIM to FLdlB, July 31, 1911, AGM, 18, Exp. 3, #18; FLdlB to FIM, July [sic] [August] 1, 1911, AGM, 22, Exp. 1, #22; FIM to FLdlB, August 2, 1911, AGM, 18, Exp. 3, #4; José Vasconcelos to *La Actualidad*, August 3, 1911, DHRM, vol. 6, #307; González Garza, *Revolución mexicana*, 245–88.

82. Alberto García Granados to FLdlB, August 10, 1911, AGM, 4, Exp. G-3, #77; Garritz, "La presidencia interina," 98.

83. Declaration of Federico González Garza, October 1911, AFGG, 22, #2162.

84. Arnulfo Pedroza to FLdlB, September 2, 1911, AGM, 14, 6, #4.

85. Abraham González to FLdlB, October 18, 1911, AGM, 19, Exp. 6, #59; FLdlB to Abraham González, October 5, 1911, AGM, 11, book 2, #287; FIM to FLdlB, October 19, 1911, AGM, 19, Exp. 6, #65.

86. FLdlB to Ambassador Gilberto Crespo y Martínez, September 21, 1911, AGM, 11, book 1, #150–51; FLdlB to Minister Sebastián B. de Mier (Paris), September 22, 1911, AGM, 11, book 1, #185.

87. Thomas Benjamin, *A Rich Land, a Poor People: Politics and Society in Modern Chiapas* (Albuquerque: University of New Mexico Press, 1989), 37–92. See also idem, "Revolución interrumpida: Chiapas y el interinato presidencial, 1911," *Historia Mexicana* 30 (July 1980): 79–98; J. B. Pineda to FLdlB, August 23, 1911, AGM, 8, Exp. P-4, #1; Carlos Flores Tavilla to FLdlB, August 12, 1911, AGM, 9, Exp. F-4, #34.

88. FIM to Indoro Castellanos, July 12, 1911, AFIM, reel 21, #3592; FIM to Governor Reinaldo Gordillo León, July 7, 1911, AFIM, reel 22, #3714; Ponciano Rojas to FLdlB, June 14, 1911, AGM, 1, Exp. R-1, #102; Policarpo Rueda to FLdlB, August 4, 1911, AGM, 1, Exp. R-3, #123.

89. Governor Manuel Rivero Arguello to FLdlB, August 28, 1911, AGM, 15, Exp. 6, #11.

90. Alberto R. Larenas to Ignacio León de la Barra, September 24, 1911, AGM, 3, Exp. L-5, #50; Benjamin, *Rich Land*, 106–8; Francisco Orozco y Jiménez to FLdlB, October 1, 1911, AGM, 21, Exp. 3, #7; T. B. Hohler to Sir Edward Grey, October 17, 1911, FO, reel 16, 371.1149/42960.

91. Alberto García Granados to Governor Rovello Arguello, September 19, 1911, AGM, 4, Exp. G-4, #86; Governor Manuel Rovello Arguello to FLdlB, September 26, 1911, AGM, 1, Exp. R-5, #10; J. Espinosa Torres to FLdlB, September 21, 1911, AGM, 15, Exp. 7, #13.

92. José Antonio Rivera G. to FLdlB, October 7, 1911, AGM, 1, Exp. R-5, #71; Francisco Orozco y Jiménez to FLdlB, September 16, 1911, AGM, 20, Exp. 1, #77; FLdlB to state legislators, October 8, 1911, AGM, 21, Exp. 3, #31. For Querido Mohero's accusation, see *Diario de los debates de la Cámara de Diputados*, September 23, 1911. Alberto García Granados to FLdlB, September 19, 1911, AGM, 4, Exp. G-4, #86.

93. M. Rovelo Arguello to FLdlB, October 10, 1911, AGM, 21, Exp. 6, #35; Benjamin, *Rich Land*, 110; Colonel Francisco Figueroa to General Merodio, October 8, 1911, AHDN, 481.5/48, #28–31; the peace arrangements in AGM, 8, Exp. P-5, #131; *El Mundo Ilustrado*, September 17, 1911, and August 13, 1911.

94. FLdlB to General Eduardo Paz, October 11, 1911, AGM, 19, Exp. 5, #48.

95. For concern about the problem, see José Antonio Rivera G. to FLdlB, October 12, 1911, AGM, 1, Exp. R-5, #47; FLdlB to Díaz et al., September 17, 1911, AdlB, 2, #138; Benjamin, *Rich Land,* 110–12.

96. Dillon Wallace, *Beyond the Mexican Sierra* (Chicago: A. C. McClurg and Company, 1910).

97. Diego Redo to FLdlB, June 6, 1911, AGM, 1, Exp. R-2, #117; Higinio Aguilar's report, August 23, 1911, AHDN, 481.5/259, 127, 159–71; Madero to de la Barra, May 30, 1911, BNAM, box 1, #170; Gilly, *Revolution,* 167–68.

98. Hector R. Olea, *Breve historia de la revolución en Sinaloa, 1910–1917* (Mexico City: Biblioteca del Instituto Nacional de Estudios Históricos de la Revolución Mexicana, 1964), 37; Manuel Bonilla to José Rentería, August 8, 1911, AGM, 31, Exp. B-2, #171. See Manuel Bonilla to FLdlB, August 8, 1911, AGM, 31, Exp. B-2, #194, and FLdlB's reply, August 9, 1911, AGM, 12, book 7, #40; FIM to FLdlB, September 17, 1911, AGM, 18, Exp. 1, #86.

99. Severiano Tamayo et al. to FLdlB, August 21, 1911, AGM, 18, Exp. 5, #10; Francisco Moncayo et al. to FLdlB, August 22, 1911, AGM, 18, Exp. 5, #42.

100. Ross, *Francisco I. Madero,* 179; Enrique de Avila to de la Barra on August 30, 1911, AGM, 5, Exp. A-4, #11; Juan Banderas to FLdlB, September 2, 1911, AGM, 15, Exp. 5, #50.

101. José Rentería to FLdlB, October 10, 1911, AGM, 18, Exp. 2, #24, and his telegram of October 12, 1911, to the president, AGM, 19, Exp. 6, #11.

102. Alberto García Granados to FLdlB, October 20, 1911, AGM, 4, Exp. G-5, #77.

103. José Rentería to FLdlB, October 10, 1911, AGM, 20, Exp. 2, #37; José Rentería to FLdlB, October 20, 1911, AGM, 19, Exp. 6, #117; Refugio Velasco to José González Salas, October 19, 1911, AHDN, 481.5/268, 131, #911; J. N. Cabanillas to FLdlB, October 23, 1911, AGM, 18, Exp. 2, #52. (Some citizens of Sinaloa had asked for Pascual Orozco to lead the troops; see the Petition dated October 3, 1911, AGM, 11, book 2, 26–64).

104. FIM to FLdlB, October 21, 1911, AGM, 19, Exp. 6, #123; FLdlB to José Rentería, October 23, 1911, AGM, 19, Exp. 7, #12; Knight, *Mexican Revolution,* 1:274–75; Olea, *Sinaloa,* 39.

105. Lowell L. Blaisdell, *The Desert Revolution: Baja California, 1911* (Madison: University of Wisconsin Press, 1962); Lawrence Douglas Taylor, *La campaña magonista de 1911 en Baja California* (Tijuana: El Colegio de la Frontera Norte, 1992); Ricardo Flores Magón to Julio Mancilla, May 27, 1911, AREM, L-E 844, 1 Leg., 124.

106. The literature on Flores Magón and anarchism in Mexico is legion. I would assert that their historical significance has been blown well out of proportion. Héctor Aguilar Camín, *La frontera nómada: Sonora y la revolución mexicana* (Mexico City: Sep Cultura, 1985), 184; General Refugio Velasco to José González Salas, September 29, 1911, AHDN, 481.5/268, 131, #859; Alexander Dye to Philander Knox, September 29, 1911, RDS, reel 14, 812.00/2398.

107. Jesús Flores Magón to FLdlB, June 4, 1911, AGM, 12, Exp. 1, #6, #12. Blaisdell, *Desert Revolution,* 175; V. Salado Alvarez to Consul in Yuma, June 9, 1911, AREM, L-E 676, Leg. 2, 31.

108. FLdlB to FIM, June 1, 1911, AGM, 15, exp. 8, #6; FIM to FLdlB, June 1, 1911, AGM, 15, Exp. 8, #5; FLdlB to FIM, June 2, 1911, AGM, 15, Exp. 8, #6, FIM to B. J. Viljoen, June 18, 1911, BNAM, 4/2156.

109. Secretary of War Eugenio Rascón to FLdlB, June 4, 1911, AGM, 22, Exp. 3, #37; FIM to FLdlB, June 3, 1911, AGM, 20, Exp. 3, #23.

110. Blaisdell, *Desert Revolution*, 140–62. Notes of Sir Cecil Spring-Rice, n.d., FO, reel 16, 371.1145/28672; Los Angeles Consul to Walter Hearn, Consul in San Francisco, June 22, 1911, FO, reel 16, 371.1149/31227. See also Lawrence D. Taylor, "Charlatán o filibustero peligroso? El papel de Richard 'Dick' Ferris en la revuelta magonista de 1911 en Baja California," *Historia Mexicana* 44 (April–June 1995): 581–616.

111. Ambassador Manuel Zamacona to FLdlB, June 20, 1911, AdlB, 1, #94; J. Díaz Priego to FLdlB, June 14, 1911, AGM, 24, Exp. D-1, #42; Taylor, *Campaña magonista*, 106–8; Celso Vega to José María Maytorena, August 5, 1911, JMMP, box 1, folder 14, #7; Luis Guzmán to FLdlB, July 1911, AGM, 4, Exp. C-2, #69.

112. Blaisdell, *Desert Revolution*, 178–81; Martín Solís et al. to FLdlB, July 28, 1911, AGM, 8, Exp. V-5, #19; Celso Vega to Zone Commander, July 26, 1911, AHDN, 481.5/11, 2, #255–58; Celso Vega to Eugenio Rascón, July 20, 1911, AHDN, 481.5/11, 2, #248.

113. Ricardo Bravo to Secretary of Foreign Relations, October 10, 1911, AREM, L-E 851R, Leg. 2, 95; Carlos Palafox, vice consul at El Paso, to Secretary of Foreign Relations, October 6, 1911, AREM, L-E 817R, Leg. 1, 200; Memorandum of Federico González Garza, n.d., AFGG, 22, #2123; Heriberto Barrón to FLdlB, September 11, 1911, AGM, 31, Exp. B-4, #361.

114. John Womack, *Zapata and the Mexican Revolution* (New York: Alfred A. Knopf, 1968); Gildardo Magaña, *Emiliano Zapata y el agrarismo en México*, 5 vols. (Mexico: Editorial Ruta, 1952).

115. Arturo Warman, *We Come to Object: The Peasants of Morelos and the National State* (Baltimore: Johns Hopkins University Press, 1980).

116. Womack, *Zapata*, 62–65.

117. Abraham Martínez (Zapata's secretary) to Alfredo Robles Domínguez, May 29, 1911, AARD, vol. 1, Exp. 6, #92; Emiliano Zapata to Alfredo Robles Domínguez, May 28, 1911, AARD, vol. 4, Exp. 17, #45.

118. Womack, *Zapata*, 93.

119. Emiliano Zapata, Alfonso Miranda, and Manuel Asúnsolo to Alfredo Robles Domínguez, May 29, 1911, AARD, vol. 4, Exp. 17, #56; Manuel Asúnsolo to Alfredo Robles Domínguez, May 29, 1911, AARD, vol. 1, Exp. 6, #89–91.

120. E. Monteón to FIM, June 5, 1911, AFIM, reel 19, #844.

121. Teofanes Jiménez to FLdlB, August 18, 1911, AGM, 6, Exp. J-3, #6.

122. José de la Macorrra to FLdlB, July 15, 1911, AGM, 7, Exp. M-2, #56; Juan Carreón to Alfredo Robles Domínguez , May 31, 1911, AARD, vol. 4, Exp. 17, #63; Samuel Brunk, *Emiliano Zapata: Revolution and Betrayal in Mexico* (Albuquerque: University of New Mexico Press, 1995), 72–75.

123. Emilio Vázquez Gómez to Emiliano Zapata (received May 31, 1911), AGM, 20, Exp. 3, #7; Memorandum of Emilio Vázquez Gómez, n.d., AFVG, box 14, #1434; Alfredo Robles Domínguez to Emiliano Zapata, May 23, 1911, AARD, vol. 4, Exp. 17, #5. Madero also expressed concern about zapatista activity in mid-June; see his letter to Juan Carreón, June 15, 1911, BNAM, 1/342.

124. Womack, *Zapata*, 96; Magaña, *Emiliano Zapata*, 1:160–61.

125. Womack, *Zapata*, 87–88; FIM to Juan M. Carreón, June 21, 1911, AFIM, reel 19, #00049.

126. Emilio Vázquez Gómez to FIM, June 14, 1911, AARD, vol. 1, Exp. 5, #81–82; Emiliano Zapata to FIM, June 21, 1911, AFIM, reel 19, #894.

127. Barrios y Murga and Fernando Doral to FLdlB, July 7, 1911, AGM, 6, Exp. V-1, #122; *El País*, June 20, 1911; Brunk, *Zapata*, 46–48; Roger Parkinson, *Zapata* (Briarcliff, NY: Stein and Day, 1975), 89; T. B. Hohler to Sir Edward Grey, June 28, 1911, FO, reel 16, 371.1148/27072.

128. See the receipts in AARD, specifically, Emiliano Zapata to Alfredo Robles Domínguez, May 29, 1911, AARD, vol. 4, Exp. 17, #59. See also Juan Pagaza to FIM, June 17, 1911, BNAM, box 3, #1603; Antonio Barrios to Alfredo Robles Domínguez, July 21, 1911, AARD, vol. 2, Exp. 8, #66–67.

129. Emiliano Zapata to Alfredo Robles Domínguez, June 3, 1911, AARD, vol. 4, Exp. 17, #103; Bryan, "Bernardo Reyes," 91–96.

130. Warman, *We Come to Object*, 114.

131. Alfredo Miranda to Editor of "El País," June 24, 1911, Genaro García Collection, University of Texas-Austin, Nettie Lee Benson Collection, no number.

132. Womack, *Zapata*, 101; FIM to Sabás Valladares Jr., June 22, 1911, AFIM, reel 19, #899.

133. Emiliano Zapata to FIM, July 11, 1911, AFIM, reel 19, #905; Womack, *Zapata*, 107; Emiliano Zapata to FIM, August 1911, AFIM, reel 19, #922; FIM to Emiliano Zapata, August 7, 1911, AFIM, reel 19, #923, #0084; Emiliano Zapata to FIM, July 3, 1911, Carlos Reyes Aviles Collection, UTEP microfilm, roll 1. Brunk, *Zapata*, 166, mentions that Zapata frequently feigned illness in 1914 and 1915 as a way of avoiding difficult situations.

134. Womack, *Zapata*, 105.

135. Francisco Javier Arenas, *Francisco Ignacio Madero, el creador de la revolución Mexicana* (Mexico: Federación Editorial Mexicana, 1977), 164; FIM to FLdlB, August 15, 1911, AdlB, 2, #120.

136. Antonio Barrios (attorney for the planters) to FLdlB, July 27, 1911, AGM, 3, Exp. C-3, #8.

137. Womack, *Zapata*, 103.

138. FIM to Ambrosio Figueroa, August 9, 1911, AGA, 1, #30. The same document can be found in AFIM, reel 18, #0099.

139. Victoriano Huerta passing on the message to FLdlB, August 19, 1911, AGM, 15, Exp. 1, #53.

140. Ian Jacobs, *Ranchero Revolt: The Mexican Revolution in Guerrero* (Austin: University of Texas Press, 1982), 87–88; General Francisco Leyva to Eugenio Rascón, May 8, 1911, AHDN, 481.5/177, 96, #59.

141. FIM to Emiliano Zapata, n.d. (but undoubtedly August 13, 1911), AFIM, reel 19, #934. The dialogue between García Granados and Zapata of August 12 and August 13 is reproduced in DHRM, vol. 6, #316, 49–50.

142. Victoriano Huerta to FLdlB, August 11, 1911, AGM, 12, Exp. 1, #17; Genovevo de la O's campaign records, August 10, 1911, Genovevo de la O Archive, box 12, Exp. 4, 1, University of Texas-El Paso microfiche.

143. FIM to FLdlB, August 14, 1911, AGM, 17, Exp. 8, #10.

144. FLdlB to FIM, August 14, 1911, AGM, 17, Exp. 8, #9.

145. FIM to FLdlB, August 15, 1911, AdlB, folder 2, #120.

146. FLdlB to FIM, August 15, 1911, AGM, 17, Exp. 8, #17. De la Barra copied Huerta in on this letter; see AGM, 14, Exp. 4, #21.

147. FLdlB to FIM, August 15, 1911, AGM, 17, Exp. 8, #12. Womack interprets this letter as evidence of de la Barra's racist attitude toward "Indians"; I believe instead that it refers to Zapata's class as well as his past untrustworthy behavior rather than to race.

148. FIM to Emiliano Zapata, n.d., AFIM, reel 19, #940.

149. Victoriano Huerto to FLdlB, August 15, 1911, AFVG, box 17, folder 7, no number.

150. FLdlB to Victoriano Huerta, August 15, 1911, AGM, 14, Exp. 3, #3.

151. FIM to FLdlB, August 15, 1911, AGM, 30, Exp. 5, #51; or AFVG, box 17, folder 7, no number.

152. FLdlB to Victoriano Huerta, August 16, 1911, AGM, 14, Exp. 3, #59.

153. Victoriano Huerta to FLdlB, August 16, 1911, AGM, 14, Exp. 3, #52.

154. Emiliano Zapata to FIM, August 16, 1911, AFIM, reel 19, #955; FIM to Emiliano Zapata, August 16, 1911, AGM, 14, Exp. 3, #43.

155. Emiliano Zapata to FLdlB, August 17, 1911, AGM, 14, Exp. 4, #23.

156. Womack, *Zapata*, 115.

157. José González Salas to Victoriano Huerta, August 17, 1911, AFIM, reel 19, #1017; Victoriano Huerta to FLdlB, August 17, 1911, AGM, 14, Exp. 4, #29.

158. FLdlB to Victoriano Huerta, August 17, 1911, AGM, 14, Exp. 4, #28.

159. Unsigned to FLdlB, August 17, 1911, AGM, 14, Exp. 4, #35.

160. FIM to Emiliano Zapata, August 17, 1911, AGA 1, #35; telegram, FIM to Zapata, August 17, 1911, AFIM, reel 19, #960.

161. FIM to FLdlB, August 18, 1911, AFIM, reel 19, #968.

162. Womack, *Zapata*, 111; Juan Vázquez to FLdlB, August 20, 1911, AGM, 6, Exp. V-4, #14; Valentín Martínez to FLdlB, August 18, 1911, AGM, 7, Exp. M-3, #128; Juan Pagaza to FLdlB, August 23, 1911, AGM, 8, Exp. P-3, #78.

163. Victoriano Huerta to FLdlB, August 18, 1911, AGM, 14, Exp. 4, #63.

164. FLdlB to FIM, August 18, 1911, AGM, 17, Exp. 8, #21.

165. FLdlB to FIM, August 19, 1911, AGM, 17, Exp. 8, #28; T. Ruiz de Velasco to FLdlB, August 21, 1911, AGM, 1, Exp. R-3, #130.

166. FIM to FLdlB, August 19, 1911, AGM, 17, Exp. 8, #23; FIM to FLdlB, August 19, 1911, AFIM, reel 19, #984; FIM to FLdlB, AGM, August 19, 1911, 17, Exp. 8, #25.

167. FIM to Gustavo Madero, August 19, 1911, AFIM, reel 19, #1027; FIM to FLdlB, August 19, 1911, AFIM, reel 19, #1029.

168. Michael C. Meyer, *Huerta: A Political Portrait* (Lincoln: University of Nebraska Press, 1972), 30–31, 46.

169. FIM to FLdlB, August 19, 1911, AGM, 17, Exp. 8, #29; Ambrosio Figueroa to FIM, August 19, 1911, AFIM, reel 19, #988; FIM to FLdlB, August 19, 1911, AFIM, reel 19, #1045.

170. FIM to Arnoldo Casso López, August 19, 1911, AFIM, reel 19, #1043; FIM to Victoriano Huerta and Aureliano Blanquet, August 19, 1911, AFIM, reel 19, #1028.

171. Ernesto Madero to FIM, August 19, 1911, AFIM, reel 19, #1001.

172. Victoriano Huerta to FLdlB, August 20, 1911, AGM, 16, Exp. 1, #25; Huerta to FLdlB, August 20, 1911, AGM, 16, Exp. 1, #2; Victoriano Huerta to José González Salas, August 24, 1911, AHDN, 481.5/177, 96, #129–34. Surprisingly, the military files on Morelos in June, July, and August are almost nonexistent. Miguel A. Sánchez Lamego, whose *Historia militar de la revolución mexicana en la epoca maderista,* 3 vols. (Mexico: Biblioteca del Instituto Nacional de Estudios Históricos de la Revolución Mexicana, 1977), is based entirely on AHDN, saw only the same few documents; see 2:31–35.

173. FLdlB to FIM, August 20, 1911, AGM, 18, Exp. 5, #1. The document also appears in AFIM, reel 19, #1083; see also FIM to FLdlB, August 20, 1911, AGM, 16, Exp. 1, #3; FIM to FLdlB, August 20, 1911, AGM, 17, Exp. 8, #36. For the order to Casso López, see José González Salas to Arnoldo Casso López, August 19, 1911, AHDN, 481.5/177, 96, #128; Magaña, *Emiliano Zapata,* 1:305–6.

174. FLdlB to FIM, August 20, 1911, AFIM, reel 19, #1063, also in AGM, 17, Exp. 8, #33; FLdlB to FIM, August 20, 1911, AFIM, reel 19, #1081; FLdlB to FIM, August 21, 1911, AGM, 17, Exp. 8, #44.

175. FLdlB to Victoriano Huerta, August 20, 1911, AFVG, box 18, folder 6, no number; Ernesto Madero to FIM, August 20, 1911, AFIM, reel 19, #1069; T. B. Hohler to Sir Edward Grey, October 28, 1911, FO, reel 17, 371.1150/44893.

176. Francisco Madero to FLdlB, August 21, 1911, AGM, 17, Exp. 8, #41.

177. FIM to FLdlB, August 21, 1911, AFIM, reel 19, 1911, #1122; or in AGM, 17, Exp. 8, #37.

178. FLdlB to Victoriano Huerta, August 21, 1911, AGM, 18, Exp. 7, #27.

179. FIM to FLdlB, August 21, 1911, AFIM, reel 19, #1101; E. M. Bonilla to the Diario del Hogar, August 21, 1911, AGM, 19, Exp. 3, #47; FIM to FLdlB, August 21, 1911, AGM, 17, Exp. 8, #40. The rebels of San José de Gracia faked their demobilization after the Cristero revolt; see Luis González, *San José de Gracia: Mexican Village in Transition* (Austin: University of Texas Press, 1974), 172.

180. Victoriano Huerta to FLdlB, August 21, 1911, AGM, 17, Exp. 11, #18. Brunk, *Zapata,* 97, is of the opinion that Zapata would have come to terms; I disagree.

181. FLdlB to FIM, August 21, 1911, AFIM, reel 19, #1093.

182. FIM to FLdlB, August 22, 1911, AGM, 18, Exp. 5, #31. See also FIM to Juan Sánchez Azcona, October 25, 1911, AFIM, reel 18, #0517.

183. FLdlB to FIM, August 22, 1911, AGM, 17, Exp. 8, #45; Meyer, *Huerta,* 23–24.

184. FLdlB to FIM, August 22, 1911, AGM, 17, Exp. 8, #49; FLdlB to FIM, August 22, 1911, and AFIM, reel 19, #1190.

185. FLdlB to Victoriano Huerta, August 24, 1911, AGM, 17, Exp. 8, #57.

186. Victoriano Huerta to FLdlB, August 26, 1911, AGM, 16, Exp. 2, #7.

187.Teofanes Jiménez to FLdlB, August 28, 1911, AGM, 6, Exp. J-4, #1; A. Falcón Roldán to FLdlB, August 30, 1911, AGM, 9, Exp. F-3, #3.

188. Victoriano Huerta to FLdlB, August 28, 1911, AGM, 12, Exp. 1, #20.

189. FLdlB to Victoriano Huerta, August 29, 1911, AGM, 16, Exp. 2, #58; FLdlB to Victoriano Huerta, August 30, 1911, AFVG, box 19, folder 8, no number.

190. Raúl Madero to FIM, August 29, 1911, AFIM, reel 19, #1224.

191. Victoriano Huerta to FLdlB, August 31, 1911, AGM, 12, Exp. 1, #21; Victoriano Huerta to FLdlB, August 30, 1911, AFVG, box 19, folder 8, no number.

192. Emiliano Zapata to FLdlB, August 31, 1911, AGM, 15, Exp. 5, #5. I have purposely repeated the words Womack uses to characterize de la Barra in order to show there are two sides to the story; see Womack, *Zapata*, 91. See also FLdlB to Zapata, September 1, 1911, AGM, 15, Exp. 5, #4.

193. Womack, *Zapata*, 120; Colonel Morales to José González Salas, September 3, 1911, AHDN, 481.5/177, 96, #135.

194. Arturo Figueroa Uriza, *Ciudadanos en armas* (Mexico City: B. Costa-Amic, 1960), 222.

195. Womack, *Zapata*, 323–30; Gilly, *Revolution*, 256.

196. Warman, *We Come to Object*, 136–42; *El País* and *El Diario*, August 31, 1911; Gilly, *Revolution*, 77.

197. Victoriano Huerto to FLdlB, September 13, 1911, AGM, 12, Exp. 1, #24.

198. FLdlB to Victoriano Huerta, September 15, 1911, AGM, 12, Exp. 1, #25; FIM to Francisco Figueroa, September 15, 1911, AFIM, reel 19, #1257; FLdlB to Alberto García Granados, September 6, 1911, AGM, 4, Exp. G-4, #36; Victoriano Huerta to FLdlB, October 5, 1911, AGM, 21, Exp. 4, #7.

199. FLdlB to Victoriano Huerta, September 15, 1911, AGM, 12, book 9, #460; Emilio R. de la Vega to FLdlB, September 22, 1911, AGM, 6, Exp. V-4, #84.

200. Agustín del Pozo to FLdlB, September 28, 1911, AGM, 21, Exp. 2, #77; Zapata's Proclamation, September 26, 1911, AGM, 24, Exp. Z-2, #7; Victoriano Huerta to FLdlB, September 26, 1911, AGM, 21, Exp. 2, #29; De la Barra to del Pozo, October 1, 1911, AGM, 21, Exp. 3, #15.

201. General Casso López to José González Salas, October 20, 1911, AHDN, 481.5/177, 96, #201; Captain Jacobo Márquez Alejandro to General Casso López, October 27, 1911, AHDN, 481.5/177, 96, #249.

202. FIM to FLdlB, August 25, 1911, DHRM, vol. 6, #331; T. B. Hohler to Sir Edward Grey, August 26, 1911, FO, reel 17, 371.1150/35718; Hohler, *Diplomatic Petrel*, 176; Fred Dearing to Philander Knox, August 30, 1911, RDS, reel 14, 812.00/2316; Dearing's note of August 21, 1911, RDS, reel 14, 812.00/2299.

203. Baron LeFavre to Baron Selves, October 26, 1911, ADRF, vol. 2, 31–33; FIM to Juan Sanchez Azcona, October 25, 1911, AFIM, reel 18, #0517, and de la Barra's reply in *El Democrático Mexicano*, October 27, 1911; Ponce de León, *El Interinato*, 178–80; *Diario de los debates*, October 26, 1911.

204. José "Che" Gómez to FLdlB, November 1, 1911, AGM, 19, Exp. 4, #4; General T. Merodio to José González Salas, October 26, 1911, AHDN, 481.5/206, 109, #609; Knight, *Mexican Revolution*, 1:374–76; Hector Gerardo Martínez Medina, "La cuestión de Don Benito Juárez Maza: La rebelión Che-Gomista y otros conflictos políticos-militares, septiembre a diciembre de 1911," in *Memoria del Congreso*, 261–98.

205. FLdlB to José Gómez, November 2, 1911, AGM, 19, Exp. 4, #13; General Enrique Toribio to José González Salas, January 20, 1912, AHDN, 481.5/206, 109, #697–99.

206. Prida, *De la dictadura*, 364–65; W. H. Dunn, *The Crimson Jester: Zapata of Mexico* (New York: R. M. McBride and Company, 1933), 109; I. V. Heredia to FLdlB, August 5, 1911, AGM, 3, Exp. H-3, #22.

207. Thomas Voetter to Philander C. Knox, June 1, 1911, RDS, reel 13, 812.00/2052; Edward D. Trowbridge, *Mexico Today and Tomorrow* (New York: Macmillan, 1920), 138.

208. Luis Cabrera (Blas Urrea, pseud.), "La revolución dentro del gobierno," in Obras politicas del Lic. Blas Urrea (Mexico City: UNAM, 1992), 335–37.

Chapter 4

1. Roderic Ai Camp, ed., *Democracy in Latin America: Patterns and Cycles* (Wilmington, DE: Scholarly Resources, 1996); Samuel P. Huntington, *The Third Wave: Democratization in the Late Twentieth Century* (Norman: University of Oklahoma Press, 1991).

2. Gabriel Almond and Sidney Verba, *The Civic Culture Revisited* (Boston: Little, Brown and Company, 1980; Alicia Hernández Chávez, *La tradición republicana del buen gobierno* (Mexico: Fondo de Cultura Económica, 1993); John Booth and Mitchell Seligson, "Political Culture of Authoritarianism in Mexico: A Re-Examination," *Latin American Research Review* 19, no. 1 (1984): 106–24.

3. Walter V. Scholes, *Mexican Politics during the Juárez Regime, 1855–1872* (Columbia: University of Missouri Press, 1957).

4. Ross, *Francisco I. Madero*, 215–16, 229; Cumberland, *Mexican Revolution*, 168–69.

5. Tannenbaum, *Peace and Bread*, 51; Hart, *Revolutionary Mexico*, 240–42.

6. Eugenio Ramírez et al. to FIM, August 3, 1911, AFIM, reel 20, #1728; "Una Señorita" to FIM, August 9, 1911, AFIM, reel 19, #1522; Venustiano Carranza to the People of Coahuila, August 1, 1911, Arch. Carranza 1, #38; Knight, *Mexican Revolution*, 1:238; Romana Falcón, "Los origines populares de la revolución de 1910: El caso de San Luis Potosí," *Historia Mexicana* 29 (October–December 1979): 197–240.

7. Manuel Garza Aldape to FLdlB, October 7, 1911, AGM, 21, Exp. 4, #43; Felipe H. Perales to FLdlB, July 12, 1911, AGM, 8, Exp. P–2, #53; Pedro Zamora to FLdlB, August 2, 1911, AGM, 24, Exp. Z-3, #18.

8. FIM to Gabriel Gavira, June 23, 1911, AFIM, reel 22, #3693; Vera Estañol, *Revolución mexicana*, 244–45.

9. Interim Governor P. Aillaud to Luis León de la Barra, August 18, 1911, AGM, 5, Exp. A-3, #133; *El Imparcial*, October 16, 1912; Salvador Sánchez Septién, *José María Lozano en la tribuna parlamentario, 1910–1913* (Mexico City: Editorial Jus, 1953).

10. Roberto Pérez to Alfredo Robles Domínguez, August 1911, AARD, vol. 2, Exp. 8, #126–27.

11. Richard Sinkin, *The Mexican Reform, 1855–1876: A Study in Liberal Nation Building* (Austin: University of Texas Press, 1979).

12. Heriberto Frías to FLdlB, November 3, 1911, AGM, 22, Exp. 6, #67; FLdlB to FIM, May 28, 1911, AGM, 17, Exp. 3, #22; FIM to FLdlB, May 28, 1911, AGM, 17, Exp. 3, #21; Aguirre Benavides, *Madero*, 485–86; T. B. Hohler to Sir Edward Grey, June 23, 1911, FO, reel 17, 371.1149/26876.

13. Ross, *Francisco I. Madero*, 231–35; Federico González Garza to FIM, July 18, 1911, AFGG, 21, #2033; González Garza, *Revolucíon mexicana*, 341–43.

14. Vera Estañol, *Revolución mexicana*, 217.

15. FLdlB to Emilia Martínez, vda. de Iglesias, July 10, 1911, AGM, 16, Exp. 4, #120; Arturo Cisneros Peña to FLdlB, June 20, 1911, AGM, 2, Exp. C-1, #140; *El Diario*, June 30, 1911.

16. J. de la Peña to FLdlB, September 6, 1911, AGM, 8, Exp. P-4, #34; FLdlB to Roque Estrada, August 4, 1911, ARE, 2, #624; Lara Pardo, *Madero*, 265–67.

17. Abraham González to Jefe Municipal of Tejolecachic, August 28, 1911, OC, reel 2(a), #971; Venustiano Carranza to Pablo González, June 14, 1911, Arch. M. González 2, #30; FIM to Luis Lara Pardo, June 21, 1911, AFIM, reel 20, #2072; FIM to Alberto Fuentes D, June 18, 1911, BNAM, 2/650.

18. *Diario de los debates*, September 21, 1911, and October 10, 1911; Francisco de Lemus to FLdlB, June 19, 1911, AGM, 3, Exp. L-1, #67.

19. C. W. Whittemore to FLdlB, May 20, 1911, AGM , 34, Exp. 3 BIS, #151; C. W. Whittemore to FLdlB, June 29, 1911, AGM, 11, Exp. W-4, #1, and de la Barra's response, July 3, 1911, AGM, 13, Exp. 4, book 4, #47.

20. Josefina MacGregor, "Madero y los diputados: En busca de una Nueva Relación," in *Memoria del Congreso Internacional sobre la Revolución Mexicana*, 2:57–79, *Diario de los debates*, October 10, 1911.

21. FLdlB to Ruperto Quintero, July 7, 1911, AGM, 13, book 4, #218; FLdlB to Evaristo Soto Véloz, September 25, 1911, AGM, 11, book 1, #337; FLdlB to León Aillaud, Interim Governor of Veracruz, August 5, 1911, AGM, 13, book 6, #381. The quotation is from FLdlB to Gregorio Torres Quintero, June 5, 1911, AGM, 10, book 1, #308.

22. Constantino Rangel to FLdlB, June 22, 1911, AGM, 1, Exp. R-2, #18.

23. William H. Beezley, "Madero: The 'Unknown' President and His Political Failure to Organize Rural Mexico," in Douglas Richmond, ed., *Essays on the Mexican Revolution* (Austin: University of Texas Press, 1979), 3–5.

24. Baron de Vaux to M. de Selves, Minister of Foreign Affairs, July 6, 1911, ADRF, vol. 3, 2–6; *Diario de los debates*, November 7, 1911; Knight, *Mexican Revolution*, I:64.

25. Circular of Emilio Vázquez Gómez to Governors, June 21, 1911, FO, reel 17, 371.1550/27069.

26. Miguel Bolanos Cacho to FLdlB, July 30, 1911, AGM, 31, Exp. B-2, #114; Silvestre Terrazas to Federico Moye, July 1, 1911, Terrazas Papers, part 1, box 81, file 1911–1912, and a reply dated July 2, 1911, Terrazas Papers, part 1, box 51, File Federico Moye.

27. Meyer, *Mexican Rebel*, 40–42.

28. Silvestre Terrazas to Miguel Bolanos Cacho, July 1, 1911, Terrazas Papers, box 81, section 1; Silvestre Terrazas to Manuel Balbas, July 1, 1911, Terrazas Papers, box 81, section 1.

29. Abraham González to Guadalupe Rivera, July 20, 1911, OC, Abraham González letterbook, reel 2(a), #440; Abraham González to C. L.

Conway, July 26, 1911, OC, Abraham González letterbook, reel 2(a), #605.

30. Rafael Zamudio to FLdlB, August 30, 1911, AGM, 24, Exp. Z-5; J. Alcocer to FLdlB, September 9, 1911, AGM, 14, Exp. 5, #36.

31. Ross, *Francisco I. Madero*, 224–25; Aguirre Benavides, *Madero*, 186.

32. Manuel Calero to Emilio Vázquez Gómez, June 16, 1911, AGM, 24, unnumbered exp., #174.

33. Alberto García Granados to FLdlB, August 6, 1911, AGM, 4, Exp. G-3, #147.

34. Antonio B. Monteverde to FLdlB, August 13, 1911, AGM, 7, Exp. M-3, #88; FLdlB to Manuel Zapata, September 30, 1911, AGM, 11, copybook 2, #121; *El Imparcial*, September 16, 1911.

35. LaFrance, *Puebla, 1908–1913*, 104–5; J. R. Isunza to FLdlB, May 27, 1911, AGM, 1, Exp. Y-2, #5; F. R. Velázquez to FIM, August 8, 1911, AFIM, reel 20, #1671.

36. *Diario de los debates*, October 4, 1911; FLdlB to Mucio Martínez, October 9, 1911, AGM, 11, book 2, #467; Calero, *Un decenio*, 67–69; *Mexican Herald*, July 18, 1911.

37. Circular of Emilio Vázquez Gómez, June 16, 1911, AFGG, 19, #1861; see also FO, reel 17, 371.1150/26877.

38. Emilio Vázquez Gómez to Governor of Zacatecas, July 6, 1911, AGM, 10, Emilio Vázquez Gómez letterbook, #431; and his letter of the same date to the Governor of Aguascalientes, #400; for the form letter see FO, reel 17, 371.1550/29161. See also Miguel Murillo to FIM, June 20, 1911, AFIM, reel 18, #0087; Adalberto Torres to FLdlB, July 1, 1911, AGM, 5, Exp. T-2, #12.

39. Jesús Munguía Santoyo to FLdlB, June 28, 1911, AGM, 7, Exp. M-2, #22.

40. Rafael Cepeda to FIM, June 30, 1911, AFIM, reel 18, #571.

41. J. Lloyd Mecham, "The Jefe Político in Mexico," *Southwestern Social Science Quarterly* 13, no. 4 (March 1933): 333–52; Cabrera, *Obras completas*, 346. Mónica Blanco, "Participación popular y revolución: La elección de los jefes políticos en Guanajuato en 1911," in *Memoria del Congreso Internacional sobre la Revolución Mexicana*, 1:135–47; Guy P. C. Thompson, with David LaFrance, *Patriotism, Politics, and Mexican Popular Liberalism in Eighteenth-Century Mexico: Juan Francisco Lucas and the Puebla Sierra* (Wilmington, DE: Scholarly Resources, 1999).

42. Ramón Carrillo to FLdlB, AGM, 2, Exp. C-1, #18; FIM to Jesús Munguía Santoyo, June 22, 1911, AFIM, reel 19, #728; E. Acosta to FLdlB, AGM, 16, Exp. 2, #50; LaFrance, *Puebla, 1908–1913*, 69–71; Jorge Vera Estañol to Porfirio Díaz, April 12, 1911, in *Últimos meses de Porfirio Díaz en el poder* (Mexico: Talleres Gráficos de la Nación, 1911), 53:205–9; Emilio Torres to Juan Sánchez Azcona, AFIM, reel 20, #1880; and Enrique Baz to FLdlB, July 18, 1911, AGM, 31, Exp. B-3, #284.

43. Ross, *Francisco I. Madero*, 203.

44. FLdlB to Emilio Vázquez Gómez, June 17, 1911, AFIM, reel 18, #0259. See also the interview with de la Barra in *Mexican Herald*, July 18, 1911.

45. Ricardo Cobamiras to FLdlB, n.d., AGM, 2, Exp. C-2, #118; J. de J. Peña to FLdlB, August 4, 1911, AGM, 8, Exp. P-3, #33; Manuel Zamacona to FLdlB, August 23, 1911, AREM, L-E 665, Leg. 99, 8–9; Aguirre Benavides, *Madero*, 42.

46. M. Marroquín y Rivera to FLdlB, June 1, 1911, AGM, 7, Exp. M-1, #38. *Diario de los debates*, October 14, 1911, and November 1, 1911.

47. Abraham González to Emilio Vázquez Gómez, July 7, 1911, OC, reel 2, #248; Abraham González to Carlos Randall, August 18, 1911, OC, reel 2(a), #866; Abraham González to Ernesto Madero, OC, González letterbook, reel 2, #87; Williams to FLdlB, August 22, 1911, AGM, 11, Exp. W-1, #6; Story, "The Genesis of Revolution."

48. Rafael Pérez de León to FLdlB, August 29, 1911, AGM, 3, Exp. L-4, #20. For the postal employees, see the discussion of Manuel Bonilla in Chapter 3.

49. FIM to Federico González Garza, July 25, 1911, AFGG, 21, #2069.

50. Francisco Elguero to FLdlB, June 2, 1911, AGM, 24, Exp. E-1, #16.

51. Vicente Garcia to FLdlB, August 16, 1911, AGM, 4, Exp. G-3, #138; Miguel Silva to FLdlB, August 14, 1911, AGM, Exp. 1, #64, and another letter dated August 16, 1911, AGM, 9, Exp. S-3, #51; Juan B. Paulin to FLdlB, August 19, 1911, AGM, 8, Exp. P-3, #69; Miguel Silva to FLdlB, September 10, 1911, AGM, Exp. 3, #3.

52. Francisco Elguero to FLdlB, September 23, 1911, AGM, Exp. E-3, #34.

53. A. M. Ugarte, Governor of Aguascalientes, to FLdlB, August 21, 1911, AGM, 18, Exp. 7, #17. J. Figueroa Domenech, *Veinte meses de anarquía* (Mexico: Herrero Hermanos Sucesores, 1913).

54. Francisco Vázquez Gómez to Emilio Vázquez Gómez, July 11, 1911, AFVG, box 14, #1409; Adrián Aguirre Benavides to Juan Sánchez Azcona, June 28, 1911, AARD, vol. 5, Exp. 21, #21-22.

55. FLdlB to Interim Governor Rafael Septién, July 13, 1911, AGM, 16, Exp. 3, #24; FIM to FLdlB, July 30, 1911, AdlB 2, #118.

56. José María Maytorena to FIM, July 28, 1911, JMMP, box 1, folder 13, #15; FIM to José María Maytorena, July 10, 1911, AFIM, reel 19, #0750.

57. FIM to FLdlB, July 24, 1911, AdlB 2, #110, and his telegram of July 29, 1911, AGM, 18, Exp. 1, #52; FLdlB to FIM, July 28, 1911, AGM, 23, Exp. 5, #12; Peter V. N. Henderson, "Un Gobernador Maderista: Benito Juárez Maza y la Revolución en Oaxaca," *Historia Mexicana* 24 (January–March 1975): 372–89.

58. Enrique Baz to FLdlB, August 15, 1911, AGM, Exp. B-2, #47; FIM to Alberto Robles Gil, October. 18, 1911, DHRM, VI, 359. Rodolfo Reyes, *De mi vida*, 3 vols. (Madrid: Biblioteca Nueva, 1929), 1:150–52, 161–65.

59. Gonzalo del Castillo Negrete to FIM, October 19, 1911, AFIM, reel 21, #3519; F. V. Aldama to FLdlB, August 23, 1911, AGM, 16, Exp. 1, #60.

60. FIM to Gonzalo del Castillo Negrete, October 23, 1911, AFIM, reel 21, #3532; Wistano L. Orozco to Ernesto Madero, September 5, 1911, AGM, 9, Exp. O-4, #12; Knight, *Mexican Revolution*, 1:402.

61. Ramón Alcázar to FLdlB, September 9, 1911, AGM, 5, Exp. A-4, #48; Manuel Villaseñor to FIM, August 26, 1911, AFIM, reel 20, #1682.

62. FLdlB to Gregorio Torres Quintero [opposition candidate for Governor of Colima], June 5, 1911, AGM, 10, book 1, #308.

63. FLdlB to Ramón Maldonado, Interim Governor of Tlaxcala, September 15, 1911, AGM, 11, book 1, #13.

64. FLdlB to Emilio Vázquez Gómez, July 14, 1911, AGM, 13, book 4, #400.

65. Raymond Buve, *El movimiento revolucionario en Tlaxcala* (Mexico: Universidad Iberoamericana, 1994); Gerzayn Ugarte to FLdlB, August 16, 1911, AGM, 11, Exp. U-3, #21.

66. Ramon Maldonado to FLdlB, September 7, 1911, AGM, 7, Exp. M-4, #43; Buve, *Tlaxcala*, 131–34.

67. Antonio Hidalgo, "Al Pueblo Tlaxcalteca," AGM, 9, Exp. S-4, #81.

68. Gerzayn Ugarte to FLdlB, September 7, 1911, AGM, 11, Exp. U-4, #8, and his letter of September 9, 1911, AGM, 11, Exp. U-4, #6.

69. Ramon Maldonado to FLdlB, September 12, 1911, AGM, 7, Exp. M-4, #80; Ramon Maldonado to FLdlB, Sept. 15, 1911, AGM, 7, Exp. M-4, #85; Agustin Sanchez to FLdlB, September 24, 1911, AGM, 9, Exp. S-4, #80.

70. Knight, *Mexican Revolution*, 1:384; Ramon Maldonado to FLdlB, October 30, 1911, AGM, 28, Exp. 11, #718; Crisanto Cuellar Abaroa, *La revolución en el estado de Tlaxcala* (Mexico: Biblioteca del Instituto Nacional de Estudios Históricos de la Revolución Mexicana, 1975), 1:96–98.

71. Hernández Chávez, *La tradición republicana*, 155–56. Even the allegedly radical Emilio Vázquez Gómez spoke about the fact that "democracy was the object of our struggle"; see Emilio Vázquez Gómez to Luis R. García, AGM, 10, Vázquez Gómez letterbook, #202.

72. Henry Lane Wilson to Philander C. Knox, October 27, 1911, RDS, reel 15, 812.00/2453; José Fernández Rojas, *De Porfirio Díaz a Victoriano Huerta* (Guadalajara: Tip. de Escuela de Artes y Oficios del Estado, 1913), 15–16; Roque Estrada to FIM, October 16, 1911, DHRM, vol. 6, #355; Manero, *El antiguo régimen*, 382; Luther Ellsworth to Philander C. Knox, July 14, 1911, RDS, reel 14, 812.00/2217.

73. Policarpio Santibáñez to FLdlB, September 1, 1911, AGM, 9, Exp. S-4, #19.

74. Luis León de la Barra to FLdlB, June 16, 1911, AGM, 5, Exp. T-1, #11; Luis León de la Barra to FLdlB, September 18, 1911, AGM, 5, Exp. T-4, #21; Ignacio León de la Barra to Federico González Garza, February 25, 1912, AFGG, 23, #2286.

75. Acuerdo from FLdlB to Secretary of War, July 4, 1911, AGM, 30, Exp. 5, #50.

76. Basilio Rojas, *Un gran rebelde: Manuel García Vigil* (Mexico: Editorial Luz, 1965), 106–7; Francisco Vázquez Gómez to David Lawrence, August 21, 1911, AFVG, box 18, folder 6, #981; Vázquez Gómez, *Memorias políticas*, 404–7, 443.

77. Francisco Vázquez Gómez to FIM, July 27, 1911, AFVG, box 15, #1618; Adrián Aguirre Benavides to Francisco Vázquez Gómez, August 5, 1911, AFVG, box 16, #0013.

78. José María Pino Suárez to Francisco Vázquez Gómez, July 13, 1911, AFVG, box 14, #1423.

79. Francisco Vázquez Gómez to José María Pino Suárez, July 25, 1911, AFVG, box 15, #1595.

80. FIM to Francisco Vázquez Gómez, August 1, 1911, AFVG, box 16, folder 1, #0005; Anti-Reelection Club to FIM, August 5, 1911, DHRM, vol. 6, #311, 36–40.

81. Francisco Vázquez Gómez to FIM, August 14, 1911, AFVG, box 17, folder 6, no #; FIM to Francisco Vázquez Gómez, August 11, 1911,

AFVG, box 17, folder 3, no #; Fernández Güell, *Revolución mexicana*, 127–28.

82. Fred Dearing to Philander C. Knox, September 4, 1911, RDS, reel 14, 812.00/2345.

83. Pablo Asconsio to Juan Sánchez Azcona, August 18, 1911, AFIM, reel 19, #1278; Lorenzo R. López to Francisco Vázquez Gómez, August 16, 1911, AFVG, box 17, folder 8, no #; Abraham González to FIM, August 22, 1911, OC, reel 2(a), González letterbook, #898.

84. Vicente Vergara to Francisco Vázquez Gómez, September 6, 1911, AFVG, box 20, folder 6, #162.

85. *Quien es Pino Súarez*? (Mexico: Imprenta Popular Nuevo México, 1911), 31–32; FIM to Citizens of Puerto Mexico, September 22, 1911, AFVG, box 21, #403; Bonilla, *Diez años*, 271–73; T. B. Hohler to Sir Edward Grey, October 16, 1911, FO, reel 17, 371.1150/42959.

86. José María Pino Suárez to Francisco Vázquez Gómez, September 28, 1911, AFVG, box 21, #522. The text of Madero's speech is in *Jalisco: Documentos de la revolución, 1910–1940* (Guadalajara: Gobierno de Jalisco, 1987), 40–52. See also Vázquez Gómez, *Memorias políticas*, 434–35; *El Diario*, October 9, 1911; Roque Estrada to FIM, October 16, 1911, DHRM, vol. 6, #355.

87. Félix N. López to Francisco Vázquez Gómez, September 25, 1911, AFVG, box 21, #437; Julian López Báez to Francisco Vázquez Gómez, September 25, 1911, AFVG, box 21, #453.

88. Juan Fortuny to Francisco Vázquez Gómez, September 18, 1911, AFVG, box 21, #365; Francisco Artiles to Francisco Vázquez Gómez, September 17, 1911, AFVG, box 21, #356; A. Guzmán to Francisco Vázquez Gómez, September 23, 1911, AFVG, box 21, #418; Lauro Villar to FLdlB, September 8, 1911, AGM, 6, Exp. V-4, #27; *El Imparcial*, October 8, 1911; Figueroa Domenech, *Veinte meses*, 39–40; Katz, *Villa*, 134.

89. Franco A. Aldama to FLdlB, October 8, 1911, AGM, 5, Exp. A-5, #54; FLdlB to Nicolás R. Arenas, September 15, 1911, AGM, 11, book 1, #29; FLdlB to FIM, July 31, 1911, AGM, 13, book 6, #103–6; *El Mañana*, September 25, 1911.

90. Alberto García Granados to FLdlB, October 18, 1911, AGM, 4, Exp. G-5, #75.

91. Unsigned to FIM, October 20, 1911, AFVG, box 23, #300.

92. Francisco O'Reilly to FLdlB, October 3, 1911, AGM, 9, Exp. 0-5, #8; Juan N. Aguirre to FIM, October 18, 1911, AFIM, reel 21, #3437.

93. Enrique Baz to FLdlB, October 15, 1911, AGM, 4, Exp. G-6, #44; Alejandro Haro to FIM, October 21, 1911, AFIM, reel 22, #3653; T. B. Hohler to Sir Edward Grey, October 4, 1911, FO, reel 17, 371.1150/41409; Baron La Faivre to Baron Selves, October 10, 1911, ADRF, vol. 3, 26–28.

94. See Francisco Vázquez Gómez to Manuel Bonilla, November 4, 1911, AFVG, box 11, #1381; Francisco Vázquez Gómez to Leopoldo Rodríguez Calderón, September 27, 1911, AFVG, box 21, #499.

95. FLdlB to Francisco Vázquez Gómez, October 30, 1911, AGM, 11, book 3, #135–36; Manuel Bonilla to Francisco Vázquez Gómez, October 31, 1911, AFVG, box 23, #497; Francisco Vázquez Gómez to El Director, December 30, 1911, AFVG, box 27, #293.

96. Bryan, "Bernardo Reyes," 221–64.

97. Madero's notes, n.d. [May 1911], BNAM, box 4, #1729; Heriberto Barrón to FLdlB, May 22, 1911, AGM, 31, Exp B-1, #77.

98. Madero's notes, May 1911, BNAM, box 4, #1728–29; FIM to Bernardo Reyes, July 13, 1911, AdlB 2, #105; Baron de Vaux to Baron Cruppi, June 13, 1911, ADRF, vol. 2, 248–50.

99. Enrique Adame Macías to FIM, July 6, 1911, AFIM, reel 20, #2288; Roque Estrada to FIM, June 26, 1911, AFIM, reel 20, #2003; Luther Ellsworth to Philander C. Knox, July 18, 1911, RDS, reel 14, 812.00/2225.

100. M. Gómez Flores to FIM, July 3, 1911, AFIM, reel 20, #2030.

101. FIM to the Anti-Reyistas, July 10, 1911, AFVG, box 14, #1344.

102. Mariano Alcérreca to Samuel Espinosa de los Monteros, August 7, 1911, Archivo de Samuel Espinosa de los Monteros, Biblioteca Manuel Orozco y Berra, Anexo a Chapultepec Castillo de Mexico City (hereafter cited as Arch. de los Monteros), vol. 5, #211–12; E. Victor Niemeyer, *El General Bernardo Reyes* (Monterrey: Biblioteca de Nueva León, 1966), 190.

103. Bernardo Reyes to FLdlB, June 19, 1911, AdlB 1, #93; Bernardo Reyes to FLdlB, July 9, 1911, AGM, 1, Exp. R-2, #60.

104. FIM to Bernardo Reyes, July 16, 1911, Archivo de Bernardo Reyes, Centro de Estudios de la Historia de Mexico, Condumex, S.A., Mexico City (hereafter cited as ABR), 40, #7941. The letter also appears in AdlB 2, #105.

105. FIM to FLdlB, July 26, 1911, AdlB 2, #115.

106. FLdlB to FIM, July 31, 1911, AGM, 13, book 6, #103–6.

107. FIM to FLdlB, August 2, 1911, AGM, 18, Exp. 3, #11. A copy is in ABR, 40, #7942. See also FIM andBernardo Reyes to FLdlB, August 2, 1911, DHRM, vol. 6, #305, 21–23.

108. FLdlB to FIM, August 2, 1911, AGM, 15, Exp. 3, #60, and 18, Exp. 3, #12. Reyes announced on August 4, 1911; see Bernardo Reyes to the Nation, August 4, 1911, DHRM, vol. 6, #309, 29–32.

109. Bernardo Reyes to Jesús Asúnsolo, n.d., ABR, copybook #46, #21487; Bernardo Reyes to Juan Sottil, August 16, 1911, ABR, copybook #46, #21226;Heriberto Barrón to FLdlB, August 16, 1911, AGM, 31, Exp. B-2, #143.

110. J. Munguía Santoyo to FLdlB, August 6, 1911, AGM, 7, Exp. M-3, #30.

111. Tomás Castilla to FLdlB, August 28, 1911, AGM, 2, Exp. C-2, #49.

112. José Narciso Zermeño to FLdlB, August 23, 1911, AGM, 24, Exp. Z-3, #31.

113. Fernando Ancira and R. E. Treviño to Bernardo Reyes, August 19, 1911, AGM, 14, Exp. 4, #95.

114. "El Corresponsal" to Juan Sánchez Azcona, August 25, 1911, AFIM, reel 19, #1666.

115. Bernardo Reyes to FLdlB, August 24, 1911, AdlB 2, #125; FLdlB to Bernardo Reyes, August 20, 1911, AGM, 12, book 7, #410; Mariano Alcérreca to Samuel Espinosa de los Monteros, August 7, 1911, Arch. de los Monteros, vol. 5, #211–12; *El País,* September 4, 1911.

116. Bernardo Reyes to FLdlB, September 6, 1911, AGM, 1, Exp. R-4, #60.

117. Bernardo Reyes to Alberto García Granados, September 10, 1911, ABR, 40, #7944.

118. Accord signed by FLdlB et al., September 12, 1911, AdlB 2, #130; ABR, 40, #7950; Ponce de León, *El interinato,* 131–35.

119. José Peón del Valle to FLdlB, September 15, 1911, AGM, 8, Exp. P-4, #61; Miguel Díaz Lombardo et al. to FLdlB, September 29, 1911, AGM,

24, Exp. D-5, #17; FLdlB to Ernesto Madero, September 25, 1911, AGM, 11, book 1, #314.

120. FLdlB to José Peón del Valle et al., September 25, 1911, AGM, 11, book 1, #313; Ernesto Madero et al. to FLdlB, September 29, 1911, AGM, 24, Exp D-4, #18.

121. Henry Lane Wilson to Philander C. Knox, September 22, 1911, RDS, reel 14, 812.00/2384; Rafael Cañete to FLdlB, September 11, 1911, AGM, 13, Exp. 3, #14; Aurelio Manrique to FLdlB, September 11, 1911, AGM, 31, Exp. B-4, #331; Eduardo Hay to FLdlB, September 23, 1911, AGM, 21, Exp. 5, #54.

122. Bernardo Reyes to Srs. Araujo and Vizcaría, September 29, 1911, ABR, book 46, #21701 (493).

123. FLdlB to Bernardo Reyes, September 29, 1911, AGM, 18, Exp. 3, #5, and in AREM, L-E 849, Leg. 2, 46; Henry Lane Wilson to Philander C. Knox, September 6, 1911, RDS, reel 14, 812.00/2348.

124. Gerónimo Treviño to FLdlB, October 9, 1911, AGM, 20, Exp. 2, #15.

125. Luis León de la Barra to FLdlB, October 26, 1911, AGM, 19, Exp. 7, #39, and a decoded version in AdlB, 2, #156.

126. Luis León de la Barra to FIM, October 27, 1911, DHRM, vol. 6, #373. See also William Carr to Philander C. Knox, November 4, 1911, RDS, reel 15, 812.00/2471.

127. E. Victor Niemeyer, "Frustrated Invasion: The Revolutionary Attempt of General Bernardo Reyes from San Antonio in 1911," *Southwestern Historical Quarterly* 47 (October 1963): 213–25.

128. FIM to Federico González Garza, July 30, 1911, AFGG, 21, #2094.

129. Jorge Adame Goddard, *El pensamiento político y social de los católicos mexicanos, 1867–1914* (Mexico City: UNAM, 1981), 164–74.

130. J. P. Alejandre to FLdlB, September 21, 1911, AGM, 5, Exp. A-4, #77; J. Vicente to FLdlB, August 16, 1911, AGM, 6, Exp. V-4, #21.

131. FLdlB to Clemente Z. Hernández, August 26, 1911, AGM, 12, book 8, #231; FLdlB to Jesús M. Rábago, August 4, 1911, AGM, 13, book 6, #259–62. See FLdlB, "Algunas páginas."

132. José Rafael de Altimira to FLdlB, August 14, 1911, AGM, 5, Exp. A-3, #77. Luis Cabrera published a famous article, "Sic vos non volis" on August 14 to dissuade de la Barra from running. See Cabrera, *Obras,* 371–75.

133. Vicente Martínez Cantú to FIM, August 21, 1911, AFIM, reel 18, #0104; Baron de Vaux to Baron de Selves, September 2, 1911, ADRF, vol. 3, 13–16.

134. Adame Goddard, *El pensamiento político,* 175–76.

135. Jorge Vera Estañol to FLdlB, August 14, 1911, JVEP, folder 2. See also AGM, 6, Exp. V-3, #28; Vera Estañol to FLdlB, June 13, 1911, AGM, 23, Exp. 10, #42.

136. FLdlB to Jorge Vera Estañol, August 15, 1911, AGM, 12, book 7, #177–80; and the copy in JVEPP, folder 2. See also Vera Estañol, *Revolución mexicana,* 227; Dearing to Philander Knox, August 4, 1911, RDS, reel 14, 812.00/2257.

137. FLdlB to Carlos Cebrián, July 17, 1911, AGM, 13, book 5, #34; Manuel Rivera Mutis to FLdlB, August 18, 1911, AGM, 1, Exp. R-3, #47; *El Mañana,* August 21, 1911.

138. Santiago Portilla Gil de Partearroyo, "La personalidad política de Francisco León de la Barra," *Historia Mexicana* 25 (October–December 1975): 232–70, 247.

139. T. B. Hohler to Sir Edward Grey, August 3, 1911, FO, reel 17, 371.1150/32135; *El Diario,* August 14, 1911; Antonio Enríquez, *La sucesión presidencial en 1911* (Mexico: Imprenta de Antonio Enríquez, 1911).

140. Ariel Rodríguez Kuri, "El discurso de Miedo: *El Imparcial* y Francisco I. Madero," *Historia Mexicana* 40 (April–June 1991): 697–740, esp. 712–14; T. B. Hohler to Sir Edward Grey, FO, reel 17, 371.1150/39853; *El País,* October 15, 1912; *Diario de los debates,* September 18 and 25, 1911.

141. Circular of Emilio Vázquez Gómez, June 19, 1911, FO, 371.1550/27069; Ponce de León, *El interinato,* 80.

142. Circular of Alberto García Granados, September 2, 1911, AFGG, 22, #2124; *Diario de los debates,* November 2, 1911.

143. Partido Liberal Estudantil to FIM, August 19, 1911, AFIM, reel 20, #1854; Lorenzo Meyer, "La revolución mexicana y sus elecciones presidenciales: Una interpretación," *Historia Mexicana* 35 (January–April 1986): 143–77. Oldtimers recalled that the Madero election was San José de Gracia's first; see González, *San José de Gracia,* 117.

144. Joaquín Rejón to FLdlB, June 7, 1911, AGM, 1, Exp. R-1, #111.

145. FIM to Colonel Martín Vicario, August 31, 1911, AFIM, reel 19, #1229.

146. Rhodes Diary, 15; T. B. Hohler to Sir Edward Grey, October 4, 1911, FO, reel 17, 371.1150/41409; Knight, *Mexican Revolution,* 1:410–11; Henry Lane Wilson to Philander Knox, October 27, 1911, RDS, reel 15, 812.00/2453; Nevin O. Winter, *Mexico and Her People of Today* (London: Cassell and Company, 1913), 409–10.

147. FIM to Francisco Vázquez Gómez, July 25, 1911, AFVG, box 15, #1597.

148. FLdlB to Juan Sánchez Azcona, August 31, 1911, AGM, 12, book 8, #410.

149. Knight, *Mexican Revolution,* 1:415; Ross, *Francisco Madero,* 176.

150. Carlos Félix Díaz, *Génesis de la revolución mexicana* (La Paz, Bolivia: El Imprenta Moderna, 1918), 80–81.

Chapter 5

1. Arredondo Muñozledo, *Historia de la revolución mexicana;* Johnson, *Heroic Mexico,* 90.

2. Ruiz, *Great Rebellion,* 147; Carlos Fuentes, *The Death of Artemio Cruz* (New York: Farrar, Straus and Giroux, 1964).

3. Ross, *Francisco I. Madero,* 241–48; *Mexican Herald,* October 5, 1911.

4. David Bushnell and Neill Macaulay, *The Emergence of Latin America in the Nineteenth Century* (New York: Oxford University Press, 1994).

5. E. Bradford Burns, *The Poverty of Progress: Latin America in the Nineteenth Century* (Berkeley and Los Angeles: University of California Press, 1980).

6. Marvin Bernstein, *The Mexican Mining Industry, 1890–1950* (Albany: State University of New York Press, 1965), 49–77.

7. Rodney Anderson, *Outcasts in Their Own Land: Mexican Industrial Workers, 1906–1911* (De Kalb: Northern Illinois University Press, 1976);

Knight, *Mexican Revolution,* 1:128–39; William E. French, *A Peaceful and Working People: Manners, Morals, and Class Formation in Northern Mexico* (Albuquerque: University of New Mexico Press, 1996).

8. Robert H. Holden, *Mexico and the Survey of Public Lands* (De Kalb: Northern Illinois University Press, 1994); Clark Reynolds, *The Mexican Economy: Twentieth-Century Structure and Growth* (New Haven: Yale University Press, 1970), 136–37.

9. Mary Kay Vaughan, *The State, Education, and Social Class in Mexico, 1880–1928* (De Kalb: Northern Illinois University Press, 1982); French, *Working People,* 35, 66–73.

10. Cumberland, *Mexican Revolution,* 225–28.

11. Ramón Ruiz, *Labor and the Ambivalent Revolutionaries: Mexico, 1911–23* (Baltimore: Johns Hopkins University Press, 1976).

12. Petition of Workers in Santiago, Hidalgo to FLdlB, June 29, 1911, AGM, 6, Exp. V-1, #111.

13. Petition of Workers in Querétaro to FLdlB, July 1, 1911, AGM, 6 Exp. V-1, #223.

14. Rafael Tapia to FLdlB, August 14, 1911, AGM, 15, Exp. 1, #75; de la Barra to Tapia, August 21, 1911, AGM, 18, Exp. 7, #3; *Mexican Herald,* August 22, 1911.

15. Pánfilo Méndez to FLdlB, September 22, 1911, AGM, 7, Exp. M-4, #144; V. Variba Bello to FLdlB, October 9, 1911, AGM, 23, Exp. 8, #61; Casamira Fuentes to FLdlB, June 6, 1911, AGM, 9, Exp. F-2, #20.

16. R. W. Wilson to T. B. Hohler, July 24, 1911, FO, reel 16, 371.1149/31153. Likewise, workers on the docks at Veracruz sought a 50 percent wage hike. See Consul Nunn to T. B. Hohler, July 14, 1911, FO, reel 16, 371.1148/30848; David LaFrance, "Francisco I. Madero and the 1911 Interim Governorship in Puebla," *The Americas* 42 (January 1986): 325–26.

17. Garritz, "La presidencia interna," 138–141; *Mexican Herald,* July 4–8, 1911; Gerald L. McGowan (ed.), *La revolución mexicana a través de sus documentos,* 5 vols. (Mexico City: UNAM, 1987), 3:240; John Lear, "Workers, Vecinos, and Citizens: The Revolution in Mexico City, 1909–1917" (Ph.D. diss., University of California-Berkeley, 1993), 63, 252–53; Meyers, *Crucible of Progress,* 242.

18. Adame Goddard, *El pensamiento político,* 184–221; Manuel Ceballos Ramírez, "La encíclica 'Rerum Novarum' y los trabajadores católicos en la Ciudad de México, 1891–1913," *Historia Mexicana* 33 (January 1985): 3–38; Randall S. Hanson, "The Day of Ideals: Catholic Social Action in the Age of the Mexican Revolution, 1867–1929" (Ph.D. diss., University of Indiana, 1994).

19. Mother Jones to Manuel Calero, October 25, 1911, in Philip S. Foner, ed., *Mother Jones Speaks: Collected Writings and Speeches* (New York: Monad Press, 1983), 580–82, and her letter to Flores Magón in the same collection, November 4, 1911, 582–86; Heriberto Barrón to FLdlB, October 10, 1911, AGM, 4, Exp. B-6, #47; Gregg Andrews, *Shoulder to Shoulder?: The American Federation of Labor, the United States, and the Mexican Revolution 1910–1924* (Berkeley and Los Angeles: University of California Press, 1991), 22.

20. J. Refugio García and other workers to FLdlB, July 2, 1911, AGM, 6, Exp. V-1, #102; Sir Edward Grey to T. B. Hohler, October 17, 1911, FO, reel 16, 371.1149/42963.

21. José María Maytorena to FLdlB, October 12, 1911, AGM, 20, Exp. 2, #55.

22. Percy Carr to FLdlB, October 6, 1911, AGM, 2, Exp. C-2, #60.

23. Rafael Zubarán Capmany to FLdlB, enclosing Holloway memo to FLdlB, August 10, 1911, AGM, 24, Exp. 3, #27; *Nueva Era,* October 3, 1911; Jonathan C. Brown, "Foreign and Native-Born Workers in Porfirian Mexico," *American Historical Review* 98 (June 1993): 786–818.

24. Rafael Pardo, attorney for the railroad, to FLdlB, August 1, 1911, AGM, 8, Exp. P-3, #27; FLdlB's notes on letter from B. E. Holloway, July 14, 1911, AGM, 16, Exp. 3, #61; T. B. Hohler to Sir Edward Grey, July 27, 1911, FO, reel 17, 371.1150/31154.

25. Rafael Hidalgo to FLdlB, July 31, 1911, AGM, 17, Exp. 1, #125, and de la Barra's response on the same day, AGM, 17, Exp. 1, #119. See also José Luis Requena to FLdlB, September 13, 1911, AGM, 1, Exp. R-4, #62.

26. FLdlB to Rafael Tapia, September 8, 1911, AGM, 14, Exp. 5, #6, and his earlier letter of August 17, 1911, AGM, 14, Exp 4, #7.

27. FLdlB to Representatives at Maritime Agency, October 4, 1911, AGM, 11, book 2, #250; Rafael Tapia to FLdlB and de la Barra's notes, August 18, 1911, AGM, 14, Exp. 4, #45.

28. FLdlB to Angel Lerdo de Tejada, July 7, 1911, AGM, 13, book 4, #206.

29. FLdlB to Martín Urrutia Escurra, June 17, 1911, AGM, 10, book 2, #353.

30. FIM to Emilio Madero, July 1, 1911, AFIM, reel 19, #749; and a follow-up letter dated July 6, 1911, AFIM, reel 19, #739.

31. Venustiano Carranza to Emilio Vázquez Gómez, July 15, 1911, AGM, 16, Exp. 3, #73; William H. Beezley, "Governor Carranza and the Revolution in Coahuila," *The Americas* 33 (July 1976): 55.

32. FIM to Mauro Martínez, President of Workers' Party, June 22, 1911, AFIM, reel 22, #3811; Francisco Madero to S. Rosas Gebadua, July 10, 1911, AFIM, 21, #2176; Lear, "Workers, Vecinos, and Citizens."

33. Circular of Emilio Vázquez Gómez, July 21, 1911, AFGG, 21, #2067.

34. *El Imparcial,* October 2, 1911, Kelley, *Blood Drenched Altars,* 219; and David LaFrance, "Labour and the Mexican Revolution: President Francisco I. Madero and the Puebla Textile Workers," *Boletín de Estudios Latinoamericanos y del Caribe,* January 1983, 62; *Diario de los debates,* September 30, 1911. See also FLdlB's speech to Congress, September 16, 1911, AFGG, 22, #2132; T. B. Hohler to Sir Edward Grey, September 21, 1911, FO, reel 17, 371.1150/38947.

35. *Diario de los debates,* September 19, 1911; Gertrude Schlicter, "European Backgrounds of American Reform, 1880–1915" (Ph.D. diss., University of Illinois, 1960).

36. Raymundo Prian to FLdlB, August 17, 1911, and August 24, 1911, AGM, 8, Exp. P-3, #67 and #87. See also *El Diario,* October 2, 1911, and *El Imparcial,* October 2, 1911, and Ceballos Ramírez, "Los trabajadores católicos," 27–29.

37. John Womack, "The Mexican Economy during the Mexican Revolution, 1910–1920, Historiography and Analysis," *Marxist Perspectives* 4 (Winter 1978): 80–123.

38. Burns, *Poverty of Progress,* 141.

39. Alzuyeta, Fernández Quiroz y Cia to FLdlB, July 13, 1911, AGM, 16, Exp. 3, #39.

40. Jorge Vera Estañol to FLdlB, October 9 and October 13, 1911, AGM, 22, Exp. 8, #66; Vera Estañol to FLdlB, August 5, 1911, AGM, 6, Exp. V-3, #27.

41. Manuel Bonilla to FLdlB, September 19, 1911, AGM, 31, Exp. B-4, #351.

42. *New York News Bureau*, October 10, 1911, AGM, 21, Exp. 8, #33.

43. J. T. Shadforth to FLdlB, August 3, 1911, AGM, 9, Exp. S-3, #17; M. E. Katze to FLdlB, August 3, 1911, AGM, 11, Exp. K-3, #2.

44. T. B. Hohler to Sir Edward Grey, November 7, 1911, FO, reel 17, 371.1150/47276.

45. A. V. Curby to FIM, July 28, 1911, AFIM, reel 19, #1303.

46. Cecilio Ocón to Minister of Treasury Rafael Hernández, August 21, 1911, AGM, 9, Exp. 0-3, #34; Ocón's memorandum to FLdlB, n.d., AGM, 9, Exp. 0-3, #57.

47. FIM to Marcos Trueba, May 29, 1911, BNAM, box 4, #2042.

48. Ernesto Madero to FLdlB, June 19, 1911, AGM, 7, Exp. M-1, #103.

49. Enrique Creel to FLdlB, June 3, 1911, AGM, 2, Exp. C-1, #52; Enrique Creel to Juan Creel, July 31, 1911, Terrazas Papers, part 2, box 1, #77.

50. Ambrosio Figueroa to FLdlB, September 23, 1911, AGM, 12, Exp. 6, #28.

51. Jacobs, *Ranchero Revolt*, 54–55.

52. FLdlB to Guadalupe González, Governor of Zacatecas, September 13, 1911, AGM, 12, book 9, #453–56.

53. FLdlB to T. B. Hohler, August 21, 1911, AGM, 12, book 8, #24–25.

54. FLdlB to Agustín M. Lazo, August 7, 1911, AGM, 23, Exp. 4, #2; Baron de Vaux to Minister of Foreign Relations Cruppi, May 29, 1911, ADRF, vol. 2, 227–28.

55. *Diario de los debates*, September 21, 1911.

56. Jonathan Brown, *Oil and Revolution in Mexico* (Berkeley and Los Angeles: University of California Press, 1993); Gilbert M. Joseph, *Revolution from Without: Yucatán, Mexico, and the United States, 1880–1924* (New York: Cambridge University Press, 1982), 68.

57. William H. Beezley, "State Reform during the Provisional Presidency: Chihuahua, 1911, *Hispanic American Historical Review* (hereafter cited as *HAHR*) 50 (April 1970): 528–30; Knight, *Mexican Revolution*, 1:421–22.

58. Antonio González to FLdlB, June 15, 1911, AGM, 4, Exp. G-1, #117.

59. Petition of Demetrio Salazar et al. to FLdlB, July 5, 1911, AGM, 6, Exp. V-1, #129.

60. Antonio Ortega to FLdlB, July 13, 1911, AGM, 9, Exp. 0-2, #19.

61. Miguel Vázquez to FLdlB, August 13, 1911, AGM, 6, Exp. V-3, #63; *Mexican Herald*, November 6, 1911.

62. Fuentes, *The Old Gringo*.

63. Frederick C. Turner, *The Dynamics of Mexican Nationalism* (Chapel Hill: University of North Carolina Press, 1968), 163–169.

64. Hart, *Revolutionary Mexico*, 10–12.

65. Alan Knight, *U.S.-Mexican Relations, 1910–1940: An Interpretation* (La Jolla, CA: Center for U.S. Mexican Studies, 1987).

66. Katz, *Secret War*, 88. Baron de Vaux to Baron Cruppi, May 18, 1911, ADRF, II, 212–14.

67. Adrián Aguirre Benavides to FIM, May 29, 1911, AFIM, reel 18, #0504-0507; T. B. Hohler to Sir Edward Grey, June 29, 1911, FO, reel 16,

371.1148/27074; Rafael Sánchez Escobar, *Narraciónes revolucionarias mexicanas, histórico-anecdóticas* (Mexico: Talleres Tipográfica de la Casa de Orientación para Varones, 1934), 17–21.

68. Heriberto Barrón to FLdlB, August 14, 1911, AGM, 31, Exp. B-2, #139.

69. Juan L. Carrillo to FIM, May 27, 1911, AFIM, reel 18, #0274.

70. L. D. Guajardo to FLdlB, September 12, 1911, AGM, 4, Exp. G-4, #89.

71. William Alger to Philander C. Knox, November 9, 1911, RDS, reel 15, 812.00/2481.

72. Louis Hosletter to Philander C. Knox, May 29, 1911, RDS, reel 14, 812.00/2088; Alexander Dye to Philander C. Knox, June 3, 1911, RDS, reel 14, 812.00/2067.

73. Carlos Randall to FLdlB, August 12, 1911, AGM, 15, Exp. 1, #45.

74. Leo M. Jacques, "The Chinese Massacre in Torreón (Coahuila) in 1911, "*Arizona and the West* 16 (1974), 233–46; Charles C. Cumberland, "The Sonora Chinese and the Mexican Revolution," *HAHR* 40 (May 1960): 191–211.

75. Douglas Richmond, "Confrontation and Reconciliation: Mexicans and Spaniards during the Revolution, 1910–1920," *The Americas* 41 (October 1984): 217.

76. LaFrance, *Puebla, 1908–1913*, 76–77; Agustín del Pozo to Alfredo Robles Domínguez, June 5, 1911, AARD, vol. 4, Exp. 19, #102. For Torreón, see D. Garza Farías to Emilio Vázquez Gómez, July 5, 1911, AFGG, 28, #1970; D. Garza Farías to FLdlB, August 1, 1911, AGM, 4, Exp. G-3, #96.

77. Henderson, "Gobernador maderista," 381; Primitivo Ortiz to FLdlB, September 19, 1911, AGM, 20, Exp. 1, #78; José González Soto to FLdlB, July 28, 1911, AGM, 4, Exp. G-3, #33.

78. T. B. Hohler to Sir Edward Grey, July 18, 1911, FO, reel 16, 371.1148/30410, Hohler's letter of August 4, 1911, FO, reel 16, 371.1148/30669, and another letter dated October 17, 1911, FO, reel 16, 371.1149/42981.

79. T. B. Hohler to Sir Edward Grey, August 2, 1911, FO, reel 16, 371.1149/32133.

80. Jorge Vera Estañol to FLdlB, September 29, 1911, AGM, 21, Exp. 8, #73; Julio Guerrero to FLdlB, June 18, 1911, AGM, 4, Exp. G-1, #90; Hohler to Sir Edward Grey, November 3, 1911, FO, reel 16, 371.1149/46233.

81. Memorandum of meeting of Lord Cowdray and Francisco Madero, September 29, 1911, Pearson Papers, box 161.

82. Eugenio D. Cagnotti to FLdlB, July 10, 1911, AGM, 16, Exp. 4, #132; G. Schulte to FIM, May 26, 1911, AFIM, reel 18, #0273; Antonio de la Peña y Reyes to Alfredo Robles Domínguez, May 29, 1911, AARD, vol. 5, Exp. 23, #8.

83. Manuel Liaguno to FLdlB, October 20, 1911, AGM, 3, Exp. L-5, #49; Luther Ellsworth to Philander C. Knox, September 17, 1911, RDS, reel 14, 812.00/2365; French, *Working People*, 141.

84. Philander C. Knox to William Howard Taft, October 28, 1911, RDS, reel 15, 812.00/2441.

85. Abraham González to FLdlB, July 22, 1911, AGM, 17, Exp. 1, #19; Abraham González to H & C Ford, June 27, 1911, OC, reel 2, #119; Abraham González to FLdlB, July 14, 1911, OC, reel 2, #367; Manuel Calero to Emilio Vázquez Gómez, June 2, 1911, AGM, 2, Exp. C-1, #41; Francisco Vázquez Gómez to Federico González Garza, March 9, 1911, AFGG, 14, #1341.

86. José Vasconcelos to José María Maytorena, September 29, 1911, JMMP, box 1, folder 15, #10; Jorge Vera Estañol to FLdlB, August 5, 1911, AGM, 6, Exp. V-3, #27; Guillermo Wood to FLdlB, August 22, 1911, AGM, 11, Exp. W-1, #6.

87. Emilio Madero to Secretary of Foreign Relations, July 10, 1911, AREM, L-E 669, Leg. 106, 132–33; Meyers, *Forge of Progress*, 240.

88. FLdlB to Lawrence Redman and Wesley Arthur Basset, August 3, 1911, AGM, 13, book 6, #255–56; *El Imparcial*, June 30, 1911.

89. Manuel M. Zamacona to FLdlB, June 20, 1911, AGM, 24, Exp. Z-4, #3.

90. Vaughan, *State Education*, 51–88.

91. Ibid., 1–77.

92. Madero's Order, May 14, 1911, BNAM, box 2, #535; FIM to Francisco Vázquez Gómez, July 31, 1911, AFGG, 21, #2095; M. González Muñoz to FLdlB, June 9, 1911, AGM, 4, Exp G-3, #70.

93. T. B. Hohler to Sir Edward Grey, June 19, 1911, FO, reel 17, 371.1149/25961; Ruiz, *Great Rebellion*, 357–59; Ramón Ruiz, "Mexico's Struggle for Rural Education, 1910–1950" (Ph.D. diss., University of California-Berkeley, 1954), 21–23.

94. Report of T. B. Hohler on Mexican Agencies, October 10, 1911, FO, reel 17, 371.1550/39852.

95. *El País*, August 26 and October 5, 1911; Richmond, *Carranza's Nationalist Struggle*, 33–34; John A. Britton, "Indian Education, Nationalism, and Federalism in Mexico, 1910–1921," *The Americas* 32 (January 1976): 445–58, esp. 445–52.

96. Francisco Vázquez Gómez to FLdlB, September 14, 1911, AGM, 6, Exp. V-4, #36; *Nueva Era*, August 11, 1911.

97. Vázquez Gómez, *Memorias políticas*, 283–84.

98. Michael E. Burke, "The University of Mexico and the Revolution, 1910–1940," *The Americas* 34 (October 1977): 252–73; *Diario de los debates*, September 23, 1911; Vázquez Gómez's article from *El País*, January 21, 1908, in AFVG, box 49, folder 1, #14; Garciadiego Dantan, "Movimientos estudiantiles," 129–30.

99. Abraham Castellanos to FLdlB, August 11, 1911, AGM, 3, Exp. C-3, #119; Gustavo E. Campa to FLdlB, September 27, 1911, AGM, 2, Exp. C-5, #4.

100. Jorge Vera Estañol to FLdlB, June 22, 1911, AGM, 23, Exp. 10, #87.

101. Manuel Ruiz to FLdlB, August 1, 1911, AGM, 1, Exp. R-1, #68; AFVG, box 49, folder 1, #10.

102. William B. Taylor, *Drinking, Homicide, and Rebellion in Colonial Mexican Villages* (Stanford: Stanford University Press, 1979); Katherine Bliss, "The Science of Redemption: Syphilis, Sexual Promiscuity, and Reformism in Revolutionary Mexico City," *HAHR* 79 (February 1999): 1–40.

103. Beezley, *Insurgent Governor*, 103–105; Abraham González to Juan T. Burns, August 11, 1911, OC, reel 2a, #791.

104. Abraham González to José de la Luz Blanco, July 4, 1911, OC, reel 2, #201; Richmond, *Carranza's Nationalist Struggle*, 32–33.

105. A. D. Gregg to FLdlB, August 20, 1911, AGM, 4, Exp. G-4, #16.

106. *Mexican Herald*, June 4, 1911; Merl Burke Cole, *Romantic Tragedies of Mexico* (Boston: Christopher Publishing House, 1956), 52.

107. Alberto García Granados to FLdlB, August 21, 1911, AGM, 4, Exp. G-3, #119; *El Mundo Ilustrado*, October 15, 1911, *El Tiempo Ilustrado*, October 15, 1911.

108. Ocampo N. Bolaños to FLdlB, October 13, 1911, AGM, 4, Exp. G-6, #29; Secundino Pérez Farías to FLdlB, October 12, 1911, AGM, 8, Exp. P-5, #27.

109. Juan García R. to FIM, August 5, 1911, AFIM, reel 19, #1398; Manuela M. Márquez to FLdlB, October 10, 1911, AGM, 21, Exp. 6, #38.

110. Francisco Vázquez Gómez to FLdlB, October 23, 1911, AGM, 22, Exp. 8, #37.

111. J. Torres C. to FLdlB, September 2, 1911, AGM, 5, Exp. T-4, #4.

112. James H. Timberlake, *Prohibition and the Progressive Movement, 1900–1920* (Cambridge: Harvard University Press, 1963).

113. *El Mundo Ilustrado*, November 5, 1911, and *Mexican Herald*, October 3, 1911.

114. *El Mundo Ilustrado*, October 1, 1911, and *El Tiempo Ilustrado*, October 1, 1911.

115. *El Tiempo Ilustrado*, October 22, 1911, *Mexican Herald*, October 20, 1911, and *El Mundo Ilustrado*, October 22, 1911.

116. Turner, *Nationalism*, 192–94; *El Imparcial*, May 31, 1911; Shirlene Ann Soto, *The Mexican Woman: A Study of Her Participation in the Revolution, 1910–1940* (Palo Alto: R & E Research Associates, 1979), 25.

117. *Mexican Herald*, June 27, 1911.

118. William French, "Prostitutes and Guardian Angels: Women, Work, and the Family in Porfirian Mexico," *HAHR* 72 (November 1992): 529–53; idem, *Working People*, 87–107.

119. Elizabeth Salas, *Soldaderas in the Mexican Military* (Austin: University of Texas Press, 1990); Anna Macías, *Against All Odds: The Feminist Movement in Mexico to 1940* (Westport, CT: Greenwood Press, 1982).

120. Ronald Waterbury, "Non-Revolutionary Peasants: Oaxaca Compared to Morelos in the Mexican Revolution," *Comparative Studies in Society and History* 17 (1975): 410–42; Knight, *Mexican Revolution*, 1:310.

121. Samuel Brunk, "Zapata and the City Boys: In Search of a Piece of the Revolution," *HAHR* 73 (February 1993): 33–65.

122. Cumberland, *Mexican Revolution*, 220, quoting González Roa, *El aspecto agrario*. The *Times* story, March 12, 1916, quotes de la Barra as saying that Mexico's problem resulted from halted reforms and the failure to create individual plots but that "there is no agrarian problem in Mexico so far as the lands providing foodstuffs are concerned." González Roa claimed de la Barra said "there was no land problem in Mexico." This allegation makes no sense in the light of de la Barra's farewell address (see Appendix E).

123. Clifton Kroeber, *Man, Land, and Water: Mexico's Farmlands Irrigation Policies, 1885–1911* (Berkeley and Los Angeles: University of California Press, 1983), 186–190.

124. Holden, *Survey of Public Land*, 133.

125. Kroeber, *Man, Land, and Water*, 219.

126. John Kenneth Turner, *Barbarous Mexico* (Austin: University of Texas Press, 1968); Herman Whitaker, "Barbarous Mexico: The Rubber Slavery of the Mexican Tropics," *American Magazine* 49 (February 1910): 546–55.

127. Katz, *Riot, Rebellion*, 533–34.

128. B. Traven, *The White Rose* (Westport, CT: Lawrence Hill, 1979).

129. Stanley Shadle, *Andrés Molina Enríquez: Mexican Land Reformer of the Revolutionary Era* (Tucson: University of Arizona Press, 1994); Jesús Silva Herzog, ed., *La cuestión de la tierra*, 5 vols. (Mexico: Instituto Mexicano de Investigaciones Económicas, 1960), esp. vol. 1 and 2.

130. Adrían Aguirre Benavides to FIM, May 29, 1911, AFIM, reel 18, #0504-0507; David MaGill to Philander C. Knox, August 5, 1911, RDS, reel 14, 812.00/2282. See also Rhodes Diary, 14–15.

131. Emiliano Zapata and Juan Andreu Almazán to Antonio Mexchaca, September 20, 1911, AGM, 28, Exp. 14, #5.

132. Knight, *Mexican Revolution*, 1:78.

133. Carlos Cruz Rugama to FLdlB, June 8, 1911, AGM, 21, Exp. 8, #98; Miguel Peón to FLdlB, n.d., AGM, 8, Exp. P-1, #90; Francisco B. de Cañedo to FLdlB, September 4, 1911, AGM, 2, Exp. C-2, #63.

134. Agustín M. Lazo to FLdlB (re Michoacán), August 16, 1911, AGM, 3, Exp. L-3, #55; Ponciano Rojas to FLdlB (re Tabasco), June 14, 1911, AGM, 1, Exp. R-1, #102; Manuel Domínguez Elizalde (Campeche) to FLdlB, June 12, 1911, AGM, 29, Exp. 9, #501; Rafael Hernández to FLdlB, October 4, 1911, AGM, 3, Exp. H-5, #21. See also David W. Walker, "Homegrown Revolution: The Hacienda Santa Catalina del Alamo y Anexas and Agrarian Protest in Eastern Durango, Mexico: 1897–1913," *HAHR* 72 (May 1992): 271.

135. Brown, *Oil*, 199.

136. Iñigo Noriega to FLdlB, October 20, 1911, AGM, 7, Exp. N-5, #16; FLdlB to Abraham González, July 22, 1911, AGM, 17, Exp. 1, #13; FLdlB to J. Valente Quevedo, June 24, 1911, AGM, 10, book 3, #211.

137. FLdlB to Governor Emiliano Zarabia (Durango), August 31, 1911, AGM, 12, book 3, #372; Agustín M. Lazo to FLdlB, August 26, 1911, AGM, 3, Exp. L-4, #1; FLdlB to Governor Guadalupe González (Zacatecas), September 13, 1911, AGM, 12, book 9, #453–56.

138. Abraham González to Emilio Madero, August 28, 1911, OC reel 2a, #992; Henry Lane Wilson to Philander Knox, July 11, 1911, RDS, reel 14, 812.00/2219; David Magill to Philander Knox, August 5, 1911, RDS, reel 14, 812.00/2299; Rhodes Diary, 3.

139. Refugio Sánchez to FLdlB, August 17, 1911, AGM, 14, Exp. 4, #1.

140. Esteban Maqueo Castellanos to FLdlB, July 26, 1911, AGM, 7, Exp. M-2, #90; Esteban Maqueo Castellanos to FLdlB, August 4, 1911, AGM, 7, Exp. M-3, #143.

141. FLdlB to Heliodoro Díaz Quintas, July 27, 1911, AGM, 17, Exp. 1, #75; FLdlB to Díaz Quintas, August 7, 1911, AGM, 14, Exp. 4, #18.

142. Heliodoro Díaz Quintas to FLdlB, August 8, 1911, AGM, 15, Exp. 2, #31.

143. Emilio Vázquez Gómez to Heliodoro Díaz Quintas, July 5, 1911 (2 letters), AGM, 10, Exp. 4, #324 and #378.

144. Enrique Creel to Juan A. Creel, July 3, 1911, Terrazas Papers, part 2, box 1, #74.

145. Enrique Creel to FLdlB, June 13, 1911, AGM, 2, Exp. C-1, #117; his letter of July 3, 1911, AGM, 2, Exp. C-4, #33; his letter of July 17, 1911, AGM, 2, Exp. C-4, #95, and Enrique Creel to Juan Creel, August 2, 1911, Terrazas Papers, part 2, box 1, #78.

146. FLdlB to Enrique Creel, July 7, 1911, AGM, 13, book 4, #212.

147. FLdlB to Abraham González, August 10, 1911, AGM, 15, Exp. 1, #6; FLdlB to Abraham González, September 6, 1911, AGM, 14, Exp. 6, #68.

148. Abraham González to FLdlB, August 10, 1911, AGM, 15, Exp. 1, #1.

149. Mark Wasserman, *Persistent Oligarchs: Elite and Politics in Chihuahua, Mexico, 1910–1940* (Durham, NC: Duke University Press, 1993).

150. Turner, *Barbarous Mexico*, 27–53; Allen Wells, *Yucatan's Gilded Age: Haciendas, Henequen, and International Harvester, 1860–1915* (Albuquerque: University of New Mexico Press, 1985), 163–65.

151. Aguilar Camín, *Frontera nómada*, 186–91; José María Maytorena to FIM, June 5, 1911, JMMP, box 1, folder 11, #2.

152. José María Maytorena to FIM, June 22, 1911, JMMP, box 1, folder 11, #15; FIM to Eugenio Gayou, June 11, 1911, AFIM, reel 22, #3674.

153. FIM to José María Maytorena, July 6, 1911, AFIM, reel 19, #740. Maytorena certainly was confident in de la Barra's ability to resolve the problem; see his letter to FLdlB, July 18, 1911, AGM, 7, Exp. M–3, #32.

154. José María Maytorena to FLdlB, July 17, 1911, AGM, 16, Exp. 3, #90; General Gonzalo Luque to José González Salas, August 31, 1911, AHDN, 481.5/268, 131, #833.

155. Carlos Randall to José María Maytorena, July 26, 1911, JMMP, box 1, folder 13, #11. For conditions, see the reports of General Luque to José González Salas, August 8, 1911, and August 28, 1911, AHDN, 481.5/268, 131, #807, 823.

156. The treaty is contained in AFGG, 22, #2121. See Planck, "The Ad Interim Regime," 46–47, and the article in *El Tiempo*, September 2, 1911.

157. Figueroa Domenech, *Veinte meses*, 23.

158. Other summaries of the problem are in Susan Deeds, "José María Maytorena and the Mexican Revolution in Sonora, Part I," *Arizona and the West* 18 (spring 1976): 21–40; Guy Weddington, *From Glory to Oblivion: The Real Truth about the Mexican Revolution* (New York: Vantage Press, 1974), 48–53.

159. José María Maytorena to FIM, June 24, 1911, JMMP, box 2, #41. The September treaty is addressed in T. B. Hohler to Sir Edward Grey, September 2, 1911, FO, 371.1149/36539.

160. José María Maytorena to General Luis Espinosa and other Yaqui officials, March 2, 1912, JMMP, box 3, folder 3, #5; José María Maytorena to FIM, September 17, 1911, AFIM, reel 18, #0510; General Gonzalo Luque to José González Salas, September 11 and 13, 1911, AHDN, 481.5/268, 131, #845 and 846.

161. Shadle, *Molina Enríquez*, 46–56; *El Imparcial*, August 25, 1911.

162. The petitions are far too numerous to cite them all. For three examples, see Francisco Gómez to FLdlB, June 12, 1911, AGM, 4, Exp. G-1, #91; Petition from Tomatlán, Jalisco to FLdlB, August 26, 1911, AGM, 8, Exp. V-5, #32; José de la Cruz Gómez et al. to FLdlB, September 14, 1911, AGM, 8, Exp. V-5, #136.

163. Tiburcio Nares to FLdlB, October 6, 1911, AGM, 21, Exp. 4, #27; Jesús Gaitán et al. to FLdlB, June 17, 1911, AGM, 23, Exp. 10, #63; Gerardo Juárez et al. to FLdlB, June 12, 1911, AGM, 22, Exp. 7, #74.

164. Alberto García Granados, *Las cajas rurales de crédito mutuo en México* (1911), in Jesús Silva Herzog, ed., *La cuestión de la tierra*, 5 vols.

(Mexico: Instituto Mexicano de Investigaciones Económicas, 1960), 1:77–108.

165. Rafael Hernández, *Política agraria* (1912), in Silva Herzog, *La cuestión*, 2:93–122.

166. Vera Estañol, *Revolución mexicana*, 201–5; Limantour, *Apuntes*, 249–62.

167. FLdlB to Eduardo Paz, October 2, 1911, AGM, 11, book 2, #160.

168. *Nueva Era*, September 15, 1911, in *Los presidentes de México: Discursos políticos, 1910–1988* (Mexico: El Colegio de México, 1988); *Nueva Era*, October 2, 1911, in AFVG, box 22, folder 2, #34. See also the interview with FLdlB in the *New York Times*, March 16, 1916.

169. Henry Lane Wilson to Philander Knox, April 3, 1911, RDS, reel 12, 812.00/1202.

170. Primitivo Orsini to FLdlB, September 21, 1911, AGM, 9, Exp. 0-5, #14; Manuel Anciola to FLdlB, October 8, 1911, AGM, 20, Exp. 2, #6.

171. Eduardo S. Paz to FLdlB, September 25, 1911, AGM, 8, Exp. P-5, #8.

172. Francisco Martínez to FLdlB, September 27, 1911, AGM, 7, Exp. M-5, #97.

173. Santiago Gómez to FLdlB, August 24, 1911, AGM, 4, Exp. G-4, #50.

174. *El País*, August 15, 1911; *Los presidentes de México*, 1:25–28, 64–66.

175. Deborah Baldwin, *Protestants and the Mexican Revolution: Missionaries, Ministers, and Social Change* (Champaign: University of Illinois Press, 1990).

176. William Lemke to M. B. Katze, enclosed in a letter to FLdlB, June 1, 1911, AGM, 11, Exp. K-1, #1.

177. M. B. Katze to William Lemke, June 27, 1911, enclosed a letter to FLdlB, AGM, 11, Exp. K-4, #6.

178. William Lemke to M. B. Katze, May 26, 1911, AGM, 11, Exp. K-1, #1.

179. FLdlB to Antonio Gaxiola, June 12, 1911, AGM, 10, book 2, #132.

180. FLdlB to Jorge Vera Estañol, June 14, 1911, AGM, 10, book 2, #297. See the response from Ignacio Cruz et al. to FLdlB, n.d. (representing 135 families), AGM, 21, Exp. 7, #21; Rafael Luna (representing thirty to fifty families) to FLdlB, July 2, 1911, AGM, 3, Exp. L-2, #15.

181. FIM to Manuel Sánchez Rivera, September 19, 1911, AFIM, reel 18, #0320.

182. Jesús Flores Magón to FLdlB, September 30, 1911, AGM, 12, Exp. 6, #36.

183. Constancio González to FLdlB, September 5, 1911, AGM, 4, Exp. G-4, #59; M. Romero Palafox to FLdlB, August 5, 1911, AGM, 1, Exp. R-3, #35.

184. Moises González Navarro, "El Maderismo y la revolución agraria," *Historia Mexicana* 37 (July–September 1987): 24. See also James Wilkie, *The Mexican Revolution: Federal Expenditure and Social Change since 1910* (Berkeley and Los Angeles: University of California Press, 1967), 44.

185. Circular of Emilio Vázquez Gómez, July 1, 1911, AGM, 10, Vázquez Gómez letterbook, #205, and in 22, Exp. 1, #85, and AFGG, 21, #2023.

186. V. Layseca to FLdlB, October 10, 1911, AGM, 3, Exp. L-5, #64.

187. M. B. Katze to FLdlB, September 1, 1911, AGM, 22, Exp. 8, #1.

188. Rafael M. Hidalgo to FLdlB, September 27, 1911, AGM, 3, Exp. H-5, #19. De la Barra's Independence Day speech, September 16, 1911, AFGG, 22, #2132; L. Palacios to FLdlB, August 26, 1911, AGM, 8, Exp. P-4, #50.

189. Emilio Vázquez Gómez to Alberto García Granados, July 1, 1911, AGM, 10, Vázquez Gómez letterbook, #198.

190. Tomás Ortega and Manuel Valadéz to FLdlB, August 7, 1911, AGM, 6, Exp. V-2, #8.

191. Jesús Martínez to FIM, August 4, 1911, AFIM. reel 20, #2100.

192. C. W. Harvey to FLdlB, July 24, 1911, AGM, 3, Exp, H-2, #36.

193. Antonio Aguilar et al. to FLdlB, August 31, 1911, AGM, 8, Exp. V-5, #45. Foreigners also observed workers' declining wages and increased costs in the Porfiriato; see T. B. Hohler to Sir Edward Grey, August 30, 1911, FO, reel 15, 371.1148/23276. For another complaint of wages of about twenty-five cents a day, see Guadalupe Galicía to FIM, June 10, 1911, AFIM, reel 20, #2028.

194. Margarita Menegus Bornemann, "Las haciendas de Mazaquiahuac y el rosario en los albores de la revolución agraria," *Historia Mexicana* 31 (January 1982): 233–50, esp. 245–49.

195. Manuel Calero to FLdlB, June 16, 1911, AGM, 2, Exp. C-1, #13; Pedro B. García to FLdlB, September 2, 1911, AGM, 15, Exp. 5, #54.

196. For the speech see Ponce de León, *El interinato*, 238–50, and excerpts in *Mexican Herald*, November 5, 1911.

197. Baron Paul LeFaivre to M. de Sches, November 10, 1911, ADRF, vol. 3, 45–46.

198. Henry Lane Wilson to Philander Knox, October 31, 1911, RDS, reel 15, 812.00/2445. The quotation is from T. B. Hohler to Sir Edward Grey, November 7, 1911, FO, reel 17, 371.1550/47274.

199. López, *El fracaso*, 14–16; Leone Moats, *Thunder in Their Veins* (New York: The Century Co., 1932), 61.

200. FLdlB, "Algunas páginas," AdlB, 6, #593.

201. Robert D. Anderson, *France 1870–1914: Politics and Society* (London: Routledge and Kegan Paul, 1977), 95–96; Roland Bonaparte et al., eds., *Le Mexique au début du 20e siècle*, 2 vols. (Paris: C. Delegrave, 1904).

202. Adrían Aguirre Benavides to FIM, May 29, 1911, AFIM, reel 18, #504.

Chapter 6

1. López, *El fracaso*, 21–25; Hugh Gibson to Philander C. Knox, November 16, 1911, Taft Papers, series 6, case file no. 40, reel 359; *El Tiempo Ilustrado*, November 19, 1911.

2. FIM to FLdlB, December 26, 1911, AdlB, 2, #165; G. A. Esteva, Minister in Italy, to FLdlB, January 10, 1912, AdlB, 2, #171; Bell, *Political Shame*, 175.

3. Secretary of Foreign Relations Manuel Calero to FLdlB, January 30, 1912, AdlB, 2, #188; G. A. Esteva to FLdlB, January 30, 1912, AdlB, 2, #190; Madero to FLdlB, January 8, 1912, AdlB, 2, #170.

4. FLdlB to Manuel Calero, February 3, 1912, AdlB, 3, #195; and FLdlB to FIM, March 2, 1912, AdlB, 3, #223.

5. FLdlB to Manuel Calero, March 2, 1912, AdlB, 3, #224; for the lack of French interest see ADRF, vol. 3.

6. Manuel Calero to FLdlB, February 22, 1912, AdlB, 3, #211; Serapio Rendón to FLdlB, March 9, 1912, AdlB, 3, #234. Portilla, "La personalidad," 258–70.

7. Hugh Gibson to Fred Dearing, April 2, 1912, enclosing the *Havana Post*, RDS, reel 17, 812.00/3545; José F. Godoy, consul in Havana to Secretary of Foreign Relations, April 3, 1912, AREM, L-E 420, 225–28; FLdlB to Serapio Rendón, March 15, 1912, AdlB, 3, #235.

8. Delbert J. Huff to Huntington Wilson, April 12, 1912, RDS, reel 18, 812.00/3821.

9. H. L. Wilson to Philander C. Knox, April 22, 1912, RDS, reel 17, 812.00/3685.

10. Meyer, *Mexican Rebel*, 53–93.

11. Sir Frances Stronge's annual report for 1912, May 29, 1913, FO, 371.1680/28626.

12. Henderson, *Félix Díaz*, 50–67; Minister Paul LeFaivre to the Minister of Foreign Relations, October 9, 1912, ADRF, vol. 3, 176–77.

13. Esteban Maqueo Castellanos to FLdlB, October 11, 1912, AdlB, 3, #252, and his defense brief, #260; *La Tribuna*, December 10, 1912, in AFVG, box 38, folder 2, #23.

14. Alberto García Granados to FLdlB, January 18, 1912, AdlB, 2, #176.

15. Bell, *Political Shame*, 258–64; Meyer, *Huerta*, 45–48; FLdlB to Felipe Angeles, October 7, 1913, AdlB, 4, #355.

16. Sir Frances Stronge's memo, February 21, 1913, FO, 371.1672/13385; Stronge to Sir Edward Grey, February 22, 1913, FO, 371.1672/13389; Meyer, *Huerta*, 45–50; General Lauro Villar to FLdlB, January 23, 1912, AdlB, 2, #179.

17. Henderson, *Félix Díaz*, 74–76; Katz, *Villa*, 862.

18. Sir Frances Stronge to Sir Edward Grey, February 16, 1913, FO, 371.1671/7624. Gonzalo Núñez de Prado, *Revolución de México: La Decena Trágica* (Mexico: Salvador Petisme, 1913), 198–200. Henry Lane Wilson to Philander C. Knox, February 14, 1913, RDS, reel 23, 812.00/6173.

19. French chargé to Secretary of Foreign Relations Jonnart, February 16, 1913, ADRF, vol. 3, 223–30; Stronge memorandum, February 21, 1913, in FO, 371.1672/13385; Hernández and Chávez, *La angosta*, 36–38.

20. Specifically, de la Barra stated that he did not know the conspirators and was ignorant of the plan, and that he was "at the British Embassy on the 18th just as he was on the 9th," implying that he had never left. FLdlB to Manuel Andrade Pliegos, editor of *El Universal*, March 14, 1918, AdlB, 8, #801; Núñez de Prado, *La Decena Trágica*, 210–13.

21. Henry Lane Wilson to Philander C. Knox, February 15, 1913, RDS, reel 23, 812.00/6176; Peter Calvert, "Frances Stronge en la decena trágica," *Historia Mexicana* 15 (July–September 1965): 57–60.

22. Haber, *Industry and Underdevelopment*, 123–32.

23. In short, the time is probably ripe for a rising young historian to undertake a new biography of Francisco Madero, if only because the three serious studies—Ross, *Francisco I. Madero*; Cumberland, *Mexican Revolution*; and Valadés, *Imaginación y realidad*—are all at least thirty years old. Despite the fact that Cumberland had fewer documentary sources to work with, I believe his portrait is truer than Ross's. Another reason for suggesting a new work is the availability of some of Madero's presidential

papers in the Archivo General de la Nación in Mexico City. See David G. LaFrance, "The Madero Collection in Mexico's Archivo General de la Nación," *Revista Interamericana de Bibliografía/Inter-American Review of Bibliography* 33, no. 2 (1983): 191–97.

24. Meyer, *Huerta*, 76–82.

25. Manuel Mondragón to FLdlB, May 23, 1914, AdlB, 5, #532.

26. Elia Kazan, "Viva Zapata," 1952.

27. Prida, *De la dictadura*, 522–36; *El Universal*, November 1917–March 1918.

28. FLdlB to Rodolfo Reyes, May 12, 1914, AdlB 5, #524; FLdlB to Jorge Vera Estañol, December 3, 1917, AdlB, 8, #783; FLdlB to Manuel Andrade Pliegos, March 14, 1918, AdlB, 8, #801; FLdlB to the Editor, *New York Times*, July 3, 1914, AdlB, 5, #537.

29. Toribio Esquivel Obregón to Jorge Vera Estañol, August 1, 1914, JVVP, folder 5, no #.

30. FLdlB to Rodolfo Reyes, May 12, 1914, AdlB, 5, #524; FLdlB to Jorge Vera Estañol, December 3, 1917, AdlB 8, #783.

31. FLdlB to Manuel Andrade Pliegos, March 14, 1918, AdlB, 8, #801; FLdlB to Rodolfo Reyes, May 12, 1914, AdlB 5, #524.

32. Rodolfo Reyes to FLdlB, May 16, 1914, AdlB, 5, #527; Reyes, *De mi vida*, 2:163–64; Toribio Esquivel Obregón to Jorge Vera Estañol, August 19, 1914, JVEP, folder 5, no #; Toribio Esquivel Obregón, *Mi labor en servicio de México* (Mexico City: Ediciones Botas, 1934), 94–96; Jorge Vera Estañol to FLdlB, June 19, 1914, AdlB, 5, #534, and in JVEP, folder 2; Vera Estañol, *Revolución mexicana*, 295–96; and Manuel Mondragón to FLdlB, May 23, 1914, AdlB, 5, #532.

33. FLdlB to Jorge Vera Estañol, September 14, 1920, AdlB, 12, #1322; FLdlB to Toribio Esquivel Obregón, August 8, 1920, AdlB, 11, #1306.

34. Memorandum to Mr. [T. B.] Hohler, February 21, 1913, FO, 371.1672/13386.

35. James Bryce to Sir Edward Grey, February 26, 1913, FO, 371.1671/11115; Henry Lane Wilson to Philander C. Knox, February 24, 1913, RDS, reel 23, 812.00/6353; Henry Lane Wilson to FLdlB, September 3, 1914, AdlB, 5, #558; O'Shaughnessy, *Intimate Pages* , 186–88.

36. Manuel Calero to FLdlB, February 5, 1914, AdlB, 5, #507; FLdlB to Manuel Pliegos, March 14, 1918, AdlB, 8, #801. Some papers lampooned de la Barra for serving all of Mexico's recent governments.

37. FLdlB to the director, *New York Times*, July 3, 1914, AdlB, 5 #537.

38. Calvert, *Mexican Revolution*, 161; and de la Barra's letter in *Revista mexicana*, May 19, 1918, AdlB #3 of Clippings, #234.

39. Sir Frances Stronge to Sir Edward Grey, June 2, 1913, FO, 371.1673/28346; FLdlB to José Yves Limantour, September 23, 1913, AdlB, 4, #347; Sir Frances Stronge to Sir Edward Grey, June 25, 1913, FO, 371.1674/32008; Sir Frances Stronge to Sir Edward Grey, March 10, 1913, FO, 371.1672/14516.

40. Henry Lane Wilson to William Jennings Bryan, March 13, 1913, RDS, reel 24, 812.00/6681.

41. Peter V. N. Henderson, "Woodrow Wilson, Victoriano Huerta, and the Recognition Issue in Mexico," *The Americas* 45 (October 1984): 151–76.

42. Sir Frances Stronge to Sir Edward Grey, May 14, 1913, FO, 371.1673/24917.

43. Henry Lane Wilson to William Jennings Bryan, March 20, 1913, RDS, reel 24, 812.00/6800; Henry Lane Wilson to William Jennings Bryan, April 12, 1913, RDS, reel 25, 812.00/7113; John Bassett Moore, Acting Secretary, to Henry Lane Wilson, May 7, 1913, RDS, reel 25, 812.00/7268; Henry Lane Wilson to William Jennings Bryan, March 11, 1913, RDS, reel 24, 812.00/6640.

44. Henry Lane Wilson to William Jennings Bryan, May 10, 1913, RDS, reel 25, 812.00/7454; Oscar Braniff to FLdlB, May 29, 1913, AdlB, 3, #275.

45. Henry Lane Wilson to William Jennings Bryan, July 8, 1913, RDS, reel 26, 812.00/7983; Undersecretary of Foreign Relations Carlos Pereyra to FLdlB, July 8, 1913, AdlB, 3, #284; Carlos Pereyra to Congress, July 15, 1913, AREM, L-E 421B, 103; Decree of Victoriano Huerta, May 27, 1913, AdlB, 3, #273; Decree of Victoriano Huerta, July 23, 1913, AREM, L-E 421B, 104; Meyer, *Huerta*, 185–87.

46. Undersecretary of Foreign Relations Manuel Garza Aldape to FLdlB, August 6, 1913, AdlB, 4, #295; FLdlB's memorandum to Secretary of Foreign Relations, August 26, 1913, AdlB, 4, #327. An official version of the same document is in AREM, L-E 421B, 157–60.

47. Victoriano Huerta's instructions, July 25, 1913, AREM, L-E 421B, #106; Manuel Garza Aldape to FLdlB, August 6, 1913, AREM, L-E 421B, #132.

48. FLdlB to Foreign Relations, August 14, 1913, AdlB, 4, #321; FLdlB report, August 9, 1913, AdlB, 4, #303; FLdlB, final report to Foreign Relations, August 26, 1913, AREM, L-E 421B, 157–60.

49. Memorandum to Secretary of Foreign Relations, December 5, 1913, AdlB, 4, #397.

50. William Howard Taft to FLdlB, October 20, 1913, AdlB, 4, #361.

51. Victoriano Huerta to FLdlB, July 10, 1913, AdlB, 3, #286; FLdlB to Joaquín Beltrán, Interim Governor, April 6, 1914, AdlB, 5, #519 and 520; *La Tribuna*, December 10, 1912.

52. Meyer, *Huerta*, 139–43.

53. Rodolfo Alanís Boyso, *El estado de México durante la revolución mexicana, 1910–1914* (Toluca: Ediciones del Gobierno del Estado de México, 1985), 181–85; Carlos Herrejón Peredo, *Historia del estado de México* (Toluca: Universidad Autónoma del Estado de México, 1985), 182–83.

54. Luis Gómez Molina to Félix Diaz, March 19, 1913, Arch. M. González, 2, #118; *El Independiente*, April 19, 1913; Nemesio García Naranjo, *Memorias de Nemesio García Naranjo*, 9 vols. (Monterrey: Talleres de "El Porvenir," n.d.) 7:52–59; De la Barra to Carlos Carballido, March 13, 1913, AREM, L-E, 421, p 44; FLdlB to José Yves Limantour, April 3, 1916, AJYL, file 2.

55. Sir Frances Stronge to Sir Edward Grey, April 26, 1913, FO, 371.1673/21899; Sir Frances Stronge to Sir Edward Grey, May 19, 1913, FO, 371.1673/26298; José Luis Requena to Francisco Vázquez Gómez, July 1, 1913, AFVG, box 40, folder 6, #2096.

56. Félix Díaz to Agustín Bolaños Cacho, June 19, 1913, Archivo Particular de Pablo González, Austin, University of Texas microfilm, 56 reels, Nettie Lee Benson Collection (hereafter cited as Arch. P. González), section E, reel 47; Agustín Bolaños Cacho to Félix Díaz, May 12, 1913, Arch. P. González, section E, reel 47, Félix Díaz to Pedro Plata, June 17, 1913, Arch. P. González, section E, reel 43.

57. Nelson O'Shaughnessy to William Jennings Bryan, August 6, 1913, RDS, reel 27, 812.00/8256; Knight, *Mexican Revolution*, 2:74.

58. FLdlB to Secretary of Foreign Relations, September 24, 1913, AREM, L-E 763, 13; FLdlB to Secretary of Foreign Relations, November 13, 1913, AREM, L-E 763, Leg. 9, 2; Victoriano Huerta to FLdlB, January 10, 1914, AdlB, 5, #502; Meyer, *Huerta*, 187–88.

59. Sir Frances Stronge to Sir Edward Grey, May 21, 1913, FO, 371.1680/126305.

60. FLdlB, "Algunas Páginas," AdlB, 25, #2976.

61. *Le Matin* (Paris), December 27, 1913, in AdlB de Impresos #1, #52; *Japan Daily News* (Tokyo), ibid., #53; FLdlB to the Secretary of Foreign Relations, January 5, 1914, AdlB, 5, #497.

62. De la Barra's secret report to Secretary of Foreign Relations, January 5, 1914, AdlB, 5, #494; Iyo Iimura Kunimoto, "Japan and Mexico: 1888–1917" (Ph.D. diss., University of Texas-Austin, 1975), 164–68.

63. Japanese Minister to Mexico to FLdlB, February 24, 1914, AdlB, 5, #512.

64. Querido Moheno to FLdlB, March 9, 1914, AdlB, 5, #515.

65. Meyer, *Huerta*, 193–96; Robert Quirk, *An Affair of Honor: Woodrow Wilson and the Occupation of Veracruz* (New York: W. W. Norton, 1967).

66. José Bernal Reyes to FLdlB, July 9, 1914, AdlB, 5, #541; Isidro Fabela to Juan Sánchez Azcona, August 26, 1914, AdlB, 5, #556.

67. Sir Frances Stronge to Sir Edward Grey, July 10, 1913, FO, 371.1674/35120.

68. Memo of William Bayard Hale, July 9, 1913, RDS, reel 27, 812.00/8203.

69. FLdlB to the editor, *New York Times*, July 3, 1914, AdlB, 5, #537.

70. Knight, *Mexican Revolution*, vol. 2. Military events are chronicled in Charles C. Cumberland *The Mexican Revolution: The Constitutionalist Years* (Austin: University of Texas Press, 1972).

71. Tello Díaz, *El exilio*, 212, 285–86; Fey, "First Tango," 195–96.

72. FLdlB to Jorge Vera Estañol, May 7, 1917, AdlB, 7, #719; Douglas Richmond, "Intentos Externos para Derrocar al Régimen de Carranza (1915–1920)" *Historia Mexicana* 32 (July–September 1982): 106–32.

73. Alfonso Acosta to Secretary of Foreign Relations, June 13, 1916, AREM, L-E 798, Leg. 35 (25) 1; the secretary's response, July 7, 1916, in ibid., p. 2. Knight, *Mexican Revolution*, 2:442–76, points out that Carranza used the fear of "reactionaries" as an integrating tool, and therefore wild accusations and sensational charges abound. Neither Knight (*Mexican Revolution*, 2:382) nor Katz (*Secret War*, 331–32) includes de la Barra as a felicista exile in 1916.

74. *New York American*, March 5, 1916, AdlB, folder 2, #140.

75. FLdlB to Manuel Calero, September 8, 1916, AdlB, 6 #660; Lord Cowdray to Maurice de Bunsen, March 22, 1916, Pearson Papers, box 161.

76. Nemesio García Naranjo to FLdlB, June 30, 1917, AdlB, 7, #726.

77. Alonso Mariscal to FLdlB, December 4, 1918, AdlB, 8, #847; Aurelio Márquez to FLdlB, December 9, 1918, AdlB, 8, #851; de la Barra to Nemesio García Naranjo, April 17, 1919, AdlB, 10, #1050; de la Barra to Félix Díaz, June 3, 1919, AdlB, 10, #1093.

78. FLdlB to Manuel Calero, September 8, 1916, AdlB, 6, #660.

79. FLdlB to Nemesio García Naranjo, November 25, 1918, AdlB, 8, #887; FLdlB to Jorge Vera Estañol, November 25, 1918, AdlB, 8, #839.

80. Nemesio García Naranjo to FLdlB, June 2, 1918, AdlB, 8, #772; Tomás MacManus to FLdlB, November 26, 1918, AdlB, 8, #840; Katz, *Villa,* 671–75.

81. Knight, *Mexican Revolution,* 2:213–14.

82. Ibid., 456–66.

83. Ibid., 470–77; E. Victor Niemeyer, *Revolution at Queretaro: The Mexican Constitutional Convention of 1916–1917* (Austin: University of Texas Press, 1974).

84. FLdlB to Nemesio García Naranjo, April 12, 1918, AdlB, 8, #807; Jorge Vera Estañol to FLdlB, May 15, 1918, AdlB, 8, #812.

85. J. M. Arriola to Cándido Aguilar, January 20, 1917, AREM, L-E 839, Leg. 7, 5–10; Report by Charles E. Jones, June 23, 1918, AREM, L-E 837, Leg. 12, 109.

86. FLdlB to Tomás MacManus, January 29, 1919, AdlB, 9, #915; FLdlB to Tomás MacManus, February 18, 1919, AdlB, 9, #948; de la Barra to Esteban Maqueo Castellanos, May 16, 1919, AdlB, 10, #1076.

87. FLdlB to the Director of *El Universal,* March 7, 1919, AdlB, 9, #1004; *Chiltipiquín,* January 19, 1920 in AdlB, folder #3, #228.

88. FLdlB to Tomás MacManus, December 9, 1918, AdlB, 8, #850. The British Public Record Office has a huge index of names of people and subjects that were involved in the Versailles Treaty, and de la Barra's name is absent. Ambassador to Earl Curzan, March 10, 1919, FO, 371.3828/ 51282.

89. House diary, December 8, 1918, Colonel Edward House Diaries, vol. 14, p. 56, Sterling Memorial Library, Yale University, New Haven.

90. FLdlB to Colonel House, February 15, 1919, Colonel Edward House Papers, series 1, box 10, folder 318, Sterling Memorial Library, Yale University, New Haven. De la Barra repeats summaries of his conversations with House in his letters to his correspondents; see FLdlB to Leopoldo Ruiz, Archbishop of Michoacán, February 12, 1919, AdlB, 9, 936; FLdlB to José Yves Limantour, December 16, 1918, AJYL, File 2.

91. FLdlB to José Peón del Valle, April 8, 1919, AdlB, 9, #1062; FLdlB to Eugenio Rascón, February 20, 1919, AdlB, 9, #955.

92. FLdlB to Archbishop Orozco y Jiménez, February 18, 1919, AdlB, 9, #951; de la Barra to Nemesio García Naranjo, March 2, 1919, AdlB, 9, #990.

93. FLdlB to Nemesio García Naranjo, March 22, 1919, AdlB, 9, #1023; FLdlB to Archbishop Francisco Orozco y Jiménez, March 2, 1919, AdlB, 9, #989; FLdlB to Orozco y Jiménez, February 14, 1919, AdlB, 9, #940; Kelley, *Blood Drenched Altars,* 311.

94. FLdlB to Antonio de la Peña y Reyes, February 18, 1919, AdlB, 9, #947; FLdlB to Juan A. Hernández, February 28, 1919, AdlB, 9, #979.

95. Jorge Vera Estañol to Nemesio García Naranjo, April 5, 1919, AdlB, 10, #1037.

96. FLdlB to Jorge Vera Estañol, May 10, 1919, AdlB, 10, #1069.

97. FLdlB to Jorge Vera Estañol, October 2, 1919, AdlB, 11, #1172; FLdlB to General Casso López, September 8, 1919, AdlB, 10, #1160.

98. Linda B. Hall, *Alvaro Obregón: Power and Revolution in Mexico, 1911–1926* (College Station: Texas A&M University Press, 1981), 247–48.

99. Secretary of the Treasury Adolfo de la Huerta to FLdlB, April 24, 1921, AdlB, 12, #1388.

100. *El Universal,* n.d., AdlB, folder #4, #339; personnel file of FLdlB, AREM, file No. L-E 421B, 221. Interestingly, the *Excélsior* defended de la Barra, AdlB, folder 4, #395.

101. FLdlB to José E. Campos, Editor of *Excélsior,* April 4, 1923, AdlB, 14, #1595.

102. *Vista de Yucatán,* March 7, 1923, in AdlB, folder #4, #384; *El Universal,* July 12, 1922 in AdlB folder #4, #364.

103. FLdlB to Roderigo de Llano, editor of *Excélsior,* April 4, 1936, AdlB, 21, #2545.

104. FLdlB's personal file, AREM, L-E420, III, 294–391; Luis G. Tornel to FLdlB, October 7, 1935, AdlB 20, #2514.

105. Wasserman, *Persistent Oligarchs.*

106. Enrique Creel to FLdlB, February 19, 1925, AdlB, 16, #1905.

107. Rodolfo Reyes to FLdlB, March 2, 1926, AdlB, 17, #2036.

108. Wasserman, *Persistant Oligarchs,* 77–93; Tobler, *Revolución mexicana,* 544–45; Benjamin, *Rich Land,* 195.

109. Haber, *Industrialization,* 169–70.

110. FLdlB, "Perceptions of the Contemporary Mexican Economy," n.d., AdlB, 16, #1967; idem, "Notes for an Interview," January 31, 1931, AdlB, 19, #2309; Marte Gómez to Secretary of Foreign Relations, December 16, 1935, AREM, L-E 42D, 321–26.

111. Brown, *Oil,* 372–73.

112. Gonzálo Fernández to FLdlB, November 5, 1936, AdlB, 21, #2582.

113. FLdlB, confidential memorandum, December 12, 1936, AdlB 21, #2588; FLdlB to A. Leñero, Mexican consul in Paris, January 22, 1937, AdlB, 21, #2596; French Oil Company memorandum, March 5, 1937, AdlB, 21, #2616.

114. FLdlB to G. Espinosa Mirales, April 11, 1938, AdlB, 22, #2702; M. Meni, Director of French Petroleum Company, to FLdlB, April 30, 1937, AdlB, 21, #2640.

115. Friedrich Schuler, *Mexico between Hitler and Roosevelt: Mexican Foreign Relations in the Age of Lázaro Cárdenas* (Albuquerque: University of New Mexico Press, 1997).

116. Lord Cowdray to FLdlB, November 26, 1915, AdlB, 6, #632, 640; Thomas W. LaMont to FLdlB, June 25, 1924, AdlB, 15, #1825.

117. FLdlB to Victoriano Salado Alvarez, July 24, 1919, AdlB, 10, #1124. His appointment to the faculty, dated December 2, 1915, is in AdlB, 6, #633. See also Lord Cowdray to FLdlB, February 1, 1917, Pearson Papers, box 162.

118. FLdlB to M. Clementel, French Minister of Finance, n.d., AdlB, 15, #1855; A. Turrettini, Bank of Paris and Low Countries to M. Rodriganez, Bank of Spain, November 17, 1917, AdlB, 7, #746, with attachments.

119. F. Larnaude to FLdlB, May 13, 1919, AdlB, 10, #1071. AdlB, 24, #2903 and 2904.

120. "Exposé de Motifs," n.d., AdlB, 24, #2888; memorandum of FLdlB, AdlB, 24, #2901; FLdlB to José Yves Limantour, December 3, 1918, AJYL, File 2.

121. FLdlB to Alfred Verdross, March 10, 1931, AdlB, 19, #2315; FLdlB to A. de La Pradelle, September 18, 1919, AdlB, 10, #1165.

122. Academy of International Law to FLdlB, October 30, 1924, AdlB, 15, #1879.

123. D. H. S. Cranage to FLdlB, February 6, 1920, AdlB, 11, #1248; FLdlB lecture, AdlB, 6, #646. See also FLdlB speech to King Edward VII and other members of the Royal Geographical Society, October 21, 1930, AdlB, 19, #2288.

124. "Le Congrès de l'union latine," clipping from Paris newspaper, n.d., AdlB, folder #3, #238; FLdlB to Hugo Barbagelata, November 9, 1925, AdlB, 17, #2002.

125. FLdlB to Dr. L. Rowe, Director of the Pan-American Union, March 11, 1927, AdlB, 17, #2100; FLdlB to Ricardo Alfaro, Secretary General of American Institute of International Rights, April 26, 1939, AdlB, 22, #2789; interview with FLdlB regarding Nicaraguan invasion, by Mr. Wadder, Associated Press, January 16, 1927, AdlB, 17, #2087; article in *La Nación* (Buenos Aires), January 17, 1927, AdlB, folder 5, #466.

126. H. E. Barrault of the University of Paris Faculty, "La Jurisprudence du tribunal arbitral mixte," publisher and date unknown, AdlB, folder #9, #786. The hundreds of decisions handed down by the various tribunals were published in a set of reports titled *Recueil des décisions des tribunaux arbitraux mixtes,* 10 vols. (Paris: Académie de Droit International, 1923–30). A complete set of these rare volumes can be found at the Library of the Peace Palace, The Hague, Netherlands, where the International Court of Justice meets. John Bassett Moore to FLdlB, November 23, 1922, AdlB, 13, #1523.

127. The tribunals have not been the subject of much recent scholarly attention. See Jean Teyssaire, *Les Tribunaux arbitraux mixtes* (Paris: Les Editions Internationales, 1931); Rudolf Bluhorn, "Le Fonctionnement et la jurisprudence des tribunaux mixte crees por les Traités de Paris," *Recueil des décisions,* 3:132, 137–244; Paul F. Simonson, *Private Property and Rights in Enemy Countries and Private Rights against Enemy Nationals* (London: Effingham Wilson, 1921); Jackson H. Ralston, *International Arbitration from Athens to Locarno* (Stanford: Stanford University Press, 1929), 246–48. See article by SWF, n.d., AdlB 11, #1232; FLdlB to Minister of Justice of France, December 20, 1920, AdlB, 12, #1342.

128. See cases cited in the *Recueil des décisions,* e.g., *Popanastassaglov v. Bulgaria* (1925), 4:479; see also Th. Theoderoff to FLdlB, March 27, 1929, AdlB, 18, #2219; Franz Scholz to FLdlB, February 9, 1923, AdlB, 13, #1562.

129. FLdlB's memorandum to the Special Anglo-Franco-Bulgarian tribunal, June 15, 1927, AdlB, 17, #2109.

130. FLdlB to Sir Eric Drummond, Secretary General of the League of Nations, August 29, 1924, AdlB, 15, #1865; J. E. Guerrero to FLdlB, January 22, 1931, AdlB, 19, #2303; FLdlB, "La evolución de la diplomacia," *Hoy,* December 1927, in AdlB, folder #8, #702.

131. Speech to French Chamber of Deputies, June 26, 1929, AdlB, 18, #2227; FLdlB to Rodolfo Lozada, January 23, 1936, AdlB, 20, #2519.

132. V. H. to Zolton Baranyai, July 4, 1923, carton R-1320, dossier 27281, no. 29262, League of Nations Archive, Geneva, Switzerland; list of candidates, September 3, 1923, carton R-1321, dossier 27281, no. 29940, League of Nations Archive.

133. Pierre Jaudan to FLdlB, January 8, 1929, AdlB, 18, #2189. The suitor governments had to bear the cost of the courts, including judicial

salaries and the office expenses at the elegant Mantignon Palace, 57 Rue de Varennes, Paris, where de la Barra worked.

134. See FLdlB's confidential memorandum, March 23, 1936, AdlB, 20, #2537, and his more discreet interview in *El Universal*, n.d., AdlB, 21, #2585. See also Pitman B. Potter, *The Wal Wal Arbitration* (Washington, DC: Carnegie Endowment for International Peace, 1938), 19, 33.

135. FLdlB to Henri Beranger, Ambassador of France, January 30, 1939, AdlB, 22, #2771; José de Yonguas Messia to FLdlB, October 9, 1936, AdlB, 21, #2579.

136. *Hoy*, June 20, 1939, in AdlB, folder 8, #726.

137. FLdlB to Carlos Keller-Sarmiento, March 28, 1928, AdlB, 18, #2152.

138. Sebastían B. de Mier to FLdlB, April 11, 1915, AdlB, 6, #604.

139. FLdlB to Sara Díaz de Rincón Gallardo, June 30, 1939, AdlB, 22, #2799. There is some dispute about the date of his death and the location of his burial. One article quotes his widow saying he died on September 3; see "Desde Tierras de Francia," AdlB, folder #8, #746. Other writers have suggested that he is buried in the Spanish church in Paris, but his tombstone at the Sabou Cemetery in Biarritz clearly reads September 22 for his date of death.

Conclusion

1. Iñigo Noriega to Porfirio Díaz, September 15, 1911, CPD, Leg. 36, reel 283, #9661–68; Enrique Creel to FLdlB, September 9, 1911, AGM, 2, Exp. C-2, #64; Henry Lane Wilson to Philander C. Knox, June 23, 1911, RDS, reel 14, 812.00/2181.

2. Knight, *Mexican Revolution*, 2:497–516.

3. Gilly, *Mexican Revolution*, 325–30, discusses the Marxist ideal of the class-based link between labor and peasants, which did not happen in Mexico. Even in Yucatán, where Salvador Alvarado, a "socialist," emerged as governor, he had no desire to overturn the basic system. Joseph, *Revolution from Without*, 102–11.

4. A perceptive contemporary who noted the various motivations behind local rebellions was Fyfe, *The Real Mexico*, 1–3, 180–83.

Bibliography

Primary Sources

Manuscripts

Mexico

Archivo General de la Nación, Mexico City. Archivo Alfredo Robles Domínguez. 5 vols.

———. Colleción Jorge Vera Estañol. 56 vols.

Biblioteca Manuel Orozco y Berra, Anexo al Castillo de Chapultepec, Mexico City. Archivo de Samuel Espinosa de los Monteros. 9 folders.

Centro de Estudios de la Historia de México, Condumex, S.A., Mexico City. Archivo Francisco León de la Barra. 25 folders.

———. Archivo de Genaro Amezcua. 15 folders.

———. Archivo de Venustiano Carranza. 371 folders.

———. Archivo de Federico González Garza. 35 folders.

———. Archivo de Manuel González. 21 folders.

———. Archivo de José Yves Limantour. 2 folders.

———. Archivo de Bernardo Reyes. 153 folders.

Secretaría de la Defensa Nacional, Mexico City. Archivo Histórico.

Secretaría de Relaciones Exteriores, Mexico City. Archivo General de la Secretaría de Relaciones de México, Ramo de Revolución.

———. Francisco León de la Barra: Su Expediente Personal. L-E 418-421B. 5 vols.

Universidad Nacional Autónoma de México, Mexico City. Archivo Particular de Gildardo Magaña. 34 boxes.

———. Archivo Particular de Roque Estrada. 4 boxes.

University of the Americas, Cholula. Colección General Porfirio Díaz. 371 reels.

United States

Bancroft Library, University of California, Berkeley. Francisco Carvajal Papers. 5 folders.

———. Great Britain, Foreign Office Reports, 1911. British Public Record Office. 8 reels.

———. Jorge Vera Estañol Papers. 5 folders.
———. Silvestre Terrazas Papers. 129 boxes.
Harry Ransom Humanities Center, University of Texas, Austin. Harriet Freedman Papers.
Honnold Library, Claremont College, Claremont, California. José María Maytorena Papers. 7 boxes.
Hoover Institution, Stanford University, Palo Alto, California. Charles Rhodes Diary.
Library of Congress, Manuscript Division, Washington, DC. Philander C. Knox Papers.
———. William Howard Taft Papers.
Love Memorial Library, University of Nebraska, Lincoln, Nebraska. Archivo Francisco I. Madero, #B1536. 22 reels.
———. Records of the Department of State Relating to the Internal Affairs of Mexico, 1910–29. Microcopy no. 274, National Archives, Washington, DC.
Morris Library, Southern Illinois University, Carbondale, Illinois. Francisco Vázquez Gómez Papers. 56 boxes.
Sterling Memorial Library, Yale University, New Haven, Connecticut. Colonel Edward House Diaries.
———. Colonel Edward House Papers.
University of Texas, Austin, Texas. Nettie Lee Benson Collection. Archivo Francisco I. Madero. Biblioteca Nacional, Mexico City. April, May, and June 1911. 4 reels.
———. Archivo Particular de Pablo González. 56 reels.
———. Great Britain, Foreign Office Reports, 1913–20. British Public Record Office. 27 reels.
———. Weetman Pearson Papers. 275 reels.
University of Texas-El Paso. Fausto Orozco Collection, Pascual Orozco Documents. Item 1, Abraham González Letterbook. Item 4, June 14, 1911, to August 29, 1911. 2 reels.
———. Carlos Reyes Avila Collection. 1 reel.
———. Genovevo de la O Archive. Microfiche.

Europe

League of Nations Archive, Geneva, Switzerland.
Public Record Office, Kew Gardens, London, England. Foreign Office Reports, 1910–1911.
Quai d'Orsay, Paris, France. Archives du Ministère des Affaires Etrangères, Mexique, Politique Intérieure. Nouvelle Series, B-25-1, vols. 2, 3.

Published Documents

Casasola, Agustín. *Historia Gráfica de la Revolución Mexicana*, 6 vols. Mexico: Archivo Casasola, 1921–50.

Diario de los debates de la Cámara de Diputados del Congreso de los Estados Unidos Mexicanos 1911. Mexico: Imprenta de la Cámara de Diputados, 1912.

Fabela, Isidro, and Josefina E., eds. *Documentos históricos de la revolución mexicana*. 27 vols. Mexico: Editorial Jus, and Fondo de Cultura Económica, 1960–73.

Foner, Philip S., ed. *Mother Jones Speaks: Collected Writings and Speeches*. New York: Monad Press, 1983.

Jalisco: Documentos de la revolución, 1910–1940. Guadalajara: Gobierno de Jalisco, 1987.

Los presidentes de México: Discursos políticos, 1910–1988. Mexico City: El Colegio de México, 1988.

McGowan, Gerald L., ed. *La revolución mexicana a través de sus documentos*. 5 vols. Mexico City: Universidad Nacional Autónoma de México, 1987.

Recueil des décisions des tribunaux arbitraux mixtes. 10 vols. Paris: Académie de Droit International, 1923–30.

Books

Abascal, Salvador. *Madero: Dictador infortunado*. Mexico: Editorial Tradición, 1983.

Adame Goddard, Jorge. *El pensamiento político y social de los católicos mexicanos, 1867–1914*. Mexico City: Universidad Nacional Autónoma de México, 1981.

Aguilar, Rafael. *Madero sin máscara*. Mexico: Imprenta Popular, 1911.

Aguilar Camín, Héctor. *La frontera nómada: Sonora y la revolución mexicana*. Mexico City: Siglo Veintiuno, 1985.

Aguirre, Amado. *Mis memorias de campaña: Apuntes para la historia*. Mexico: Private Printing, 1985.

Aguirre Benavides, Adrián. *Errores de Madero*. Mexico City: Editorial Jus, 1980.

———. *Madero el Inmaculado*. Mexico City: Editorial Diana, 1962.

Alanís Boyso, Rodolfo. *El estado de México durante la revolución mexicana, 1910–1914*. Toluca: Ediciones del Gobierno del Estado de México, 1985.

Almada, Francisco R. *La revolución en el estado de Chihuahua*. Vol. 1, *1910–1913*. Mexico City: Biblioteca del Instituto Nacional de Estudios Históricos de la Revolución Mexicana, 1965.

Almond, Gabriel, and Sidney Verba. *The Civic Culture Revisited*. Boston: Little, Brown and Company, 1980.

Anderson, Robert D. *France, 1870–1914: Politics and Society*. London: Routledge and Kegan Paul, 1977.

Anderson, Rodney. *Outcasts in Their Own Land: Mexican Industrial Workers, 1906–1911*. De Kalb: Northern Illinois University Press, 1976.

Andrews, Gregg. *Shoulder to Shoulder? The American Federation of Labor, the United States, and the Mexican Revolution, 1910–1924*. Berkeley and Los Angeles: University of California Press, 1991.

Angel Aguilar, José. *La decena trágica*. 2 vols. Mexico City: Biblioteca del Instituto Nacional de Estudios Históricos de la Revolución Mexicana, 1981.

———. *La revolución en el estado de México*. Mexico City: Biblioteca del Instituto Nacional de Estudios Históricos de la Revolución Mexicana, 1976.

Arredondo Múñozledo, Benjamín. *Historia de la revolución mexicana*. Mexico City: Librería de Porrúa, 1971.

Atkin, Ronald. *Revolution: Mexico, 1910–1920*. New York: The John Day Company, 1970.

Baldwin, Deborah. *Protestants and the Mexican Revolution: Missionaries, Ministers, and Social Change*. Champaign: University of Illinois Press, 1990.

Ballesteros, Leonardo. *Apuntes biográficos de los Señores Lic. Emilio Vázquez Gómez y Doctor Francisco Vázquez Gómez*. Mexico: Talleres Tipográficos de El Tiempo, 1911.

Balmori, Diane, and Stuart Voss. *Notable Family Networks in Latin America*. Chicago: University of Chicago Press, 1984.

Bazant de Saldana, Mílada. *Historia de la educación durante el Porfiriato*. Mexico: El Colegio de México, 1993.

Beals, Carleton. *Porfirio Díaz, Dictator of Mexico*. Philadelphia: J. B. Lippincott Company, 1932.

Beezley, William H. *Insurgent Governor: Abraham González and the Mexican Revolution in Chihuahua, 1910–1913*. Lincoln: University of Nebraska Press, 1973.

———. *Judas at the Jockey Club and Other Episodes of Porfirian Mexico*. Lincoln: University of Nebraska Press, 1987.

Bell, Edward. *The Political Shame of Mexico*. New York: McBride, Nast and Company, 1914.

Benjamin, Thomas. *A Rich Land, a Poor People: Politics and Society in Modern Chiapas*. Albuquerque: University of New Mexico Press, 1989.

———, ed. *Provinces of the Revolution: Essays on Regional Mexican History*. Albuquerque: University of New Mexico Press, 1990.

Bernstein, Marvin. *The Mexican Mining Industry, 1890–1950*. Albany: State University of New York Press, 1965.

Bethel, Leslie, ed. *Chile since Independence*. New York: Cambridge University Press, 1993.

Blaisdell, Lowell L. *The Desert Revolution: Baja California, 1911*. Madison: University of Wisconsin Press, 1962.

Bonaparte, Roland, ed. *Le Mexique au début du 20e siècle*. 2 vols. Paris: C. Delagrave, 1904.

Bonilla, Manuel. *Diez años de guerra*. Mazatlán: Imprenta Avendaño, 1922.

———. *El régimen maderista*. Mexico: Editorial Arana, 1962.

Bose, Ellen. *Farewell to Durango*. New York: Doubleday and Company, 1927.
Brading, David. *Caudillo and Peasant in the Mexican Revolution*. New York: Cambridge University Press, 1980.
Breceda, Alfredo. *Don Venustiano Carranza*. Mexico: Talleres Gráficos de la Nación, 1930.
Brown, Jonathan. *Oil and Revolution in Mexico*. Berkeley and Los Angeles: University of California Press, 1993.
Brunk, Samuel. *Emiliano Zapata: Revolution and Betrayal in Mexico*. Albuquerque: University of New Mexico Press, 1995.
Bulnes, Francisco. *El verdadero Díaz y la revolución mexicana*. Mexico: Gómez de la Puente, 1920.
Burns, E. Bradford. *The Poverty of Progress: Latin America in the Nineteenth Century*. Berkeley and Los Angeles: University of California Press, 1980.
Bush, Ira. *Gringo Doctor*. Caldwell, ID: Caxton Printers, 1939.
Bushnell, David, and Neill Macaulay. *The Emergence of Latin America in the Nineteenth Century*. New York: Oxford University Press, 1994.
Buve, Raymond. *El movimiento revolucionario en Tlaxcala*. Mexico: Universidad Iberoamericana, 1994.
Cabrera, Luis (Blas Urrea, pseud.). *Obras politicas del Lic. Blas Urrea*. Mexico City: Universidad Nacional Autónoma de México, 1992.
———. *The Mexican Situation from a Mexican Point of View*. New York: L. Middleditch Co., 1920.
Calero, Manuel. *Un decenio de política mexicana*. New York: L. Middleditch Company, 1920.
Callahan, James Morton. *American Foreign Policy in Mexican Relations*. New York: MacMillan, 1932.
Calvert, Peter. *The Mexican Revolution, 1910–1914: The Diplomacy of the Anglo-American Conflict*. New York: Cambridge University Press, 1968.
Camp, Roderic Ai, ed. *Democracy in Latin America: Patterns and Cycles*. Wilmington, DE: Scholarly Resources, 1996.
———. *Political Recruitment across Two Centuries: Mexico, 1884–1991*. Austin: University of Texas Press, 1995.
Carr, Albert H. *The World and William Walker*. New York: Harper and Row, 1963.
Carr, Barry. *El movimiento obrero y la política en México*. 2 vols. Mexico: Sep-Setentas, 1976.
Castilla Echánove, Manuel. *Apuntes para la biografía del Sr. Doctor Don Francisco León de la Barra y Quijano, presidente interino de la república*. Mexico City: Imprenta Universal, 1911.
Chávez, Federico, and Alfonso López. *Fracaso y desastre del gobierno Maderista*. Mexico: Tipografía de Humboldt, 1913.
Choate, Joseph H. *The Two Hague Conferences*. Princeton: Princeton University Press, 1913.
Cole, Merl Burke. *Romantic Tragedies of Mexico*. Boston: Christopher Publishing House, 1956.

Cosío Villegas, Daniel, ed. *Historia moderna de México: El Porfiriato: La vida económica*. Mexico: Editorial Hermes, 1965.
———. *Historia moderna de México: El Porfiriato: La vida política interior*. Mexico: Editorial Hermes, 1972.
———. *Historia moderna de México: El Porfiriato: La vida social*. Mexico: Editorial Hermes, 1965.
———. *Historia moderna de México: La república restaurada*. 9 vols. Mexico: Editorial Hermes, 1955.
Cuéllar Abaroa, Crisanto. *La revolución en el estado de Tlaxcala*. Mexico: Biblioteca del Instituto Nacional de Estudios Históricos de la Revolución Mexicana, 1975.
Cumberland, Charles C. *The Mexican Revolution: Genesis under Madero*. Austin: University of Texas Press, 1952.
———. *The Constitutionalist Years*. Austin: University of Texas Press, 1972.
Davis, Calvin DeArmond. *The United States and the First Hague Peace Conference*. Ithaca, NY: Cornell University Press, 1962.
———. *The United States and the Second Hague Peace Conference: American Diplomacy and International Organization, 1899–1914*. Durham, NC: Duke University Press, 1975.
de Beer, Gabriella. *Luis Cabrera: Un intelectual de la revolución mexicana*. Mexico: Fondo de Cultura Económica, 1984.
de Kay, John. *Dictators of Mexico*. London: Effingham Wilson, 1914.
del Castillo, José R. *Historia de la revolución social de México: Primera etapa*. Mexico: Private Printing, 1915.
del Castillo, Porfirio. *Puebla y Tlaxcala en los días de la revolución*. Mexico: Zavala, 1953.
Díaz, Carlos Félix. *Génesis de la revolución mexicana*. La Paz, Bolivia: El Imprenta Moderna, 1918.
Díaz y Ovando, Clementina. *La Escuela Nacional Preparatoria*. 2 vols. Mexico: UNAM, 1972.
Dromundo, Baltazar. *Vida de Emiliano Zapata*. Mexico: Editorial Guaranía, 1961.
Dunn, W. H. *The Crimson Jester: Zapata of Mexico*. New York: R. M. McBride and Company, 1933.
Enríquez, Antonio. *La sucesión presidencial en 1911*. Mexico: Imprenta de Antonio Enríquez, 1911.
Esquivel Obregón, Toribio. *Democracia y personalismo*. Mexico: Imprenta de A. Carranza e Hijos, 1911.
———. *Mi labor en servicio de México*. Mexico City: Ediciones Botas, 1934.
Estrada, Roque. *La Revolución y Francisco I. Madero*. Guadalajara: Imprenta Americana, 1912.
Fernández Güell, Rogelio. *La revolución mexicana: Episodios*. San José: Editorial Costa Rica, 1973.
Fernández Rojas, José. *De Porfirio Díaz a Victoriano Huerta*. Guadalajara: Tip. de Escuela de Artes y Oficios del Estado, 1913.

Ferrer de Mendiolea, Gabriel. *Presencia de Don Francisco I Madero.* Mexico: Colección Metropolitana, 1973.

Figueroa Domenech, J. *Veinte meses de anarquia.* Mexico: Herrero Hermanos Sucesores, 1913.

Figueroa Uriza, Arturo. *Ciudadanos en armas.* Mexico City: B. Costa-Amic, 1960.

Franck, Harry. *Tramping through Mexico, Guatemala, and Honduras.* New York: The Century Company, 1916.

French, William E. *A Peaceful and Working People: Manners, Morals, and Class Formation in Northern Mexico.* Albuquerque: University of New Mexico Press, 1996.

Fuentes, Carlos. *The Old Gringo.* New York: Harper and Row, 1985.

———. *The Death of Artemio Cruz.* New York: Farrar, Straus, and Giroux, 1964.

Furber, Percy N. *I Took Chances, from Windjammers to Jets.* Leicester, England: E. Backus, 1953.

Fyfe, J. Hamilton. *The Real Mexico.* New York: McBride, Nast and Company, 1914.

García Granados, Alberto. *Las cajas rurales de crédito mutuo en México.* 1911. In Jesús Silva Herzog, ed., *La cuestión de la tierra,* 5 vols. (Mexico: Instituto Mexicano de Investigaciones Económicas, 1960), 1:77–108.

García Granados, Ricardo. *Por qué y como cayó Porfirio Díaz.* Mexico: A. Botas e Hijos, 1928.

García Naranjo, Nemesio. *Memorias de Nemesio García Naranjo.* 9 vols. Monterrey: Talleres de "El Porvenir," n.d.

Garibaldi, Giuseppe. *A Toast to Rebellion.* Indianapolis: Bobbs-Merrill Company, 1935.

Gilly, Adolfo. *The Mexican Revolution.* London: Thetford Press, 1983.

González Pacheco, Cuahtémoc. *Capital extranjero en la selva de Chiapas, 1863–1982.* Mexico: UNAM, 1983. 2 vols. Mexico: UNAM, 1972.

González Garza, Federico. *La revolución mexicana, Mi contribución político-literaria.* Mexico: A. del Bosque, 1936.

González Ramírez, Manuel. *La revolución social de México.* Mexico: Fondo de Cultura Económica, 1960.

González Roa, Federico. *El aspecto agrario de la revolución mexicana.* Mexico: Departmento de Aprovisionamientos Generales, Dirección de Talleres Gráficos, 1919.

González y González, Luis. *San José de Gracia: Mexican Village in Transition.* Austin: University of Texas Press, 1974.

Gruening, Ernest. *Mexico and Its Heritage.* New York: The Century Company, 1928.

Guerra, François-Xavier. *Le Mexique: De l'ancien régime à la révolution.* 2 vols. Paris: Editions L'Harmattan, 1985.

Haber, Stephen. *Industrialization and Underdevelopment: The Industrialization of Mexico, 1890–1940.* Stanford: Stanford University Press, 1989.

Hale, Charles. *The Transformation of Liberalism in Late Nineteenth-Century Mexico*. Princeton: Princeton University Press, 1989.

Hall, Linda B. *Alvaro Obregón: Power and Revolution in Mexico, 1911–1926*. College Station: Texas A&M University Press, 1981.

Hamill, Hugh. *The Hidalgo Revolt: Prelude to Mexican Independence*. Gainesville: University of Florida Press, 1966.

Hart, John Mason. *Revolutionary Mexico: The Coming and the Process of the Mexican Revolution*. Berkeley and Los Angeles: University of California Press, 1987.

Henderson, Peter V. N. *Félix Díaz, the Porfirians, and the Mexican Revolution*. Lincoln: University of Nebraska Press, 1981.

———. *Mexican Exiles in the Borderlands, 1910–1913*. Southwestern Studies. El Paso: Texas Western Press, 1979.

Hernández, Rafael. *Política agraria*. 1912. In Jesús Silva Herzog, ed., *La cuestión de la tierra*, 5 vols. (Mexico: Instituto Mexicano de Investigaciones Económicas, 1960), 2:93–122.

Hernández Chávez, Alicia. *La tradición republicana del buen gobierno*. Mexico: Fondo de Cultura Económica, 1993.

Herrejón Peredo, Carlos. *Historia del estado de México*. Toluca: Universidad Autónoma del Estado de México, 1985.

Hobsbawm, Eric J. *Bandits*. London: Penguin Books, 1972.

Hohler, Thomas Beaumont. *Diplomatic Petrel*. London: John Murray, 1942.

Holden, Robert H. *Mexico and the Survey of Public Lands*. De Kalb: Northern Illinois University Press, 1994.

Hundley, Norris. *Dividing the Waters: A Century of Controversy between the United States and Mexico*. Berkeley and Los Angeles: University of California Press, 1966.

Huntington, Samuel P. *The Third Wave: Democratization in the Late Twentieth Century*. Norman: University of Oklahoma Press, 1991.

Huntington-Wilson, Frances M. *Memoirs of an Ex-Diplomat*. Boston: Bruce Humphreys, 1945.

Iturbide, Eduardo. *Mi paso por la vida*. Mexico: Editorial Cultura, 1941.

Jacobs, Ian. *Ranchero Revolt: The Mexican Revolution in Guerrero*. Austin: University of Texas Press, 1982.

Jane, Cecil. *Liberty and Despotism in Spanish America*. New York: Cooper Square Publishers, 1966.

Johns, Michael. *The City of Mexico in the Age of Díaz*. Austin: University of Texas Press, 1997.

Johnson, William Weber. *Heroic Mexico*. Garden City, NY: Doubleday, 1968.

Joseph, Gilbert M. *Revolution from Without: Yucatán, Mexico, and the United States, 1880–1924*. New York: Cambridge University Press, 1982.

Katz, Friedrich. *The Life and Times of Pancho Villa*. Stanford: Stanford University Press, 1998.

———. *The Secret War in Mexico: Europe, the United States, and the Mexican Revolution*. Chicago: University of Chicago Press, 1981.

———, ed. *Riot, Rebellion, and Revolution: Rural Social Conflict in Mexico*. Princeton: Princeton University Press, 1988.

Kelley, Francis C. *Blood Drenched Altars*. Milwaukee: Bruce Publishing, 1935.

King, Rosa. *Tempest over Mexico*. Boston: Little, Brown and Co., 1935.

Knight, Alan. *The Mexican Revolution*. 2 vols. New York: Cambridge University Press, 1986.

———. *U.S.-Mexican Relations, 1910–1940: An Interpretation*. La Jolla, CA: Center for U.S. Mexican Studies, 1987.

Kroeber, Clifton. *Man, Land, and Water: Mexico's Farmland Irrigation Policies, 1885–1911*. Berkeley and Los Angeles: University of California Press, 1983.

LaFrance, David. *The Mexican Revolution in Puebla, 1908–1913: The Maderista Movement and the Failure of Liberal Reform*. Wilmington, DE: Scholarly Resources, 1989.

Langle Ramírez, Arturo. *Huerta contra Zapata: Una campaña desigual*. Mexico: Universidad Nacional Autónoma de México, 1981.

Lara Pardo, Luis. *De Porfirio Díaz a Francisco I. Madero: La sucesión dictatorial de 1911*. New York: Polyglot Publishing, 1912.

———. *Madero: Esbozo político*. Mexico: Ediciones Botas, 1938.

León de la Barra, Francisco. *Algunas consideraciones acerca de la historia diplomática de México*. Mexico: Editorial Polis, 1938.

———. *Estudio sobre la ley mexicano de extradición*. Mexico: Imprento de Gobierno Federal, 1897.

———. *La geografía, el derecho de gentes y la política internacional*. Mexico: Imprenta Mundial, 1933.

———. *La igualdad jurídica de los estados, base del derecho internacional moderno*. Mexico: Eusebio Gómez de la Puente, 1912.

———. *La inmigración en la República Argentina*. Buenos Aires: Compañía Sud-Americana de Billetes de Banco, 1904.

———. *La Médiation et la conciliation internationales*. Paris: Imprimeria Jean Cussac, 1925.

———. *El sistema de reciprocidad en el derecho civil mexicano*. Mexico: Oficina de la Secretaría de Fomento, 1887.

———. *Los neutrales y el derecho internacional*. Paris: Imprimerie Jean Cussac, 1917.

León de la Barra, Luis. *Historia de un linaje*. Mexico: Editorial Luis Foja, 1958.

———. *Memorias de la Academia Mexicana de Genealogía y Heráldica*. Vol. 1, no. 1. Mexico: Private Printing, 1945.

Limantour, José Yves. *Apuntes sobre mi vida pública*. Mexico: Editorial Porrúa, 1965.

Liss, Sheldon. *A Century of Disagreement: The Chamizal Conflict, 1864–1964*. Washington, DC: University Press of Washington, DC, 1965.

Luna Morales, Ricardo. *Mi vida revolucionaria*. Mexico: Private Printing, 1943.

Macías, Anna. *Against All Odds: The Feminist Movement in Mexico to 1940*. Westport, CT: Greenwood Press, 1982.
Madero, Francisco I. *Las memorias y las mejores cartas de Francisco I. Madero*. Mexico: Libro-Mex Editores, 1956.
Madero, Gustavo. *Gustavo A. Madero: Epistolario*. Mexico: Editorial Diana, 1991.
Magaña, Gildardo. *Emiliano Zapata y el agrarismo en México*. 5 vols. Mexico: Editorial Ruta, 1952.
Magdaleno, Mauricio. *Instantes de la revolución*. Mexico: Biblioteca del Instituto Nacional de Estudios Históricos de la Revolución Mexicana, 1981.
Manero, Antonio. *El antiguo régimen y la revolución*. Mexico: Tipografía y Litografía "La Europea" 1911.
Márquez Sterling, Manuel. *Los ultimas días del Presidente Madero*. Mexico: Editorial Porrúa, 1958.
Martínez Vásquez, Victor Raúl. *La revolución en Oaxaca, 1900–1930*. Oaxaca: Instituto de Administración Pública de Oaxaca, 1985.
Meyer, Michael C. *Huerta: A Political Portrait*. Lincoln: University of Nebraska Press, 1972.
———. *Mexican Rebel: Pascual Orozco and the Mexican Revolution, 1910–1915*. Lincoln: University of Nebraska Press, 1967.
Meyers, William K. *Forge of Progress, Crucible of Revolt: The Origins of the Mexican Revolution in La Comarca Laguna, 1880–1911*. Albuquerque: University of New Mexico Press, 1994.
Moats, Leone. *Thunder in Their Veins*. New York: The Century Company, 1932.
Molina Enríquez, Andrés. *La revolución agraria en México*. Mexico: Liga de Economistas Revolucionarios de la República Mexicana, 1976.
Needell, Jeffrey D. *A Tropical Belle Epoque: Elite Culture and Society in Turn-of-the Century Río de Janeiro*. New York: Cambridge University Press, 1987.
Niemeyer, E. Victor. *El General Bernardo Reyes*. Monterrey: Biblioteca de Nuevo León, 1966.
———. *Revolution at Queretaro: The Constitutional Convention of 1916–1917*. Austin: University of Texas Press, 1974.
Núñez de Prado, Gonzalo. *Revolución de México : La decena trágica*. Barcelona: F. Granada, 1913.
Olea, Hector R. *Breve historia de la revolución en Sinaloa, 1910–1917*. Mexico City: Biblioteca del Instituto Nacional de Estudios Históricos de la Revolución Mexicana, 1964.
Ortiz Rubio, Pascual. *La revolución de 1910*. Mexico: Ediciones Botas, 1937.
O'Shaughnessy, Edith. *Intimate Pages of Mexican History*. New York: George H. Doran Company, 1920.
Parkinson, Roger. *Zapata*. Briarcliff, NY: Stein and Day, 1975.
Perry, Laurens B. *Juárez and Díaz: Machine Politics in Mexico*. De Kalb: Northern Illinois University Press, 1978.

Pilcher, Jeffrey. *Que vivan los tamales: Food and the Making of Mexican Identity*. Albuquerque: University of New Mexico Press, 1998.

Piña, Joaquín, et al. *Memorias del General Victoriano Huerta*. Mexico: Librería de Quiroga, n.d.

Pollard, Hugh B. C. *A Busy Time in Mexico*. New York: Duffield and Company, 1913.

Ponce de León, Gregorio. *El interinato presidencial de 1911*. Mexico: Imprenta y Fototipia de la Secretaría de Fomento, 1912.

Potash, Robert. *The Mexican Government and Industrial Development in the Early Republic: The Banco de Avío*. Amherst: University of Massachusetts Press, 1983.

Potter, Pitman B. *The Wal Wal Arbitration*. Washington, DC: Carnegie Institute for International Peace, 1938.

Prida, Ramón. *De la dictadura a la anarquía*. Mexico: Ediciones Botas, 1958.

Putnam, Samuel. *Paris Was Our Mistress*. New York: The Viking Press, 1947.

Py, Pierre. *Francia y la revolución mexicana*. Mexico: Fondo de Cultura Económica, 1991.

Quirk, Robert. *An Affair of Honor: Woodrow Wilson and the Occupation of Veracruz*. New York: W. W. Norton, 1967.

———. *The Mexican Revolution and the Catholic Church, 1910–1929*. Bloomington: Indiana University Press, 1973.

Raat, William. *El positivismo durante el Porfiriato, 1876–1910*. Mexico: Sep-Setentas, 1975.

———. *Revoltosos: Mexico's Rebels in the United States, 1903–1923*. College Station: Texas A&M University Press, 1981.

Ralston, Jackson H. *International Arbitration from Athens to Locarno*. Stanford: Stanford University Press, 1929.

Rasgos biográficos del Sr. Lic. Emilio Vázquez Gómez. Mexico: Imprenta La Voz de Juárez, 1911.

Reyes, Rodolfo. *De mi vida*. 3 vols. Madrid: Biblioteca Nueva, 1929.

Reynolds, Clark. *The Mexican Economy: Twentieth-Century Structure and Growth*. New Haven: Yale University Press, 1970.

Ribot, Héctor. *Las últimas revoluciónes*. Mexico: Imprenta de Humboldt, 1912.

Richmond, Douglas W. *Carlos Pellegrini and the Crisis of Argentine Elites, 1880–1916*. New York: Praeger, 1989.

———, ed. *Essays on the Mexican Revolution: Revisionist Views of the Leaders*. Austin: University of Texas Press, 1979.

———. *Venustiano Carranza's Nationalist Struggle, 1893–1920*. Lincoln: University of Nebraska Press, 1983.

Rivero, Gonzalo G. *Hacia la verdad: Episodios de la revolución*. Mexico: Companía Editora Nacional, 1911.

Rodríguez O, Jaime. *The Emergence of Spanish America: Vicente Rocafuerte and Spanish Americanism, 1808–1835*. Berkeley and Los Angeles: University of California Press, 1975.

———. *The Revolutionary Process in Mexico: Essays on Political and Social Change, 1890–1940*. Los Angeles: UCLA Latin American Center Publications, 1990.
Rojas, Basilio. *Un gran rebelde: Manuel García Vigil*. Mexico: Editorial Luz, 1965.
Romero Flores, Jesús. *Anales históricos de la revolución mexicana*. Mexico: Ediciones Encuadernables, 1939.
Ross, Stanley R. *Francisco I. Madero: Apostle of Mexican Democracy*. New York: Columbia University Press, 1955.
Rouaix, Pastor. *La revolución maderista y constitucionalista en Durango*. Mexico: Editorial Cultura, 1931.
Ruiz, Ramón. *The Great Rebellion, Mexico, 1905–1924*. New York: W. W. Norton, 1980.
———. *Labor and the Ambivalent Revolutionaries: Mexico, 1911–23*. Baltimore: Johns Hopkins University Press, 1976.
———. *The People of Sonora and the Yankee Capitalists*. Tucson: University of Arizona Press, 1988.
Salado Álvarez, Victoriano. *Memorias*. 2 vols. Mexico: E.d.i.a.p, S.A., 1946.
Salas, Elizabeth. *Soldaderas in the Mexican Military*. Austin: University of Texas Press, 1990.
Salvucci, Richard J. *Textiles and Capitalism in Mexico: An Economic History of the Obrajes, 1539–1840*. Princeton: Princeton University Press, 1987.
Sánchez Azcona, Juan. *Apuntes para la Historia de la Revolución Mexicana*. Mexico: Biblioteca del Instituto Nacional de Estudios Históricos de la Revolución Mexicana, 1961.
———. *La etapa maderista de la revolución mexicana*. Mexico: Biblioteca del Instituto Nacional de Estudios Históricos de la Revolución Mexicana, 1960.
Sánchez Escobar, Rafael. *Narraciones Revolucionarias mexicanas, Histórico-Anécdotas*. Mexico: Talleres Tipográfica de la Casa de Orientación para Varones, 1934.
Sánchez Lamego, Miguel A. *Historia militar de la revolución mexicana en la epoca maderista*. 3 vols. Mexico: Biblioteca del Instituto Nacional de Estudios Históricos de la Revolución Mexicana, 1976.
Sánchez Septién, Salvador. *José María Lozano en la tribuna parlamentario, 1910–1913*. Mexico City: Editorial Jus, 1953.
Scholes, Walter, and Marie Scholes. *The Foreign Policy of the Taft Administration*. Columbia: University of Missouri Press, 1966.
Schuler, Friedrich. *Mexico between Hitler and Roosevelt: Mexican Foreign Relations in the Age of Lázaro Cárdenas*. Albuquerque: University of New Mexico Press, 1997.
Scobie, James T. *Buenos Aires: Plaza to Suburb, 1870–1910*. Oxford: Oxford University Press, 1974.
———. *Revolution on the Pampas: A Social History of Argentine Wheat*. Austin: University of Texas Press, 1964.

Shadle, Stanley. *Andrés Molina Enríquez: Mexican Land Reformer of the Revolutionary Era*. Tucson: University of Arizona Press, 1994.

Sherman, William L., and Richard Greenleaf. *Victoriano Huerta: A Reappraisal*. Mexico City: Mexico City College Press, 1960.

Silva Herzog, Jesús, ed. *La cuestión de la tierra*. 5 vols. Mexico: Instituto Mexicano de Investigaciones Económicas, 1960.

———. *Breve historia de la revolución mexicana*. Mexico: Fondo de Cultura Económica, 1960.

Simonson, Paul F. *Private Property and Rights in Enemy Countries and Private Rights against Enemy Nationals*. London: Effingham Wilson, 1921.

Sinkin, Richard. *The Mexican Reform, 1855–1876: A Study in Liberal Nation Building*. Austin: University of Texas Press, 1979.

Soto, Shirlene Ann. *The Mexican Woman: A Study of Her Participation in the Revolution, 1910–1940*. Palo Alto, CA: R & E Research Associates, 1979.

Starr, Frederick. *Mexico and the United States*. Chicago: The Bible House, 1914.

Taracena, Alfonso. *La verdadura revolución mexicana*. 5 vols. Mexico: Biblioteca del Instituto Nacional de Estudios Históricos de la Revolución Mexicana, 1960.

Taylor, Lawrence Douglas. *La campaña magonista de 1911 en Baja California*. Tijuana: El Colegio de la Frontera Norte, 1992.

Taylor, William B. *Drinking, Homicide, and Rebellion in Colonial Mexican Villages*. Stanford: Stanford University Press, 1979.

Tello Díaz, Carlos. *El exilio: Un relato de familia*. Mexico: Cal y Arena, 1993.

Teyssaire, Jean. *Les Tribuneaux arbitraux mixtes*. Paris: Les Editions Internationales, 1931.

Thompson, Wallace. *The People of Mexico*. New York: Harper and Brothers, 1921.

Timberlake, James H. *Prohibition and the Progressive Movement, 1900–1920*. Cambridge: Harvard University Press, 1963.

Tobler, Hans Werner. *La revolución mexicana: Transformación social y cambio político, 1876–1940*. Mexico: Editorial Alianza, 1994.

Traven, B. *The White Rose*. Westport CT: Lawrence Hill, 1979.

Trowbridge, Edward D. *Mexico Today and Tomorrow*. New York: Macmillan, 1920.

Turner, Frederick C. *The Dynamic of Mexican Nationalism*. Chapel Hill: University of North Carolina Press, 1968.

Turner, John Kenneth. *Barbarous Mexico*. Austin: University of Texas Press, 1968.

Ulloa, Berta. *La revolución intervenida: Relaciones diplomáticas entre México y los Estados Unidos, 1910–1914*. Mexico: El Colegio de México, 1971.

Ultimos meses de Porfirio Díaz en el poder. Mexico: Talleres Gráficos de la Nación, 1911.

Valadés, José C. *Imaginación y realidad de Francisco I. Madero*. 2 vols. Mexico: Antiguo Librería Robredo, 1960.

———. *Historia general de la revolución mexicana*. 5 vols. Mexico: M. Quesada Brandi, 1963–65.

Van Young, Eric. *Hacienda and Market in Eighteenth Century Mexico: The Rural Economy of the Guadalajara Region, 1675–1820*. Berkeley and Los Angeles: University of California Press, 1981.

Vanderwood, Paul. *Disorder and Progress: Bandits, Police, and Mexican Development*. 1981. Reprint, Wilmington, DE: Scholarly Resources, 1992.

Vaughan, Mary Kay. *The State, Education, and Social Class in Mexico, 1880–1928*. De Kalb: Northern Illinois University Press, 1982.

Vázquez Gómez, Francisco. *Memorias políticas, 1909–1913*. Mexico: Imprenta Mundial, 1933.

Vela González, Francisco. *Diario de la revolución*. Monterrey: Patronato Universitario de Nuevo León, 1971.

Vera Estañol, Jorge. *La revolución mexicana: Origenes y resultados*. Mexico City: Editorial Porrúa, 1957.

Wallace, Dillon. *Beyond the Mexican Sierra*. Chicago: A. C. McClurg Company, 1910.

Warman, Arturo. *We Came to Object: The Peasants of Morelos and the National State*. Baltimore: Johns Hopkins University Press, 1980.

Wasserman, Mark. *Capitalists, Caciques, and Revolution: The Native Elite and Foreign Enterprise in Chihuahua, Mexico, 1854–1911*. Chapel Hill, University of North Carolina Press, 1984.

———. *Persistent Oligarchs: Elite and Politics in Chihuahua, Mexico, 1910–1940*. Durham, NC: Duke University Press, 1993.

Weddington, Guy. *From Glory to Oblivion: The Real Truth about the Mexican Revolution*. New York: Vantage Press, 1974.

Wells, Allen. *Yucatan's Gilded Age: Haciendas, Henequen, and International Harvester, 1860–1915*. Albuquerque: University of New Mexico Press, 1985.

Wilkie, James. *The Mexican Revolution: Federal Expenditure and Social Change since 1910*. Berkeley and Los Angeles: University of California Press, 1967.

Wilson, Henry Lane. *Diplomatic Episodes in Mexico, Belgium, and Chile*. New York: Doubleday and Page, 1927.

Winter, Nevin O. *Mexico and Her People of Today*. London: Cassell and Company, 1913.

Womack, John. *Zapata and the Mexican Revolution*. New York: Alfred A. Knopf, 1968.

Zook, David. *Zarumilla-Marañón: The Ecuador-Peru Dispute*. New York: Bookman Associates, 1964.

Zuno Hernández, José G. *Historia de la revolución en el Estado de Jalisco*. Mexico: Biblioteca Nacional del Instituto Nacional de Estudios Históricos de la Revolución Mexicana, 1964.

Articles

Beezley, William H. "Governor Carranza and the Revolution in Coahuila." *The Americas* 33 (July 1976): 50–61.

———. "Madero: The 'Unknown' President and his Political Failure to Organize Rural Mexico." In Douglas Richmond, ed., *Essays on the Mexican Revolution* (Austin: University of Texas Press, 1979), 1–19.

———. "State Reform during the Provisional Presidency: Chihuahua, 1911." *Hispanic American Historical Review* 50 (1970): 524–37.

Benjamin, Thomas. "Revolución interrumpida: Chiapas y el Interinato presidencial, 1911." *Historia Mexicana* 30 (July 1980): 79–98.

Berbusse, Edward. "Neutrality Diplomacy of the United States and Mexico, 1910–1911." *The Americas* 12 (January 1956): 265–83.

Blaiser, Cole. "Studies of Social Revolution: Origins in Mexico, Bolivia, and Cuba." *Latin American Research Review* 2, no. 3 (1967): 28–64.

Blanco, Mónica. "Participación Popular y revolución: La elección de los jefes políticos en Guanajuato en 1911." In *Memoria de Congreso Internacional sobre la revolución mexicana*, 1:135–47.

Bliss, Katherine. "The Science of Redemption: Syphilis, Sexual Promiscuity, and Reformism in Revolutionary Mexico City." *Hispanic American Historical Review* 79 (February 1999): 1–40.

Booth, John, and Mitchell Seligson. "Political Culture of Authoritarianism in Mexico: A Re-Examination." *Latin American Research Review* 19, no. 1 (1984): 106–24.

Breymann, Walter N. "The Científicos: Critics of the Díaz Regime, 1892–1903." *Proceedings of the Arkansas Academy of Science* 7 (1954): 91–97.

Britton, John A. "Indian Education, Nationalism, and Federalism in Mexico, 1910–1921." *The Americas* 32 (January 1976): 445–58.

Brown, Jonathan C. "Foreign and Native-Born Workers in Porfirian Mexico." *American Historical Review* 98 (June 1993): 786–818.

Brunk, Samuel. "Zapata and the City Boys: In Search of a Piece of the Revolution." *Hispanic American Historical Review* 73 (February 1993): 33–65.

Burke, Michael E. "The University of Mexico and the Revolution, 1910–1940." *The Americas* 34 (October 1977): 252–73.

Buve, Raymond. "State Governors and Peasant Mobilization in Tlaxcala." In David A. Brading, ed., *Caudillo and Peasant in the Mexican Revolution* (Cambridge: Cambridge University Press, 1980), 222–45.

Calvert, Peter. "Frances Stronge en la Decena Trágica." *Historia Mexicana* 15 (July 1965): 47–68.

Ceballos Ramírez, Manuel. "La encíclica 'Rerum Novarum' y los trabajadores católicos en la Ciudad de México, 1891–1913." *Historia Mexicana* 33 (January 1985): 3–38.

Cumberland, Charles C. "The Sonora Chinese and the Mexican Revolution." *Hispanic American Historical Review* 40 (May 1960): 191–211.

Deeds, Susan. "José María Maytorena and the Mexican Revolution in Sonora, Part I." *Arizona and the West* 18 (Spring 1976): 21–40.

Falcón, Romana. "Los origenes populares de la revolución de 1910: El caso de San Luis Potosí." *Historia Mexicana* 29 (October 1979): 197–240.

French, William. "Prostitutes and Guardian Angels: Women, Work, and the Family in Porfirian Mexico." *Hispanic American Historical Review* 72 (November 1992): 529–53.

González Navarro, Moises. "El maderismo y la revolución agraria." *Historia Mexicana* 37 (July–September 1987): 5–28.

Hale, Charles A. "Scientific Politics and the Continuity of Liberalism in Mexico, 1867–1910." In *Proceedings of the Fifth International Conference of Mexicanists* (Austin: University of Texas Press, 1982).

Henderson, Peter V. N. "Un gobernador maderista: Benito Juárez Maza y la revolución en Oaxaca." *Historia Mexicana* 24 (January–March 1975): 372–89.

———. "Woodrow Wilson, Victoriano Huerta, and the Recognition Issue in Mexico." *The Americas* 45 (October 1984): 151–76.

Iturribarría, Jorge Fernando. "Limantour y la caída de Porfirio Díaz." *Historia Mexicana* 10 (October–December 1960): 243–81.

———. "La versión de Limantour." *Historia Mexicana* 16 (January 1967): 382–418.

Jacques, Leo M. "The Chinese Massacre in Torreón (Coahuila) in 1911." *Arizona and the West* 16 (1974): 233–46.

Knudson, Jerry. "When Did Francisco I. Madero Decide on Revolution?" *The Americas* 30 (April 1974): 529–34.

LaFrance, David. "Francisco I. Madero and the 1911 Interim Governorship in Puebla." *The Americas* 42 (January 1986): 311–31.

———. "Germany, Revolutionary Nationalism, and the Downfall of President Francisco I. Madero: The Covadonga Killings." *Mexican Studies, Estudios Mexicanos* 2, no. 1 (Winter 1986): 59–82.

———. "Labour and the Mexican Revolution: President Francisco I. Madero and the Puebla Textile Workers." *Boletín de Estudios Latinoamericanos y del Caribe* (January 1983): 59–74.

———. "The Madero Collection in Mexico's Archivo General de la Nación." *Revista Interamericana de Bibliografía/Inter-American Review of Bibliography* 33, no. 2 (1983): 191–97.

MacGregor, Josefina. "Madero y los Diputados: En busca de una nueva relación." In *Memoria del Congreso Internacional Sobre la Revolución Mexicana* (1991), 2:57–79.

Mecham, J. Lloyd. "The Jefe Político in Mexico." *Southwestern Social Science Quarterly* 13, no. 4 (March 1933): 333–52.

Menegus Bornemann, Margarita. "Las haciendas de mazaquiahuac y el rosario en los albores de la revolución agraria." *Historia Mexicana* 31 (January 1982): 233–50.

Meyer, Lorenzo. "La revolución mexicana y sus elecciones presidenciales: Una interpretación (1911–1940)." *Historia Mexicana* 32 (October–December 1982): 143–97.

Meyers, William K. "Politics, Vested Rights, and Economic Growth in Porfirian Mexico: The Company of Tlahualilo in the Comarca Lagunera, 1885–1911." *Hispanic American Historical Review* 57 (1977): 425–54.

Niemeyer, E. Victor. "Frustrated Invasion: The Revolutionary Attempt of General Bernardo Reyes from San Antonio in 1911." *Southwestern Historical Quarterly* 47 (October 1963): 213–25.

Portilla Gil de Partearroyo, Santiago. "La personalidad política de Francisco León de la Barra." *Historia Mexicana* 25 (October–December 1975): 232–75.

Powell, T. G. "Mexican Intellectuals and the Indian Question." *Hispanic American Historical Review* 48 (February 1968): 19–36.

Richmond, Douglas. "Confrontation and Reconciliation: Mexicans and Spaniards during the Revolution, 1910–1920." *The Americas* 41 (October 1984): 215–28.

———. "Intentos externos para derrocar al régimen de Carranza." *Historia Mexicana* 32 (July–September 1982): 102–32.

Rodríguez Kuri, Ariel. "El discurso de miedo: *El Imparcial* y Francisco I. Madero." *Historia Mexicana* 40 (April–June 1991): 697–740.

Schmitt, Karl M. "Catholic Adjustment to the Secular: The Case of Mexico, 1867–1911." *Catholic Historical Review* 482 (1962): 182–204.

Super, John C. "Querétaro Obrajes: Industry and Society in Provincial Mexico, 1600–1810." *Hispanic American Historical Review* 56 (May 1976): 197–216.

Taylor, Lawrence D. "Charlatán o filibustero peligroso? El papel de Richard 'Dick' Ferris en la Revuelta Magonista de 1911 en Baja California." *Historia Mexicana* 44 (April–June 1995): 581–616.

Ulloa, Berta, "Las relaciones Mexicanos-Norteamericanas, 1910–1911." *Historia Mexicana* 15 (July 1965): 25–46.

Vanderwood, Paul. "Response to Revolt: The Counter-Guerrilla Strategy of Porfirio Díaz." *Hispanic American Historical Review* 56 (November 1976): 551–79.

———. "Mexico's Rurales: Reputation versus Reality." *The Americas* 34 (July 1977): 102–13.

Walker, David W. "Homegrown Revolution: The Hacienda Santa Catalina del Alamo y Anexas and Agrarian Protest in Eastern Durango, Mexico, 1897–1913." *Hispanic American Historical Review* 72 (May 1992): 239–73.

Waterbury, Ronald. "Non-Revolutionary Peasants: Oaxaca Compared to Morelos in the Mexican Revolution." *Comparative Studies in Society and History* 17 (1975): 410–42.

Whitaker, Herman. "Barbarous Mexico: The Rubber Slavery of the Mexican Tropics." *American Magazine* 49 (February 1910): 546–55.

Womack, John. "The Mexican Economy during the Mexican Revolution, 1910–1920: Historiography and Analysis." *Marxist Perspectives* 4 (Winter 1978): 80–123.

Newspapers

El Diario (Mexico City), 1911.
Frivolidades (Mexico City), 1911.
El Imparcial (Mexico City), 1911–1912.
El Mañana (Mexico City), 1911.
Mexican Herald (Mexico City), 1911.
El Mundo Ilustrado (Mexico City), 1911.
New York Times (New York), 1911–1920.
El País (Mexico City), 1911–1912.
El Tiempo (Mexico City), 1910–1911.
El Tiempo Ilustrado (Mexico City), 1911.

Dissertations and Unpublished Memoirs

Alexius, Robert. "The Army and Politics in Porfirian Mexico." Ph.D. diss., University of Texas-Austin, 1976.

Bryan, Anthony T. "Mexican Politics in Transition, 1900–1913: The Role of General Bernardo Reyes." Ph.D. diss., University of Nebraska-Lincoln, 1970.

Caleca, John. "The Vázquez Gómez Brothers and Francisco I. Madero: Conflict within the Mexican Revolution, 1909–1913." Master's thesis, University of Nebraska-Lincoln, 1970.

Fey, Ingrid. "First Tango in Paris: Latin Americans in Turn-of-the-Century France, 1880–1920." Ph.D. diss., UCLA, 1996.

Garritz Ruiz, Amaya. "La presidencia interina de Francisco León de la Barra: Política interina." Master's thesis, Universidad Nacional Autónoma de México, 1965.

Hanson, Randall S. "The Day of Ideals: Catholic Social Action in the Age of the Mexican Revolution, 1867–1929." Ph.D. diss., University of Indiana, 1994.

Hernández-González, Virginia. "Guía comentada del archivo documental Francisco León de la Barra, fondo condumex." Master's thesis, Universidad Nacional Autónoma de México, 1978.

Kunimoto, Iyo Iimura. "Japan and Mexico, 1888–1917." Ph.D. diss., University of Texas-Austin, 1975.

Lear John. "Workers, Vecinos, and Citizens: The Revolution in Mexico City, 1909–1917." Ph.D. diss., University of California-Berkeley, 1993.

León de la Barra, Francisco. "Algunas páginas de la historia de México." Unpublished manuscript, Archivo Francisco León de la Barra, Centro de Estudios de la Historia de México, Condumex, S.A., Mexico City.

———. "Mi labor como embajador en Washington, 1908–1911." Unpublished manuscript, Archivo Francisco León de la Barra, folder 1, #89, Centro de Estudios de la Historia de México, Condumex, S.A., Mexico City.

Maytorena, José María. "Mi Gobierno en Sonora." Unpublished memoirs, Maytorena Papers, Honnold Library, Claremont College, Claremont, California.

Planck, James. "The Ad Interim Regime of Francisco León de la Barra." Master's thesis, University of the Americas, 1966.

Ruiz, Ramón. "Mexico's Struggle for Rural Education, 1910–1950." Ph.D. diss., University of California-Berkeley, 1954.

Schlicter, Gertrude. "European Backgrounds of American Reform, 1880–1915." Ph.D. diss., University of Illinois, 1960.

Secrest, Louis James. "The End of the Porfiriato: The Collapse of the Díaz Government, 1910–1911." Ph.D. diss., University of New Mexico, 1970.

Story, Victor Obe. "The Genesis of Revolution in the Tamaulipas Sierra: Campesinos or Shopkeepers in the Carrera Torres Uprising, 1907–1911." Ph.D. diss., University of North Carolina, 1991.

Index

Latin American Silhouettes
Studies in History and Culture

William H. Beezley and
Judith Ewell
Editors

Volumes Published

Silvia Marina Arrom and Servando Ortoll, eds., *Riots in the Cities: Popular Politics and the Urban Poor in Latin America, 1765–1910* (1996). Cloth ISBN 0-8420-2580-4 Paper ISBN 0-8420-2581-2

Roderic Ai Camp, ed., *Polling for Democracy: Public Opinion and Political Liberalization in Mexico* (1996). ISBN 0-8420-2583-9

Brian Loveman and Thomas M. Davies, Jr., eds., *The Politics of Antipolitics: The Military in Latin America*, 3d ed., revised and updated (1996). Cloth ISBN 0-8420-2609-6 Paper ISBN 0-8420-2611-8

Joseph S. Tulchin, Andrés Serbín, and Rafael Hernández, eds., *Cuba and the Caribbean: Regional Issues and Trends in the Post-Cold War Era* (1997). ISBN 0-8420-2652-5

Thomas W. Walker, ed., *Nicaragua without Illusions: Regime Transition and Structural Adjustment in the 1990s* (1997). Cloth ISBN 0-8420-2578-2 Paper ISBN 0-8420-2579-0

Dianne Walta Hart, *Undocumented in L.A.: An Immigrant's Story* (1997). Cloth ISBN 0-8420-2648-7 Paper ISBN 0-8420-2649-5

Jaime E. Rodríguez O. and Kathryn Vincent, eds., *Myths, Misdeeds, and Misunderstandings: The Roots of Conflict in U.S.-Mexican Relations* (1997). ISBN 0-8420-2662-2

Jaime E. Rodríguez O. and Kathryn Vincent, eds., *Common Border, Uncommon Paths: Race, Culture, and National Identity in U.S.-Mexican Relations* (1997). ISBN 0-8420-2673-8

William H. Beezley and Judith Ewell, eds., *The Human Tradition in Modern Latin America* (1997). Cloth ISBN 0-8420-2612-6 Paper ISBN 0-8420-2613-4

Donald F. Stevens, ed., *Based on a True Story: Latin American History at the Movies* (1997). Cloth ISBN 0-8420-2582-0 Paper ISBN 0-8420-2781-5

Jaime E. Rodríguez O., ed., *The Origins of Mexican National Politics, 1808–1847* (1997). Paper ISBN 0-8420-2723-8

Che Guevara, *Guerrilla Warfare*, with revised and updated introduction and case studies by Brian Loveman and Thomas M. Davies, Jr., 3d ed. (1997). Cloth ISBN 0-8420-2677-0 Paper ISBN 0-8420-2678-9

Adrian A. Bantjes, *As If Jesus Walked on Earth: Cardenismo, Sonora, and the Mexican Revolution* (1998). ISBN 0-8420-2653-3

Henry A. Dietz and Gil Shidlo, eds., *Urban Elections in Democratic Latin America* (1998). Cloth ISBN 0-8420-2627-4 Paper ISBN 0-8420-2628-2

A. Kim Clark, *The Redemptive Work: Railway and Nation in Ecuador, 1895–1930* (1998). ISBN 0-8420-2674-6

Joseph S. Tulchin, ed., with Allison M. Garland, *Argentina: The Challenges of Modernization* (1998). ISBN 0-8420-2721-1

Louis A. Pérez, Jr., ed., *Impressions of Cuba in the Nineteenth Century: The Travel Diary of Joseph J. Dimock* (1998). Cloth ISBN 0-8420-2657-6 Paper ISBN 0-8420-2658-4

June E. Hahner, ed., *Women through Women's Eyes: Latin American Women in Nineteenth-Century Travel Accounts* (1998). Cloth ISBN 0-8420-2633-9 Paper ISBN 0-8420-2634-7

James P. Brennan, ed., *Peronism and Argentina* (1998). ISBN 0-8420-2706-8

John Mason Hart, ed., *Border Crossings: Mexican and Mexican-American Workers* (1998). Cloth ISBN 0-8420-2716-5 Paper ISBN 0-8420-2717-3

Brian Loveman, *For* la Patria: *Politics and the Armed Forces in Latin America* (1999). Cloth ISBN 0-8420-2772-6 Paper ISBN 0-8420-2773-4

Guy P. C. Thomson, with David G. LaFrance, *Patriotism, Politics, and Popular Liberalism in Nineteenth-Century Mexico: Juan Francisco Lucas and the Puebla Sierra* (1999). ISBN 0-8420-2683-5

Robert Woodmansee Herr, in collaboration with Richard Herr, *An American Family in the Mexican Revolution* (1999). ISBN 0-8420-2724-6

Juan Pedro Viqueira Albán, trans. Sonya Lipsett-Rivera and Sergio Rivera Ayala, *Propriety and Permissiveness in Bourbon Mexico* (1999). Cloth ISBN 0-8420-2466-2 Paper ISBN 0-8420-2467-0

Stephen R. Niblo, *Mexico in the 1940s: Modernity, Politics, and Corruption* (1999). ISBN 0-8420-2794-7

David E. Lorey, *The U.S.-Mexican Border in the Twentieth Century* (1999). Cloth ISBN 0-8420-2755-6 Paper ISBN 0-8420-2756-4

Joanne Hershfield and David R. Maciel, eds., *Mexico's Cinema: A Century of Films and Filmmakers* (2000). Cloth ISBN 0-8420-2681-9 Paper ISBN 0-8420-2682-7

Peter V. N. Henderson, *In the Absence of Don Porfirio: Francisco León de la Barra and the Mexican Revolution* (2000). ISBN 0-8420-2774-2

Mark T. Gilderhus, *The Second Century: U.S.-Latin American Relations since 1889* (2000). Cloth ISBN 0-8420-2413-1 Paper ISBN 0-8420-2414-X

Catherine Moses, *Real Life in Castro's Cuba* (2000). Cloth ISBN 0-8420-2836-6 Paper ISBN 0-8420-2837-4

K. Lynn Stoner, ed./comp., with Luis Hipólito Serrano Pérez, *Cuban and Cuban-American Women: An Annotated Bibliography* (2000). ISBN 0-8420-2643-6

Thomas D. Schoonover, *The French in Central America: Culture and Commerce, 1820–1930* (2000). ISBN 0-8420-2792-0